WORLD COURT DECISIONS AT THE TURN OF THE MILLENNIUM (1997-2001)

WORLD COURT DECISIONS
AT THE TURN OF THE MILLENNIUM
(1997-2001)

PIETER H.F. BEKKER

MARTINUS NIJHOFF PUBLISHERS
THE HAGUE / LONDON / NEW YORK

A C.I.P. Catalogue record for this book is available from the Library of Congress.

ISBN 90-411-1791-1

Published by Kluwer Law International,
P.O. Box 85889, 2508 CN The Hague, The Netherlands.

Sold and distributed in North, Central and South America
by Kluwer Law International,
101 Philip Drive, Norwell, MA 02061, U.S.A.
kluwerlaw@wkap.com

In all other countries, sold and distributed
by Kluwer Law International,
P.O. Box 85889, 2508 CN The Hague, The Netherlands.

Lay-out and camera-ready copy: Anne-Marie Krens – Oegstgeest – The Netherlands

Printed on acid-free paper

This book is dedicated to the memory of
Abram Chayes (1922-2000) and
Keith Highet (1933-2000)

FOREWORD

By Stephen M. Schwebel, Judge of the International Court of Justice (1981-2000); Vice President (1994-1997); President (1997-2000).

Writing at the end of the first year of the Twenty-First Century, and looking back on the history of the Twentieth Century to appraise sweepingly the place of international adjudication, the retrospective is mixed. It began auspiciously, with The Hague Peace Conferences of 1899 and 1907 and the establishment of the Permanent Court of Arbitration. It is a measure of how recent an innovation in the history of mankind is international organization and adjudication to recall that The Hague Peace Conference of 1907 was the first diplomatic conference to which all States then in existence were invited (and the first at which consideration was given to the establishment of a world court). At the outset of the Twentieth Century, the "peace movement" of that era focused its hopes on international arbitration and adjudication as the principal means for the peaceful settlement of international disputes and the prevention of international warfare.

The Twentieth Century too soon however was marked and marred by World War I, and the rise thereafter of the totalitarian States. Twenty years after the end of World War I, they plunged the world into World War II, and engaged in mass murder and other atrocities in the course of it on a scale unknown to previous centuries. International tensions provoked by the expansionist aims of the totalitarian States in the interwar years, and by the policies of the surviving totalitarian Power after World War II, hardly conduced to international adjudication.

The Permanent Court of International Justice (PCIJ), which functioned in the years 1922-1940, was not, and was not seen to be, a factor in the prevention of war. The hopes that international adjudication would be the antidote to war proved misplaced. The PCIJ nevertheless was a significant and successful institution. It adjudicated a substantial number of international disputes and rendered a stream of advisory opinions, and in the process demonstrated that a world court could work. It demonstrated as well that a world court could not only resolve international disputes but contribute to the development of international law. Thus when at the end of World War II it was accepted that the League of Nations would be replaced by another international organization, it was no less accepted that the World Court would be maintained. It essentially was maintained, the Statute of the International Court of Justice being expressly based on that of the Permanent Court.

The International Court of Justice has a record, in the large, more significant and successful still than that of the PCIJ. It has functioned for fifty-five years. The flow of cases submitted to it has waxed and waned but, since 1984, has mounted remarkably, despite the fact that its compulsory jurisdiction has not.

The increase in the caseload of the Court is especially notable in the years 1997-2001, those that are addressed in this study by Dr. Pieter Bekker. Attention of international lawyers has moved from concern over how to increase recourse to the Court to how the Court may more expeditiously and effectively handle its burgeoning caseload.

The explanation of why the Court has in recent years been so busy, while earlier it was so sparsely used, is uncertain. In my view, the likeliest reasons are two. The first is that the end of the Cold War has reduced international tensions; as the interwar years tend to suggest, States are more prone to have recourse to international adjudication in times of détente (as in the 1920's) than high international tension (as in the 1930's). The second reason is that the States that became independent the last forty years, after some years of suspicion of an international law that they did not fashion, have become increasingly confident in that law as they have contributed to its refashioning and in the place of the Court as its most authoritative interpreter.

Whatever the reasons for the impressive number, consequence and worldwide provenance of the cases before the Court, there is ground for hoping that the Court will continue to maintain a high level of activity. As States increasingly send cases to the Court, their example should generate more such recourse. The Court itself has revised its Rules to expedite its procedures. And the amelioration of the fiscal drought that has crippled the United Nations for years promises a continuing increase in the modest financial resources of the Court that began with the election of Kofi Annan as Secretary-General of the United Nations in 1997.

Pieter Bekker in this study of the work of the Court in the years 1997-2001 analyzes its activity in depth and breadth. His introduction provides a useful survey and commentary; his annual analyses of the Court's judgments, advisory opinions and orders are comprehensive and perceptive. He has included a discussion of a panel of the Annual Meeting of the American Society of International Law that he chaired, in which a number of worthwhile observations are made about the product and prospects of the Court.

Dr. Bekker, who served as a valued member of the staff of the Registry of the Court in his capacity of special assistant to the then Registrar, in the years since has established himself as an industrious and lucid expositor of the work of the Court. He has done so despite the demands of an international legal practice. It is to be expected that this latest contribution of Dr. Bekker to a wider understanding of the work of the Court will not be his last.

Stephen M. Schwebel
December 31, 2001

ABOUT THE AUTHOR

PIETER H.F. BEKKER (LL.B., Ph.D. (Int'l Law), Leiden University, The Netherlands; LL.M., Harvard Law School) is a Dutch attorney in the International Arbitration Group at White & Case LLP, the New York City based global law firm (<www.whitecase.com>), and is a former staff lawyer in the Registry of the International Court of Justice (1992-1994). He serves as ICJ Reporter for The American Society of International Law, whose 94th Annual Meeting he co-chaired in April 2000. He is the author of two books – *The Legal Position of Intergovernmental Organizations – A Functional Necessity Analysis of Their Legal Status and Immunities* (1994) and, as editor and principal author, *Commentaries on World Court Decisions (1987-1996)* (1998) – published by Martinus Nijhoff Publishers/Kluwer Law International and of numerous articles and shorter notes on international law and adjudication.

The views expressed in this book are those of the author in his individual capacity and not of The American Society of International Law or any national or international organization, institution, law firm or governmental body with which the author was or currently is affiliated.

This book generally conforms to the style of the *American Journal of International Law* published by the American Society of International Law.

TABLE OF CONTENTS

PREFACE

1 Introduction

This book records and analyzes the judicial activity of the International Court of Justice (ICJ) during the five-year period from January 1, 1997, to December 31, 2001. It contains summaries, complete with commentary, of the 11 Judgments, one Advisory Opinion and 19 Orders disposing of substantive issues delivered by the Court during the busiest period in its history. Commentaries on seven decisions[1] previously were published between 1997 and 2000 as part of the International Decisions section of the *American Journal of International Law*. Reviews of the remaining, more recent decisions were added, together with introductory notes describing the judicial activity of the Court in a given year.[2]

The book is divided into five chapters covering each of the years 1997-2001, following the structure of an earlier volume describing the Court's decisions during the years 1987-1996.[3] The idea for publishing the earlier volume, the format of which has been retained in this book, arose from my work as Special Assistant to the then Registrar of the International Court of Justice and from my desire to create a complete overview of the work of the Court in a user-friendly format. It is one of the functions of the Registrar to keep the General List of cases up-to-date and to prepare an annual report for submission to the UN General Assembly. I assisted the Registrar in this task by creating a ledger

---

1   *See* 92 AJIL 273 (1998); 92 AJIL 508 (1998); 92 AJIL 503 (1998); 92 AJIL 751 (1998); 93 AJIL 913 (1999); 93 AJIL 928 (1999); and 94 AJIL 707 (2000).

2   Similar summaries of the judicial work of the ICJ during 1997-1999 previously were published in 92 AJIL 350 (1998), 93 AJIL 534 (1999), and 94 AJIL 412 (2000).

3   *See* COMMENTARIES ON WORLD COURT DECISIONS (1987-1996) (P.H.F. Bekker ed., 1998). I decided to retain this structure due to its accessibility, allowing a seamless review by way of a uniform format of the Court's decisions since 1987. This volume nevertheless has been set up as a stand-alone work and, while there may be overlap in structure, its focus is entirely and exclusively on the years 1997-2001.

containing the information found in the opening section of each chapter of this book. These sections consist of concise summaries of the judicial activity of the Court during a given year, using the General List of cases, pleadings filed, Orders and Judgments or Advisory Opinions issued, and hearings held at the Peace Palace in The Hague (The Netherlands) to describe the Court's record for that year. In this manner, a complete and up-to-date overview is presented of the judicial activity of the Court between January 1, 1997, and December 31, 2001. The book thus covers the Eighteenth Period (1997-2000) and part of the Nineteenth Period (2000-2003) of the Court under the presidencies of Judges Stephen Schwebel (U.S.A.) and Gilbert Guillaume (France), respectively.[4]

Additional information on the work and composition of the Court during the period covered is offered by way of an introductory chapter and the annexes found at the end of this book. In this way, both the practitioner before, and the student of, the Court will find essential information on the work of the Court during the period reviewed.

Most of the period covered in this book formed part of the United Nations Decade of International Law (1990-1999), which was promulgated by UN General Assembly Resolution 44/23 of November 17, 1989. According to Paragraph 2(b) of Resolution 44/23, one of the main purposes of the Decade was "to promote means and methods for the peaceful settlement of disputes between States, including resort to and full respect of the International Court of Justice."[5]

An assembly of unofficial summaries of the substantive Orders, Judgments and Advisory Opinions of the Court that are prepared and issued by the Court's Registry was published by the United Nations in 1992 under the title "*Summaries of Judgments, Advisory Opinions and Orders of the International Court of Justice 1948-1991*."[6] This publication, containing some 225 pages of unofficial summaries, is available in all of the official languages of the United Nations (English, French, Spanish, Arabic, Chinese and Russian).

---

4   The First Period started on February 6, 1946. "Periods" correspond to the three-year cycles of the Court, one-third of the Court being elected or re-elected, as the case may be, every three years.

5   For the Secretary-General's final report on the United Nations Decade of International Law, see UN Docs. A/54/362 & Add.1 (1999). For the General Assembly's formal conclusion of the Decade at its plenary meeting held on November 17, 1999, see UN Docs. A/54/PV.54-55 (1999).

6   UN Doc. ST/LEG/SER.F/1 (1992).

By offering a series of summaries, commentaries and statistics relating to a diverse jurisprudence, this book presents concise insights into the decisions in various cases that were pending between 1997 and 2001, with references to the earlier jurisprudence of the World Court. However, a word of caution is in place here. Convenient as summaries and commentaries may be, it is important to gain first-hand knowledge of the decisions of the Court. An in-depth understanding can be attained only by reading the full text of such decisions, including the declarations and separate and dissenting opinions of individual judges attached to them, which in recent years have been particularly voluminous. The publications of the Court, where the official text of its decisions and a description of its work may be found, are described at the end of the introductory chapter.

2 Tribute to Abram Chayes and Keith Highet

During the period reviewed in this book, the ICJ "Bar" lost its two most senior and prominent American members within a short period of time. On April 16, 2000, Abram Chayes died at age 77. Chayes' death was followed, on July 12, 2000, by the passing of his friend and colleague Keith Highet at age 67. Both men died after a brave struggle with cancer. Abe Chayes and Keith Highet, who both were born at a time when the Permanent Court of International Justice was still in existence, were remarkable individuals and formidable mentors to whom I am forever indebted. An entire volume could be written about the extraordinary international law accomplishments of both men, but I will confine myself here to a description of some of their many contributions to the ICJ. It is to the loving memory of these two mentors *extraordinaires* that I dedicate this book.

Abram Chayes (1922-2000)

A leading expert on civil procedure, arms control, conflict prevention and environmental law, Abe Chayes will be remembered especially for his role in the case concerning *Military and Paramilitary Activities in and against Nicaragua* (Nicaragua v. United States), in which he appeared as Counsel and Advocate for Nicaragua, marking the first time that a former Legal Adviser of one country (he served in that capacity in the Kennedy and Johnson administrations during 1961-1965), appeared in proceedings against his country on behalf of the government of another country. Notwithstanding the U.S. withdrawal from the Court's Optional Clause system during the proceedings, Abe was successful in bringing Nicaragua the relief it sought.[7] During the period reviewed in this book, he was involved in his second and third cases before the Court, appearing on behalf of Namibia in the case concerning *Kasikili/ Sedudu Island* (Botswana/Namibia) and representing Croatia in *Application of the Convention on the Prevention and Punishment of the Crime of Genocide* (Croatia v. Yugoslavia). Despite his fine advocacy work, he was unable to repeat for Namibia the success he helped achieve in the *Nicaragua* Case several years earlier, which prompted him to comment to me shortly after the Court handed down its judgment, in typical no-nonsense fashion: "Oh well, I am still one-and-one before the World Court!"

In his foreword to the volume of Commentaries preceding the present work, Abe complained about what he believed was an *ad hominem* attack on the Judges of the Court by his country in the aftermath of the *Nicaragua* Case. Putting that precedent in its proper perspective, he made a convincing argument for the proposition that the case actually rehabilitated the Court's authority.[8] His words, written in September 1997, stand out for their clarity and wisdom and will retain their value for many years to come.

A former president of the prestigious Harvard Law Review, Professor Chayes was the most inspiring and engaging teacher imaginable, who shared his wealth of scholarly insights and practical and life experience generously with his students during his long tenure as the Felix Frankfurter Professor of Law at Harvard Law School. As Dean Clark put it during Abe's memorial celebration at Harvard on September 27, 2000, "Abe Chayes is part of the pantheon of god-like leading citizens who define the Harvard Law School." In recognition of his extraordinary service to the legal profession and Harvard Law School, Abe was given the Harvard Law School Association Award in April 1999. I will never forget the ease with which he navigated, in traditional Socratic teaching style, through some of the broadest and most complex inter-national law topics in the two courses that I took with him at Harvard Law School during 1990-1991. As a student, you realized that you were being taught by a genuine giant of the law. He also was remarkably frank and modest, as became clear from a story he told his students during the first day of class. Relying on his razor-sharp mind, he was reminiscing about his Senate confirma-

---

7 For a tribute to Prof. Chayes, including a description of his role in the *Nicaragua* Case, see 42 HARV. INT'L L.J. 1 (2001).

8 *See* COMMENTARIES ON WORLD COURT DECISIONS (1987-1996) ix (P.H.F. Bekker ed., 1998).

tion hearing as the Legal Adviser to the U.S. Department of State in the Kennedy administration in 1961. According to his own admission, he did not know too much about international law at that time, let alone the World Court. In fact, he had never taken an international law class. Toward the end of the hearing, after he made an unsolicited statement about the meager U.S. record before the World Court, a senator asked him how many judges serve on the World Court. Rather than taking a wild guess, he gracefully admitted that he did not know the answer. He certainly made up for this deficit in later years, when he became a prominent commentator and advocate himself before the Court. As Associate Justice Stephen Breyer of the U.S. Supreme Court commented during his memorial celebration, Abe was "a model for what a dedicated, practical idealist can achieve in the law."

His arguments before the Court were consistently crisp and wrought with astute observations evidencing his wisdom and sense of reality. In his final appearance before the Court, as Counsel and Advocate for Namibia in *Kasikili/Sedudu Island* (Botswana/Namibia), a case involving a tiny island, he reminded the Court that "small places do not necessarily make small cases" and that "the size of the place does not measure its meaning to those who may be affected by the judgment."[9]

Keith Highet (1933-2000)

Keith Highet appeared in more cases before the Court than any other American lawyer. However, it was not only the quantity of cases that was so impressive, representing a number of governments in some 15 cases over a 40-year period, the quality of his representations is what really stands out. He represented the applicants in the *South West Africa* (Ethiopia v. South Africa; Liberia v. South Africa) (Second Phase) Cases, probably the most controversial litigation ever to come before the Court and his first introduction to this Hague institution. Keith was immensely proud of this particular representation and would tell anyone who wanted to listen his many ICJ "war stories" from the 1960s (evidence of which can be found throughout his remarks during the 94th Annual Meeting of The American Society of International Law set forth as an Addendum to Chapter 4 of this book – remarks that turned out to be his final ones made in public). A humorous drawing that he made during the *South West Africa* hearings, depicting the main players and scenes of the case, was prominently displayed in his office.

---

9   ICJ Doc. CR 99/1, at 14, para. 4 (1999).

In addition to the *South West Africa* Cases, Keith was involved in the following cases before the Court: *Continental Shelf* (Tunisia/Libya) (for Libya); *Application for Permission to Intervene in the Case concerning the* Continental Shelf (Tunisia/Libya) (for Libya); *Application for Revision and Interpretation of the Judgment of 24 February 1982 in the Case concerning the* Continental Shelf (Tunisia/Libya) (Tunisia v. Libya) (for Libya); *Elettronica Sicula S.p.A.* (U.S. v. Italy) (for Italy); *Arbitral Award of 31 July 1989* (Guinea-Bissau v. Senegal) (for Guinea-Bissau); *Land, Island and Maritime Frontier Dispute* (El Salvador/Honduras) (for El Salvador); *Application of Nicaragua to Intervene in the Case concerning the* Land, Island and Maritime Frontier Dispute (El Salvador/Honduras) (for El Salvador); *Maritime Delimitation in the Area between Greenland and Jan Mayen* (Denmark v. Norway) (for Norway); *Maritime Delimitation and Territorial Questions between Qatar and Bahrain* (Qatar v. Bahrain) (for Bahrain); *Land and Maritime Boundary between Cameroon and Nigeria* (Cameroon v. Nigeria) (for Cameroon); *Request for Interpretation of the Judgment of 11 June 1998 in the Case concerning the* Land and Maritime Boundary between Cameroon and Nigeria (Cameroon v. Nigeria), *Preliminary Objections* (Nigeria v. Cameroon) (for Cameroon); *Application for Permission to Intervene in the Case concerning the* Land and Maritime Boundary between Cameroon and Nigeria (Cameroon v. Nigeria) (for Cameroon); *Fisheries Jurisdiction* (Spain v. Canada) (for Spain); and *Sovereignty over Pulau Ligitan and Pulau Sipadan* (Indonesia/Malaysia) (for Indonesia).

A former president of The American Society of International Law (1986-1988), Keith was best known for his knowledge of what is one of the most complicated aspects of public international law, namely, the law of the sea and, within that particular field, maritime delimitation. As such, he was prominently involved in the *Continental Shelf* cases during the 1980s, which firmly shaped the Court's jurisprudence on maritime delimitation. In recognition of his maritime expertise, Yemen appointed him as an arbitrator in its arbitration with Eritrea, the first international arbitration to deal with both matters of sovereignty to land territory and maritime boundaries conducted under the auspices of the Permanent Court of Arbitration, in which he proudly served with ICJ Judges Schwebel, Higgins and Sir Robert Jennings as his fellow arbitrators between 1997 and 2000.[10]

---

10 For the text of the arbitral awards issued by the tribunal formed to deal with the Eritrea/Yemen case, see the PCA's Web site, <www.pca-cpa.org>.

I was privileged to assist him in various phases of the cases concerning *Fisheries Jurisdiction* (Spain v. Canada) and *Land and Maritime Boundary between Cameroon and Nigeria* (Cameroon v. Nigeria) in 1998. Even though his illness interfered abruptly with our cooperation, the lessons learnt from him during that time will forever strengthen my understanding of litigating cases before the Court, adding a critical dimension to my perspective "from the inside" as a former ICJ official.

In recognition of his contributions to international law in the Western Hemisphere, Keith was elected to serve on the Inter-American Juridical Committee of the Organization of American States, of which he was the distinguished chairman at the time of his death.

Keith enjoyed every aspect of ICJ litigation. The Hague truly had become his "home away from home," and he loved staying at the grand *Hotel Des Indes* in the center of town during the hearings of a case. His incredible gift for foreign languages resulted in his ability to address almost all of his clients in their native language. As a result of his extensive stays in The Hague over the years, he even was able to utter some words in my native language, Dutch. His favorite Dutch word was *prima* (which means "very good"), because of its expressiveness and positive connotation – characteristics that both were represented in his own personality. His oral interventions before the Court always were wrought with Latin expressions (probably inspired by his father, Gilbert Highet, who was a well-known professor of Latin at Columbia and Oxford Universities) and citations from English literature, especially Shakespeare (his mother, Helen MacInnes, was a successful author of novels).[11] Keith was the *complete* international lawyer and quintessential "ICJ Bar" member, being polished, elegant and articulate (he was born in Oxford and educated at Harvard and Oxford Universities) and, above all, a true believer in international law and adjudication. The fact that, by contrast to most of his opponents in the Great Hall of Justice, he was a practitioner and not an international law academic never was a handicap to him. As his good friend and former ICJ President Stephen Schwebel commented in Keith's obituary in The New York Times, Keith appeared in his record number of cases before the

---

11 A good example from one of his interventions of recent date, referring to one of Nigeria's preliminary objections as a Shakespearean "play within a play," is found in the hearing record on Nigeria's preliminary objections in *Land and Maritime Boundary between Cameroon and Nigeria (Cameroon v. Nigeria)* (ICJ Doc. CR 98/4, at 40, para. 28 (1998)) and was referred to by Germany in its oral argument on the merits of the *LaGrand Case (Germany v. U.S.). See* ICJ Doc. CR 2000/26, at 22, para. 25 (2000).

Court "always with great scholarship, insight and legal flair."[12] I will forever remember the brilliant display of all of these elements during his interventions as Counsel and Advocate for Norway in the case concerning *Maritime Delimitation in the Area between Greenland and Jan Mayen* (Denmark v. Norway), which I witnessed as a young official in the ICJ Registry in 1992.

At the time of his passing, Keith was involved in two cases, *Land and Maritime Boundary between Cameroon and Nigeria* (Cameroon v. Nigeria) and *Sovereignty over Pulau Ligitan and Pulau Sipadan* (Indonesia/Malaysia), both of which are featured in this book. When he died, the unofficial "ICJ Bar" lost its proud *de facto* Dean and this author, and numerous others with him, a dear friend, mentor and colleague.

3 Acknowledgment

The American Society of International Law kindly has granted its permission to republish certain of my writings that previously were published in the *American Journal of International Law* and the *ASIL Proceedings*, as indicated throughout this book.

I am grateful to Kluwer Law International for publishing this work, my third with this leading publisher on works on the International Court.

Last but not least, I wish to pay special tribute to three individuals who played important supporting roles in my development as an international lawyer: Ms. Martine van Leeuwen Boomkamp-Oppenhuis de Jong, of the Leiden University Law School, Univ.Prof.Dr. Ignaz Seidl-Hohenveldern, of the Univer-

---

12   N.Y. TIMES, July 15, 2000, at C16. Keith displayed his scholarship in a number of writings, of which two, both published in 1991, stand out: *Winning and Losing: The Commitment of the United States to the International Court – What Was It, What Is It and Where Has It Gone?* 1 TRANSNAT'L L. & CONTEMP. PROB. 157 (1991) and *The Peace Palace Heats Up: The World Court in Business Again?*, 85 AJIL 646 (1991). I had the honor of co-authoring the following pieces with him: *International Court of Justice Orders U.S. to Stay Execution of Paraguay National in Virginia* (April 1998, available from the Web site of The American Society of International Law, <www.asil.org>), *International Courts and Tribunals*, 31 INT'L LAW. 599 (with Roger Alford), and an article on the Court's decisions on jurisdiction in the case between Qatar and Bahrain in COMMENTARIES ON WORLD COURT DECISIONS (1987-1996) 191 (P.H.F. Bekker ed., 1998).

sity of Vienna, and Ambassador Achol Deng of the Sudan. All three individuals, dedicated international lawyers and Friends of the International Court, passed away at this book was being readied for publication.

Pieter H.F. Bekker
New York City
January 2002

INTRODUCTION

AN OVERVIEW OF THE WORK
OF THE COURT (1997-2001)

1 Introduction

1.1 Judicial Statistics

The International Court of Justice has an essential role to play in the maintenance of the international legal order as well as in the enunciation and development of international law and jurisprudence. The very existence of the Court
is considered to be one of the main factors for the promotion of world peace
and justice and for strengthening the rule of law among nations. The Court's
jurisprudence is an important element in developing the climate of respect for
the peaceful legal order within the framework of which individual nations and
other subjects of international law should conduct themselves. The Court's
Judgments, Advisory Opinions and Orders that dispose of substantive issues
(such as those concerning counterclaims and requests for the indication of
provisional measures of protection) have had fundamental significance for the
development of international law and the maintenance of peace and security.
In this field, it has no equal, being truly situated at the apex of an ever-growing
number of international courts and tribunals. The Court's decisions have assisted
in decreasing regional conflict and tension and in promoting regional peace
and stability by impartially and authoritatively adjudicating sensitive matters
of eminent importance to the states involved and, indeed, the world community-
at-large. In this process, the Court also has drawn legitimate criticism from

P.H.F. Bekker, World Court Decisions at the Turn of the Millennium (1997-2001), p. 3-40.
© 2002 *Kluwer Law International. Printed in the Netherlands.*

time to time, including especially from international law scholars.[1] The commentaries contained in this book seek to present a critical but fair appraisal of the Court's work in the light of its earlier decisions and its docket in general. An interesting discussion of the Court's recent work is included at the end of Chapter 4, reflecting a unique exchange of views by both representatives of the Court and scholars participating in the legal process that the Court administers.

An ever-increasing interest in the work of the Court is displayed by a worldwide audience, consisting of government officials, lawyers, academic institutions, university libraries, teachers, students, the press and the general public. If the ICJ is to function as a genuine "World Court," it is imperative that its decisions be understood by the widest possible audience, so as to increase public awareness and appreciation of the work of the Court and international law generally the world over and to facilitate access to, and understanding of, its jurisprudence for all those concerned and interested. It is hoped that summaries and commentaries in the form contained in this book and statistics on the work of the Court will furnish the key for opening up the Court's work to larger areas of the world legal community and to the public in general. At a time when the world is paying greater attention to the activity of the Court, it is essential that its jurisprudence and work be explained to, and understood by, a wide audience.

Between 1997 and 2001, the Court had a longer and more diverse case list than at any previous stage in its 55-year history. Cases that were dealt with in one way or another by the Court during this period ranged from 9 to 29, and 39 states from all five different regions represented in the United Nations participated in ICJ proceedings covering the most diverse topics ranging from questions on the legality of using force and the expropriation of foreign property to complicated maritime and territorial boundary disputes. This attests to the increasing trust and confidence that the world community is placing in the work of the Court and reflects a rising willingness to submit to its procedures and

---

1   According to Art. 38(1)(d) of the ICJ Statute, the Court is to apply, as secondary sources of law, "the teachings of the most highly qualified publicists of the various nations" in its judicial work. *See supra* section 2.8. Even though such sources are hardly ever cited by the Court in its decisions, it is clear that it is influenced by the literature. For example, in its Judgment of June 27, 2001 in the *LaGrand Case* (reviewed in Chapter 5 below), the Court noted that the interpretation of the article in its Statute that governs the indication of provisional measures, "has been the subject of extensive controversy in the literature." LaGrand Case (Ger. v. U.S.), Merits, Judgment, at para. 99 (June 27, 2001), *available from* <www.icj-cij.org>.

authority. By the end of 2001, 23 cases were pending before the Court, three involving African states, one featuring Asian states, two each between Latin American states and 12 involving European states, the remainder being of an intercontinental nature. The Court's recent docket is thus evidence of the fact that the ICJ is effectively operating in far more widely spread areas of the world than ever before, involving the Americas and the Pacific, and Asian, Middle Eastern, African, and Western and Eastern European regions. The 37 countries representing these various regions that were parties to cases before the Court between 1997 and 2001 are listed in Annex C to this book. Of these countries, Bosnia-Herzegovina, Cameroon, the Democratic Republic of the Congo, Germany, Nigeria, Spain and Yugoslavia are the only states that appeared before the Court in both capacities of applicant and respondent during the five-year period reviewed. Yugoslavia had the most appearances as applicant and the United States was most frequently seen as respondent before the Court.

This record can be appreciated only against the background of previous decades. In the four decades prior to 1997, some 78 states appeared as parties in cases before the Court, compared to 37 states from all over the world during the most recent period reviewed in this book, 25 percent of which were first-time litigants before the Court. The number of pending cases averaged two or three during the 1950s, but fell to none or one in the 1960s. From mid-1962 to January 1967, no new proceedings were instituted at all, and the same situation applied between early 1967 and late 1971. As of 1972, the number of cases brought before the Court increased steadily, and new cases began to average from one to three each year. Between 1987 and 1997, the total number of cases that the Court had to deal with at any particular time stood between six and 17.

Annex E to this book gives an overview of some basic statistics concerning the General List of cases between 1987 and 2001. Several observations may be made based on that table.

Between 1997 and 2001, a total of 36 cases appeared on the General List at any particular time, 35 of which are contentious and one advisory. The General List developed steadily from 9 cases in 1997 to a record of 29 cases in 1999. Since 1991, the Court has had a steady workload of nine or more cases appearing on the General List. Between 1997 and 2001, the Court delivered 11 Judgments, one Advisory Opinion and 19 Orders disposing of substantive issues, including 14 Orders regarding requests for the indication of provisional measures of protection.

In terms of new cases brought, 1999 was the top year, with 17 new proceedings instituted in that year.[2]

1998 is the only year besides 1996 in which the Court issued four decisions in one year (all contentious). In each of the other years during the period covered by this book, with the exception of 2001, the Court never issued more than two decisions (in contentious cases) a year.

During the five-year period covered, advisory proceedings were instituted only once, in 1998. An Advisory Opinion was issued in 1999.

No *ad hoc* Chamber has been formed since 1992.

The highest number of Orders was issued in 1999 (35), with 2000 ranking second with 20 Orders issued. The average number of Orders issued annually was 19.

Discontinuance of cases occurred in 1998, 1999 and 2001. As former ICJ President Sir Robert Jennings has pointed out, discontinuance of proceedings is part of the Court's broader role, which includes the encouragement of states parties in cases pending before it to try to negotiate a friendly settlement. In doing so, the Court is, in an important sense, still productively at work.[3] The official titles of the cases that were discontinued are listed in Annex B.

Although the strength and authority of the Court, as any other tribunal, lies in the quality of its decisions,[4] the statistical data contained in the introductory notes to the various chapters of this book demonstrate that during the period 1997-2001, several quantitative records were broken by the Court in its judicial work, which betokens a strong basis for the continued success of

---

2   This unusually high number is caused mainly by the fact that Yugoslavia instituted separate but similar proceedings against 10 member states of the North Atlantic Treaty Organization (NATO) on April 29, 1999, as described in Chapter 3.

3   Statement by the President of the International Court of Justice, Sir Robert Jennings, to the United Nations General Assembly, Oct. 21, 1992, UN Doc. A/47/PV.43, at 11. In its jurisprudence, the ICJ continually has maintained that judicial settlement is only an alternative to settlement by the parties themselves. *See*, e.g., Aerial Incident of 10 August 1999 (Pakistan v. India), Jurisdiction, Judgment, at para. 52 (June 21, 2000) reviewed in Chapter 4 of this book.

4   As Shabtai Rosenne has pointed out, "in the long run, the bare figures may be misleading as the point of departure for an evaluation of the role of the Court in the international scene today." SHABTAI ROSENNE, THE WORLD COURT – WHAT IT IS AND HOW IT WORKS 225 (5th rev. ed., The Hague, 1995). By way of illustration, the statistical fact that only five cases were terminated by a Judgment on the merits or Advisory Opinion in the five-year period reviewed obscures the wealth of jurisprudence offered by the totality of the Court's decisions issued during this period, as described in this book.

this unique judicial institution in the 21st century. The commentaries found in the five chapters of this book each reflect on the quality aspect of the decisions of the Court.

The most fascinating aspect of the work of the World Court is that, with few exceptions, its decisions feature issues, whether of a procedural/jurisdictional kind or of a substantive nature, that never before have been submitted to, or addressed by, the Court.[5] As a consequence, there is some novel element in almost every decision. As described below, the years 1997-2001 were no exception to this phenomenon.

1.2   Procedural/Jurisdictional Developments

A prominent place was claimed once again by procedural and jurisdictional issues. This is no surprise, given that, of the more than 30 contentious cases appearing on the General List during the period reviewed, only two cases were of the "voluntary" kind, having been submitted jointly by the litigating states.[6] In "involuntary" cases, jurisdictional and procedural obstacles invariably will be introduced and pleaded by unwilling respondent states, if only to create delay.[7] The aspect of delay, including the Court's recent initiatives to combat it, is commented on throughout this book.

First and foremost, the Court made important contributions to its jurisprudence on "Optional Clause" declarations accepting the Court's compulsory jurisdiction, and reservations contained in declarations, through several decisions reviewed in this book.[8]

---

5   This is explained by the fact cases usually reach the Court only after years, or even decades, of negotiations or debates.

6   Gabčíkovo-Nagymaros Project (Hungary/Slovakia); Sovereignty over Pulau Ligitan and Pulau Sipadan (Indonesia/Malaysia). On the distinction between "voluntary" and "involuntary" cases, see Keith Highet's observations in COMMENTARIES ON WORLD COURT DECISIONS (1987-1996), at 204-07 (P.H.F. Bekker ed., 1998).

7   *Id.* at 207. Notable exceptions to this practice during the period reviewed were LaGrand Case (Ger. v. U.S.) and Arrest Warrant of 11 April 2000 (Dem. Rep. of the Congo v. Bel.), which proceeded straight to a hearing.

8   *See infra* section 2.2. See, especially, Land and Maritime Boundary between Cameroon and Nigeria (Cameroon v. Nigeria), Preliminary Objections, Judgment, 1998 ICJ REP. 275 (June 11); Fisheries Jurisdiction (Spain v. Canada), Jurisdiction, Judgment, 1998 ICJ REP. 432 (Dec. 4); and Aerial Incident of 10 August 1999 (Pakistan v. India), Jurisdiction, Judgment of June 21, 2000. *See also* Legality of Use of Force (Yugo. v. Bel.) (Yugo. v. Neth.) (Yugo. v. Port.) (Yugo. v. Spain)

For the first time since 1952, the Court had an opportunity to develop its hitherto limited jurisprudence on counterclaims, not once, but four times in the period reviewed, so that a more sophisticated jurisprudence has emerged on this aspect of the Court's incidental jurisdiction.[9] In one of these cases, the Court for the first time upheld the admissibility of counterclaims at a preliminary stage under the 1978 version of the Rules of Court.[10]

Besides the wide variety of substantive developments concerning the General List of cases between 1997 and 2001 discussed below, the Court continued to develop and modify the law governing its own procedure.[11] This development is linked with the frequent invocation of counterclaims in the period reviewed, in that the latest revision of the Rules of Court was concerned mainly with the provisions governing counterclaims found in Article 80 of the Rules.[12] In addition, Article 79 governing preliminary objections was amended to introduce a time limit for the filing of such objections.[13] The revisions to the Rules of Court, adopted on December 5, 2000 and effective February 1, 2001, marked the first revision since 1978.[14] With regard to the Court's internal procedure, it also was announced that the Court intends to abolish the practice of Notes by individual Judges in the preliminary phase of proceedings involving objections to the Court's jurisdiction or the admissibility of the application and that it has decided that Judges' declarations and separate and

---

(Yugo v. UK), 1999 ICJ REP. 124, 542, 761, 826 (Orders of June 2).

9   *See* Application of the Convention on the Prevention and Punishment of the Crime of Genocide (Bosnia-Herzegovina v. Yugoslavia), 1997 ICJ REP. 243 (Order of Dec. 17); Oil Platforms (Iran v. U.S.), 1998 ICJ REP. 190 (Order of Mar. 10); Land and Maritime Boundary between Cameroon and Nigeria (Cameroon v. Nigeria), Order of June 30, 1999; Armed Activities on the Territory of the Congo (Dem. Rep. of the Congo v. Uganda), Order of Nvember 29, 2001.

10   *See* Application of the Convention on the Prevention and Punishment of the Crime of Genocide (Bosnia-Herzegovina v. Yugoslavia), 1997 ICJ REP. 243 (Order of Dec. 17).

11   *See* ICJ Communiqués 98/14 (April 6, 1998), 2001/1 (January 12, 2001) and 2001/32 (October 31, 2001).

12   *See infra* section 2.4.5.

13   *See infra* section 2.4.1.

14   *See* ICJ Communiqué 2001/1 (January 12, 2001). *See also* "Background Note by the Registry Indicating the Rules of Court (1978) Amended on 5 December 2000," available from the Court's Web site, <www.icj-cij.org.>. ICJ Rules of Court, *reprinted in* 73 AJIL 748, 761 (1979) [as amended as of February 1, 2001, hereinafter R .les of Court].

dissenting opinions will no longer be presented sequentially, but will feature in the order of precedence of their authors.[15]

The Court also made the first site visit in its history.[16]

The Court had another opportunity to address the question of the position of third states in ICJ proceedings, as well as the effect of their absence.[17] In *Land and Maritime Boundary between Cameroon and Nigeria* (Cameroon v. Nigeria),[18] the full Court for the first time allowed a third state (Equatorial Guinea) to intervene as a nonparty in the main proceedings.[19]

The case concerning *Land and Maritime Boundary between Cameroon and Nigeria* (Cameroon v. Nigeria) was perhaps the most remarkable in the period reviewed, given the wide variety of procedural phases of incidental jurisdiction featured in this case: preliminary objections, interpretation, counterclaims and intervention, all of which were before the Court during 1998-1999.[20] Of these various instances, interpretation and intervention were the most prominent: the Court never before had been seised of a request to interpret a judgment on preliminary objections while the related proceedings on the merits were still pending, and no third party ever before had been granted permission to intervene as a nonparty in a case before the full Court. The Court's March 25, 1999

---

15 *See infra* section 2.5. *See also* ICJ Communiqués 98/14 (April 6, 1998), 2000/40 (December 8, 2000), 2001/1 (January 12, 2001), and 2001/32 (October 31, 2001).

16 *See* Gabčíkovo-Nagymaros Project (Hungary/Slovakia), 1997 ICJ REP. 3 (Order of Feb. 5).

17 *See*, e.g., Land and Maritime Boundary between Cameroon and Nigeria (Cameroon v. Nigeria), Preliminary Objections, Judgment, 1998 ICJ REP. 275, at 311-13, paras. 79-81 and 324-25, paras. 116-17 (June 11); Maritime Delimitation and Territorial Questions between Qatar and Bahrain (Qatar v. Bahrain), Judgment of March 16, 2001, at para. 221 (on the absence of Saudi Arabia).

18 *See* Order of Oct. 21, 1999.

19 Two years later, the Court found that the Philippines' Application for permission to intervene as a non-party in *Sovereignty over Pulau Ligitan and Pulau Sipadan (Indonesia/Malaysia)* could not be granted (Judgment of Oct. 23, 2001, reviewed in Chapter 5 below).

20 *See* Land and Maritime Boundary between Cameroon and Nigeria (Cameroon v. Nigeria), Preliminary Objections, Judgment, 1998 ICJ REP. 275 (June 11); Request for Interpretation of the Judgment of 11 June 1998 in the Case concerning the *Land and Maritime Boundary between Cameroon and Nigeria (Cameroon v. Nigeria)*, Preliminary Objections (Nigeria v. Cameroon), Interpretation, Judgment, 1999 ICJ REP. 31 (Mar. 25); Land and Maritime Boundary between Cameroon and Nigeria (Cameroon v. Nigeria), Counterclaims, Order of June 30, 1999; and Land and Maritime Boundary between Cameroon and Nigeria (Cameroon v. Nigeria), Application to Intervene, Order of Oct. 21, 1999.

Judgment declaring inadmissible Nigeria's request for interpretation was the first ever judgment that was not preceded by hearings.

The Court was faced with a record number of urgent requests for the indication of provisional measures of protection, all of which are reviewed in this book.[21] Of the Orders issued in response to such requests, the unanimous ones rendered in the so-called death penalty cases undoubtedly were the most prominent.[22] In one of these, the *LaGrand Case*, the Court made use, for the first time in its history, of the power conferred upon it by Article 75, paragraph 1 of the Rules of Court to indicate provisional measures *proprio motu* without holding a hearing.[23] In *Legality of Use of Force*, the Court for the first time dismissed requests for the indication of provisional measures for lack of *prima facie* jurisdiction.[24]

1.3   Substantive Legal Developments

Even though the Court issued only four Judgments on the merits of a case and one Advisory Opinion between 1997 and 2001, the various decisions featured in this book, especially those dealing with issues of incidental jurisdiction, evidence the wide range of substantive legal issues dealt with by, or presented to, the Court in the period reviewed.

Several cases involved situations of armed conflict or the use of force,[25]

---

21 *See infra* section 2.4.3.

22 *See* Vienna Convention on Consular Relations (Paraguay v. U.S.), Provisional Measures, 1998 ICJ REP. 248 (Order of Apr. 9) and LaGrand Case (Germany v. U.S.), Provisional Measures, 1999 ICJ REP. 9 (Order of Mar. 3).

23 *See* LaGrand Case (Germany v. U.S.), Provisional Measures, 1999 ICJ REP. 9 (Order of March 3).

24 *See* Legality of Use of Force (Yugoslavia v. Belgium), Legality of Use of Force (Yugoslavia v. Canada), Legality of Use of Force (Yugoslavia v. France), Legality of Use of Force (Yugoslavia v. Germany), Legality of Use of Force (Yugoslavia v. Italy), Legality of Use of Force (Yugoslavia v. The Netherlands), Legality of Use of Force (Yugoslavia v. Portugal), Legality of Use of Force (Yugoslavia v. Spain), Legality of Use of Force (Yugoslavia v. United Kingdom), Legality of Use of Force (Yugoslavia v. United States), Applications filed on April 29, 1999, Orders of June 2, 1999, 1999 ICJ REP. 124, 259, 363, 422, 481, 542, 656, 761, 826, 916.

25 *See*, e.g., Application of the Convention on the Prevention and Punishment of the Crime of Genocide (Bosnia-Herzegovina v. Yugoslavia), Preliminary Objections, Judgment, 1996 ICJ REP. 595 (July 11); Oil Platforms (Iran v. United States), Preliminary Objection, Judgment, 1996 ICJ REP. 803 (Dec. 12); Land and Maritime

many in the context of a territorial dispute, and most cases presented issues connected with the law of treaties and state responsibility,[26] the latter having gained an incidental environmental perspective as part of the Court's body of work.[27]

Boundary between Cameroon and Nigeria (Cameroon v. Nigeria), Application filed on March 29, 1994 (and supplemented on June 6, 1994); Legality of Use of Force (Yugoslavia v. Belgium), Legality of Use of Force (Yugoslavia v. Canada), Legality of Use of Force (Yugoslavia v. France), Legality of Use of Force (Yugoslavia v. Germany), Legality of Use of Force (Yugoslavia v. Italy), Legality of Use of Force (Yugoslavia v. The Netherlands), Legality of Use of Force (Yugoslavia v. Portugal), Legality of Use of Force (Yugoslavia v. Spain), Legality of Use of Force (Yugoslavia v. United Kingdom), Legality of Use of Force (Yugoslavia v. United States), Applications filed on April 29, 1999; Armed Activities on the Territory of the Congo (Dem. Rep. of the Congo v. Burundi), Armed Activities on the Territory of the Congo (Dem. Rep. of the Congo v. Rwanda), Armed Activities on the Territory of the Congo (Dem. Rep. of the Congo v. Uganda), Applications filed on June 23, 1999; Application of the Convention on the Prevention and Punishment of the Crime of Genocide (Croatia v. Yugoslavia), Application filed on July 2, 1999; Aerial Incident of 10 August 1999 (Pakistan v. India), Application filed on September 21, 1999, Jurisdiction, Judgment of June 21, 2000.

26 *See*, e.g., Application of the Convention on the Prevention and Punishment of the Crime of Genocide (Bosnia-Herzegovina v. Yugoslavia), Preliminary Objections, Judgment, 1996 ICJ REP. 595 (July 11); Application of the Convention on the Prevention and Punishment of the Crime of Genocide (Croatia v. Yugoslavia), Application filed on July 2, 1999; Questions of Interpretation and Application of the 1971 Montreal Convention arising from the Aerial Incident at Lockerbie (Libya v. United Kingdom) and (Libya v. United States), Preliminary Objections, Judgments, 1998 ICJ REP. 9 and 115 (Feb. 27); Fisheries Jurisdiction (Spain v. Canada), Jurisdiction, Judgment, 1998 ICJ REP. 432 (Dec. 4); Kasikili/Sedudu Island (Botswana/Namibia), Merits, Judgment of Dec. 13, 1999; Ahmadou Sadio Diallo (Guinea v. Dem. Rep. of the Congo), Application filed on December 28, 1998; Vienna Convention on Consular Relations (Paraguay v. U.S.), Application filed on April 3, 1998; LaGrand Case (Germany v. U.S.), Application filed on March 2, 1999, Judgment of June 27, 2001; Certain Property (Liechtenstein v. Germany), Application filed on June 1, 2001.

27 Especially, Gabčíkovo-Nagymaros Project (Hungary/Slovakia), Judgment, 1997 ICJ REP. 7 (Sept. 25). For additional statements on the environment, see Request for an Examination of the Situation in Accordance with Paragraph 63 of the Court's Judgment of 20 December 1974 in the *Nuclear Tests (New Zealand v. France)* Case, 1995 ICJ REP. 288, at 306, para. 64 (Order of Sept. 22), and Legality of the Threat or Use of Nuclear Weapons, 1996 ICJ REP. 226, at 241, para. 29 (Advisory Opinion of July 8).

Another group of cases, representing a classic type of dispute, involved complaints by applicant states of the treatment suffered by their nationals at the hands of the respondent states.[28]

The Court's Judgment of March 16, 2001 in *Maritime Delimitation and Territorial Questions between Qatar and Bahrain* (Qatar v. Bahrain) was its first decision involving maritime delimitation and other law of the sea issues since 1985.[29] The Court's decision fixing a single maritime boundary in this case for the first time relied entirely on customary international law. In addition, the Court received two new cases involving issues relating to the international law of the sea and maritime delimitation.[30]

For the first time since 1985, the Court received an application for revision of a decision previously rendered by it.[31]

In its decision on the merits of the *LaGrand Case* (Germany v. U.S.), rendered on June 27, 2001, the Court pointed out, for the first time in its history, that its Orders indicating provisional measures are legally binding.[32]

Through various decisions rendered between 1997 and 2001, the Court continued to develop the law relating to the United Nations, its principal organs and persons employed by it.[33] The Court received its second request from

28 *See*, e.g., Ahmadou Sadio Diallo (Guinea v. Dem. Rep. of the Congo), Application filed on December 28, 1998; LaGrand Case (Germany v. U.S.), Application filed on March 2, 1999, Judgment of June 27, 2001; Certain Property (Liechtenstein v. Germany), Application filed on June 1, 2001.

29 On the contribution of the ICJ to the development of the law of the sea, see a paper published by the Netherlands Institute for the Law of the Sea (authored by Barbara Kwiatkowska), available from <www.law.uu.nl/english/isep/nilos/Stockhol.pdf>. *See also* Barbara Kwiatkowska, *The Law-of-the-Sea-Related Cases in the International Court of Justice during the Presidency of Judge Stephen M. Schwebel*, 16 INT'L J. MAR. & COAST. L. 1 (2001).

30 *See* Maritime Delimitation between Nicaragua and Honduras in the Caribbean Sea (Nicar. v. Hond.), Application filed on December 8, 1999, and a case concerning title to territory and maritime delimitation in the western Caribbean filed by Nicaragua against Colombia on December 6, 2001.

31 *See* Application for Revision of the Judgment of 11 July 1996 in the Case concerning *Application of the Convention on the Prevention and Punishment of the Crime of Genocide (Bosnia-Herzegovina v. Yugoslavia)*, Preliminary Objections (Yugoslavia v. Bosnia-Herzegovina), Application of April 24, 2001.

32 *See* LaGrand Case (Ger. v. U.S.), Judgment of June 27, 2001.

33 *See* Questions of Interpretation and Application of the 1971 Montreal Convention Arising from the Aerial Incident at Lockerbie (Libya v. UK), Preliminary Objections, Judgment, 1998 ICJ REP. 9 (Feb. 27); Questions of Interpretation and Application of the 1971 Montreal Convention Arising from the Aerial Incident at Lockerbie

the Economic and Social Council (ECOSOC) for an Advisory Opinion relating to the legal position of a UN Special Rapporteur, its first binding advisory opinion issued under Section 30 of the General Convention on the Privileges and Immunities of the United Nations.[34]

The various proceedings before the Court presented many interesting examples and lasting lessons of judicial reasoning and litigation strategy before the principal judicial organ of the United Nations, many of which are highlighted in this book.

2   The ICJ in a Nutshell

In order to provide a basic understanding of the functioning of the Court as described in the present book, this section will present a concise overview of the Court's role and procedures, with references to its work from 1997 through 2001. Technicalities have been avoided as much as possible.[35]

The International Court of Justice, popularly known as the World Court, which has its seat at the Peace Palace in the Dutch city of The Hague,[36] is the principal judicial organ of the United Nations.[37] The ICJ replaced the Permanent Court of International Justice (PCIJ), whose Statute entered into force in 1921. The PCIJ operated under the auspices of the League of Nations, without

---

(Libya v. U.S.), Preliminary Objections, Judgment, 1998 ICJ REP. 115 (Feb. 27); Difference Relating to Immunity from Legal Process of a Special Rapporteur of the Commission on Human Rights, 1999 ICJ REP. 62 (Advisory Opinion of Apr. 29); Armed Activities on the Territory of the Congo (Dem. Rep. of the Congo v. Uganda), Provisional Measures, Order of July 1, 2000.

34 *See* Difference Relating to Immunity from Legal Process of a Special Rapporteur of the Commission on Human Rights, 1999 ICJ REP. 62 (Advisory Opinion of Apr. 29). For the first request, see Applicability of Article VI, Section 22, of the Convention on the Privileges and Immunities of the United Nations, Advisory Opinion, 1989 ICJ REP. 177 (Dec. 15).

35 For further reading, see the works listed in Annex D to this book and, especially, ARTHUR EYFFINGER, THE INTERNATIONAL COURT OF JUSTICE 1946-1996, at 401-13 (1996).

36 ICJ STATUTE Art. 22, para. 1.

37 UN CHARTER Art. 92; ICJ STATUTE Art. 1. According to Art. 7 of the UN Charter, the six principal organs of the United Nations are: the General Assembly, the Security Council, the Economic and Social Council, the Trusteeship Council, the Secretariat, and the ICJ. Of these, the ICJ is the only principal organ located outside New York.

ever becoming an official part (i.e., organ) of the League. The PCIJ sat between 1920 and 1942.[38] The ICJ was founded in 1945 upon the entry into force of the United Nations Charter on October 24th of that year. The ICJ Statute forms an integral part of the UN Charter, which means that the member states of the United Nations (currently numbering 189) automatically are parties to the Statute. The inaugural public sitting of the Court took place on April 18, 1946.

According to the Statute, the Court has a dual role: (1) to decide in accordance with international law the legal disputes submitted to it by sovereign states (*contentious jurisdiction*);[39] and (2) to give Advisory Opinions on legal questions referred to it by certain organs and agencies within the UN system (*advisory jurisdiction*).[40]

The functioning of the Court is governed by the United Nations Charter, the Statute, the Rules of Court (most recently revised in December 2000)[41] and a "Resolution concerning the International Judicial Practice of the Court."[42] The Statute has never been amended since it entered into force in 1945.

2.1   Composition

The Court is composed of 15 independent judges ("Members of the Court") from different countries. The composition of the Court as a whole is meant to reflect the main forms of civilization and the principal legal systems of the world.[43] This should ensure equitable geographical distribution of seats. Consequently, ICJ judges represent the following five regions: Africa (3 judges),

---

38   *See* MANLEY O. HUDSON, THE PERMANENT COURT OF INTERNATIONAL JUSTICE 1920-1942 (repr., 1972).

39   *See* ICJ STATUTE Art. 38, para. 1.

40   *See* ICJ STATUTE Arts. 65-68; UN CHARTER Art. 96.

41   Amendments to Arts. 79-80 of the Rules of Court, adopted on December 5, 2000, with effect from February 1, 2001, ICJ Communiqué 2001/1 (January 12, 2001). *See also* Eduardo Jiménez de Aréchaga, *The Amendment to the Rules of Procedure of the International Court of Justice*, 67 AJIL 1 (1973); SHABTAI ROSENNE, PROCEDURE IN THE INTERNATIONAL COURT OF JUSTICE – A COMMENTARY ON THE 1978 RULES OF THE INTERNATIONAL COURT OF JUSTICE (1982).

42   *See* Jennings, *infra* note 93.

43   *See* ICJ STATUTE Art. 9. The principal legal systems of the world include: Civil law, Common law, and Hindu, Islamic, Bhuddist, Confucian and Socialist legal traditions.

Asia (3 judges), Eastern Europe (2 judges), Latin America (2 judges), and Western Europe and other states (5 judges).

In accordance with United Nations practice, each of the five permanent members of the UN Security Council (China, France, the Russian Federation, the United Kingdom and the United States) has a judge of its nationality on the bench. Judges are elected to nine-year terms of office by the Security Council and the General Assembly of the United Nations voting simultaneously but independently of each other.

Candidates are nominated by the national groups in the Permanent Court of Arbitration[44] and need an absolute majority (fifty percent of the parties to the Statute plus one) in the General Assembly and a minimum of eight votes in the Security Council in order to be elected.[45] Elections are held at United Nations Headquarters in New York in the Fall every three years for one-third

---

44   The Permanent Court of Arbitration (PCA) was founded in 1899. It is not a court in the strict sense of the word, but consists of a list of some 265 jurists ("Members of the Court") from which states parties to the 1899 and 1907 Conventions on the Pacific Settlement of International Disputes may choose in case they wish to submit their disputes to arbitration by the PCA. Each state party may designate up to four jurists to be Members of the PCA for six-year terms. Appointments are renewable. Together, they form a "national group." Each national group may designate up to four candidates for election to the ICJ, whose names are communicated to the UN Secretary-General a few months before elections are held at United Nations Headquarters in New York. States that do not participate in the PCA may make ICJ nominations in a similar way. For a description of the nominating process within the U.S. National Group, see Lori Fisler Damrosch, *The Election of Thomas Buergenthal to the International Court of Justice*, 94 AJIL 579 (2000). For a discussion of the selection process, see INCREASING THE EFFECTIVENESS OF THE INTERNATIONAL COURT OF JUSTICE 165-206 (C. Peck & R. Lee eds., 1997). The PCA has adopted Optional Rules for Arbitration between states, between two parties of which only one is a state, involving international organizations and states, and between international organizations and private parties. In addition, the PCA has put in place Optional Conciliation Rules and Optional Rules of Procedure for Fact-Finding Commissions of Inquiry and Optional Rules for Arbitration of Disputes Relating to Natural Resources and/or the Environment. For detailed information on the PCA, which enjoys permanent observer status with the UN General Assembly, see the organization's Web site, <www.pca-cpa.org>.

45   According to Art. 2 of the ICJ Statute, candidates must be "persons of high moral character, who possess the qualifications required in their respective countries for appointment to the highest offices, or are jurisconsults of recognized competence in international law." In the General Assembly, Switzerland, which is the only non-member state that is a party to the ICJ Statute, also participates in the vote. *See* UNJYB 274 (1986) (opinion by the UN Office of Legal Affairs of May 9, 1986).

of the seats on the Court and whenever a vacancy needs to be filled due to the death[46] or resignation[47] of a judge.

Retiring judges may be re-elected. A judge who retires from the Court may only continue to sit in a case if oral proceedings in that case took place before the expiration of his or her term.

Immediately following the start of office of one-third of the Members of the Court at each triennial election (usually during the first week of February), the Court elects by secret ballot a president and vice president who serve on three-year terms.

Whenever a state party to a case before the Court has no judge of its nationality represented on the bench, it is entitled to appoint a person to sit as judge *ad hoc* for the purpose of that case. No nationality restrictions apply in such case.[48] Annex A to this book sets forth the composition of the Court between 1997 and 2001.

At regular intervals, the Judges meet to elect the members of the Court's standing chambers (2) and internal committees (6), namely, the Chamber of Summary Procedure,[49] the Chamber for Environmental Matters,[50] the Budget-

---

46 Between 1997 and 2001, no ICJ Judges died in office.

47 Between 1997 and 2001, the two immediate past presidents resigned. Judge Stephen Schwebel resigned immediately after his term as president (1997-2000) ended, with effect from February 29, 2000. *See* ICJ Communiqué 99/54 (Dec. 15, 1999). His predecessor, Judge Mohammed Bedjaoui, who was the Court's president during the seventeenth period (1994-1997), resigned with effect from September 30, 2001. *See* ICJ Communiqués 2001/20 (July 6, 2001) & 2001/25 (Oct. 12, 2001); *see also Election of a member of the International Court of Justice – Memorandum by the Secretary-General*, UN Docs. A/56/372 & S/2001/881 (2001).

48 *See* ICJ STATUTE, Art. 31. According to Article 3, paragraph 1 of the ICJ Statute, no two of the 15 *elected* Judges may be nationals of the same state. Judges *ad hoc*, who are *appointed* by states, are not considered regular "Members" of the Court, but otherwise take part in the proceedings on terms of complete equality with the regular ICJ Judges. *See also* Stephen M. Schwebel, *National Judges and Judges Ad Hoc*, in: MÉLANGES EN L'HONNEUR DE NICOLAS VALTICOS – DROIT ET JUSTICE 319 (1999).

49 According to Art. 29 of the ICJ Statute, "[w]ith a view to the speedy dispatch of business, the Court shall form annually a chamber composed of five judges which, at the request of the parties, may hear and determine cases by summary procedure." The president and vice president are members *ex officio* and the other three members, together with three substitutes, are elected. *See* Rules of Court, Art. 15, para. 1.

50 This Chamber, the seven members (the president, the vice president and five judges) of which are elected every three years, is the only one to have been established by the Court pursuant to Art. 26 of the ICJ Statute, according to which the Court

ary and Administrative Committee (chaired by the ICJ president *ex officio*), the Rules Committee, the Committee on Relations, the Library Committee, the Computerization Committee and the Committee on the Court's Museum.[51]

2.2   Contentious Jurisdiction

The Court is competent to entertain a legal dispute in a *contentious* case only if the states involved have accepted its jurisdiction. There must be jurisdiction both *ratione personae* and *ratione materiae*.

As regards the requirement of jurisdiction *ratione personae*, only sovereign states may apply to and appear before the Court.[52] The Court's potential clientèle is made up as follows. As stated above, the 189 member states of the United Nations are *ipso facto* parties to the Statute.[53] In addition, states not members of the United Nations (currently only Switzerland) which have become parties to the Statute, have standing before the Court.[54] Nonmember states may acquire access to the Court without becoming a party to the Statute, by depositing with the ICJ Registrar a general or particular statement accepting

---

may "form one or more chambers, composed of three or more judges as the Court may determine, for dealing with particular categories of cases; for example, labour cases and cases relating to transit and communications." The Chamber for Environmental Matters was established on July 19, 1993. *See* ICJ Communiqué 93/20 (July 19, 1993). Recourse to this Chamber is voluntary. No cases have as yet been submitted to it.

51 *See*, e.g., ICJ Communiqué 2000/3 (February 10, 2000).

52 *See* ICJ STATUTE Art. 34, para. 1. Private persons and international organizations are not entitled to institute contentious proceedings before the ICJ. The Court receives over 1,000 requests a year from private persons, who have to be informed that they lack standing. However, an individual's case may be taken up by his or her government against another government through the exercise of every government's inherent right to exercise diplomatic protection on behalf of its citizens.

53 *See* UN CHARTER Art. 93, para. 1.

54 States that become parties to the ICJ Statute must comply with certain conditions determined by the General Assembly upon the recommendation of the Security Council: (1) acceptance of the Court's jurisdiction in accordance with the provisions of the ICJ Statute; (2) acceptance of all the obligations of a UN member state under Article 94 of the Charter; and (3) an undertaking to contribute to the expense of the Court such equitable amount as the General Assembly may assess from time to time after consultation with the government of the state concerned. *See* SC Res. 91 (1946), UN Doc. A/64/Add.1, at 182 (1947).

the Court's jurisdiction and undertaking to comply with its decision and to accept the obligations of a UN member under Article 94 of the Charter.[55]

The requirement of jurisdiction *ratione materiae* reflects a fundamental principle governing the settlement of international disputes by the Court, i.e., the Court's jurisdiction depends in the last resort on the consent of the sovereign states concerned.[56] Generally speaking, such consent may be expressed in one of three ways:

1   by the conclusion between or among states of a "Special Agreement" (*compromis*) whereby they jointly express their consent to submit their dispute to the Court;[57]
2   by virtue of a jurisdictional or compromissory clause in an existing bilateral or multilateral treaty to which the disputing states are parties;[58] or
3   through the reciprocal effect of voluntary (optional) declarations made by some of the states parties to the Statute whereby one such state has accepted

---

55   *See* SC Res. 9 (1946), UN Doc. S/INF/2/Rev. 1(I), at 13 (1946). *See also* ICJ STATUTE Art. 35, para. 2; Rules of Court, Art. 26, para. 1(c), Art. 41.
56   The equality of sovereign states is a fundamental principle of international law. This means also that if the Court's decision in a given case necessarily would involve a determination of the rights and obligations of a third state which is absent from the proceedings, and such a determination would not only affect and have legal implications for the interests or rights and obligations of the absent state, but form the very subject matter of the Court's decision on the merits, the Court has no jurisdiction to entertain the dispute. See, e.g., Indonesia's absence in the proceedings blocking jurisdiction in East Timor (Port. v. Austl.), Judgment, 1995 ICJ REP. 90 (June 30).
57   *See* ICJ STATUTE Art. 36, para. 1. Between 1997 and 2002, only one case was instituted on this basis: Sovereignty over Pulau Ligitan and Pulau Sipadan (Indo./ Mala.) (Nov. 2, 1998). In addition, Slovakia filed a request for an additional judgment in the case it brought with Hungary on September 3, 1998.
58   *See* ICJ STATUTE Art. 36, para. 1. Some 260 treaties currently contain a clause of this kind. Between 1997 and 2001, the following cases were brought on this basis: *Vienna Convention on Consular Relations (Paraguay v. U.S.)*; *LaGrand Case (Germany v. U.S.)*; *Application of the Convention on the Prevention and Punishment of the Crime of Genocide (Croatia v. Yugoslavia)*; *Armed Activities on the Territory of the Congo (Dem. Rep. of the Congo v. Burundi)*; *Armed Activities on the Territory of the Congo (Dem. Rep. of the Congo v. Rwanda)*; *Maritime Delimitation between Nicaragua and Honduras in the Caribbean Sea (Nicaragua v. Honduras)*; *Certain Property (Liechtenstein v. Germany); and the case brought by Nicaragua against Colombia on December 6, 2001. See also* the cases concerning *Legality of Use of Force* (except for the ones against Spain and the U.S.).

the Court's jurisdiction as compulsory in the event of a dispute with another state which has made a similar declaration (so-called Optional Clause acceptance of the Court's compulsory jurisdiction).[59]

The declarations of some 63 states are in force at present, a number of them having been made subject to reservations excluding certain categories of dispute. Declarations take effect upon their deposit with the Secretary-General of the United Nations in New York.[60] Through the principle of reciprocity, the narrower of two declarations dictates the Court's jurisdiction.[61] This means that the Court's jurisdiction in a particular case based on Optional Clause declarations is restricted to those classes of dispute that are not excluded by way of any reservations attached to the declarations of the states involved and only insofar as the declarations coincide or

---

59 *See* ICJ STATUTE Art. 36, para. 2. Between 1997 and 2001, the following cases were brought on this basis: *Ahmadou Sadio Diallo (Guinea v. Dem. Rep. of the Congo)*; *Legality of Use of Force (Yugoslavia v. Belgium)*; *Legality of Use of Force (Yugoslavia v. Canada)*; *Legality of Use of Force (Yugoslavia v. The Netherlands)*; *Legality of Use of Force (Yugoslavia v. Portugal)*; *Legality of Use of Force (Yugoslavia v. Spain)*; *Legality of Use of Force (Yugoslavia v. United Kingdom)*; *Armed Activities on the Territory of the Congo (Dem. Rep. of the Congo v. Uganda)*; *Aerial Incident of 10 August 1999 (Pakistan v. India)* (Pakistan's Application relied also on the 1928 General Act for Pacific Settlement of Disputes and on Art. 36, para. 1 of the Statute); *Maritime Delimitation between Nicaragua and Honduras the Caribbean Sea (Nicaragua v. Honduras)*; and the case brought by Nicaragua against Colombia on December 6, 2001.

60 *See* Land and Maritime Boundary between Cameroon and Nigeria (Cameroon v. Nigeria), Preliminary Objections, Judgment, 1998 ICJ REP. 275, at 290-96, paras. 21-35 (June 11).

61 *See id.* at 298-300, paras. 41-46. Under Article 36 of the Statute, reciprocity is expressed in two ways in that declarations apply "in relation to any other state accepting the same obligation" (para. 2) and are allowed to be made "on condition of reciprocity on the part of several or certain states" (para. 3). As at December 31, 2001, the following 63 states had accepted the Optional Clause jurisdiction of the ICJ, in one form or another: Australia, Austria, Barbados, Belgium, Botswana, Bulgaria, Cambodia, Cameroon, Canada, Colombia, Costa Rica, Cyprus, Democratic Republic of the Congo, Denmark, Dominican Republic, Egypt, Estonia, Finland, Gambia, Georgia, Greece, Guinea, Guinea-Bissau, Haiti, Honduras, Hungary, India, Japan, Kenya, Lesotho, Liberia, Liechtenstein, Luxembourg, Madagascar, Malawi, Malta, Mauritius, Mexico, Nauru, Netherlands, New Zealand, Nicaragua, Nigeria, Norway, Pakistan, Panama, Paraguay, Philippines, Poland, Portugal, Senegal, Somalia, Spain, Sudan, Suriname, Swaziland, Sweden, Switzerland, Togo, Uganda, United Kingdom, Uruguay, and Yugoslavia. The text of the declarations may be found in the ICJ YEARBOOK.

overlap. Reservations can be of a wide variety and may exclude from the Court's jurisdiction disputes involving certain treaties, states, hostilities situations or categories.[62]

When proceedings have been instituted by one state against another on the basis of the Optional Clause, the latter may seek to defeat the Court's jurisdiction by invoking any reservations contained in its own declaration and, through the effect of reciprocity, any reservation excluding disputes contained in the Applicant's declaration. The effect of this mechanism is that the broader a state's reservations are, the less likely it will be able to have recourse to the Court by instituting proceedings against another state. Thus, the protective shield of reservations to a state's declaration may effectively hinder its ability to use the Court.

Although the number of declarations increased from 46 in 1987 to 63 in 2000-2001, this increase is less impressive when viewed against the sharp increase in membership in the United Nations from 159 in 1986 to 189 in 2001. Consequently, only one-third of the UN member states have accepted the Optional Clause jurisdiction of the Court. At the same time, it should be remembered that of all the cases that have ever been brought before the Court, only one-third were based on Optional Clause jurisdiction, while the other two-thirds relied on jurisdictional clauses in bilateral or multilateral treaties and on special agreements.

Technically speaking, there is yet a fourth option to consent to the Court's jurisdiction, namely that of *forum prorogatum*, where an Applicant (the name for the plaintiff in an ICJ case) submits a unilateral Application to the Court naming another state as Respondent (the name for the defendant), thereby as it were inviting that state to accept the Court's jurisdiction in this case, and the state named as Respondent subsequently recognizes the Court's jurisdiction either explicitly or tacitly (e.g., by pleading on the merits of the case).[63]

---

62 *See*, e.g., Fisheries Jurisdiction (Spain v. Canada), Jurisdiction, Judgment, 1998 ICJ REP. 432 (Dec. 4); Aerial Incident of 10 August 1999 (Pakistan v. India), Jurisdiction, Judgment of June 21, 2000, at paras. 29-44. *See*, generally, STANIMIR A. ALEXANDROV, RESERVATIONS IN UNILATERAL DECLARATIONS ACCEPTING THE COMPULSORY JURISDICTION OF THE INTERNATIONAL COURT OF JUSTICE (1995).

63 *See* Rules of Court, Art. 38, para. 5; ICJ YEARBOOK 1996-1997 at 216-34. Examples of this category are Yugoslavia's Applications naming France, Germany, Italy and the United States as Respondent, filed in the Registry on April 29, 1999, and Eritrea's Application naming Ethiopia as Respondent, filed in the Registry on February 16, 1999 (*see* ICJ Communiqué 99/4 (Feb. 16, 1999)). By contrast to the

Each means of establishing the Court's jurisdiction *ratione materiae*, i.e., of expressing the requisite consent, forms a "basis of jurisdiction." However, independently of the basis of jurisdiction invoked by an Applicant against a Respondent, there must be a valid procedural act instituting proceedings before the Court.[64] The Court is unable to entertain a case so long as the relevant basis of jurisdiction has not been supplemented by what is called an act of "seisin." Seisin relates to procedure. Valid seisin of the Court is possible only when there exists a prior basis of jurisdiction (except for *forum prorogatum* cases, where jurisdiction follows seisin). There are two modalities of seisin: unilateral seisin and joint seisin.

Unilateral seisin is accomplished by means of the filing in the Registry of an "Application." The Application must describe the name of the state against which proceedings are brought, the subject of the dispute, the basis of jurisdiction and the facts and grounds on which the Applicant relies. In cases of unilateral seisin, it is the practice of the Court to separate the parties by the abbreviation of the Latin word *versus* ("A *v.* B") in the official title of the case. The related bases of jurisdiction for unilateral seisin are Optional Clause declarations and jurisdictional clauses in bilateral or multilateral treaties.

Joint seisin is accomplished by the notification by either of the states parties to the proceedings or by both of a "Special Agreement." The Special Agreement must describe the subject of the dispute and the parties thereto. The related basis of jurisdiction in such instance is the agreement itself, which qualifies as an *ad hoc* bilateral treaty and defines the question that the parties request the Court to decide. In cases of joint seisin, it is the practice of the Court to separate the names of the parties by an oblique stroke ("A/B") in the official title of the case. Once the Court has been validly seised, the parties to a case are bound by the procedural and substantive consequences that the Statute and the Rules of Court attach to the method of seisin employed. The Court always has the final say in matters relating to its jurisdiction.[65]

---

latter, the Court did take some action on the former cases, considering and rejecting Yugoslavia's request for provisional measures in these cases, before removing the case brought against the United States from the General List by its Order of June 2, 1999.

64 *See* ICJ STATUTE Art. 40 and Part III, Section C, Subsection I, and Arts. 38-39, of the Rules of Court.

65 *See* ICJ STATUTE Art. 36, para. 6. For a discussion of the concept of seisin, see Maritime Delimitation and Territorial Questions between Qatar and Bahrain (Qatar v. Bahrain), Judgment (Jurisdiction and Admissibility), 1995 ICJ REP. 6, at 17, paras. 30-42 (Feb. 15).

The above concise outline can be misleading in its simplicity: the issue of the Court's jurisdiction in fact has developed into an extremely difficult and technical area of international law, which plays a critical part in most of the cases that are submitted to the Court, especially those that are brought unilaterally against "involuntary" respondents.

2.3   Main Proceedings

The main proceedings before the Court are divided into a written phase and an oral phase. A state may refuse to appear in the proceedings before the Court, but this does not prevent the Court from rendering a decision on the merits after it has satisfied itself that it has jurisdiction over the case and that the claim is well founded in fact and in law.[66]

During the written phase, the parties file pleadings that include detailed statements of the points of fact and of law in a case. The written pleadings are generally prepared by special teams in the ministries of foreign affairs of the parties, assisted by experts typically drawn from the academic world. Orders issued by the Court or its president shortly after a case has been brought fix time limits for the filing of pleadings, which may be extended by the Court or its president upon request of either party. Time limits range from three to eighteen months and are usually the same in length for both parties. The Applicant usually files a Memorial, followed by a Counter-Memorial of the Respondent. If the parties so request or if the Court deems it necessary, the Court may order a second round of written pleadings, in which the Applicant files a Reply and the Respondent submits a Rejoinder. In cases brought by Special Agreement, the parties themselves usually fix in advance the number, order and time limits of the pleadings in their agreement. In such cases, both parties file a Memorial, a Counter-Memorial, and sometimes a Reply and a Rejoinder. Each party must file 125 copies of its pleading including annexes in the Registry. Any document not in English or French must be accompanied by a certified translation into one of those languages. Pleadings are confidential. According to Article 53 of the Statute, it is for the Court to decide, after

---

66 *See* ICJ STATUTE Art. 53. On non-appearance, *see* Stanimir A. Alexandrov, *Non-Appearance before the International Court of Justice*, 33 COLUM. J. TRANSNAT'L L. 41 (1995), referring to additional literature. *See also* Keith Highet, *Nonappearance and Disappearance Before the International Court of Justice*, 81 AJIL 237-54 (1987).

consultation with the parties, whether copies of the written pleadings filed in a case are made available, before or after the oral proceedings, to a state entitled to appear before the Court which has requested to be furnished with such copies, or, on or after the opening of the hearings, to the public.[67]

As soon as all the written pleadings have been filed, a case becomes ready for hearing, constituting the oral phase of an ICJ case. At public sittings in the "Great Hall of Justice" of the Peace Palace in The Hague, the parties' representatives (Agents, counsel and advocates) address the Court by presenting official statements prepared in advance. Judges may pose questions, to which the parties are expected to respond in writing before the end of the hearings or within a reasonable time period afterwards. There is no active bench. Hearings usually last between one and three weeks: during the first phase, the Applicant presents its oral argument, followed by the Respondent's reply during the second phase.[68] A third phase usually is reserved for rebuttal and surrebuttal by each party. The Court and the parties may call witnesses and/or experts to testify at the hearings. The hearings end with the presentation by the Agents of the parties of their "final submissions" describing the formal decision requested from the Court.

2.4   Incidental or interlocutory proceedings[69]

There are five principal types of incidental or interlocutory proceedings at the Court: (1) Preliminary Objections; (2) "Initial Phase" procedure (questions of jurisdiction and/or admissibility); (3) Provisional Measures; (4) Intervention; and (5) Counterclaims. Each of them will be discussed briefly below.

---

67 *See* Sovereignty over Pulau Ligitan and Pulau Sipadan (Indo./Mala.), Judgment of October 23, 2001 (discussed in Chapter 5 below).

68 As announced in April 1998, the Court in recent cases has attempted to restrict the time allocated to hearing the parties in an effort to accelerate the proceedings. *See* ICJ Communiqués 98/14 (April 6, 1998) and 2001/1 (January 12, 2001) (announcing a revision to the "Note" containing recommendations to the parties to a new case, which provides that, in cases involving objections of lack of jurisdiction or of inadmissibility, "oral proceedings must be limited to statements on the objections and observe the requisite degree of brevity."). For the most recent comprehensive overhaul of the "Note" to new parties to cases and the introduction of "Practice Directions," see ICJ Communiqué 2001/32 (October 31, 2001) (summarized at the end of the introductory section to Chapter 5 below).

69 *I.e.*, proceedings that do not address or dispose of the merits of a case.

2.4.1 Preliminary Objections

The Respondent has the right to file one or several objections to the Court's jurisdiction and/or the admissibility of the Application in an effort to prevent the Court from rendering a judgment on the merits of a case. The right to file Preliminary Objections must be exercised "as soon as possible, and not later than three months after the delivery of the Memorial."[70] They may even be filed before the filing of a Memorial by the Applicant.[71] Once Preliminary Objections are filed, the proceedings on the merits are automatically suspended and a trial within a trial occurs, governed by Article 79 of the Rules of Court. In such Preliminary Objections, the party making these may argue that the basis of jurisdiction on which the other party relies is absent or no longer in force, that the dispute is beyond the scope of the basis of jurisdiction invoked, or that the claim is inadmissible, because local remedies have not been exhausted or there is no "legal" or justiciable dispute. An Order issued by the Court or its president will determine the time limit within which the Applicant may submit its written "observations and submissions" on the Preliminary Objections filed by the Respondent.[72] The oral proceedings will be limited to the Preliminary Objections and the judgment rendered by the Court will stipulate whether the Preliminary Objection concerned will be upheld (in which case the proceedings are terminated), rejected, or declared not to possess an exclusively pre-

---

70 Rules of Court, Art. 79, para. 1 (amendment effective February 1, 2001). Prior to February 1, 2001, and with respect to cases pending as of that date, the right to file Preliminary Objections had to be exercised before the expiration of the time limit fixed for the delivery of the Counter-Memorial. *See* ICJ Communiqué 2001/1 (January 12, 2001).

71 *See,* e.g., Monetary Gold Removed from Rome in 1943 (Italy v. France/UK/U.S.), 1954 ICJ REP. 19 (June 15); Aerial Incident of 3 July 1988 (Iran v. U.S.), 1989 ICJ REP. 132, at 134 (Order of Dec. 13). If a Preliminary Objection is made by a party other than the Respondent, it must be filed within the time limit fixed for the delivery of that party's first pleading. *See* Rules of Court, Art. 79, para. 1 (final sentence).

72 In an effort to accelerate the proceedings on Preliminary Objections, the Court revised its "Note" containing recommendations to the parties in a case (provided to all parties to a new case) to indicate that the time limit for the presentation of a written statement of one party's observations and submissions to another party's Preliminary Objections generally should not exceed four months. *See* ICJ Communiqué 2001/1 (January 12, 2001). *See also* ICJ Communiqué 2001/32 (October 31, 2001), introducing a new set of "Practice Directions" (summarized at the end of the introductory note to Chapter 5 below).

liminary character. In the last two scenarios, the proceedings on the merits will be resumed. In case the Respondent decides to raise certain objections during its argument on the merits (and not as Preliminary Objections under Article 79 of the Rules of Court), as did Australia in *East Timor* (Portugal v. Australia), the Court still must decide upon these objections *proprio motu* before it can decide on the merits of the case. Significantly, *Aerial Incident of 10 August 1999* and *Fisheries Jurisdiction* are the only contentious cases in which the Court decided not to exercise its jurisdiction during the period reviewed, a result that had not been seen in The Hague, except for *East Timor*, since 1978, when the Court found that it was without jurisdiction to entertain the Application filed by Greece against Turkey in *Aegean Sea Continental Shelf*.[73]

Between 1997 and 2001, Preliminary Objections were introduced and rejected in the following three cases: *Questions of Interpretation and Application of the 1971 Montreal Convention arising from the Aerial Incident at Lockerbie* (Libya v. United Kingdom) and (Libya v. United States);[74] and *Land and Maritime Boundary between Cameroon and Nigeria* (Cameroon v. Nigeria).[75] Moreover, Belgium, Canada, France, Germany, Italy, The Netherlands, Portugal and the United Kingdom filed Preliminary Objections in the *Legality of Use of Force* cases initiated against each of them by Yugoslavia in July 2000.

2.4.2 Initial Phase Procedure

The parties to a case may request the Court to decide, or the Court may direct on its own motion, that the first phase of the proceedings be devoted entirely to the issues of the Court's jurisdiction to entertain the dispute and the admissibility of the Application. Similar to Preliminary Objections procedure, this also operates like a trial within a trial, but with the addition of one or two full rounds of written pleadings. Initial Phase procedure has developed from practice since 1972 and until February 2001 was not dealt with in the Statute

---

73 *See* Aegean Sea Continental Shelf (Greece v. Turk.), Jurisdiction, Judgment, 1978 ICJ REP. 3 (Dec. 19).

74 1998 ICJ REP. 9 and 115, respectively (Feb. 27).

75 1998 ICJ REP. 275 (June 11).

or Rules of Court.[76] It was first adopted in the *Fisheries Jurisdiction* (UK v. Iceland) and (Fed. Rep. of Germany v. Iceland) cases and was followed in a line of cases up to *Aerial Incident of 10 August 1999* (Pakistan v. India), where an Initial Phase procedure limited to the issue of the Court's jurisdiction was commenced in 1999 and concluded in 2000.[77]

Initial Phase procedure began as a way of dealing first with questions of jurisdiction and admissibility in instances where the Respondent, having declined to appear, decided not to file Preliminary Objections, but indicated unofficially that it disputed the Court's jurisdiction to entertain the dispute and/ or the admissibility of the Application. The procedure later was extended to instances where the Respondent had not declined to appear and where the Court by its own motion directed that the initial proceedings be addressed to complicated issues of jurisdiction and admissibility. Under the Initial Phase procedure, the initiative remains with the Court. While either party may suggest the opening of an Initial Phase, the Court decides. The decision of the Court is embodied in an Order opening the Initial Phase procedure and suspending the proceedings on the merits. The Memorial and the Counter-Memorial, as well as the Reply and the Rejoinder if necessary, address jurisdiction and/or admissibility issues only. The same applies to the Court's Judgment. If the Judgment upholds the Court's jurisdiction to entertain the dispute and the admissibility of the Application, the case will proceed to the merits.

---

76 *See* ICJ Communiqué 2001/1 (January 12, 2001). For a clear statement on the distinction between Initial Phase procedure and Preliminary Objections, see Military and Paramilitary Activities in and against Nicaragua (Nicar. v. U.S.), Jurisdiction and Admissibility, Judgment, 1984 ICJ REP. 392, at 425, para.76 (Nov. 26).

77 In the following ten Initial Phase cases, the Applicant was ordered to file the initial pleading arguing in favor of jurisdiction/admissibility: *Fisheries Jurisdiction (Germany v. Iceland)*; *Fisheries Jurisdiction (United Kingdom v. Iceland)*; *Nuclear Test (Australia v. France)*; *Nuclear Tests (New Zealand v. France)*; *Trial of Pakistani Prisoners of War (Pakistan v. India)*; *Aegean Sea Continental Shelf (Greece v. Turkey)*; *Military and Paramilitary Activities in and against Nicaragua (Nicaragua v. U.S.)*; *Maritime Delimitation and Territorial Questions between Qatar and Bahrain (Qatar v. Bahrain)*; *Fisheries Jurisdiction (Spain v. Canada)*; *Aerial Incident of 10 August 1999 (Pakistan v. India)*. In the remaining three Initial Phase cases, the Respondent objecting to jurisdiction/admissibility was ordered to file the initial pleading: *Border and Transborder Armed Actions (Nicaragua v. Honduras)*; *Armed Activities on the Territory of the Congo (Dem. Rep. of the Congo v. Burundi)*; *Armed Activities on the Territory of the Congo (Dem. Rep. of the Congo v. Rwanda)*.

With effect from February 1, 2001, the Rules of Court were amended to codify the above practice whereby the Court may decide that any questions of jurisdiction and admissibility shall be determined separately.[78]

Between 1997 and 2001, Initial Phase procedure applied in the following cases: *Maritime Delimitation and Territorial Questions between Qatar and Bahrain* (Qatar v. Bahrain)*; Fisheries Jurisdiction* (Spain v. Canada) (jurisdiction only); *Armed Activities on the Territory of the Congo* (Democratic Republic of the Congo v. Burundi) (jurisdiction only); *Armed Activities on the Territory of the Congo* (Democratic Republic of the Congo v. Rwanda); and *Aerial Incident of 10 August 1999* (Pakistan v. India) (jurisdiction only).[79] *Maritime Delimitation and Territorial Questions between Qatar and Bahrain* is the only case in the history of the Court in which it ordered *proprio motu* that a full second round of written pleadings be held in an Initial Phase case.[80]

2.4.3   Provisional Measures

A state party to a case may at any time during the proceedings request the Court to indicate interim measures of protection, a form of injunctive relief.[81] If the Court considers that there is urgency and a risk of irremediable harm to the subject matter of the case (i.e., where the respective rights of either party are in immediate danger and deserve to be preserved), it will issue an Order indicating protective measures, usually after hearings are held on a priority

---

78   *See* ICJ Communiqué 2001/1 (January 12, 2001). The amendment, which is found in paragraphs 2 and 3 of Art. 79 of the Rules of Court, applies only to cases submitted after February 1, 2001. According to paragraph 2, "(...) following the submission of the application and after the President has met and consulted with the parties, the Court may decide that any questions of jurisdiction and admissibility shall be determined separately." Paragraph 3 provides that "[w]here the Court so decides, the parties shall submit any pleadings as to jurisdiction and admissibility within the time-limits fixed by the Court and in the order determined by it (...)."

79   In addition, in *Arrest Warrant of 11 April 2000*, Belgium accepted to address both questions of jurisdiction and admissibility and the merits of the dispute, but this cannot be said to transform the proceedings into an Initial Phase case properly so-called.

80   By contrast, in its Order of May 8, 1996, the Court rejected Spain's request to be authorized to file a Reply as part of a second round of written pleadings on the question of the Court's jurisdiction in Fisheries Jurisdiction (Spain v. Canada). *See* 1996 ICJ REP. 58.

81   *See* ICJ STATUTE Art. 41.

basis.[82] At this stage, the Court must satisfy itself that it does not manifestly lack jurisdiction in the case. However, the Court's Order itself cannot be taken as establishing jurisdiction in a case; it does not preclude a subsequent finding that the Court lacks jurisdiction or that the application is inadmissible. In other words, an Order indicating provisional measures leaves unaffected any future findings that the Court might make on its jurisdiction, the admissibility of the application introducing the proceedings, or the merits.

Between 1997 and 2001, the Court dealt with requests for interim measures in the following cases: on April 3, 1998, Paraguay filed a request in *Vienna Convention on Consular Relations* (Paraguay v. United States), which the Court upheld by its Order of April 9, 1998;[83] on March 2, 1999, Germany filed a request in the *LaGrand Case* (Germany v. United States), which the Court upheld by its Order of March 3, 1999;[84] on April 29, Yugoslavia filed requests in *Legality of Use of Force* against ten NATO member states, which the Court rejected by its Orders of June 2, 1999; on June 19, 2000, the Democratic Republic of the Congo filed a request in *Armed Activities on the Territory of the Congo* (Dem. Rep. of the Congo v. Uganda), which led to certain measures indicated by the Court in its Order of July 1, 2000, and on October 17, 2000, the Democratic Republic of the Congo filed a request in *Arrest Warrant of 11 April 2000* (Dem. Rep. of the Congo v. Belgium), which the Court rejected by its Order of December 8, 2000.

2.4.4   Intervention

If a state believes that it has a legal interest in a pending case to which it is not a party, it may submit to the Court an "Application for Permission to Intervene" in that case.[85] The Court decides upon such a request after granting

---

82   *But see* LaGrand Case (Germany v. U.S.), Provisional Measures, 1999 ICJ REP.
      9 (Order of Mar. 3), in which no hearing was held due to the extreme urgency of
      the request.

83   1998 ICJ REP. 248.

84   1999 ICJ REP. 9.

85   During the period reviewed, the Court received two such applications, namely one
      dated June 30, 1999 by Equatorial Guinea in *Land and Maritime Boundary between
      Cameroon and Nigeria (Cameroon v. Nigeria)* and the other dated March 13, 2001
      by the Philippines in *Sovereignty over Pulau Ligitan and Pulau Sipadan (Indonesia/
      Malaysia). See* ICJ Communiqués 99/35 (June 30, 1999) and 2001/17 (March 15,
      2001).

the parties an opportunity to express their views.[86] Until 1999, *Land, Island and Maritime Frontier Dispute* (El Salvador/Honduras) was the only case in which a Chamber of the Court granted a third state (Nicaragua) such permission to intervene.[87] The full Court finally followed the 1990 example set by this Chamber in *Land and Maritime Boundary between Cameroon and Nigeria* (Cameroon v. Nigeria) in 1999, granting Equatorial Guinea permission to intervene as a non-party.[88] However, the Court rejected the contested Application of the Philippines in *Sovereignty over Pulau Ligitan and Pulau Sipadan* (Indonesia/Malaysia) two years later.[89]

In addition, if a case involves the construction of a multilateral treaty to which third states are parties, such states are notified of the pending case and have the right to file a declaration of intervention in the proceedings (subject to the Court's examination of the admissibility of the intervention), in which case they accept to be bound by the Judgment.[90]

2.4.5   Counterclaims

A party in a pending case has the right to present a counterclaim against the other party if such a claim satisfies three basic requirements, one *ratione temporis* and the other two *ratione materiae*: (1) the counterclaim must be made in the counter-memorial of the party presenting the counterclaim as part of that party's submissions; (2) the counterclaim must come within the Court's jurisdiction; and (3) it must be directly connected with the subject matter of the other party's claim.[91] Thus, a party cannot use a counterclaim to introduce

---

86 *See* ICJ STATUTE Art. 62.
87 1990 ICJ REP. 92 (Sept. 13).
88 Order of Oct. 21, 1999. *See* ICJ Communiqué 2001/17 (March 15, 2001).
89 *See* Judgment of October 23, 2001. On March 13, 2001, the Philippines filed an Application for permission to intervene in *Sovereignty over Pulau Ligitan and Pulau Sipadan (Indo./Mala.)*, aimed at preserving its long-standing claims to dominion and sovereignty over territory in North Borneo. Whereas Cameroon and Nigeria had no objection in principle to the Application for permission to intervene of Equatorial Guinea in their case, Indonesia and Malaysia both successfully opposed the Application of the Philippines in 2001.
90 *See* ICJ STATUTE Art. 63.
91 *See* Rules of Court, Art. 80, paras. 1-2. With effect from February 1, 2001, Art. 80 of the Rules of Court governing counterclaims was amended to reverse the order in which the basic requirements must be fulfilled (assigning priority to the jurisdiction requirement over the "direct connection" requirement) (para. 1), to preserve

claims that exceed the limits of the Court's jurisdiction as recognized by the parties. The extent of the connection required by the third condition is assessed by the Court both in fact and in law based on the parties' submissions and usually is satisfied if the parties' claims rest on facts of the same nature forming part of the same factual complex and pursue the same legal aim. The party against whom the counterclaim is introduced may assert both lack of jurisdiction and lack of connection, so long as this is done at the preliminary stage of the order ruling on the admissibility of the counterclaims, i.e., usually through its written observations on the counterclaim(s).[92]

---

the right of the party against which counterclaims are raised to present its views on the counterclaim in an additional pleading (para. 2), and to indicate that, where an objection is raised concerning the application of the first paragraph or whenever the Court deems it necessary, the Court shall take its decision thereon after hearing the parties (para. 3). The amendments to Art. 80 apply only to cases submitted after February 1, 2001. *See* ICJ Communiqué 2001/1 (January 12, 2001).

92   *See id.* Art. 80, para. 3. In practice, the Court has dispensed with holding a public hearing on counterclaims, preferring instead to be informed by the parties in writing. *See* Application of the Convention on the Prevention and Punishment of the Crime of Genocide (Bosnia-Herzegovina v. Yugoslavia), 1997 ICJ REP. 243 (Order of Dec. 17); Oil Platforms (Iran v. U.S.), 1998 ICJ REP. 190 (Order of Mar. 10); Land and Maritime Boundary between Cameroon and Nigeria (Cameroon v. Nigeria), Order of June 30, 1999; Armed Activities on the Territory of the Congo (Dem. Rep. of the Congo v. Uganda), Order of November 29, 2001. These four decisions are reviewed in Chapters 2, 3 and 5 below. Reflecting the Court's jurisprudence on counterclaims, Art. 80, para. 2 of the Rules of Court was revised, with effect from February 1, 2001, to state expressly that the right of the party against whom a counterclaim is made to present its views on the counterclaim in an additional pleading is preserved. *See* ICJ Communiqué 2001/1 (Jan. 12, 2001). In implementation of this revision, and notwithstanding the Court's announcement that the 1978 version of the Rules of Court would continue to apply to all cases submitted to the Court prior to February 1, 2001, the Court's Order of February 20, 2001 fixed a time limit for the filing by Cameroon of an additional pleading in *Land and Maritime Boundary between Cameroon and Nigeria (Cam. v. Nig.)* (Order of Feb. 20, 2001). The same arrangement was followed in *Oil Platforms (Iran v. U.S.)* through the Vice President's Order of August 28, 2001. *See* ICJ Communiqué 2001/ 21 (August 30, 2001). *See also* Armed Activities on the Territory of the Congo (Dem. Rep. of the Congo v. Uganda), Order of November 29, 2001. The President's Order of September 10, 2001 officially recorded the withdrawal by Yugoslavia of its counterclaims in the *Genocide (Bosnia)* case, marking the first time in the Court's history that counterclaims have been withdrawn.

2.5   Deliberations

Upon the conclusion of the oral proceedings, the Court enters into deliberations. Deliberations are secret. This stage of the proceedings is governed by a "Resolution concerning the Internal Judicial Practice of the Court" adopted in revised form by the Court in 1976.[93] Deliberations typically take about three to six months and are divided into the following phases. First, the President submits to his fellow judges an outline of the issues dividing the parties. The President's outline is discussed and commented on by the judges during the initial deliberative meeting at which individual judges state their preliminary views. Judges then have several weeks to prepare their individual Written Notes in which they give their tentative views on the issues presented in the President's outline.[94] After the conclusion of a case, these confidential notes are destroyed by the Registry. Deliberative meetings then are resumed and judges express their views orally and in inverse order of seniority. After this session, the Court proceeds to elect a Drafting Committee consisting of three judges. Two members of the Drafting Committee are elected by secret ballot from among those judges whose views most closely reflect the opinion of the apparent majority position within the Court. The president will act as chairman *ex officio* of the Drafting Committee, unless he shares the minority opinion, in which case the vice president will preside over the meetings of the Drafting Committee.[95] A regular Member of the Court also will be elected by secret ballot if both the president and the vice president appear to hold minority views in a case. The Drafting Committee then prepares a preliminary draft judgment on which individual judges may make written suggestions. The Drafting Committee subsequently issues a fresh draft which it submits for first reading. That draft is discussed at several private meetings of the Court. At this stage, declarations[96] and separate[97] or dissenting[98] opinions are made available by indi-

---

93   *See* Sir Robert Jennings, *The Internal Judicial Practice of the International Court of Justice*, BYBIL 31 (1989).

94   However, the Court announced in 1998 that, as part of the ongoing revision of its working methods designed to expedite the examination of contentious cases, it intends to abolish the practice of Notes by individual judges in the preliminary phase of proceedings involving objections to the Court's jurisdiction or the admissibility of the application. *See* ICJ Communiqué 98/14 (April 6, 1998); *see also* ICJ Communiqués 2001/1 (January 12, 2001) and 2001/32 (October 31, 2001).

95   If the vice president also shares the minority opinion, the most senior member of the Court elected to sit on the Drafting Committee will preside over its meetings.

96   These are individual statements of a judge that briefly explain his or her vote.

vidual judges.[99] Each paragraph of the draft judgment is read aloud in the two official languages of the Court, is discussed and is either left unchanged, amended or referred back to the Drafting Committee. Finally, an amended draft judgment is distributed to the judges, which is then given a page-by-page second reading and may be commented on by the judges. At the end of the second reading, a final vote is taken on the points raised by the parties in their final submissions, as reflected in the draft judgment. Judges vote either "yes" or "no" orally on separate holdings, in inverse order of seniority (i.e., the President is the last to vote and may use his casting vote in case the judges are split evenly on a particular holding).[100]

2.6   Decision; Enforcement

After the deliberations are concluded and the case has not been settled or discontinued,[101] the Court delivers a Judgment at a public sitting. Judgments of the Court are final and without appeal.[102] A victorious state may proceed

---

97 A judge may append a separate opinion if he or she supports the holding adopted by the majority, but disagrees in whole or in part with the reasoning behind it.

98 A judge may append a dissenting opinion if he or she disagrees with the holding adopted by the majority of the Court.

99 In December 2000, the ICJ Registry announced that, following a decision of the Court, declarations and separate and dissenting opinions no longer are presented sequentially, but will feature in the order of precedence of their authors. *See* ICJ Communiqué 2000/40 (Dec. 8, 2000).

100 President Bedjaoui used his casting vote in the Court's Advisory Opinion on Legality of the Threat or Use of Nuclear Weapons, issued on July 8, 1996. *See* 1996 ICJ REP. 226 (July 8).

101 Discontinuance is officially recorded in an Order issued by the Court or its president, which removes the case of the General List of cases as of the date on which the Order is signed.

102 *See* ICJ STATUTE Art. 60. At the request of either party to a case, the Court may interpret its judgment if the parties differ as to the meaning or scope of the Court's decision. Between 1997 and 2001, this occurred only once. *See* Request for Interpretation of the Court's Judgment of July 11, 1998, in the Case concerning the *Land and Maritime Boundary between Cameroon and Nigeria (Cameroon v. Nigeria)*, Preliminary Objections (Nigeria v. Cameroon), Judgment, 1999 ICJ REP. 31 (Mar. 25) (declaring Nigeria's request inadmissible). Either party may also request the Court to revise its Judgment, "upon the discovery of some fact of such a nature as to be a decisive factor, which fact was, when the judgment was given, unknown to the Court" and provided that such ignorance was not due to the negligence of

to request the Court to fix monetary or other compensation in subsequent proceedings.[103]

In case one of the states parties to a case should fail to comply with the Judgment, the other party may have recourse to the UN Security Council. The Security Council may then make recommendations or decide upon measures to be taken to give effect to the Judgment. Such measures could include the use of military force, but this kind of enforcement action has never occurred in practice.[104] The Court's decisions generally are complied with by states due to political pressures within the world community.

---

the party claiming revision. *Id.* Art. 61, para. 1. On April 24, 2001, Yugoslavia filed an application for revision of the Judgment delivered by the Court on July 11, 1996 in *Application of the Convention on the Prevention and Punishment of the Crime of Genocide (Bosnia-Herzegovina v. Yugoslavia)*, rejecting Yugoslavia's Preliminary Objections. *See* ICJ Communiqué 2001/12 (April 24, 2001). On revision and the finality of decisions, see Effect of Awards of Compensation Made by the United Nations Administrative Tribunal, 1954 ICJ REP. 47, at 55 (Advisory Opinion of July 13); Application for Revision and Interpretation of the Judgment of 24 February 1982 in the Case concerning the *Continental Shelf (Tunisia/Libyan Arab Jamahiriya)*, Judgment, 1985 ICJ REP. 192 (Dec. 10); Monastery of Saint Naoum, Advisory Opinion, 1924 PCIJ (ser. B), No. 9, at 22.

103 In order for the Court to award compensation, the claimant must present detailed evidence relating to each head of damage suffered and must request, preferably in the Memorial, that the Court receive evidence and assess compensation in a separate phase of the proceedings. *See* Fisheries Jurisdiction (Fed. Rep. of Germany v. Iceland), Merits, Judgment, 1974 ICJ REP. 175, at 204, para. 76 (July 25); Military and Paramilitary Activities in and against Nicaragua (Nicar. v. U.S.), Merits, Judgment, 1986 ICJ REP. 14, at 142-43, paras. 283-85 (June 27). There is no provision in the Statute or Rules of Court either specifically empowering the Court to award any specific type of damages or debarring it from doing so. The only Judgment in the history of the ICJ containing a determination of monetary relief is Corfu Channel (UK v. Albania), Damages, Judgment, 1949 ICJ REP. 244 (Dec. 15). For the leading monetary compensation precedent in the PCIJ, see S.S. "Wimbledon" (France, UK, Italy, Japan v. Germany; Poland intervening), Judgment, 1923 PCIJ (ser. A) No. 1 (Merits) at 15 (Aug. 17). Between 1997 and 2001, no case included a compensation phase.

104 *See* UN CHARTER Art. 94, para. 2. It must be kept in mind that the veto power of the five permanent members of the Security Council applies in these situations.

2.7   Advisory Jurisdiction

The Court's dual role is evidenced by its power to give *Advisory Opinions* on
legal questions referred to it by any of 21 duly authorized United Nations
organs and agencies.[105] Only those organizations have standing in advisory
proceedings before the Court. The Security Council and General Assembly
of the United Nations have the authority to request Advisory Opinions on any
legal question.[106] The other organizations may only request Advisory Opinions
"on legal questions arising within the scope of their activities."[107] Under the
UN Charter and the Statute, Advisory Opinions rendered by the Court are non-
binding. But a provision contained in an international instrument governing
the request for an Advisory Opinion may explicitly confer binding force on
the Advisory Opinion for the parties involved.[108] Moreover, despite the non-
binding character of Advisory Opinions, the legal reasoning found in them
reflects the Court's authoritative views on important issues of international law
and in arriving at them, the Court follows the same rules and procedures that
govern its binding Judgments delivered in contentious cases submitted to it
by sovereign states.

After a written request for an Advisory Opinion has been received by the
Registry, the Court issues an Order inviting any state entitled to appear before

---

105 *See* UN CHARTER Art. 96 and ICJ STATUTE Arts. 65-68. All of the principal organs
      of the United Nations (with the exception of the Secretary-General representing
      the UN Secretariat), the 16 UN Specialized Agencies and the Interim Committee
      of the General Assembly may submit requests for advisory opinion. Until 1996,
      the Committee on Applications for Review of Administrative Tribunal Judgements
      also was authorized to request Advisory Opinions of the Court. This review proced-
      ure was terminated by UN General Assembly Resolution 50/54 of December 11,
      1995, with effect from January 1, 1996. *See* UN Doc. A/RES/50/54 (1995). Thus,
      Application for Review of Judgement No. 333 of the United Nations Administrative
      Tribunal (1987 ICJ REP. 18) (Advisory Opinion of May 27) was the last of its kind.
106 *See* UN CHARTER Art. 96, para. 1.
107 *Id.*, Art. 96, para. 2.
108 *See Difference Relating to Immunity from Legal Process of a Special Rapporteur
      of the Commission on Human Rights*, Advisory Opinion, 1999 ICJ REP. 62 (Apr.
      29), discussed in Chapter 3 below; *see also* Roberto Ago, *"Binding" Advisory
      Opinions of the International Court of Justice*, 85 AJIL 439 (1991), and response
      by Derek Bowett in 86 AJIL 342 (1992); Charles N. Brower & Pieter H.F. Bekker,
      Understanding "Binding" Advisory Opinions of the International Court of Justice,
      in: LIBER AMICORUM JUDGE SHIGERU ODA (N. Ando, E. McWhinney & R. Wolfrum
      eds., 2002).

it and international organizations selected by it to file written statements concerning the request. Those organizations and states that have submitted written statements also may submit written comments on each other's statements. The Court subsequently may decide to hold public hearings. After deliberations are held, the Advisory Opinion is then delivered at a public sitting of the Court.

Between 1997 and 2001, the Court delivered only one Advisory Opinion, namely, *Difference Relating to Immunity from Legal Process of a Special Rapporteur of the Commission on Human Rights.*[109]

2.8 Applicable Law

According to Article 38, paragraph 1 of the Statute, the Court is to decide in accordance with international treaties and conventions in force, international custom as evidence of a general practice accepted as law, the general principles of law recognized by civilized nations and, as subsidiary means,[110] judicial decisions and the teachings of the most highly qualified scholars.

2.9 *Ad hoc* Chambers

At the request of the parties to a case, the Court may establish an *ad hoc* Chamber to deal with a particular case.[111] *Ad hoc* Chambers combine many of the characteristics of arbitration and judicial settlement. The number and names of the judges constituting each Chamber (usually five) is determined by the Court after consultation with the parties. The exact number of Chamber judges must be approved by the parties. The parties to a Chamber case thus are granted a voice in the composition of the Chamber. Chamber judges are elected by the Court by secret ballot. If the Court does not elect a national of one of the states parties to the Chamber case, that state is entitled to appoint

---

109 1999 ICJ REP. 62 (Apr. 29).

110 I.e., they are only *evidence of* international law, but they do not qualify as free-standing sources of such law and therefore cannot be relied upon independently. In addition, Article 59 of the Statute dictates that the Court's own decisions in a particular case have binding force only between the parties in that case. Consequently, no formal rule of binding precedent (*stare decisis*) applies before the Court.

111 ICJ STATUTE Art. 26, paras. 2-3. *Ad hoc* Chamber procedure, which is practically the same as in regular cases before the full Court, is governed by Arts. 17-18 and 90-93 of the Rules of Court.

a judge *ad hoc*. Elected Chamber judges continue to sit on that Chamber until the Chamber delivers its final judgment, even if the judge's term of office on the full Court has expired while the Chamber case is pending. *Ad hoc* Chambers were formed only in 1982 (*Delimitation of the Maritime Boundary in the Gulf of Maine Area (Canada/United States)*), 1985 (*Frontier Dispute (Burkina Faso/ Mali)*), and 1987 (*Elettronica Sicula S.p.A. (ELSI) (United States v. Italy)* and *Land, Island and Maritime Frontier Dispute (El Salvador/Honduras)*).[112]

2.10   Finances

According to Article 33 of the Statute, the expenses of the Court are borne by the United Nations, as determined by the General Assembly. The Court's budget, which is drawn up on a biennial basis, thus is part of the budget of the United Nations and its member states contribute to the expenses of the Court in the same proportion as they do to those of the General Assembly. Non-member states that participate in the Court pay a fixed contribution toward the Court's expenses. The Court's budget represents around one percent of the total budget of the United Nations.

"The expenses of the Court" mentioned in Article 33 concern only the Court's internal administrative costs, including the salaries and pensions of the Judges and the staff of the Registry. The parties to a case must finance the preparation of the written and oral pleadings and the expenses incurred by their delegations before the Court. The cost of printing the pleadings, including translation of documents that are not in English or French, also is borne by the parties. If the parties wish to present witnesses or experts, they must bear their travel expenses, accommodations and fees. Amounts payable to witnesses and experts appearing at the initiative of the Court are borne by the United Nations. The parties may face the further expense of producing technical materials, such as cartographic evidence, especially in boundary delimitation cases. Finally, the parties must meet costs relating to the execution of a Judgment, such as fees of scientific and technical experts (e.g., geographers and geologists).

---

112 *See* FIFTY YEARS OF THE INTERNATIONAL COURT OF JUSTICE at 503 (Vaughan Lowe & Malgosia Fitzmaurice eds., 1996).

2.11   ICJ Trust Fund

On November 1, 1989, the Secretary-General of the United Nations announced the establishment of a "Trust Fund to Assist States in the Settlement of Disputes through the International Court of Justice" (Trust Fund).[113] The Trust Fund was set up as a device to help overcome financial impediments to the judicial settlement of international disputes between states by providing financial assistance to less fortunate states as an inducement for submitting their disputes before the Court. The Trust Fund, the operation of which is governed by its own "Terms of Reference, Guidelines and Rules," is managed by the Secretary-General through the United Nations Office of Legal Affairs. The Secretary-General submits an annual report on the activities of the Trust Fund, which is subject to internal UN auditing, to the General Assembly of the United Nations. The Trust Fund is financed by voluntary contributions from states, intergovernmental organizations, national institutions and nongovernmental organizations, as well as individuals and corporations. Cases that are eligible for funding are limited to those brought by Special Agreement, so that states that institute proceedings by unilateral Application may, in principle, not be funded through the Trust Fund.[114] The Secretary-General is assisted in his task of assessing applications for funding by a special three-member "Panel of Experts" formed to deal with a particular application. Ultimately, the Secretary-General decides whether or not to grant assistance from the Trust Fund and with him lies also the determination of the exact amount and types of expenses. States can be reimbursed only for actual expenditures incurred in submitting a case to the Court or in implementing a Judgment of the Court. A limited number of African states have been able to profit from the Trust

---

113 *See* Peter H.F. Bekker, *International Legal Aid in Practice: The ICJ Trust Fund,* 87 AJIL 659 (1993). This author serves as ICJ Trust Fund Reporter for the Committee on International Dispute Settlement within the American Branch of the International Law Association.

114 An interesting question is whether unreserved, unconditional Optional Clause declarations may be said to constitute acceptance in advance of the Court's jurisdiction, so that a case brought on this basis is eligible for funding under the ICJ Trust Fund.

Fund in preparing their ICJ cases relating to territorial disputes.[115] However, the Trust Fund remains severely under-funded and under-utilized to date.[116]

3   ICJ Publications

It is of critical importance to the rule of international law that wider dissemination of, and easier access to, the work of the International Court of Justice is attained. The present book seeks to contribute to this goal.

The publications and documents of the Court are distributed free of charge to the governments of all states entitled to appear before the Court, to the major law libraries of the world and to interested persons. The sale of those publications is entrusted to the Sales Sections of the United Nations Secretariat in New York and the UN Office in Geneva (Sales Section, United Nations Secretariat, New York, NY 10017, USA; Sales Section, Office of the United Nations, CH-1211 Geneva 10, Switzerland). The decisions of the Court can also be found on WESTLAW, the on-line legal service (Database Identifier: INT-ICJ). Basic data relating to the Court also are available as part of a home page maintained on the Internet by the Court.[117]

---

115 According to information obtained from the UN Secretariat, during the period reviewed, Botswana and Namibia each received $250,000 in connection with the case concerning *Kasikili/Sedudu Island* (Botswana/Namibia), a boundary dispute involving neighboring states (reviewed in Chapter 3 below). The first two awards were made to developing countries in 1991.

116 Contributions by bank transfer may be sent to: Account no. 485-001969 (account code TJA), Account name: United Nations General Trust Fund Account, Chase Manhattan Bank, United Nations Branch, New York, NY 10017, ABA routing number: 021-000-021, SWIFT code: CHASUS33. According to the most recent report of the Secretary-General, the total balance of the Fund was $1,602,734 as at June 30, 2001. *See* UN Doc. A/56/456 (Oct. 10, 2001).

117 The Court's Web site, the establishment of which was announced on September 25, 1997 (<HTTP://WWW.ICJ-CIJ.ORG>), carries the text of the decisions of, and general information on, the ICJ. In addition, it makes available most of the relevant documents in past and pending cases. *See* ICJ Communiqué No. 97/11 (Sept. 25, 1997). Another useful Web site on the ICJ maintained by Cornell University is <HTTP://WWW.LAW.CORNELL.EDU/ICJ/HOME.HTM> (in English). For French texts on the ICJ, see also <HTTP://WWW.LAW.CORNELL.EDU/ICJ/F.HOME.HTM>. Requests for information may be sent by e-mail to: <information@icj-cij.org>.

The publications of the Court, consisting of printed and published materials in bound form for which the Court's Registry is responsible, include three annual series in the two official languages of the Court (English and French):

a) *Reports of Judgments, Advisory Opinions and Orders* containing the full bilingual text of the Court's decisions and Orders (including declarations and separate and dissenting opinions of individual judges) during any given year (published since 1948);
b) *Yearbook* of the International Court of Justice (published annually since 1946-1947) describing the Court's work during the period August 1–July 31; and
c) *Bibliography* of works and documents relating to the Court (issued annually).

In connection with the above documents, the Court also publishes an annual index and a catalogue of publications.

A fairly complete record of the Court's proceedings in a particular case is published by the Court sometime after the end of the proceedings in a series entitled *Pleadings, Oral Arguments, Documents*.

Another series, entitled *Acts and Documents concerning the Organization of the Court*, contains all the basic instruments governing the Court's functioning and practice, including the United Nations Charter, the Statute, the Rules of Court and the Resolution concerning the Internal Judicial Practice of the Court.

An off-print of the Rules of Court is available in French and English. Unofficial Arabic, Chinese, German, Russian and Spanish translations of the Rules of Court also are available.

Since 1968, the Court has been submitting voluntarily, in French and English, an annual *Report of the International Court of Justice* to the General Assembly of the United Nations, covering the Court's work from August 1 of one year to July 31 of the following year.[118] This Report appears as a Supplement to the *Official Records* of the General Assembly.

The Registry also distributes press communiqués, background notes and an unofficial handbook on the Court's work and functions. The fourth and most

---

118 One major inconvenience connected with some of the Court's main publications is that they cover the period July 31-August 1, as opposed to the regular calendar year. The present work adheres to the latter form of reporting in order to enable a review of the various calendar years during 1997-2001.

recent edition of the handbook (sometimes referred to as the "Blue Book") appeared in July 1997, on the occasion of the Court's 50th anniversary, in English and French. Arabic, Chinese, Russian and Spanish translations of the third edition were published in 1990. A German version also is available.

Annex D provides a selection of some of the most informative writings on the work of the World Court.[119]

---

119 On ICJ publications, see also Ignaz Seidl-Hohenveldern, *Changes in the Publications of I.C.J. Reports: Effects of these Suggestions on Teaching International Law*, 10 MICH. J. INT'L L. 679 (1989); Shabtai Rosenne, *Publications of the International Court of Justice*, 81 AJIL 681 (1987).

1

THE YEAR 1997

THE 1997 JUDICIAL ACTIVITY OF
THE INTERNATIONAL COURT OF JUSTICE[*]

This introductory section summarizes the judicial work of the International Court of Justice during 1997,[1] using the updated General List, pleadings filed, Orders and Judgments given and hearings held at the Peace Palace in The Hague to describe the Court's record in 1997.

THE WORK OF THE COURT

General List

During the calendar year 1997, the Court was seized of no new cases. In 1997 a total of nine cases appeared on the General List. The contentious proceedings before the full Court were *Gabčíkovo-Nagymaros Project (Hungary/Slovakia)*, *Maritime Delimitation and Territorial Questions between Qatar and Bahrain (Qatar v. Bahrain)*, *Questions of Interpretation and Application of the 1971 Montreal Convention arising from the Aerial Incident at Lockerbie (Libya v. United Kingdom)* and *(Libya v. United States)*, *Oil Platforms (Iran v. United States)*, *Application of the Convention on the Prevention and Punishment of the Crime of Genocide (Bosnia-Herzegovina v. Yugoslavia)* (hereinafter *Geno-*

---

[*] Reproduced with permission from 92 AJIL 350 (1998). © The American Society of International Law.

[1] For a summary of the jurisprudence and judicial activity of the ICJ for the period 1987-1996, see COMMENTARIES ON WORLD COURT DECISIONS (1987-1996) (P.H.F. Bekker ed., 1998). *See also* P.H.F. Bekker, *Recent Developments in the International Court of Justice (1987-1998)*, in XXV CURSO DE DERECHO INTERNACIONAL 355 (1998) (Organization of American States, 1999).

P.H.F. Bekker, World Court Decisions at the Turn of the Millennium (1997-2001), p. 43-47.
© 2002 *Kluwer Law International. Printed in the Netherlands.*

cide (Bosnia) case), *Fisheries Jurisdiction (Spain v. Canada)*, *Land and Maritime Boundary between Cameroon and Nigeria (Cameroon v. Nigeria)* and *Kasikili/Sedudu Island (Botswana/Namibia)*.

During 1997 no cases were pending before any ICJ chamber and no requests for an advisory opinion were received by the Court.

Pleadings

In 1997 pleadings were filed in the following instances. On February 28, Botswana and Namibia each filed a Memorial in *Kasikili/Sedudu Island*, followed by their Counter-Memorials on November 28. On June 23, the United States filed a Counter-Memorial in *Oil Platforms*. The Counter-Memorial included a counterclaim requesting that the Court adjudge and declare "[t]hat in attacking vessels, laying mines in the Gulf and otherwise engaging in military actions in 1987-88 that were dangerous and detrimental to maritime commerce, the Islamic Republic of Iran breached its obligations to the United States under Article X of the 1955 Treaty [of Amity, Economic Relations and Consular Rights]," for which Iran must make full reparation to the United States.[2] Iran and the United States each submitted written observations on the question of the admissibility of the U.S. counterclaim on November 18 and December 18, respectively. Yugoslavia filed a Counter-Memorial in the *Genocide (Bosnia)* case on July 22, including counterclaims whereby it requested that the Court hold Bosnia-Herzegovina responsible for certain acts of genocide allegedly committed against the Serbs in Bosnia-Herzegovina and for other violations of the obligations established by the 1948 Convention on the Prevention and Punishment of the Crime of Genocide. Bosnia-Herzegovina and Yugoslavia each submitted written observations on the question of the admissibility of the Yugoslav counterclaims on October 9 and 23, respectively. Qatar and Bahrain each filed a Counter-Memorial in their case on December 23.

---

2   The Rules of Court require that a counterclaim be directly concerned with the subject matter of the claim of the other party. It must also come within the Court's jurisdiction. *See* ICJ Rules of Court, Apr. 14, 1978, Art. 80, para. 1, *reprinted in* 73 AJIL 748, 761 (1979). A recent amendment to Art. 80 reversed the order in which these conditions are listed. *See* ICJ Communiqué 2001/01 (Jan. 12, 2001).

Orders

Two Orders were made by the full Court and none by its president in 1997. The Court issued an Order on February 5, in which it decided to accept the invitation of the parties in *Gabčíkovo-Nagymaros Project* to visit the site of the disputed project.[3] This visit *in situ*, the first in the history of the ICJ, took place on April 1-4. On December 17, the Court issued an Order in the *Genocide (Bosnia)* case in which it held, by 13 votes to 1, that the counterclaims filed by Yugoslavia on July 22 are admissible as such and form part of the proceedings in the *Genocide* case because they are directly connected with the subject matter of Bosnia-Herzegovina's claims and constitute separate claims seeking relief beyond the dismissal of the applicant's claims. This is the first time in the Court's history that it has upheld the admissibility of counterclaims at a preliminary stage under the 1978 version of the Rules of Court.[4]

Hearings

In 1997 the full Court held public sittings (hearings) in three cases: *Gabčíkovo-Nagymaros Project* (Merits) (March 3-7, March 24-27, April 10-11 and April 14-15) and *Lockerbie (Libya v. United Kingdom)* and *(Libya v. United States)* (Preliminary Objections) (October 13-22).

Decisions

The ICJ handed down one decision in 1997. On September 25, the Court issued its Judgment on the merits in *Gabčíkovo-Nagymaros Project (Hungary/ Slovakia)*.[5]

---

3   *See* 1997 ICJ REP. 3. *See also* Peter Tomka & Samuel S. Wordsworth, *The First Site Visit of the International Court of Justice in Fulfillment of Its Judicial Function*, 92 AJIL 133 (1998).

4   *See* 1997 ICJ REP. 243; ICJ Communiqué No. 97/18 (Dec. 17, 1997). In its Order, the Court also fixed January 23, 1998, and July 23, 1998, as the time limits within which Bosnia-Herzegovina and Yugoslavia were to submit a Reply and a Rejoinder, respectively, stating their views. These time limits later were extended by the President's Order of January 22, 1998. *See* 1998 ICJ REP. 3. The President's Order of September 10, 2001 officially recorded the withdrawal by Yugoslavia of its counterclaims.

5   *See* 1997 ICJ REP. 7.

ELECTIONS

On February 6, the Court elected Stephen Schwebel (United States) as its president and Christopher Weeramantry (Sri Lanka) as its vice president to serve on three-year terms.

PRESIDENT'S ADDRESS

On October 27, Judge Stephen Schwebel addressed the General Assembly for the first time as ICJ president on the occasion of the Assembly's consideration of the Court's annual report.[6] He reminded the Assembly that the tradition of the Court's president speaking to the General Assembly was initiated by Sir Robert Jennings during his presidency (1991-1994).

President Schwebel focused his discussion of the Court's judicial work on its September 25, 1997 Judgment in *Gabčíkovo-Nagymaros Project (Hungary/ Slovakia)*, which he said was particularly noteworthy for various reasons. First, that case produced the first site visit in the history of the ICJ. Provided the situation on the ground lends itself to carrying out a site visit and the states involved can cooperate in organizing such a visit, a working visit to the site of a dispute can be a valuable procedure for the Court. Second, this Judgment is notable because of the breadth and depth of the importance given in it to the work of the International Law Commission, especially on state succession in respect of treaties and the law of international watercourses, illustrating the influence that both institutions can assert over each other.[7] Third, this Judgment is the first decision to be placed on the Court's own Web site on the day of its delivery. Finally, the case is a further demonstration of the Court's potential as a "partner in preventive diplomacy" and facilitator of negotiations, as opposed to being a mere judicial "last resort" for states.

While referring to the severe resource constraints from which the Court continues to suffer, especially in the area of translation, President Schwebel reminded the Assembly of the unique strengths of the Court. Being productively

6   The full text of the Address by the President of the International Court of Justice, Judge Stephen M. Schwebel, to the United Nations General Assembly, Oct. 27, 1997, is available on the ICJ's Web site, <www.icj-cij.org>.

7   *See also* Stephen M. Schwebel, *The Influence of the International Court of Justice on the Work of the International Law Commission and the Influence of the Commission on the Work of the Court*, in: THE INTERNATIONAL LAW COMMISSION AT 50, at 161 (1998) (text of keynote speech by Judge Schwebel).

at work even when it is not publicly sitting, the ICJ not only can claim to be truly universal, its Members representing the main forms of civilization and principal legal systems of the world, its judicial process also marries the key features of the common and civil law systems by combining both oral and written phases of procedure and offering a flexible approach to evidence. Moreover, its deliberative process permits each judge to participate on an equal footing in the Court's drafting work.

Acting on its desire to deal with cases as expeditiously as possible and to accelerate the judicial process to the extent allowed by the framework of the Statute, the president announced that the Court was in the process of implementing a range of alterations to its working procedures, involving changes in the Court's administrative and internal practices. For example, the Court has decided to proceed in deliberations without written Notes by individual judges in suitable cases concerning the Court's jurisdiction or the admissibility of the application. Moreover, appropriate cases on jurisdiction in the future may be heard "back to back," i.e., in immediate succession, enabling work on cases to proceed concurrently. Finally, the Court will engage in "forward planning" by giving the parties notice of its intended schedule for the next three cases.

◊

Law of treaties – grounds for treaty termination – effect of environmental duties on treaty obligations – state responsibility – state succession – countermeasures – lawfulness of Hungary's abandonment of 1977 Treaty for development of Danube River and Czechoslovakia's unilateral diversion of the river

GABČÍKOVO-NAGYMAROS PROJECT (Hungary/Slovakia)
Judgment
1997 ICJ REP. 7
International Court of Justice, September 25, 1997[*]

On July 2, 1993, Hungary and Czechoslovakia instituted proceedings before the International Court of Justice on the basis of a special agreement signed by both countries in Brussels on April 7, 1993. The Court held, by clear majorities, that both Hungary and Slovakia had breached their obligations under the bilateral Treaty on the Construction and Operation of the Gabčíkovo-Nagymaros System of Locks (Treaty) signed on September 16, 1977, with effect from June 30, 1978. It found unlawful Hungary's unilateral suspension and subsequent abandonment of the project contemplated by the Treaty, as well as Slovakia's subsequent unilateral diversion of the Danube. Most important, the Court concluded that the Treaty is still in force and that its object and purpose must be carried out in good faith by both parties.[1]

Several dates are material to this case. In chronological order, these dates are: (1) September 16, 1977: Hungary and Czechoslovakia sign the Treaty;

---

[*] Reproduced with permission from 92 AJIL 273 (1998). © The American Society of International Law.

[1] Vice President Weeramantry and Judges Bedjaoui and Koroma appended separate opinions. Judges Oda, Ranjeva, Herczegh, Fleischhauer, Vereshchetin and Parra-Aranguren and Judge *ad hoc* Skubiszewski appended dissenting opinions. President Schwebel and Judge Rezek appended brief declarations explaining their votes. A first round of public hearings was held in the Peace Palace in The Hague on March 3-7 and March 24-27, 1997, after which the ICJ Judges made a visit *in situ* under Article 66 of the Rules of Court in order to obtain evidence at the place to which the case relates (April 1-4, 1997). This was the first site visit in the history of the ICJ. *See* 1997 ICJ REP. 3 (Order of Feb. 5). A second round of oral proceedings took place on April 10, 11, 14 and 15, 1997. *See* 1997 ICJ REP. 7, at 13-14, paras. 10-11.

P.H.F. Bekker, World Court Decisions at the Turn of the Millennium (1997-2001), p. 49-58.
© 2002 *Kluwer Law International. Printed in the Netherlands.*

(2) October 27, 1989: Hungary decides to abandon its part of the project; (3) November 1991: Czechoslovakia begins work on an alternative solution ("Variant C"); (4) May 19, 1992: Hungary's notification of termination of the Treaty; (6) October 1992: Czechoslovakia puts Variant C into operation by diverting the Danube; and (7) January 1, 1993: Slovakia succeeds Czechoslovakia as a sovereign state.

The Treaty was originally concluded between Hungary and Czechoslovakia for the construction and joint operation of a large, integrated complex of structures and installations on certain parts of the territories of the two countries along the Danube, Europe's second longest river. The Court characterized the Treaty as constituting an integrated joint project containing a joint investment program and also as establishing a regime. Its objectives were the production of hydroelectric power, improvement of navigation on a 200km-stretch of the Danube between Bratislava (Slovakia) and Budapest (Hungary), and flood control. In particular, it provided for the building of two series of locks at Gabčíkovo (Slovakia) and Nagymaros (Hungary), which together were to constitute a single and indivisible operational system of works financed, constructed, operated and owned by both states. The Treaty also established the navigational regime for parts of the Danube and relocated the main shipping lane.

The two countries commenced work on the project in 1978. On Hungary's initiative, the parties agreed to slow down the project in October 1983 and to accelerate it in February 1989. However, in response to domestic pressure, the Hungarian Government decided to abandon the works at Nagymaros on October 27, 1989, stating economic and environmental reasons. Czechoslovakia immediately protested. Negotiations between the two countries to address the situation failed.

In 1991 Czechoslovakia proceeded to develop an alternative solution (Variant C) that included the unilateral diversion of the Danube on its territory and the construction of an overflow dam, a levee linking the dam to a bypass canal and ancillary works. In response, Hungary claimed that its access to the water of the Danube would be affected adversely by Variant C and terminated the Treaty with effect from May 25, 1992. Czechoslovakia then proceeded to dam the Danube, beginning on October 23, 1992.

The Judgment is divided into two parts: the first part deals with the conduct of Hungary and Slovakia between 1989 and 1992, while the second part addresses the consequences of such conduct and the Court's findings in relation thereto for the *future* conduct of the parties.

First, as to Hungary's unilateral suspension and subsequent abandonment of the project in 1989, the Court indicated that the provisions of the 1969 Vienna Convention on the Law of Treaties concerning the termination and the suspension of the operation of treaties might "in many respects" be considered as a codification of existing customary law.[2] It explained that a distinction must be made between, on the one hand, a determination under the law of treaties of whether a treaty is in force and has been properly suspended or denounced, and, on the other hand, an evaluation under the law of state responsibility of the extent to which the suspension or denunciation of a treaty, in violation of the law of treaties, engages the responsibility of the state concerned. The law of state responsibility emphasizes the effects of an unlawful suspension or denunciation.

Hungary contended that, although it had suspended or abandoned certain works, it never suspended the application of the Treaty itself. In the Court's view, however, the effect of Hungary's conduct, which the Court interpreted as an expression of Hungary's unwillingness to comply with at least some of the provisions of the Treaty, was to render impossible the accomplishment of the system of works that Article 1, paragraph 1 of the Treaty expressly described as "single and indivisible."[3]

The Court rejected Hungary's reliance on "a state of ecological necessity" as a justification for Hungary's failure to comply with its treaty obligations. Hungary and Slovakia agreed that the existence of a state of necessity must be evaluated in the light of the criteria laid down by the International Law Commission in Article 33 of the draft articles on the international responsibility of states adopted on first reading.[4] The Court found that, although the environmental concerns expressed by Hungary related to an "essential interest," the perils that in Hungary's view threatened that interest were not sufficiently

---

2   *Id.* at 38, para. 46. The Court thus adopted the cautious attitude that Hungary had requested it to take in this respect. *See id.* at 36, para. 42.

3   *Id.* at 29, para. 28 and 39, para. 48.

4   The Court disagreed with Slovakia that ecological necessity/risk could not constitute a circumstance precluding wrongfulness of an act, but wrongfulness could be precluded only if the strictly defined criteria laid down in ILC draft Article 33 (reflecting customary law) were cumulatively satisfied. *Id.* at 37, para. 44 and 40, para. 51. *See also* Report of the International Law Commission on the work of its thirty-second session, [1980] 2 Y.B. INT'L L. COMM'N 34, UN Doc. A/CN.4/SER.A/ 1980/Add.1 (Part 2).

established in 1989,[5] nor were they real "grave and imminent" perils as opposed to perceived ones. Suspension and abandonment had not been the only way out for Hungary: it should have awaited the outcome of the bilateral negotiation process. Having rejected Hungary's reliance on a state of necessity as a ground for precluding wrongfulness, the Court held, by 14 votes to 1, that Hungary had not been entitled to suspend and subsequently abandon the works on the Nagymaros Project and on the part of the Gabčíkovo Project for which it was responsible.

Noting that the Treaty does not contain any provision regarding its termination and that there is no indication of the parties' intention to admit denunciation or withdrawal, the Court concluded that the Treaty could be terminated only on the limited grounds enumerated in Articles 60-62 of the Vienna Convention, which are declaratory of customary law.[6] The Court rejected all of the treaty law defenses that Hungary advanced in support of the lawfulness and effectiveness of its notification of termination; namely (1) the existence of a state of necessity,[7] (2) the impossibility of performance of the Treaty,[8] (3) the occurrence of a fundamental change in circumstances,[9] (4) the material

---

5   Hungary argued that the building of the Nagymaros dam would cause the bed of the Danube to silt up, negatively affecting the quality of the water collected in the bank-filtered wells. *Id.* at 35, para. 40.

6   *Id.* at 62-63, paras. 99-100. The 1969 Vienna Convention is not directly applicable to the 1977 Treaty because both parties ratified the Convention only after the conclusion of the 1977 Treaty. For the Convention, *opened for signature* May 23, 1969, see 1155 UNTS 331 (entered into force Jan. 27, 1980).

7   The Court agreed with Slovakia that a state of necessity is not a ground for the termination of a treaty; it may be invoked only to relieve a state of responsibility for failure to implement a treaty. *Id.* at 63, para. 101.

8   Hungary relied on Article 61 of the Vienna Convention, *supra* note 6. That provision requires the "permanent disappearance or destruction of an object indispensable for the execution" of a treaty. However, the Court noted that the Treaty provides means for any required readjustments. *Id.* at 63-64, paras. 102-03.

9   Hungary relied on Article 62 of the Vienna Convention, *supra* note 6, and cited profound political changes, the project's diminishing economic viability, the progress of environmental knowledge and the development of new norms and prescriptions of international environmental law. However, the Court considered that these events could not be said to have been completely unforeseen in 1977, nor did the existence of the stated circumstances at the time of the Treaty's conclusion constitute an essential basis of the consent of the parties to be bound by the Treaty. *Id.* at 64, para. 104.

breach of the Treaty by Czechoslovakia,[10] and (5) the development of new norms of international environmental law.[11] On the last point, the Court pointed out that newly developed norms of environmental law could be incorporated by the parties into their "Joint Contractual Plan" through existing provisions of the Treaty.[12] In sum, the Court found, by 11 votes to 4, that the parties' reciprocal wrongful conduct had not brought the Treaty to an end or justified its termination, thereby emphasizing the rule *pacta sunt servanda*.[13]

By 9 votes to 6, the Court confirmed Slovakia's right to proceed to develop an alternative solution that was as close to the original project as possible.[14] It based this finding on a fundamental distinction between the actual commission of a wrongful act (whether instantaneous or continuous) and the conduct prior to that act, which is of a preparatory character but does not qualify as a wrongful act.

In defending its actual implementation of Variant C, Slovakia relied principally on what it described as a "principle of approximate application" referred to by Judge Lauterpacht in 1956.[15] According to the Court, however, even

10 Hungary relied on Article 60 of the Vienna Convention, *supra* note 6. However, in the Court's view, Czechoslovakia's material breach of the Treaty (the actual putting into operation of Variant C) did not occur until October 1992, making the notification of termination by Hungary on May 19, 1992, premature. Besides, Hungary, by its own conduct, had prejudiced its right to terminate the Treaty. *Id.* at 65-67, paras. 105-10.

11 Hungary argued that the previously existing obligation not to cause substantive damage to the territory of another state had evolved into an *erga omnes* obligation of prevention of damage pursuant to the "precautionary principle." The Court considered that it was not required to examine the scope of Article 64 of the Vienna Convention on the Law of Treaties, given that neither Hungary nor Slovakia contended that new peremptory norms of environmental law had emerged since the conclusion of the 1977 Treaty. *Id.* at 62, para. 97 and 67, para. 112.

12 *Id.* at 67, para. 112. According to Article 1, paragraph 4 of the Treaty, the Joint Contractual Plan (JCP), as an instrument complementing the Treaty, was to set forth the technical specifications and operating and maintenance rules for the system of works in conformity with which the joint investment was to be carried out. Apparently, the complete text of the JCP was never submitted to the Court.

13 *Id.* at 68-69, paras. 114-15. This rule is expressed in Article 26 of the Vienna Convention on the Law of Treaties which provides: "Every treaty in force is binding upon the parties to it and must be performed by them in good faith."

14 "[I]n so far as [Czechoslovakia] then confined itself to undertaking works which did not determine the final decision to be taken by it." *Id.* at 57, para. 88.

15 *Id.* at 53, para. 75 (citing Admissibility of Hearings of Petitioners by the Committee on South West Africa, 1956 ICJ REP. 23, at 46 (Advisory Opinion of June 1) (Separate opinion of Judge Lauterpacht)).

if such a principle existed, it could by definition only be employed within the limits of the Treaty, a cardinal condition that Variant C failed to satisfy.

Slovakia also argued that Variant C could be justified as a countermeasure. Referring to its prior jurisprudence and to Articles 47-50 of the ILC's draft articles on state responsibility, the Court observed that a countermeasure must be taken in response to a previous internationally wrongful act of another state and must be directed against that state; that the injured state must have called upon the state committing the wrongful act to discontinue its wrongful conduct or make reparation for it; that the effects of a countermeasure must commensurate with the injury suffered, taking account of the rights in question; and, finally, that as its purpose must be to induce the wrongdoing state to comply with its obligations under international law, the countermeasure must be reversible. The Court pointed out that the Danube is not only a shared international watercourse, but also an international boundary river to which the principle of the perfect equality of all riparian states applies. It considered that Czechoslovakia, by its unilateral diversion of the Danube and by unilaterally assuming control of a shared resource, had deprived Hungary of its right to an equitable and reasonable share of the natural resources of the river and had failed to respect the requirement of proportionality. Moreover, the Court found that, even if Czechoslovakia was under a duty to mitigate the damage resulting from Hungary's unlawful actions, that duty could not justify an otherwise wrongful act on its part. The Court held, by 10 votes to 5, that Variant C, including the unilateral damming and diversion of the Danube from October 1992, did not meet the cardinal condition of the Treaty that a joint system of locks be constructed that would constitute a single and indivisible operational system of works. By definition, this could not be attained by unilateral action.[16]

In the second part of the decision, the Court addressed the legal consequences of its Judgment for the future conduct of both parties. First, the Court confirmed, by 12 votes to 3, that Slovakia had become a party to the Treaty as successor to Czechoslovakia upon the dissolution of the latter state on January 1, 1993, on the basis of the particular nature of the Treaty. The Treaty had established a territorial and navigational regime and created rights and

---

16　*Id.* at 53, para. 77 and 56, para. 85.

obligations attaching to the relevant parts of the Danube, leaving it unaffected by a succession of states.[17]

Observing that its findings on the past conduct of the parties between 1989 and 1992 have a declaratory character and do not determine what the future conduct should be the Court reiterated that the Treaty is still in force and, as a *lex specialis*, governs the relationship between the parties. The factual situation that has developed since 1989 must be placed within the context of the Treaty relationship, with a view to achieving the Treaty's object and purpose insofar as that is feasible.[18]

The Court concluded, by 13 votes to 2, that both parties are under a legal obligation to negotiate in good faith to determine in what way the Treaty's multiple objectives can best be carried out. These objectives must be attained in an integrated and consolidated program, to be developed in the Joint Contractual Plan. Most important, the Court determined, by 13 votes to 2, that the joint operational regime that the Treaty seeks to establish should be restored by both parties, and any works carried out so far should be made to comply with it.

The Court recognized that the project's implications for the environment are of necessity a key issue in the parties' negotiations. It stressed that current environmental standards must be taken into consideration by both parties, so that the quality of the water of the Danube and nature in general are protected and a satisfactory solution is found for the volume of water to be released into the old bed of the Danube and into the side-arms of that international waterway. Referring to the concept of sustainable development as aptly expressing the need to reconcile economic development with protection of the environment, the Court suggested that the parties could, by agreement, incorporate newly developed norms of environmental law through the application of several of the Treaty's provisions.

---

17 This is reflected in Article 12 of the 1978 Vienna Convention on Succession of States in respect of Treaties, *opened for signature* Aug. 23, 1978, 17 ILM 1488 (1978), which according to the Court reflects a rule of customary international law. The Court thus rejected Hungary's argument that sought to distinguish between, on the one hand, rights and obligations such as "continuing property rights" under the Treaty, and, on the other hand, the Treaty itself. *Id.* at 71-72, para. 123.

18 *Id.* at 76, para. 133. Hungary argued that future relations between the parties, as far as Variant C is concerned, are not governed by the 1977 Treaty. *Id.* at 73, para. 125.

While the Court deferred to the parties' ultimate power to determine the modalities for executing its decision, as laid down in their special agreement, the Judgment indicates some guidelines for their subsequent negotiations on future cooperative arrangements. Thus, the Court stated that there is no longer any point in building a power plant at Nagymaros on Hungarian territory, and that some performance obligations relating to the construction of the system of locks may have been overtaken by events. In its view, "[i]t would be an administration of the law altogether out of touch with reality if the Court were to order those obligations to be fully reinstated and the works [on Slovak territory] to be demolished ... ."[19] The parties should look afresh at the environmental effects of the Gabčíkovo power plant. The works at Cunovo on Slovak territory should become a jointly operated unit.

As to the legal effects of the internationally wrongful acts committed by both parties, the Court summarized its position as follows:

> Reparation must, "as far as possible," wipe out all the consequences of the illegal act. In this case, the consequences of the wrongful act of both Parties will be wiped out "as far as possible" if they resume their co-operation in the utilization of the shared water resources of the Danube, and if the multi-purpose programme, in the form of a co-ordinated single unit, for the use, development and protection of the watercourse is implemented in an equitable and reasonable manner. What it is possible for the Parties to do is to re-establish co-operative administration of what remains of the Project.[20]

The Court observed that the issue of compensation, which both parties are under an obligation to pay and which both are entitled to obtain, could be resolved satisfactorily in the framework of an overall settlement if each party were to renounce or cancel all financial claims and counterclaims. The Court's vote on this point, which was combined in one of the operative paragraphs, was 12 to 3.[21]

---

19 *Id.* at 76-77, paras. 134-136.
20 *Id.* at 80, para. 150.
21 Through the dissents we learn that there was disagreement among the Judges on whether to separate the operative paragraph that deals with the compensation issue into two paragraphs so that it could be voted on as two separate issues. Apparently, the majority was in favor of a single vote, prompting several Judges to dissent where they otherwise agreed, at least in part, with the operative paragraph concerned. *See* Dissenting opinions of Judges Oda (para. 2), Vereshchetin (final para.), and Parra-Aranguren (para. 21).

Finally, the Court held, by 13 votes to 2, that the settlement of accounts for the construction of the works must be resolved in accordance with the Treaty and related instruments and that Hungary must pay a proportionate share of the costs related to the works already constructed on Slovak territory if it is to share in their operation and benefits.[22]

* * * *

This case is a good example of how the ICJ gives and takes with a view to achieving a result that is acceptable to both litigants and that, consequently, stands the best chance of being complied with by the two sovereign litigants. Judging from the reactions of the media in Hungary and Slovakia in the aftermath of the Court's Judgment, both countries welcomed the outcome of the case. This is somewhat surprising, especially as regards Hungary, given that the pivotal holding of the Judgment is that, in stark contrast to what Hungary argued, the Treaty still governs the relationship between the two countries and that all of its objectives must be carried out. Inevitably, this means that Hungary must return to the project that it abandoned in 1989 in order to complete, in one form or another, its part of the project contemplated by the Treaty. But the Judgment also gives the Hungarian Government some space to negotiate a result that is different from that originally contemplated by the Treaty and that it can "sell" to the Hungarian people as being just and favorable.

Notwithstanding elaborate treatment of environmental issues in the Judgment, this was not an environment case. First and foremost, the dispute involved issues of the law of treaties and the law of state responsibility. Because the Special Agreement reserved to the parties the power to determine the modalities of implementing the Judgment, the Court's pronouncements on the environment are necessarily more recommendatory than prescriptive, which somewhat diminishes their value.

The case highlights the unique role that the ICJ may play when two interdependent states have reached a stalemate after lengthy negotiations. Through their Special Agreement, Hungary and Slovakia asked the Court to define and resolve the legal aspects of their dispute. But the Special Agreement also provided that the parties shall "[i]mmediately after the transmission of the Judgment ... enter into negotiations on the modalities for its execution" and that "[i]f they are unable to reach agreement within six months, either Party may request the Court to render an additional Judgment to determine the

---

22 *Id.* at 81, para. 154.

modalities for executing its Judgment." In this way, both parties are actively using the principal judicial organ of the United Nations to assist them in defining the fundamental legal parameters of a process of ongoing negotiations geared toward achieving a political result that is mutually acceptable.

◊

New ICJ jurisprudence on counterclaims – interpretation of Article 80 of Rules of Court – Yugoslav and U.S. counterclaims within the Court's jurisdiction and directly connected with the subject matter of the applicant's claim

APPLICATION OF THE CONVENTION ON THE PREVENTION AND PUNISHMENT OF THE CRIME OF GENOCIDE (Bosnia-Herzegovina v. Yugoslavia)

Counterclaims, Order
1997 ICJ REP. 243
International Court of Justice, December 17, 1997

OIL PLATFORMS (Islamic Republic of Iran v. United States)
Counterclaims, Order
1998 ICJ REP. 190
International Court of Justice, March 10, 1998[*]

Through Orders in each of the cases concerning *Application of the Convention on the Prevention and Punishment of the Crime of Genocide (Bosnia-Herzegovina v. Yugoslavia)* and *Oil Platforms (Islamic Republic of Iran v. United States of America)*, the International Court of Justice upheld the admissibility of the counterclaims filed by the respondent states as part of their counter-memorials in both cases, and thus allowed these claims to form part of the proceedings on the merits. In both Orders the Court developed, for the first time since 1952, the limited jurisprudence concerning the admissibility of counterclaims as part of the incidental jurisdiction conferred upon the Court by the ICJ Statute.[1]

---

[*] Reproduced with permission from 92 AJIL 508 (1998). © The American Society of International Law.

[1] The only two ICJ precedents are Asylum (Peru v. Colom.), 1950 ICJ REP. 266 (Nov. 20) and Rights of Nationals of the United States of America in Morocco (Fr. v. U.S.), 1952 ICJ REP. 176 (Aug. 27). Judge Oda discusses these precedents in paras. 6-7 of part III of his separate opinion appended to the *Oil Platforms* Order, *infra* note 7. However, in contrast to the recent Orders, counterclaims were not dealt with as a preliminary matter in the 1950s cases, which were also governed by Rules of Court that were worded slightly differently. *See also* United States Diplomatic and Consular Staff in Tehran (U.S. v. Iran), Provisional Measures, 1979 ICJ REP.

P.H.F. Bekker, World Court Decisions at the Turn of the Millennium (1997-2001), p. 59-74.
© 2002 *Kluwer Law International. Printed in the Netherlands.*

The Court's Order in the Genocide *Case*

On July 22, 1997, the Government of the Federal Republic of Yugoslavia (Yugoslavia) filed a counter-memorial with the ICJ Registry responding to the Application filed by Bosnia-Herzegovina (Bosnia) on March 20, 1993, in which Bosnia asked the Court to hold Yugoslavia responsible for alleged acts of genocide committed against the Bosnian population. Part of the submissions contained in the Yugoslav Counter-memorial alleged violations by Bosnia of the 1948 Convention on the Prevention and Punishment of the Crime of Genocide (Genocide Convention) through acts of direct and public incitement to commit genocide and its actual commission against the Serbs in Bosnia. Yugoslavia asked the Court to declare that Bosnia has itself violated the Genocide Convention, to order Bosnia to prevent the repetition of acts constituting such violations, and to declare that Bosnia had incurred international responsibility for which it must provide adequate compensation.

Bosnia indicated its objections to Yugoslavia's counterclaims when the parties met with ICJ President Schwebel on September 22, 1997, triggering the first application of paragraph 3 of Article 80 of the 1978 version of the Rules of Court.[2] Through a letter of September 26, 1997, from the ICJ Registrar, Bosnia and Yugoslavia were both invited to submit to the Court their written observations on the question of the admissibility of the Yugoslav counterclaims

---

7, 15, para. 24 (Order of Dec. 15). For a brief description of the three precedents (the *Chorzów Factory* (Merits), *Diversion of Water from the Meuse* and *Panevezys-Saldutiskis Railway* cases) in the Permanent Court of International Justice (1920-1945), see SHABTAI ROSENNE, 3 THE LAW AND PRACTICE OF THE INTERNATIONAL COURT, 1920-1996, at 1274 (3rd. ed. 1997) and GENEVIEVE GUYOMAR, COMMENTAIRE DU REGLEMENT DE LA COUR INTERNATIONALE DE JUSTICE ADOPTÉ LE 14 AVRIL 1978 – INTERPRÉTATION ET PRATIQUE 519-522 (1983). *See also* MANLEY O. HUDSON, THE PERMANENT COURT OF INTERNATIONAL JUSTICE, 1920-1942, at 292, 430, 539 (1943); A. Miaja de la Muela, *La Reconvención ante el Tribunal internacional de Justicia*, in *Estudios de derecho procesal en honor de Niceto Alcalá-Zamora y Castillo*, 24 BOLETÍN MEXICANO DE DERECHO COMPARADO 757 (1975).

2   ICJ Rules of Court, Apr. 14, 1978, Art. 80, para. 3, *reprinted in* 73 AJIL 748, 761 (1979) ("In the event of doubt as to the connection between the question presented by way of counter-claim and the subject-matter of the claim of the other party the Court shall, after hearing the parties, decide whether or not the question thus presented shall be joined to the original proceedings."). The original Rules of Court, adopted by the ICJ in 1946, dealt with counterclaims in Article 63, which remained unchanged in Article 68 of the 1972 amendment of the Rules. Art. 80 subsequently was amended. *See* ICJ Communiqué 2001/01 (Jan. 12, 2001).

to the Court no later than October 10, 1997 (Bosnia) and October 24, 1997 (Yugoslavia).

Bosnia's principal objection to the admissibility of the Yugoslav counter-claims was that they do not satisfy the conditions laid down in Article 80, paragraph 1 of the Rules of Court,[3] because they are not "directly connected" with the subject matter of the initial proceedings instituted by Bosnia. Bosnia based this objection on the structure and content of Yugoslavia's Counter-memorial. Except for one reference in the introduction, that document does not specifically refer to any "counterclaims" (it does not even mention Article 80 of the Rules of Court), but merely claims, in Part II, that Bosnia is itself responsible for violating the Genocide Convention. Bosnia argued that the facts submitted by Yugoslavia were totally different from those on which the initial claim of Bosnia had relied. According to Bosnia, the test should be whether examining either of the two sets of facts (i.e., those presented by the applicant in the application and memorial and those presented by the respondent in the counter-memorial containing the counterclaim) is of help in the judicial analysis of the other set and can determine or influence its outcome in any manner. In addition, Bosnia inferred from the *erga omnes* and non-reciprocal nature of the obligations embodied in the Genocide Convention that the Convention leaves no place for the reciprocity implied by the introduction of counterclaims derived from its provisions.[4] Bosnia further alleged that a counterclaim must have the objective of countering the applicant's principal claim (i.e., it must oppose it in order to block the principal claim or to reduce its effects, as opposed to formulating an autonomous dispute relating to different facts) and it must claim something more, in particular a judgment against the applicant in the principal proceedings.

Yugoslavia maintained that Bosnia's original claim and the Yugoslav counterclaim are both based on the same legal ground, namely, the Genocide Convention and the rules of state responsibility, and that the disputed facts of both claims relate to the war in Bosnia. Hence, there was a legal and factual connection.

According to the Court, it needed first to consider whether the Yugoslav claims constitute "counterclaims" within the meaning of Article 80 of the Rules

---

3   Rules of Court, *supra* note 2, Art. 80, para. 1 ("A counter-claim may be presented provided that it is directly connected with the subject-matter of the claim of the other party and that it comes within the jurisdiction of the Court.").

4   Yugoslavia agreed with Bosnia that a breach of the Genocide Convention cannot serve as an excuse for another breach of the same treaty, a point confirmed by the Court in paragraph 35.

of Court and, if so, whether they satisfy the conditions embodied in Article 80. As to the nature of a counterclaim, the Court explained that it has a dual character in relation to the applicant's claim: a counterclaim is independent of the applicant's claim in that it constitutes a separate claim (i.e., an autonomous legal act aimed at submitting a new claim) and, at the same time, it is linked to the other party's claim in that it reacts to it. Moreover, a counterclaim is distinguishable from a defense on the merits in that it widens the original subject matter of the dispute by pursuing objectives other than the mere dismissal of the applicant's claim. The Court also pointed out that the instrument of counterclaims has been admitted to ensure better administration of justice in appropriate cases so as to achieve a procedural economy and present the Court with an overview of the parties' respective claims conducive to consistent decision-making.[5] On this basis, the Court noted that, whereas the first two of Yugoslavia's submissions in its Counter-Memorial relate exclusively to the dismissal of Bosnia's claims, submissions 3-6 set out separate claims seeking relief beyond the dismissal of Bosnia's claims, qualifying them as counterclaims within the meaning of the Rules of Court.[6]

The Court next observed that Article 80 of the Rules of Court requires that a claim that constitutes a "counterclaim" satisfy three basic conditions, one *ratione temporis* and two *ratione materiae*: (1) the counterclaim must be made in the counter-memorial of the party presenting the counterclaim as part of that party's submissions; (2) it must come within the Court's jurisdiction; and (3) it must be directly connected with the subject matter of the other party's claim. The Court explained that the rationale for the latter two conditions is that a counterclaim cannot be used to introduce claims that exceed the limits of its jurisdiction as recognized by the parties. Moreover, the respondent cannot use a counterclaim to impose on the applicant any claim it chooses.[7]

---

5   Order of Dec. 17, 1997, 1997 ICJ REP. 243, 256-57, paras. 26-30 [hereinafter *Genocide* Order].

6   It is not entirely clear from the operative paragraph 43(A) of the Order which of the Yugoslav submissions referred to in paragraph 29 are considered acceptable counterclaims. The Court merely referred to "the counter-claims submitted by Yugoslavia."

7   *Genocide* Order, *supra* note 5, at 257-58, para. 31. The Court cited this statement in its entirety in the *Oil Platforms* Order. Order of Mar. 10, 1998, 1998 ICJ REP. 190, 203, para. 31 (released Mar. 19, 1998) [hereinafter *Oil Platforms* Order]. Judge Oda's separate opinion indicates that Iran already had been informed of the Order on March 10, 1998.

Given that in its view the first two conditions were not disputed, the Court focused on Bosnia's principal objection, namely, that the Yugoslav counterclaims were not "directly connected" to Bosnia's claims. In the absence of a definition of what constitutes such a direct connection, the Court has full discretion to make its own assessment, taking account of the particular aspects of each case. The extent of this connection must be assessed both in fact and in law.

As to the factual element of the connection, the Court observed that it emerges from the parties' submissions that their respective claims rest on facts of the same nature, forming part of the same factual and time complex, i.e., the war in Bosnia.[8]

The Court pointed out that the argument that Bosnia drew from the absence of reciprocity in the Genocide Convention is not determinative for the assessment of the existence or absence of a legal connection between the applicant's claim and the counterclaim, in light of the fact that both parties are effectively pursuing the same legal aim: the establishment of legal responsibility for violations of the Genocide Convention.[9] On this basis, and referring to its earlier statements in a previous stage of the proceedings, the Court, by 13 votes to 1,[10] concluded that the Yugoslav counterclaims are directly connected with the subject matter of Bosnia's claims and, as counterclaims, are admissible as such and form part of the main proceedings instituted by Bosnia.[11] The Court thus decided to rule on the claims of Bosnia and Yugoslavia in a single set of proceedings. By 13 votes to 1, the Court directed Bosnia to submit a reply by January 23, 1998, and it ordered Yugoslavia to submit a rejoinder by July 23, 1998, relating to the respective claims of both parties.[12]

---

8   *Genocide* Order, *supra* note 5, at 258, para. 34. This means that a counterclaim does not have to be limited exclusively to facts presented by the applicant in the main proceedings and that the respondent is entitled to submit new facts by a counterclaim in its counter-memorial, so long as the counterclaim can be said to be directly connected with the applicant's claim and come within the Court's jurisdiction.

9   *Id.*, para. 35.

10   Only Vice President Weeramantry dissented. Judge *ad hoc* Kreća (appointed by Yugoslavia) appended a declaration and Judge Koroma and Judge *ad hoc* Lauterpacht (appointed by Bosnia) appended separate opinions to the Order.

11   *Genocide* Order, *supra* note 5, at 260, para. 43 (operative subpara. (A)).

12   *Id.*, at 261 (operative subpara. (B)).

The Court's Order in the Oil Platforms *Case*

On June 23, 1997, the United States filed a document entitled "Counter-Memorial and Counter-Claim" with the ICJ Registry. The case had been brought by Iran on November 2, 1992, and concerns the destruction of certain Iranian oil platforms by the U.S. Navy in 1987-1988. Part VI introduced a counterclaim requesting that the Court adjudge and declare "[t]hat in attacking vessels, laying mines in the Gulf and otherwise engaging in military actions in 1987-88 that were dangerous and detrimental to maritime commerce, the Islamic Republic of Iran breached its obligations to the United States under Article X" of the Treaty of Amity, Economic Relations and Consular Rights between the United States and Iran of August 15, 1955 (Treaty),[13] for which Iran must make full reparation to the United States.

Iran informed the Court of its objection to the U.S. counterclaim by letter of October 2, 1997. Subsequent to a meeting between Vice President Weeramantry, acting as president in the case, and the agents of both parties on October 17, 1997, Iran and the United States were both invited, through a letter of October 21, 1997, from the ICJ Registrar, to submit their written observations to the Court on the admissibility of the U.S. counterclaim no later than November 18, 1997 (Iran), and December 18, 1997 (United States).

In its written observations, Iran argued, first, that the U.S. counterclaim and Iran's original claim lack any direct connection and, second, that the counterclaim does not come within the Court's jurisdiction, as required by Article 80, paragraph 1 of the Rules of Court. Iran accused the United States of seeking to widen the dispute to paragraphs 2-5 of Article X of the Treaty. Referring to the Judgment of December 12, 1996, in which the Court had ruled that only Article X, paragraph 1 of the Treaty was applicable to the Iranian claim, Iran pointed out that paragraphs 2-5 had never been in question in the proceedings until the filing of the U.S. counterclaim. According to Iran, the general assertion of the violation of freedom and commerce in the U.S. counterclaim is not sufficiently specific to enable the Court to determine whether the requisite connection exists. Iran also argued that the alleged attacks by Iranian gunboats on U.S. vessels during 1987-1988 described in the U.S. counterclaim, in alleged violation of the freedom of commerce guaranteed by Article X, paragraph 1 of the Treaty, lack any legal and factual connection with the U.S. attacks on the platforms that form the basis of Iran's complaint. Moreover, the alleged Iranian attacks involved vessels that were not engaged in commerce

---

13   8 UST 899, 284 UNTS 93.

or navigation *between Iran and the United States*, and thus fall outside the realm of application of the Treaty.

In response, the United States objected to Iran's jurisdictional arguments as seeking to force the entire U.S. counterclaim into the confines of Article X, paragraph 1 of the Treaty. It argued that Article 80 of the Rules of Court requires that the counterclaim be directly connected with the *subject matter* of the claim, not with the claim itself, so that a proper counterclaim need not be a mirror image of the claim or rest upon precisely the same theory or facts. The United States argued that there is a direct connection between the subject matter of Iran's claim and the U.S. counterclaim, given that the facts and circumstances that caused the United States to attack Iran's oil platforms are at the heart of the U.S. defense to Iran's claims and, at the same time, form the basis of its counterclaim. It also argued that paragraphs 2-5 of Article X of the Treaty are not, as Iran had claimed, limited to commercial vessels involved in trade between the United States and Iran.

As regards the meaning of Article 80 of the Rules of Court, the United States maintained that the Court's Order should be limited to the question of whether there is doubt as to the direct connection between its counterclaim and Iran's claim required by Article 80, paragraph 3 of the Rules. By contrast, Iran claimed that it was entitled to address both the issue of direct connection *and* the Court's jurisdiction and that the decision that the Court is required to make under Article 80, paragraph 3 after a hearing exclusively concerns whether or not the counterclaim should be joined to the main proceedings. In Iran's view, this provision does not prejudice the right of the party opposing the counterclaim in a *subsequent* phase of the proceedings to advance any defense relating either to the admissibility or to the merits of the counterclaim. Consequently, Iran reserved the right to lodge preliminary objections with regard to the U.S. counterclaim. In response, the United States argued that Iran drew false analogies between the preliminary objections procedure described in Article 79 of the Rules and the procedure governing counterclaims laid down in Article 80. It claimed that Iran's objections to jurisdiction and admissibility involved contested matters of fact that the Court could not effectively address and decide in the context of the abbreviated procedure of Article 80, paragraph 3. According to the United States, Iran's position was not whether the U.S. counterclaim is connected with the subject matter of Iran's claim, but whether there is a valid counterclaim at all, which goes to the merits of the counterclaim and could not be determined by the Court at this stage of the proceedings.

In only fifteen short paragraphs of legal reasoning embodied in an Order issued four months after receipt of the U.S. written observations, the Court failed to address explicitly a number of the above points that were raised by both parties. However, the Court's treatment of some of these issues in the Order implies that it agreed with Iran that the applicant may assert both lack of connection and lack of jurisdiction, but that this can be done only at the preliminary stage of the Order ruling on admissibility of the respondent's counterclaims. The Court simply stated that a decision on the admissibility of a counterclaim taking account of the requirements of Article 80 in no way prejudges any question that the Court will have to deal with during the remainder of the proceedings.[14]

Referring to its Judgment of December 12, 1996, the Court agreed with Iran that its jurisdiction in the present case covers only claims made by Iran under Article X, paragraph 1 of the Treaty, and under no other provision.[15] According to that provision, as interpreted by the Court, there shall be *freedom* of commerce (which includes commercial activities in general) and navigation between Iran and the United States, prohibiting any act that would impede that freedom. The Court considered that the allegations made in the U.S. counterclaim of Iranian attacks on shipping, the laying of mines, and other military actions said to be dangerous and detrimental to maritime commerce are capable of falling within the scope of Article X, paragraph 1. Consequently, the Court found that it has jurisdiction to entertain the U.S. counterclaim "in so far as the facts alleged may have prejudiced the freedoms guaranteed by Article X, paragraph 1."[16]

---

14 *Oil Platforms* Order, *supra* note 7, at 205, para. 41. Paragraph 38 of the *Genocide* Order contains nearly identical language. It remains to be seen how the Court will interpret this statement in any subsequent stages of a case, especially in light of the explicit reservations made by Iran and the United States in their written observations.

15 *See* Oil Platforms (Iran v. U.S.), Preliminary Objection, Judgment, 1996 ICJ REP. 803, para. 55(2) (Dec. 12, 1996).

16 *Oil Platforms* Order, *supra* note 7, at 204, paras. 34-36 (issue of jurisdiction). In her separate opinion, Judge Higgins took issue with this part of the Order. According to her, the Court should have addressed the U.S. arguments based on Article X, paragraphs 2-5 of the Treaty and the Order should have contained a reasoned decision on the Court's apparent rejection of those arguments. Judge Higgins also did not understand why the Court allowed Iran's jurisdictional argument concerning the question whether Article X(1) of the Treaty is restricted to commerce "between" the parties to go to the merits, whereas it had declined to enter into a discussion of the same question in its decision on jurisdiction of December 12, 1996. Similarly, she disagreed with the Court's silence on Iran's argument that certain vessels featured in the U.S. counterclaim and identified as warships are excluded from the reach of Article X(1).

The Court considered that the U.S. counterclaim is directly connected with Iran's original claim both in fact and in law, given that the parties' claims rest on facts of the same nature forming part of the same factual complex (having occurred in the Persian Gulf during the same period) and that both pursue the same legal aim, namely, the establishment of legal responsibility for violations of the Treaty.[17]

Consequently, the Court, by 15 votes to 1,[18] found that the U.S. counterclaim is admissible as such and forms part of the main proceedings instituted by Iran.[19] The Court thus decided to rule on the claims of Iran and the United States in a single set of proceedings. Unanimously, the Court directed Iran to submit a reply by September 10, 1998, and it ordered the United States to submit a rejoinder by November 23, 1999, relating to the respective claims of both parties.[20]

* * * *

This new jurisprudence on counterclaims is particularly relevant in light of the possible effects of the recent increase in the use of this instrument in "involuntary" cases in which the Court had previously rejected preliminary objections to its jurisdiction.[21] Counterclaims are likely to emerge as an important new tool for respondents whose preliminary objections have been rejected, as part of an effort to delay the merits phase of a case involuntarily brought against them.[22] These two Orders are as interesting for what they

---

17 *Oil Platforms* Order, *supra* note 7, at 204-05, paras. 37-39 (issue of connection, reflecting paras. 33-34 of the *Genocide* Order, *supra* note 5).

18 Only Judge *ad hoc* Rigaux (appointed by Iran) dissented. Judges Oda and Higgins appended separate opinions to the Order.

19 *Oil Platforms* Order, *supra* note 7, at 206, para. 46 (operative subpara. (A)).

20 *Id.* at 207 (operative subpara. (B)).

21 In the *Genocide* case, the Court dismissed Yugoslavia's preliminary objections in its Judgment of July 11, 1996. *See* 1996 ICJ REP. 595. See my casenote in 91 AJIL 121 (1997) (co-authored with Paul Szasz), *reprinted in* COMMENTARIES ON WORLD COURT DECISIONS (1987-1996) 253 (P.H.F. Bekker ed., 1998). In the *Oil Platforms* case, the Court dismissed the preliminary objection of the United States in its Judgment of December 12, 1996. See my casenote in 91 AJIL 518 (1997), *reprinted in* COMMENTARIES ON WORLD COURT DECISIONS (1987-1996) 263 (P.H.F. Bekker ed., 1998).

22 As Vice President Weeramantry and Judge Koroma complain in their respective opinions appended to the *Genocide* Order, the Order was issued more than four years after proceedings were instituted by Bosnia and the case still is not ready

state with regard to counterclaims as for the many important issues of international due process and procedure that the Court *failed* to address despite the arguments of the parties. Given the incomplete terms of Article 80 of the Rules of Court, the Court's interpretative statements become even more significant in cases involving counterclaims. In dealing with counterclaims, the Court is faced with different, often conflicting considerations: the principles of the equality of the parties and of material truth and judicial economy, the interest of the applicant in having its claims decided within a reasonable period of time, and the interest of the sound administration of justice, including the guarantee of due process and the prevention of abuse of court procedures.

While the Court's decisions on counterclaims are embodied in orders and not in judgments, and thus strictly speaking are issued without the force of *res judicata*, the Court's statements embodied in them are as authoritative as any other decision by the principal judicial organ of the United Nations, being directed to parties that have already been found to be subject to its jurisdiction.

The main difference between these cases is that, in contrast to Bosnia in the *Genocide* case, Iran did not dispute that the U.S. claim was presented in its Counter-Memorial as a "counterclaim" (as opposed to as a defense on the merits).[23] Moreover, unlike Bosnia, Iran claimed that the U.S. counterclaim does not fall within the Court's jurisdiction *and* that it lacks any direct connection to the original claim. Otherwise, the two Orders are practically identical in their legal reasoning: the *Oil Platforms* Order drew obvious inspiration from the *Genocide* Order issued three months earlier.

Significantly, in an apparent effort to ensure due process and strict equality between the parties, the Court decided in each case to reserve the applicant's right to present its views on the respondent's counterclaim a second time in an additional written document.[24] In each case, it also instructed the Registrar

---

for hearings on the merits.

23   The Court's statement in paragraph 32 of the *Genocide* Order that "in the present case it is not disputed that the Yugoslav counter-claims were 'made in the Counter-Memorial of the Party presenting it, and ... appear as part of the submissions of that Party', in accordance with Article 80, paragraph 2, of the Rules of Court," stands in direct contrast with the Court's earlier summary of Bosnia's position in paragraphs 11-14.

24   See the identical concluding words of paragraphs 42 and 45 of the *Genocide* and *Oil Platforms* Orders, respectively. The Court sought to remedy the effect that joinder of the counterclaim to the main proceedings might have on the equality of the parties, stemming from the fact that the respondent could address its counterclaims in both the counter-memorial and the rejoinder, whereas the applicant could respond only once in writing through its reply.

to transmit a copy of the Order to third states entitled to appear before the Court with a view to protecting any interests they might have.[25]

The Court did not address the argument advanced by Iran that no counterclaim may be filed after submission of the Counter-Memorial and that the United States was precluded from reserving to add further instances of Iranian attacks on U.S. vessels in the future. The Court should have made clear, as it did in the *Genocide* Order, that Article 80, paragraph 2 of the Rules of Court contains a requirement *ratione temporis* precluding the United States from submitting counterclaims after the filing of its Counter-Memorial.

Although both Orders suggest that the counterclaimant is not restricted to the exact same facts on which the applicant relied, so long as they form part of the same "factual complex" (i.e., same place and time), the Court's statements on jurisdiction in the *Oil Platforms* Order suggest that the jurisdictional basis established by the Court for the applicant's claim also sets the limits for the counterclaim. Judge Higgins rightly challenged this part of the *Oil Platforms* Order in her separate opinion. It is not clear how to interpret the condition that the counterclaim "come[ ] within the Court's jurisdiction" (Art. 80, paragraph 1 of the Rules of Court) in light of the Court's statement in both Orders that "the Respondent cannot use a counterclaim as a means of referring to an international court claims which exceed the limits of its jurisdiction *as recognized by the parties*."[26] Judge Higgins argued that the Court's jurisdiction with regard to counterclaims should be determined by reference to the usual jurisdictional principles rather than by reference to the basis of jurisdiction that the applicant happened to have relied on in relation to its particular facts.[27] The Court's rather broad holding on what constitutes a "direct connection" on the facts, allowing the respondent to introduce different facts, dictates that

---

25 See the identical wording of paragraphs 39 and 42 of the *Genocide* and *Oil Platforms* Orders, respectively. Both Bosnia and Iran sought to avoid a joinder of the counterclaims and the original claims by pointing to the detrimental effects that it could have for the rights and interests of third states, which would not be informed of any counterclaims, but only of any new case pursuant to Article 40, paragraph 3 of the Statute. *See Genocide* Order, *supra* note 5, at 253, para. 15 and *Oil Platforms* Order, *supra* note 7, at 199, para. 20.

26 *Genocide* Order, *supra* note 5, at 257-58, para. 31, and *Oil Platforms* Order, *supra* note 7, at 203, para. 33 (emphasis added).

27 According to Judge Higgins, the correct interpretation of the requirement that the counterclaim "come[ ] within the jurisdiction of the Court" is to inquire whether the Court would have had jurisdiction to deal with the claims of the United States, as they related to Article X, paragraphs 2-5 of the Treaty, had they been the subject of an ordinary application to the Court.

the respondent should not be restricted to the jurisdictional basis of the specific facts on which the applicant's claim relies. Hence, the *Oil Platforms* Order is inconsistent, or at best unclear, on this important point, with detrimental effect to the counterclaimant. This Order indicates that the apparent flexibility that the Court allows in its interpretation of the requirement that there be a "direct connection" is severely curtailed by its interpretation of the second important condition that the counterclaim "come[ ] within the jurisdiction of the Court," if indeed it meant to say that the counterclaim cannot be based on a wider, or simply different, jurisdictional basis from the one that the Court has already upheld with regard to the applicant's claim.[28]

Apart from this potentially detrimental effect, counterclaims can be beneficial to respondents by enabling them to profit from the jurisdictional case already argued by the applicant in establishing, and sometimes extending, jurisdiction over claims by way of *forum prorogatum*. Especially in cases in which the respondent's preliminary objections have been rejected by the Court, counterclaims can provide an effective tool of litigation strategy available to respondent states for making the applicant a defendant in its own case and simultaneously delaying the proceedings on the merits.

Another due process point of interest raised by these two recent cases is the Court's refusal to hold oral proceedings on the admissibility of the respondents' counterclaims, even if one or both parties request that they be held. The Orders shed some light on the Court's interpretation of the words "to hear the parties" in Article 80, paragraph 3 of the Rules of Court when the admissibility of counterclaims is disputed. The Orders refer to letters of the Registrar informing the parties that the Court would decide the remainder of the procedure on the basis of the documents (i.e., their written observations) before the Court at that time.[29] In both Orders, the Court considered that, having received full and detailed written observations from each of the parties, it was sufficiently well informed about their positions and, accordingly, did not need to hear from them "otherwise"[30] or "further"[31] on the subject, i.e., presumably, through

---

28   Manley Hudson believed that the proviso that the counterclaim must "come within the jurisdiction of the Court" was quite unnecessary "as to *direct* counter-claims, for once established the jurisdiction of the Court would seem to extend to any counter-claim directly connected with the subject of the application." HUDSON, *supra* note 1, at 292-93 (emphasis added). It is unclear from this statement whether Hudson also accepted "indirect" counterclaims, for which the proviso might make sense.

29   *Genocide* Order, *supra* note 5, at 254, para. 17, and *Oil Platforms* Order, *supra* note 7, at 199, para. 21.

30   *Genocide* Order, *supra* note 5, at 256, para. 25.

public hearings in the Peace Palace. The words "otherwise" and "further" imply that the Court attributes a broad meaning to the word "hearing," and that the filing of written observations in its view forms part of "hearing" the parties. Article 80, paragraph 3 of the Rules of Court requires that the Court decide on joining the counterclaim to the original proceedings "after hearing the parties" if there is doubt as to the connection between the counterclaim and the applicant's claim. But that provision does not specify how such a hearing is to be effected: it does not indicate whether oral proceedings must be held in the Great Hall of Justice. This necessarily means that the Court has full discretion to decide as to how it will hear the parties.[32] The Orders indicate that the Court is keen on retaining this discretion in deciding whether to join a counterclaim to the main proceedings.[33]

In his commentary on Article 80 of the Rules of Court, which was published before the issuance of these two Orders, Shabtai Rosenne states with regard to the expression "after hearing the parties" that "[t]his means that in future there will always be some oral proceedings in the event of doubt – by whom is not stated – as to the connection."[34] The Court's most authoritative com-

---

31 *Oil Platforms* Order, *supra* note 7, at 203, para. 31.
32 This discretion derives from Article 30 of the ICJ Statute. In establishing the Rules of Court, the Court retained this basic discretion. The Statute itself is completely silent on the issue of counterclaims. However, it is true that Articles 43, paragraph 5, and 45-47 of the Statute employ the word "hearing" to denote oral proceedings.
33 Judge *ad hoc* Lauterpacht devoted the first part of his separate opinion to the *Genocide* Order to this procedural issue, in which he argued that the Court should have granted the parties an opportunity to comment orally, i.e., at a public hearing, on each other's position. In his separate opinion to the *Oil Platforms* Order, Judge Oda argued that all issues relating to the respondent's counterclaim should be discussed in parallel with the original claim of the applicant in the written and oral proceedings on the *merits*, support for which he found in precedent. According to the senior judge, the procedure by which the Court determines the admissibility of a counterclaim in the form of an order at a preliminary stage is irregular. Instead, the Court should give its decision on the admissibility of a counterclaim in its judgment on the merits.
34 SHABTAI ROSENNE, PROCEDURE IN THE INTERNATIONAL COURT: A COMMENTARY ON THE 1978 RULES OF THE INTERNATIONAL COURT OF JUSTICE 171 (1983). The same statement is repeated in ROSENNE, *supra* note 1, at 1273. Presumably, it is the Court's doubt that counts, stemming from the initial opposing views expressed by the parties to the President of the Court. Hence, the provision is triggered by the applicant's indicating its opposition to the counterclaims filed by the respondent. Judge *ad hoc* Lauterpacht acknowledged in paragraph 4 of his separate opinion to the *Genocide* Order that the Court's practice in relation to Articles 36, paragraph

mentator will have to revise his comments in the light of the new jurisprudence discussed above.[35] Given that the 1978 Rules replaced the words "after due examination" in the 1972 Rules with "after hearing the parties," there is some confusion as to whether public hearings in the Great Hall of Justice are called for, as opposed to a private "hearing" of the parties through their written observations.[36]

Not surprisingly, several judges indicated that they favor revising Article 80 of the Rules of Court. Such a revision could address the issues referred to above and could clarify the procedure applicable to counterclaims within the context of international due process. Not only is there no provision describing the procedure in case the Court concludes that the counterclaim is not directly connected with the applicant's claim (so that presumably joinder is not directed),[37] it also is unclear what happens if there is no doubt as to such a connection (because the applicant does not object to the filing of the counterclaim or the Court has no doubt). One might assume that in the latter case the counterclaim is joined automatically to the main proceedings without the need to issue an order recording that result.[38] However, the Court's statements in both Orders imply that the strict fulfillment of the conditions laid down in Article 80 may not be sufficient to effect an automatic joinder and that the Court wishes to reserve to itself a margin of discretion to ensure that the higher goal of the sound administration of justice is served. Perhaps that is what is

---

2, 56, paragraph 2, and 67 of the Rules of Court, which all contain the words "after hearing the parties," has been merely to give the parties the opportunity to present their views in writing.

35 *See*, in fact, Shabtai Rosenne, *Controlling Interlocutory Aspects of Proceedings in the International Court of Justice*, 94 AJIL 307, at 309 (2000).

36 In the *Oil Platforms* case, the record indicates that Iran unsuccessfully requested a hearing no less than four times: namely, in a letter of October 2, 1997; during the meeting with the Vice President on October 17, 1997; in a letter of October 27, 1997; and finally, in its written observations filed on November 18, 1997, entitled "Request for hearing in relation to the United States counter-claim pursuant to Article 80(3) of the Rules of Court." The United States argued that a hearing is required only where there is doubt as to the direct connection between the counter-claim and the original claim, which doubt it maintained was lacking in this instance.

37 *See* ROSENNE, *supra* note 1, at 1274.

38 The Court's treatment of the U.S. counterclaim in *Rights of Nationals of the United States of America in Morocco (Fr. v. U.S.)* lends support to this conclusion. In dealing with the various submissions in that case, the Court did not address the connection of the U.S. counterclaim with the French claim. 1952 ICJ REP. 176 (Aug. 27). *See also* Judge *ad hoc* Kreca's declaration appended to the *Genocide* Order, *supra* note 5, at 262.

meant by the words "a counter-claim *may* be *presented*" (emphasis added) in Article 80, paragraph 1: after a claim is presented, it is for the Court to decide whether it will allow that claim to be joined as a counterclaim to the main proceedings, employing the conditions laid down in Article 80 as the principal, but not exclusive, yardstick. Nothing in Article 80 suggests that the Court could not examine *proprio motu* the conditions that it sees fit to attach to counter-claims in exercising its broader role as guardian and master of its own proced-ure.

The Court granted both parties over fourteen months to file their second round of written pleadings in the *Oil Platforms* case. Thus, the case brought by Iran on November 2, 1992, will not be ready for hearing on the merits before the year 2000, i.e. eight years after the commencement of proceedings. In the *Genocide* case, which was initiated on March 20, 1993, hearings are not likely to start until the new millennium, or more than six years after Bosnia filed its Application. Whereas in the *Genocide* case several judges complained about this delay, the even more significant delay through new time limits adopted unanimously in the *Oil Platforms* case was not commented on at all.[39]

The resemblance between the two Orders indicates that the current Court is keen to develop a procedural jurisprudence on counterclaims from which at least some general principles may be extracted that are likely to be applied in other cases. The Orders demonstrate that the Court prefers to settle the issue of the admissibility of counterclaims at a preliminary stage of the proceedings through a short Order, on the basis of the parties' written observations and without oral proceedings. In general, the Court's views on counterclaims stated in these Orders do not indicate that it intends to reverse the flexibility that has long been a feature of the treatment of counterclaims by both litigants and the Court itself. That being said, it is still unclear why the Court did not address the many fundamental issues of due process and procedure that were raised by the parties.

As a postscript to the above, it is noted that Article 80 of the Rules of Court was amended in December 2000, with effect from February 1, 2001, as described in section 2.4.5 of the Introduction to this book. The issues raised

---

39 Further to a request from Bosnia as applicant in the *Genocide* case, President Schwebel issued an Order on January 22, 1998, extending the time limit for the filing of the reply of Bosnia to April 23, 1998, and the time limit for the filing of the rejoinder of Yugoslavia to January 22, 1999. *See* 1998 ICJ REP. 3; ICJ Com-muniqué No. 98/01 (Jan. 22).

in connection with Yugoslavia's counterclaims in the *Genocide* case became moot with their withdrawal in September 2001, as officially recorded by the President's Order of September 10, 2001.

2

THE YEAR 1998

THE 1998 JUDICIAL ACTIVITY OF
THE INTERNATIONAL COURT OF JUSTICE[*]

This introductory section summarizes the judicial work of the International Court of Justice during 1998,[1] using the updated General List, pleadings filed, Orders and Judgments given, and hearings held at the Peace Palace in The Hague to describe the Court's record in 1998.

THE WORK OF THE COURT

General List

During the calendar year 1998, the Court was seized of six new cases: five are contentious: *Vienna Convention on Consular Relations* (*Paraguay v. United States*);[2] *Gabčíkovo-Nagymaros Project* (*Slovakia v. Hungary*);[3] *Request for Interpretation of the Court's Judgment of June 11, 1998, in the Case Concerning the* Land and Maritime Boundary between Cameroon and Nigeria (Cameroon v. Nigeria), Preliminary Objections (*Nigeria v. Cameroon*) (hereinafter *Request for Interpretation*);[4] *Sovereignty over Pulau Ligitan and Pulau Sipadan*

---

[*]   Reproduced with permission from 93 AJIL 534 (1999). © The American Society of International Law.

[1]   Most of the information contained in this Note is available from the ICJ's Web site, <www.icj-cij.org>.

[2]   Application of Paraguay filed in the ICJ Registry on April 3. *See* ICJ Communiqué No. 98/13 (Apr. 3, 1998).

[3]   Request for an additional judgment filed by Slovakia on September 3. *See* ICJ Communiqué No. 98/28 (Sept. 3, 1998).

[4]   Application of Nigeria filed on October 28. *See* ICJ Communiqué No. 98/34 (Oct. 29, 1998).

P.H.F. Bekker, World Court Decisions at the Turn of the Millennium (1997-2001), p. 77-82.
© 2002 *Kluwer Law International. Printed in the Netherlands.*

(*Indonesia/Malaysia*);[5] and *Ahmadou Sadio Diallo (Guinea v. Democratic Republic of the Congo)*.[6] The sixth is a request for an advisory opinion brought by the Economic and Social Council of the United Nations entitled *Difference Relating to Immunity from Legal Process of a Special Rapporteur of the Commission on Human Rights* (hereinafter *Difference Relating to Immunity*).[7] In 1998 a total of fourteen cases appeared on the General List at any particular time. Besides the six new cases referred to, the contentious proceedings before the full Court were *Maritime Delimitation and Territorial Questions between Qatar and Bahrain (Qatar v. Bahrain), Questions of Interpretation and Application of the 1971 Montreal Convention arising from the Aerial Incident at Lockerbie (Libya v. United Kingdom)* and *(Libya v. United States)* (hereinafter *Lockerbie* cases), *Oil Platforms (Iran v. United States)* (hereinafter *Oil Platforms* case), *Application of the Convention on the Prevention and Punishment of the Crime of Genocide (Bosnia-Herzegovina v. Yugoslavia)* (hereinafter *Genocide* case), *Fisheries Jurisdiction (Spain v. Canada), Land and Maritime Boundary between Cameroon and Nigeria (Cameroon v. Nigeria)*, and *Kasikili/ Sedudu Island (Botswana/Namibia)*. During 1998, no cases were pending before any chamber of the Court.

Pleadings

In 1998 pleadings were filed in the following instances. On April 23, Bosnia-Herzegovina filed its Reply in the *Genocide* case. On September 30, Qatar filed an interim report on disputed documents in *Maritime Delimitation and Territorial Questions between Qatar and Bahrain*. On October 9, Paraguay filed its Memorial in *Vienna Convention on Consular Relations*. Botswana and Namibia each filed a Reply in *Kasikili/Sedudu Island* on November 27. In *Difference Relating to Immunity*, written statements by the UN Secretary-General and Costa Rica, Germany, Italy, Malaysia, Sweden, the United Kingdom and the United States were received by October 7, and Greece was given leave for late filing on October 12. A related letter was received from Luxembourg

---

5   Special Agreement of May 31, 1997 (entered into force May 14, 1998), notified to the Court on November 2. *See* ICJ Communiqué No. 98/35 (Nov. 2, 1998). Pulau Ligitan and Pulau Sipadan are two islands located in the Celebes Sea off the east coast of Indonesia's Kalimantan province and Malaysia's east coast of Sabah.

6   Application of Guinea filed on December 28. *See* ICJ Communiqué No. 98/46 (Dec. 30, 1998).

7   The request was filed on August 10 and is embodied in ECOSOC Decision 1998/297 (Aug. 5, 1998). *See* ICJ Communiqué No. 98/26 (Aug. 10, 1998).

on October 29, 1998. Written comments by the Secretary-General and Costa Rica, Malaysia and the United States, together with a written communication from Luxembourg, were submitted by November 6. On November 12, Cameroon filed its written observations on Nigeria's Application in *Request for Interpretation*. On December 7, Hungary filed a written statement of its observations on Slovakia's request for an additional judgment in *Gabčíkovo-Nagymaros Project*.

Orders

Nineteen Orders were made by the Court, the President, the Vice President and the senior judge in 1998, most of which concerned time limits.[8] The Court's Order of March 10 upheld the admissibility of the counterclaim filed by the United States in the *Oil Platforms* case.[9] On March 30, the Court issued two separate Orders fixing time limits for the filing of the Counter-Memorials of the United Kingdom and the United States in the *Lockerbie* cases.[10] On April 9, the Court issued a unanimous Order indicating provisional measures of protection in *Vienna Convention on Consular Relations*.[11] The case was subsequently discontinued at the request of Paraguay and removed from the General List by the Court's Order of November 10.[12]

---

8   Full Court Orders fixing time limits were issued in *Kasikili/Sedudu Island*, 1998 ICJ REP. 6 (Feb. 27), *Maritime Delimitation and Territorial Questions between Qatar and Bahrain*, 1998 ICJ REP. 243 (Mar. 30), *Land and Maritime Boundary between Cameroon and Nigeria*, 1998 ICJ REP. 420 (June 30), and *Sovereignty over Pulau Ligitan and Pulau Sipadan*, 1998 ICJ REP. 429 (Nov. 10). Orders extending time limits were issued in the *Oil Platforms*, 1998 ICJ REP. 740 (Dec. 8) and *Genocide*, 1998 ICJ REP. 743 (Dec. 11) cases. President's Schwebel's Order of January 22 extended time limits in the *Genocide* case. 1998 ICJ REP. 3. Vice President Weeramantry issued three such Orders, in *Vienna Convention on Consular Relations*, 1998 ICJ REP. 266 (Apr. 9, fixing time limits), *Oil Platforms*, 1998 ICJ REP. 269 (May 26, extending time limits), and *Vienna Convention on Consular Relations*, 1998 ICJ REP. 272 (June 8, extending time limits); and the senior judge, Judge Oda, issued four such Orders in *Difference Relating to Immunity*, 1998 ICJ REP. 423 (Aug. 10, fixing time limits); *Request for Interpretation* (Oct. 29, fixing time limits), and *Lockerbie (Libya v. UK)* and *(Libya v. U.S.)* (Dec. 17, extending time limits) (1998 ICJ REP. 746 and 1998 ICJ REP. 749, respectively).
9   1998 ICJ REP. 190. For a summary of this decision, see 92 AJIL 508 (1998), *reprinted in* Chapter 1 above.
10   1998 ICJ REP. 237 and 240, respectively.
11   1998 ICJ REP. 248.
12   1998 ICJ REP. 426.

Hearings

In 1998 the full Court held public sittings (hearings) in four cases: *Land and Maritime Boundary between Cameroon and Nigeria* (Preliminary Objections) (March 2-11), *Vienna Convention on Consular Relations* (Provisional Measures) (April 7), *Fisheries Jurisdiction* (Preliminary Objections) (June 9-17) and *Difference Relating to Immunity* (December 7-8 and 10).

Decisions

In 1998 the Court handed down three decisions on preliminary objections, one on jurisdiction and none on the merits of a case. On February 27, the Court issued two separate Judgments rejecting the preliminary objections raised by the United Kingdom and the United States, respectively, in the *Lockerbie* cases.[13] The Court's Judgment of June 11 rejected Nigeria's preliminary objections in *Land and Maritime Boundary between Cameroon and Nigeria (Cameroon v. Nigeria).*[14] Finally, on December 4, the Court issued a Judgment holding that it lacked jurisdiction over Spain's Application in *Fisheries Jurisdiction (Spain v. Canada)* on the basis of a reservation contained in Canada's declaration accepting the Court's compulsory jurisdiction.[15]

PRESIDENT'S ADDRESS

In October, President Stephen M. Schwebel addressed the General Assembly of the United Nations on the occasion of the presentation of the Court's annual report.[16] He explained that, while the number of cases before the Court and

---

13 1998 ICJ REP. 9 and 115, respectively.
14 1998 ICJ REP. 275 (rejecting seven of Nigeria's eight preliminary objections and declaring that the eighth preliminary objection did not have, in the circumstances of the case, an exclusively preliminary character).
15 1998 ICJ REP. 432.
16 The full texts of the Address by the President of the International Court of Justice, Judge Stephen M. Schwebel to the General Assembly of October 27, 1998 [hereinafter President's Address] and Statement by Judge Schwebel to the Sixth Committee of October 30, 1998, are available at the ICJ's Web site, *supra* note 1. *See also* UN Doc. A/53/PV.44 (1998). Attached to the Court's annual report is its response to General Assembly Resolution 52/161, para. 4 (Dec. 15, 1997) inviting the Court to submit its "comments and observations on the consequences that the increase in the volume of cases before the Court has on its operation." *See* Consequences

the range of issues involved have significantly increased, the Court has not enjoyed a proportional growth in its resources; its current annual budget of around $11 million represents a smaller percentage of the total United Nations budget than in 1946. At the same time, the international community, including the United Nations, has established other tribunals to adjudicate international disputes and international crimes. He expressed the view that "[t]he proliferation of international courts at the same time raises the question of the role of the International Court of Justice, and of problems proliferation may pose."[17] Although he pledged that the Court would work harmoniously with other international tribunals, the President stressed the unique characteristics of the ICJ as the principal judicial organ of the United Nations: (1) it is a factor and actor in the maintenance of international peace and security; (2) it is the most authoritative interpreter of the legal obligations of states in disputes between them; (3) it has acted as the supreme interpreter of the United Nations Charter; and (4) it is the only truly universal judicial body of general jurisdiction.

The relative erosion of the ICJ's funding has resulted in an enlarging gap between the conclusion of the written proceedings and the opening of the hearings in cases. Reminding the Assembly that the Court must be afforded the resources to work with full effectiveness and dispatch, the President complained of the shortage of staff, especially translators, secretaries and clerks for judges, and of funds for the Court's publication program, among other concerns. He warned that justice delayed due to the inadequacy of resources may be justice denied. This could discourage states from resorting to the Court.

COMPENSATION

On the occasion of its three-year review of the conditions of service of the Members of the Court, the Fifth Committee of the General Assembly, at its forty-third meeting on December 14, adopted, without a vote, a draft resolution that approved the recommendations of the Advisory Committee on Administrative and Budgetary Questions,[18] inter alia, to increase the judges' annual re-

---

that the increase in the volume of cases before the International Court of Justice has on the operations of the Court, Report of the Secretary-General, UN Doc. A/53/326/corr.1 (1998).

17 President's Address, *supra* note 16.

18 *See* UN Docs. A/53/7/Add.6 (1998) and A/C.5/53/L.27 (1998). For the Report of the Secretary-General containing slightly different proposals, see UN Doc. A/C.5/53/11 (1998).

muneration from $145,000 to $160,000, effective January 1, 1999.[19] This draft resolution was adopted as Resolution 53/214 by the General Assembly at its ninety-third plenary meeting on December 18. In addition, the Assembly adopted a fundamental change in the retirement pension regime for ICJ judges, abolishing the fixed-amount system that had been in place since 1990.[20] Effective January 1, 1999, the annual pension of an ICJ judge equals half of the annual salary of a judge who has completed a full nine-year term. A proportional reduction applies to a judge who has not completed a full term. The new scheme represents a departure from current practice in that a reelected judge who joined the Court after January 1, 1999, will no longer receive any increase in pension. The new pension system was applied with prospective effect, so that it is inapplicable to serving judges currently in office who have been or are reelected. The old pension regime therefore continued to apply to the Members of the Court in office on January 1, 1999.[21]

---

19 *See* UN Doc. A/C.5/53/L.27, at 14, paras. 26-28 (1998). For the text of the draft resolution, see *id.* at 20, and UN Doc. A/C.5/L.25 (1998). In accordance with Article 32, paragraph 5 of the ICJ Statute, the salaries, allowances and compensation of the Members of the Court shall be fixed by the General Assembly and may be decreased during their term of office.

20 *See* GA Res. 45/250B (Dec. 21, 1990). Under the old regime, a judge who had served one full nine-year term received a pension of $50,000 and a judge who had completed two full terms received $75,000, with proportionate reductions for judges having served less than a full term. According to Article 32, paragraph 7 of the ICJ Statute, Members of the Court are entitled to retirement pensions whose specific conditions are governed by regulations adopted by the General Assembly. The Assembly adopted a change in Article 7, paragraph 2 of the Pension Scheme Regulations whereby any revision of pension payments will automatically be based on the same percentage and the same effective date as salary adjustments. *See* UN Doc. A/C.5/53/L.27, at 20 (1998).

21 These judges will continue to be entitled to receive one three-hundredth of the pension benefit for each further month of service past nine years, up to a maximum pension of two-thirds of annual salary. The new pension regime was implemented in three stages: (1) January 1, 1999, pension level increases by 20% to $60,000; (2) January 1, 2000, level increases another 16.7% to $70,000; and (3) January 1, 2001, level increases by a further 14.3% to $80,000. *See* UN Doc. A/53/7/Add.6, at 4, para. 17 (1998). Finally, the Assembly decided to maintain the level of the special allowances of the president ($15,000 a year) and the vice president when acting as president ($94 a day, subject to a maximum of $9,400 a year) and the compensation system for judges *ad hoc* (one three-hundred-and-sixty-fifth of the annual salary of a member of the Court for each day they exercise their functions in the case for which they were appointed).

◊

Preliminary objections to Court's jurisdiction and admissibility of application – existence of dispute under 1971 Montreal Convention – objections not "exclusively" preliminary – effect of Security Council resolution requiring Libya to extradite suspects in Lockerbie disaster

QUESTIONS OF INTERPRETATION AND APPLICATION OF THE 1971 MONTREAL CONVENTION ARISING FROM THE AERIAL INCIDENT AT LOCKERBIE (Libyan Arab Jamahirya v. United Kingdom) and (Libyan Arab Jamahirya v. United States)

Preliminary Objections, Judgments
1998 ICJ REP. 9 and 115
International Court of Justice, February 27, 1998[*]

On March 3, 1992, Libya filed two separate applications instituting proceedings before the International Court of Justice against the United Kingdom and the United States, asserting claims arising from the aftermath of the crash of Pan Am Flight 103 over Lockerbie, Scotland, on December 21, 1988. The respondent states believe that the incident, which claimed 270 lives, was caused by a bomb placed on board the aircraft by two Libyan nationals (allegedly intelligence agents). The two Libyans were subsequently indicted by the Lord Advocate of Scotland and by a Grand Jury of the District of Columbia. Subsequent to the incident, the UN Security Council, with the support of the two respondent states, adopted several resolutions demanding that Libya surrender the two accused for trial outside Libya and imposing economic sanctions against that state. Libya has asked the Court to declare that it has fully complied with its obligations under the only treaty applicable between the parties, the 1971 Montreal Convention for the Suppression of Unlawful Acts against the Safety of Civil Aviation (Montreal Convention); that the United Kingdom and the United States have breached a number of provisions of that treaty; and that they must cease and desist from such breaches and from the threat or use of force against Libya designed to compel it to surrender the two Libyan nationals for trial in either the United States or the United Kingdom (Scotland).

---

[*]   Reproduced with permission from 92 AJIL 503 (1998). © The American Society of American Law.

P.H.F. Bekker, World Court Decisions at the Turn of the Millennium (1997-2001), p. 83-91.
© 2002 *Kluwer Law International. Printed in the Netherlands.*

On June 16 and 20, 1995, respectively, the United Kingdom and the United States filed preliminary objections alleging that (1) the Court lacked jurisdiction; (2) the Libyan Application was inadmissible; and (3) the Libyan claims had become moot, as having been rendered without object because of the adoption of certain resolutions by the UN Security Council. Hearings on the preliminary objections were held in The Hague on October 13-22, 1997.

On February 27, 1998, almost six years after Libya instituted proceedings, the Court ruled, by clear majorities, that it has jurisdiction and that the Libyan Application is admissible in both cases. The Court proceeded to consider the merits of the two cases.

First, the respondents argued that the Court lacked jurisdiction. They claimed that Libya had not complied with the conditions of Article 14, paragraph 1 of the Montreal Convention on which Libya has relied as the basis for the Court's jurisdiction.[1] They maintained that no legal dispute existed between the parties, in any event not one concerning the interpretation or application of the Montreal Convention. In their view, the Montreal Convention is not relevant because, instead of involving bilateral differences, the case concerns a threat to international peace and security resulting from state-sponsored terrorism. Libya, on the other hand, maintained that the Montreal Convention is the only instrument applicable to the Pan Am disaster and that the respondent states are attempting to prevent its application.

The Court considered that Libya had complied with Article 14 of the Montreal Convention and that its claim was positively opposed by the claims of the respondents.[2] In the Court's view, a dispute exists between the parties as to whether the destruction of the Pan Am aircraft is governed by the Montreal Convention. Apart from this general dispute, the Court also found that specific disputes exist between the parties concerning certain provisions of the Montreal Convention relating to the place of prosecution (Article 7, read

---

1   Article 14(1) reads: "Any dispute between two or more Contracting States concerning the interpretation or application of this Convention which cannot be settled through negotiation, shall, at the request of one of them, be submitted to arbitration. If within six months from the date of the request for arbitration the Parties are unable to agree on the organization of the arbitration, any one of those Parties may refer the dispute to the International Court of Justice by request in conformity with the Statute of the Court." Convention for the Suppression of Unlawful Acts against the Safety of Civil Aviation, Sept. 23, 1971, 24 UST 564.

2   *See* Questions of Interpretation and Application of the 1971 Montreal Convention arising from the Aerial Incident at Lockerbie (Libya v. U.S.), Preliminary Objections, Judgment, 1998 ICJ REP. 115, at 122-23, paras. 20-21 (Feb. 27).

in conjunction with Articles 1, 5, 6 and 8) and to assistance in connection with criminal proceedings (Article 11). Article 7 of the Montreal Convention imposes on a state in whose territory an alleged offender is found the obligation either to prosecute that person before its domestic courts or to extradite him. Libya claimed that it had submitted the two accused Libyans to its competent authorities for prosecution under Libyan law, in accordance with the Montreal Convention, and that the Libyan Constitution does not permit their extradition. The respondents' position was that Libya is not now justified in exercising domestic jurisdiction under the Montreal Convention, as this would be contrary to binding Security Council resolutions, which have overriding effect in accordance with the UN Charter.

The Court found that it can decide, on the basis of Article 14 of the Montreal Convention, on the lawfulness of the respondents' actions criticized by Libya, insofar as those actions violate the Convention.[3]

The respondents also claimed that, even if the Montreal Convention did confer the rights it claims on Libya, those rights could not be exercised because they were superseded by Security Council Resolution 748 (1992) of March 31, 1992, and Resolution 883 (1993) of November 11, 1993, which, by virtue of Articles 25 and 103 of the UN Charter, take priority over all rights and obligations arising out of the Montreal Convention.[4] In any event, the adoption of those resolutions meant that the only dispute that might exist is between Libya and the Security Council as a whole, falling outside Article 14, paragraph 1 of the Montreal Convention. The Court pointed out that both resolutions were adopted after the date on which Libya filed its Application. On that date, which alone is relevant, the Court had jurisdiction.[5]

---

3   *Id.* at 128, paras. 33-35.
4   In the two Orders that the Court issued in response to Libya's request for provisional measures, it observed that both Libya and the respondent states, as member states of the United Nations, are obliged to accept and carry out resolutions issued by the UN Security Council in accordance with Article 25 of the Charter. Moreover, the Court pointed out that "in accordance with Article 103 of the Charter, the obligations of the Parties in that respect prevail over their obligations under any other international agreement, including the Montreal Convention." *See* 1992 ICJ REP. 3, at 15, para. 39 (Libya v. UK), and 1992 ICJ REP. 114, at 126, para. 42 (Libya v. U.S.) (Orders of Apr. 14).
5   1998 ICJ REP. 115, at 129, para. 37 (citing Nottebohm (Liechtenstein v. Guatemala), Preliminary Objection, Judgment, 1953 ICJ REP. 111, at 122 (Nov. 18) and Right of Passage over Indian Territory (Portugal v. India), Preliminary Objections, Judgment, 1957 ICJ REP. 125, at 142 (Nov. 26)).

Consequently, a majority of thirteen judges rejected the respondents' objections to jurisdiction and found that the Court has jurisdiction on the basis of Article 14, paragraph 1 of the Montreal Convention.[6]

Second, the respondents claimed that Libya's Application was inadmissible. They argued that, by bringing its case before the Court, Libya was endeavoring to undo the actions taken by the Security Council under Resolutions 731 (1992), 748 (1992) and 883 (1993),[7] and that Libya's claims under the Montreal Convention were superseded by those resolutions, which alone defined the obligations of the parties. Libya argued that the Court must interpret those resolutions in accordance with the UN Charter and that the Charter prohibits the Security Council from requiring Libya to surrender its nationals to the United Kingdom or the United States. In any event, the respondents' arguments based on the Charter raised problems that did not possess an exclusively preliminary character and should thus be decided in the merits phase of the dispute.[8]

The Court agreed with Libya that the critical date for determining the admissibility of an application is the date on which it is filed, in this case March 3, 1992. Resolutions 748 and 883 were adopted after March 3, 1992, and Resolution 731, although adopted before the Application was filed, was a mere recommendation without binding effect.[9] Consequently, a majority of twelve judges rejected the respondents' objection to admissibility derived from Security

---

6   The vote was 13-3 in *Libya v. UK* (President Schwebel, Judge Oda and Judge *ad hoc* Jennings dissenting) and 13-2 in *Libya v. U.S.* (President Schwebel and Judge Oda dissenting). Judge Oda pointed out in his dissenting opinion that it was only in Libya's letter of January 18, 1992, to the respondents that the Montreal Convention was mentioned, which letters had met with no response by the time Libya filed its Applications. Hence, he wondered, how could there be a "dispute" under the Montreal Convention at the time of the filing of the Applications? President Schwebel and Judge *ad hoc* Jennings stated in their dissenting opinions that none of the provisions of the Montreal Convention invoked by Libya impose obligations on the respondent states in the circumstances of this case and that, if any dispute exists, it is between Libya and the Security Council as a whole, not over the Montreal Convention, but over the legality of the Council's adoption of certain resolutions.

7   For SC Res. 731 and 748, respectively, see UN SCOR, 47th Sess., Res. At 51, 52, UN Doc. S/INF/48 (1992), 31 ILM 732, 750 (1992). For SC Res. 883, see UN SCOR, 48th Sess., Res. At 113, UN Doc. S/INF/49 (1993).

8   1998 ICJ REP. 115, at 129-30, paras. 40-41.

9   *Id.*, at 130-31, para. 43.

Council Resolutions 748 and 883 and found that the Libyan Application is admissible.[10]

Third, the respondents advanced the objection, by way of a fallback position, that intervening Security Council resolutions have left the Libyan claims without object. They argued that the Libyan claims have been rendered moot, and Libya has been precluded from obtaining the relief it seeks, by the subsequent adoption of resolutions 748 and 883. The effect of these binding resolutions was that any judgment on Libya's claims would be devoid of practical purpose.

The Court acknowledged that events subsequent to the filing of an application may render it without object, precluding a case from being adjudicated on the merits. It determined that the respondents' objection qualified as a "preliminary objection" under Article 79, paragraph 1 of the Rules of Court. However, the parties differed on the question of whether the objection was of an "exclusively" preliminary character under Article 79, paragraph 7 of the Rules of Court, which was therefore for the Court to interpret. The Court pointed out that objections are not "exclusively" preliminary, and hence must be dealt with at the merits stage, if they contain both preliminary aspects and other aspects relating to the merits. It considered that Libya's rights on the merits not only would be affected by a decision not to proceed to judgment on the merits, but would constitute, in many respects, the very subject matter of that decision. In this light, the objection is inextricably interwoven, or at least closely interconnected, with the merits.[11]

Finally, the Court dismissed the U.S. alternative request to resolve the case in substance at the preliminary stage by deciding that the relief sought by Libya was precluded. The Court pointed out that, by raising preliminary objections,

---

10 The vote was 12-4 in *Libya v. UK* (President Schwebel, Judges Oda and Herczegh, and Judge *ad hoc* Jennings dissenting), and 12-3 in *Libya v. U.S.* (President Schwebel and Judges Oda and Herczegh dissenting). As President Schwebel rightly pointed out in his dissenting opinion, there appears to be an inconsistency in the Court's present holding in that "the whole basis on which the Court in 1992 proceeded in approving its Order rejecting the provisional measures sought by Libya was that of the applicability, as of the date of its Order, of Security Council resolution 748, adopted after the date of the filing of Libya's Application and Libya's request for the indication of provisional measures."

11 1998 ICJ REP. 115, at 133-34, para. 49. Interestingly, this test is practically identical to that used by the Court in administering the "necessary third-party rule." *See* East Timor (Port. v. Austl.), 1995 ICJ REP. 90 (June 30), and my analysis at 90 AJIL 94, at 95 (1996), *reprinted in* COMMENTARIES ON WORLD COURT DECISIONS (1987-1996) at 209 (P.H.F. Bekker ed., 1998).

the United States made a procedural choice leading to the automatic suspension of the proceedings on the merits pursuant to the Rules of Court.

Consequently, the Court declared, by a majority of ten judges, that the respondents' objection according to which Libya's claims became moot because Security Council Resolutions 748 and 883 rendered them without object, does not, in the circumstances of the case, have an exclusively preliminary character, and can be considered at the merits stage.[12]

* * * *

It is interesting to compare the voting pattern of these two Judgments with those of the Orders rejecting Libya's request for provisional measures that the Court issued in April 1992.[13] By its Orders of 1992, the Court found that the circumstances of the case were not such as to require the exercise of its power to indicate provisional measures under Article 41 of the ICJ Statute. Five of the sixteen judges voted against the operative paragraph and seven appended opinions.[14] One may safely assume that the Court's drafting committee that prepared the text of the Judgments included one or more judges who appended individual opinions to the 1992 Orders. Thus, in a sense the judges who voted

---

12 The vote was 10-6 in *Libya v. UK* (President Schwebel, Judges Oda, Guillaume, Herczegh and Fleischhauer and Judge *ad hoc* Jennings dissenting), and 10-5 in *Libya v. U.S.* (President Schwebel and Judges Oda, Guillaume, Herczegh and Fleischhauer dissenting). In their joint declaration, Judges Bedjaoui, Ranjeva and Koroma explained their view that this holding means that it is not sufficient to invoke Chapter VII provisions of the UN Charter so as to bring to an end, *ipso facto* and with immediate effect, all argument on the decisions of the Security Council. By contrast, Judges Guillaume and Fleischhauer stated in their joint declaration that the objection based on mootness did have an exclusively preliminary character which the Court could and should have decided on. Judge Herczegh went one step further in his declaration, expressing his view that the objection was exclusively preliminary and should have been upheld to reject the Libyan claim. The dissenting judges reached similar conclusions.

13 *See* 1992 ICJ REP. 3 (Libya v. UK) and 1992 ICJ REP. 114 (Libya v. U.S.) (Orders of Apr. 14).

14 Judges Bedjaoui, Weeramantry, Ranjeva, Ajibola and Judge *ad hoc* El-Kosheri (appointed by Libya) appended dissenting opinions to the 1992 Orders. Judge Ajibola retired from the Court in 1994. For the grounds of the dismissal, see *supra* note 4. Only Judges Schwebel, Weeramantry, Oda, Bedjaoui, Guillaume and Ranjeva (together with Judge *ad hoc* Jennings in the *Libya v. UK* case), who were on the bench in 1992, were still Members of the Court in 1998, making this a rather different Court. Half of these six remaining judges dissented in 1992.

against, or otherwise expressed a concern with, the Orders in 1992 were vindicated six years later.

The Court has not previously had an opportunity in contentious cases to pass on the question of whether it possesses judicial review power over decisions of the Security Council. It is by no means certain that the Court will address this issue directly now that it has allowed the case to proceed to the merits stage. The individual opinions do, however, shed some light on this aspect of the proceedings.

Judge Kooijmans, who voted with the majority, made clear in his separate opinion to both Judgments that the Court's jurisdiction should be confined to the issues of applicability of, and compliance with, the Montreal Convention. In his view, the question whether the specific acts of alleged non-compliance are at variance with the UN Charter and with general international law lies outside the Court's jurisdiction in this case.[15]

President Schwebel and Judge *ad hoc* Jennings both stated in their dissenting opinions that the Court is not generally empowered to review the decisions of the Security Council and particularly lacks any power to overrule or undercut that organ's decisions under Chapter VII of the Charter. President Schwebel pointed out that the United Nations is far from being a government and that it is not democratic, having to rely instead on self-censorship by the organ concerned or on review by its members or another political organ. According to Judge *ad hoc* Jennings, the Court must administer and apply the law, including the applicable United Nations law as it has been laid down in the Charter, of which Chapter VII forms a key part. President Schwebel and Judge *ad hoc* Jennings both argued that, apart from the absence of any dispute under the Montreal Convention, it is questionable whether that treaty applies to situations where individuals accused of destroying an aircraft are alleged to have acted as agents of one of the parties to the Convention.[16] Both are concerned that these decisions allow recalcitrant nations to invoke jurisdictional clauses in

---

15 *See* separate opinion of Judge Kooijmans, 1998 ICJ REP. 115, at 146, para. 8.

16 The dissenting judges also believed that there was nothing contrary to the Montreal Convention in the respondents' requesting Libya to extradite the two Libyan suspects. The Convention is silent on the issue of priority or exclusivity of jurisdiction. *See also* Sami Shuber, *The contribution of the International Court of Justice to air law, in* FIFTY YEARS OF THE INTERNATIONAL COURT OF JUSTICE 316, 325 (Vaughan Lowe & Malgosia Fitzmaurice eds., 1996).

bilateral or multilateral treaties to frustrate, delay and defy binding Security Council resolutions through an appeal to the ICJ.[17]

According to Judge Oda, the dissenting senior judge in both cases, the issues in the cases relate solely to the demand by the respondents that Libya surrender the two Libyan suspects and Libya's refusal to accede to the respondents' demand; the effect of the Security Council resolutions, which have a political connotation in dealing with broader aspects of threats to or breaches of the peace, is a matter quite irrelevant to these cases.

Interestingly, the Court has not ordered a formal joinder of these cases filed by the same applicant against different respondents. However, a joinder would undoubtedly have served judicial economy at a time when the Court has been complaining of financial hardship. Both cases arose out of a single set of facts, rely on the same title of jurisdiction, are directed to the same object and assert identical claims and submissions. The Orders and Judgments rendered and pleadings filed over a period of six years demonstrate how similar they are. However, it is understandable from a political perspective that Libya prefers two decisions to one. Moreover, the United Kingdom presumably would not want to give up its right to have a British judge *ad hoc* participate in the proceedings. Whereas in case of a joinder both respondents might be considered parties in the same interest, the Court in this instance did not treat the British judge *ad hoc* as in the same interest as the sitting U.S. national judge. While one may assume that the ground for failure to order a joinder was the desire conveyed to the Court by the parties, there is no record of it. Instances of joinder in the Hague Court remain extremely scarce.[18]

---

17 Judge *ad hoc* Jennings gave expression to the feeling of confusion among the general public caused by these cases, when he stated that it "is indeed ironic that the jurisdictional clause of a Convention whose whole purpose is to control international terrorism over aircraft, should be thus employed, it seems successfully, to afford protection to persons alleged to have been involved in such terrorism who are nationals and officials of a State also alleged itself to have been thus involved." 1998 ICJ REP. 9, at 105.

18 The ICJ has ordered a formal joinder of the proceedings in two cases only: *South West Africa* and *North Sea Continental Shelf*. The arguments that dissenting Judges Forster, Gros, Petrén and Ignacio-Pinto advanced in favor of a formal joinder of the *Nuclear Tests* cases all appear to be applicable here. *See* Nuclear Tests (NZ v. Fr.), 1973 ICJ REP. 135, at 148, 149, 159, 163 (Order of June 22).

The recent record demonstrates that the Unites States has not been very successful as a litigant before the ICJ.[19] After the *Nicaragua* Judgments of 1984 and 1986, the Court opined in *Applicability of the Obligation to Arbitrate under Section 21 of the United Nations Headquarters Agreement of 26 June 1947*[20] that the U.S. was obligated to enter into arbitration with the United Nations in connection with the U.S. announcement on closing the UN Observer Mission of the Palestine Liberation Organization in 1988. In 1989, a chamber of the Court rejected the U.S. claims in *Elettronica Sicula S.p.A. (United States v. Italy)*.[21] As in *Lockerbie*, the Court rejected the preliminary objection raised by the Clinton administration against Iran in the *Oil Platforms* case in 1996.[22] Finally, on April 9, 1998, the Court adopted, unanimously, an Order indicating provisional measures of protection in *Vienna Convention on Consular Relations (Paraguay v. United States)*, over the objections of the United States. But it is important and encouraging to note that successive U.S. administrations are appearing again in these post-*Nicaragua* cases and are participating in the proceedings before the Court. The United States is to be commended for this co-operative attitude toward a judicial institution whose creation it so strongly advocated. One must hope that the *Lockerbie* Judgments, rendered during the presidency of the American member of the Court, will not cause the U.S. administration to change this positive attitude.

It should be stressed that the Court's preliminary ruling leaves unaffected any defenses on the merits that the two respondent states may wish to advance in the subsequent written proceedings and hearings on the merits. It would thus be desirable for the United Kingdom and the United States to continue to defend their positions. The respondents will also have a chance to submit counterclaims as part of their counter-memorials, for which the Court fixed new time limits.[23]

---

19 For a detailed appraisal of the U.S. involvement in ICJ cases, see Keith Highet, *Winning and Losing: The Commitment of the United States to the International Court – What Was It, What Is It and Where Has It Gone?* 1 TRANSNAT'L L. & CONTEMP. PROB. 157 (1991).

20 *See* 1988 ICJ REP. 12 (Advisory Opinion of Apr. 26). See the case note by Paul C. Szasz in COMMENTARIES ON WORLD COURT DECISIONS (1987-1996) at 53 (P.H.F. Bekker ed., 1998).

21 *See* 1989 ICJ REP. 15 (July 20) *summarized in* 84 AJIL 249 (1990), *reprinted in* COMMENTARIES ON WORLD COURT DECISIONS (1987-1996) at 75 (P.H.F. Bekker ed., 1998).

22 *See* 1996 ICJ REP. 803 (Dec. 12) *summarized in* 91 AJIL 518 (1997), *reprinted in* COMMENTARIES ON WORLD COURT DECISIONS (1987-1996) at 263 (P.H.F. Bekker ed., 1998).

23 *See* 1998 ICJ REP. 237 and 240, respectively (Orders of Mar. 30).

Provisional measures – prima facie jurisdiction – U.S. failure of notification to detained Paraguayan national under Vienna Convention on Consular Relations – remedies for non-notification

VIENNA CONVENTION ON CONSULAR RELATIONS (Paraguay v. United States)

Provisional Measures, Order
1998 ICJ REP. 248
International Court of Justice, April 9, 1998

On April 3, 1998, the Republic of Paraguay (Paraguay) filed an Application in the Registry of the International Court of Justice instituting proceedings against the United States of America in connection with a dispute over alleged violations by the U.S. of the Vienna Convention on Consular Relations (Vienna Convention).[1] On that same date, Paraguay submitted a request for the indication of provisional measures pursuant to Article 41 of the Court's Statute, asking the Court to order the United States to stay the execution of Angel Francisco Breard (Breard), a Paraguayan citizen who at that time was on death row in Virginia prison. This request resulted in the Order discussed below. Simultaneous proceedings were pending before the U.S. Supreme Court in Washington, D.C.[2]

The violations arose out of the alleged failure by the Commonwealth of Virginia, the U.S. state in which Breard was arrested, charged, tried, convicted of homicide and sentenced to death in 1992-1993, to advise him of his right to communicate with, and receive assistance from, the consular officers of

---

1   Convention on Consular Relations, done at Vienna, Apr. 24, 1963, 21 UST 77, 596 UNTS 261. Both Paraguay and the United States are parties to the Convention.

2   *See* William J. Aceves' summary in 92 AJIL 517 (1998). For a range of views and commentaries on the decisions of the ICJ and U.S. courts relating to the *Breard* case, see "*Agora: Breard*," 92 AJIL 666-712 (1998). *See also* Sean D. Murphy, *Contemporary Practice of the United States Relating to International Law*, 93 AJIL 161, 170 (1999).

P.H.F. Bekker, World Court Decisions at the Turn of the Millennium (1997-2001), p. 93-102.
© 2002 *Kluwer Law International. Printed in the Netherlands.*

Paraguay and to advise such officers of Breard's arrest and detention.[3] The parties differed on what remedies, if any, are available under international law for a failure to comply with the notification obligation under the Vienna Convention. Paraguay, which did not learn of Breard's detention until 1996, asked the Court to declare that it was entitled to the reestablishment of the situation that existed before the United States, as the country responsible for the acts or omissions of its federal states, failed to provide the notification required by the Vienna Convention. Through its Application, Paraguay sought to have the conviction and death penalty imposed upon Breard revoked. However, the U.S. argued that, when a claim for failure to notify is made, the only remedy available under common state practice is that apologies are presented by the responsible government together with an undertaking to ensure improved future compliance. The U.S. claimed that it had already offered such a remedy to Paraguay.

On April 9, 1998, the Court issued an Order ruling, unanimously, that, pending final judgment in the case, the U.S. should take all measures at its disposal to prevent Breard's execution scheduled for April 14, 1998.

At the outset, the Court had to determine whether Article I of the Vienna Convention's Optional Protocol concerning the Compulsory Settlement of Disputes of April 24, 1963,[4] on which Paraguay sought to base the Court's jurisdiction, appeared, *prima facie*, to afford a basis on which its jurisdiction might be founded.

At the hearing in The Hague on April 7, 1998, the United States denied the existence of a dispute under Article I. In the light of its admission of the failure to notify the Paraguayan consular officers, the U.S. argued that there could not be a dispute as to the "interpretation or application" of the Vienna Convention. The U.S. contended that Paraguay had no legal recognizable claim to the relief it requested, given that neither the Vienna Convention nor state practice provide for entitlement to *restitutio in integrum* or the return to the *status quo ante* sought by Paraguay. It pointed out that, even though, admittedly,

---

3   Art. 36(1)(b) of the Vienna Convention, *supra* note 1, provides that the competent authorities of the receiving state have an active duty to inform a detained national of the sending state of his right to communicate with the consular officers of the sending state and must permit such detainee without delay to communicate with the relevant consular post.

4   Art. I reads: "Disputes arising out of the interpretation or application of the Convention shall lie within the compulsory jurisdiction of the International Court of Justice and may accordingly be brought before the Court by an application made by the party to the dispute being a Party to the present Protocol."

Breard had not been informed of his rights under the Vienna Convention, this omission was not deliberate and the assistance of Paraguayan consular officers would not have altered the outcome of the proceedings brought against Breard, so that in consequence he had not been prejudiced by the absence of notification. Moreover, the U.S. had apologized to Paraguay and had taken steps to ensure future compliance with the Vienna Convention at both the federal and state level. It has done so, *inter alia*, by providing pocket-sized reference cards for law enforcement officers to carry on the street. The U.S. warned the Court that the indication of provisional measures in this case would severely intrude upon the criminal justice systems of the states parties to the Vienna Convention and the workload of the Court, pointing to the risk of proliferation of cases.[5] Finally, the U.S. claimed that, in any event, it would be unable to stay Breard's execution, as such a stay is the prerogative of the U.S. Supreme Court and the governor of Virginia.

Paraguay argued that any criminal liability imposed upon Breard should be recognized as void by the legal authorities of the U.S. and that the *status quo ante* should be restored by granting Breard the benefit of the protections of the Vienna Convention in any renewed proceedings brought against him. Thus, Paraguay did not contend that Breard was not subject to re-trial or future prosecution for the act with which he was charged.

On the basis of the above contentions, the Court was satisfied that there existed a dispute as to whether the relief sought by Paraguay is a remedy available under the Vienna Convention, which is a dispute arising out of the application of the Convention within the meaning of Article I of the Optional Protocol. Consequently, the Court found that, *prima facie*, it had jurisdiction to decide the dispute brought by Paraguay.

---

5   The U.S. contended that, once the Court opens itself to the process of reviewing, staying and reversing domestic criminal court decisions, it can be expected that many defendants will press the states of their nationality to take recourse to the Court. However, by failing to distinguish between pressure and right, the U.S. ignored the Court's established jurisprudence on the exercise of diplomatic protection. Such exercise is the absolute prerogative of the sovereign state, and, once diplomatic protection is granted, the claim becomes exclusively the state's claim and ceases to be that of the national. *See* Barcelona Traction, Light and Power Company, Limited (Second Phase) (Belgium v. Spain), Judgment, 1970 ICJ REP. 3, at 44, para. 79 (Feb. 5) ("The State must be viewed as the sole judge to decide whether its protection will be granted, to what extent it is granted, and when it will cease. It retains in this respect a discretionary power ... . Since the claim of the State is not identical with that of the individual or corporate person whose cause is espoused, the State enjoys complete freedom of action.").

The Court next considered that its power to indicate provisional measures of protection under Article 41 of the Statute in cases of urgency is intended to preserve the respective rights of the parties pending its decision and presupposes that irreparable prejudice shall not be caused to the rights that are the subject of the dispute in pending proceedings. The Court was satisfied that Breard's execution ordered for April 14, 1998, would render it impossible for the Court to render the relief that Paraguay sought and thus cause irreparable harm to the rights it claimed.

Finally, the Court pointed out that the issues in this case did not concern the entitlement of the federal states of the United States, including Virginia, to resort to the death penalty "for the most heinous crimes."[6] The Court emphasized that its function is not to act as a universal supreme court of criminal appeal, but to resolve international legal disputes between sovereign states.

* * * *

In this first death penalty related case to reach the International Court, the Court merely needed to satisfy itself that it had *prima facie* jurisdiction on the basis of (i) the existence of a dispute between Paraguay and the United States as to whether the specific relief sought by Paraguay is a remedy available under the Vienna Convention, qualifying as a dispute arising out of the application of the Convention within the meaning of Article I of the Optional Protocol; and (ii) there being urgency and a risk of irremediable harm to the subject matter of the case. An Order of this kind cannot be taken itself as establishing jurisdiction in a case; it does not preclude a subsequent finding that the Court lacks jurisdiction or that the application is inadmissible. In other words, the Court's Order left unaffected any future findings that the Court might have made on its jurisdiction, the admissibility of Paraguay's Application or the merits; on these issues the United States could have advanced any defenses in the subsequent stages of the proceedings.

Breard was executed by lethal injection on April 14, 1998, in accordance with an order of February 25, 1998, issued by the Circuit Court of Arlington County, Virginia, the court that sentenced him. Given that the ICJ had held that Breard's execution would render it impossible for it to render the relief that Paraguay sought, a matter reserved for the merits stage, the announcement of

---

6   1998 ICJ REP. 248, at 257, para. 38.

the discontinuance of the proceedings, by the Court's Order of November 10, 1998, hardly came as a surprise.[7]

Breard's execution triggered the non-compliance by the United States with the Court's Order of April 9, 1998. At the time of the U.S. breach, it was unclear what the legal ramifications of such non-compliance are within the framework of the Court's Statute and the United Nations Charter of which it forms an integral part. Pursuant to Article 94, paragraph 1 of the Charter, each UN member state has undertaken to comply with the Court's decision in any case to which it is a party. Does an Order of the Court, as opposed to a judgment, constitute a "decision" that must be complied with at a stage where the Court's jurisdiction is still open to challenge by the state named as defendant?

A comparison of the text of Article 94 of the Charter with that of Article 41 of the Statute, in particular the second paragraphs of these provisions, might lend support for the argument that an Order is an enforceable decision, given that both provisions refer to the Security Council. According to the second paragraph of Article 41 of the Statute, notice of the measures adopted by the Court shall be given to the parties and to the Security Council. Article 94, paragraph 2 of the Charter entitles a party to have recourse to the Security Council for enforcement action if the other party fails to comply with a judgment. However, it is true that Article 41, paragraph 2 of the Statute merely refers to *notification* of the Security Council, without indicating whether the Council has any enforcement powers with regard to provisional measures indicated by the Court. Perhaps that is why Rosenne believes that political expediency rather than legal considerations will carry more weight when it comes to enforcing a state's refusal to observe interim measures indicated by the Court.[8] In practice, the presiding judge usually issues a letter to the parties

---

7   Paraguay duly filed its Memorial on November 9, 1998, in accordance with the Court's Order issued on June 8, 1998. *See* 1998 ICJ REP. 272. An earlier Order of April 9, 1998, had fixed October 9, 1998, as the time limit within which Paraguay was to file its Memorial, and April 9, 1999, for the filing of the Counter-Memorial of the United States. *See* 1998 ICJ REP. 266.

8   *See* SHABTAI ROSENNE, THE LAW AND PROCEDURE OF THE INTERNATIONAL COURT 428 (2nd rev. ed. 1985). According to Professor Louis Henkin, one of America's leading international legal scholars, the *Breard* Order was intended to be, and was, legally binding on the United States (including the Commonwealth of Virginia and U.S. courts). Prof. Henkin based his conclusion on the status of the ICJ Statute (including Art. 41, paragraph 1 governing provisional measures) as a treaty of the United States, which, according to Article VI of the U.S. Constitution, is the supreme law of the land. *See* Louis Henkin, *Provisional Measures, U.S. Treaty Obligations, and the States*, 92 AJIL 679, at 680 (1998).

drawing their attention to the need to act in such a way as to enable any Order that the Court will make on the request for provisional measures to have its appropriate effects.[9]

Too often it is forgotten that it was Elihu Root, the great American secretary of state and war, 1912 Nobel Peace Prize winner and co-founder of The American Society of International Law, who was the driving force behind the creation of a permanent international court. Aspects of the formula that Root devised for the composition of a permanent court in his instructions for the U.S. delegation to the Second Hague Peace Conference served as a source of inspiration for the drafting of the Statute of the Permanent Court of International Justice.[10] It is important to keep in mind that the Committee of Jurists appointed by the League of Nations to frame a plan for an international court, of which Root and Lord Phillimore were the chief architects, came up with a Statute establishing a strong court. In fact, it was so strong that the League struck out the provision for the general obligatory jurisdiction of the Court favored by Root to replace it with what is known today as the Optional Clause.[11] Viewed in this historical perspective, it is hard to imagine that the drafters of the Statute had wanted to create a court whose orders, the only form besides a judgment through which the Court speaks to the parties in contentious cases, would not be binding.

The elaborate judicial process that lies behind the Court's adoption of an Order disposing of substantive issues in a contentious case, including provisional measures, is practically the same as the one through which the Court arrives at a Judgment that settles with finality the legal issues dividing the parties. The legal reasoning leading to the conclusion found in the operative paragraph of an Order indicating provisional measures reflects the Court's authoritative views on the request before it. In this sense, an Order indicating provisional measures is hardly different from a Judgment that unquestionably is binding.[12] At the same time, the important thing to keep in mind in under-

---

9   *See* 1998 ICJ REP. 248, at 252, para. 12 (referring to letters that Vice President Weeramantry addressed to both parties on April 3, 1998).

10 *See* THE INTERNATIONAL COURT OF JUSTICE 13 (4th ed. 1996) (published by the ICJ Registry). The PCIJ has been referred to as the "Root Court." *See* MICHAEL DUNNE, THE UNITED STATES AND THE WORLD COURT (1920-1935) at 17 (1988).

11 *See* PHILIP C. JESSUP, ELIHU ROOT 421-22 (1938).

12 It is worth recalling the statement by the UK representative in the UN Security Council during the Council's discussions of Iran's non-compliance with the provisional measures ordered in the *Tehran Hostages* case in 1979, referred to by Sir Gerald Fitzmaurice in his treatise on the ICJ:

standing the incidental relief known as "provisional measures" of protection is that, in order to issue an Order for such relief, the Court needs to satisfy itself that *prima facie* jurisdiction exists in the case, and that unless such an Order were issued, there would be a risk of irremediable harm to the subject matter of an urgent case. An Order indicating provisional measures can never be taken itself as establishing jurisdiction in the case and, therefore, does not preclude a subsequent finding that the Court lacks jurisdiction.[13] However, Judge Tarazi's 1980 statement that the parties "must refrain from taking any decisions on the planes of *either domestic or international law* which could have the effect of impeding the proper administration of justice"[14] is as accurate at the main jurisdictional stage as it is at the *prima facie* jurisdictional stage. It would be wrong to use the "interim" status of an Order indicating provisional measures, which usually remains in effect for the duration of *the case* (i.e., through the reading of the final judgment), to deny the binding effect of such an Order.

It is difficult to understand the U.S. administration's argument that the Court regarded its Order as merely "precatory" because it only "indicated" certain actions that the United States "should" take.[15] The less assertive statement by Professors Bradley and Goldsmith that it is not clear whether the ICJ itself *intended* the *Breard* Order to be binding also misses the point.[16] The words

---

"... clearly there would be no point in making the final judgment binding if one of the parties could frustrate that decision in advance by actions which would render the final judgment nugatory. It is therefore a necessary consequence ... of the bindingness of the final decision that the interim measures intended to preserve its efficacy should equally be binding."
GERALD FITZMAURICE, 2 THE LAW AND PROCEDURE OF THE INTERNATIONAL COURT OF JUSTICE 549 (repr. 1995) (citing Sir Gladwyn Jebb, Security Council Records, UN Doc. S/PV 559, at 20).

13 Thus, Professor Vázquez's statement that "it seems strange to regard an order of provisional measures not to be compulsory where, as in *Breard*, ... the ICJ's juris-diction over the dispute was compulsory" is inaccurate. *See* Carlos Manuel Vázquez, *Breard and the Federal Power to Require Compliance with ICJ Orders of Pro-visional Measures*, 92 AJIL 683, at 686 (1998). The same author was more accurate in stating that "[t]he binding quality of the Order ... does not turn on one party's views about whether the Court possessed jurisdiction." *Id.*, at 686, n. 19.

14 United States Diplomatic and Consular Staff in Tehran (U.S. v. Iran), Judgment, 1980 ICJ REP. 3, at 63 (May 24) (Tarazi J., diss. op.) (emphasis added).

15 Brief for the United States as Amicus Curiae, at 51, *Breard v. Greene*, 11 S.Ct. 1352 (1998) (Nos. 97-1390, 97-8214).

16 *See* Curtis A. Bradley & Jack L. Goldsmith, *The Abiding Relevance of Federalism to U.S. Foreign Relations*, 92 AJIL 675, at 678, n. 25 (1998).

"indicate" and "should" are "terms of art" used in Article 41 of the ICJ Statute and nothing special should be read into them.[17] The Rules of Court do not prescribe any particular form in which the Court may take the measures that the Statute empowers it to take.[18] The Rules merely refer to a *decision* concerning provisional measures which, in the Court's practice, takes the form of an Order.[19] By an Order, the Court *orders* sovereign states to do, or to refrain from doing, certain things that otherwise might frustrate the legal process that the Court is to administer. In a case the very subject matter of which revolves around the legality of the execution of a foreigner who is said to have been denied his international rights (a fact admitted by the respondent in this case), it may be assumed that this legal process is frustrated once one of the parties takes unilateral action that destroys the subject matter. In these circumstances, how can the Court be said to have meant to merely "suggest" or "request" that the respondent take certain actions without binding effect being attached to its Order, especially when the Rules of Court stipulate that a "request for the indication of provisional measures shall have *priority over all other cases*"[20] and the Court delivered its Order in a record time of four busi-

---

17 It is true, however, that the Statute refers at one point to "measures suggested." *See* ICJ STATUTE June 26, 1945, Art. 42, para. 2, 59 Stat. 1055, TS No. 993 [hereinafter ICJ STATUTE].

18 *See* ICJ Rules of Court, Arts. 73-78, *reprinted in* 73 AJIL 748, 761 (1979).

19 Notice incidentally that Article 59 of the Statute uses the word "decision" and not "judgment." *See* ICJ STATUTE Art. 41, para. 2. As noted, the fact that the Statute directs the Court to give notice of any provisional measures to the UN Security Council lends support to the argument that the Council may have an enforcement role in the matter of such measures. Enforceability, while fundamentally different from the issue of the binding effect of a legal instrument, depends on such instrument to be legally binding.

20 ICJ Rules of Court, *supra* note 18, Art. 74, para. 1 (emphasis added). As Sir Gerald Fitzmaurice, *supra* note 12, at 548, has convincingly argued:
    "The whole logic of the jurisdiction to indicate interim measures entails that, when indicated, they are binding – for this jurisdiction is based on the absolute necessity, when the circumstances call for it, of being able to preserve, and to avoid prejudice to, the rights of the parties, as determined by the final judgment of the Court. To indicate special measures for that purpose, if the measures, when indicated, are not even binding (let alone enforceable), lacks all point, except in so far as the parties may be expected to give a voluntary compliance to the Order of the Court. Even so, such a position in no way accords with the urgency and importance so clearly and deliberately imparted to the matter by the language ... of the Rules of Court."

ness days after Paraguay filed its request? Why would the Rules refer to "measures which ought to be taken or complied with"?[21]

The problem is that the Court, until the *LaGrand Case* discussed in Chapter 5 below, had not really had a chance to pronounce itself in explicit terms on whether or not Orders on provisional measures are binding, presumably because it is obvious to the Judges of the Court that such Orders are binding.[22] However, there are two important instances that the United States should have remembered when it considered how to respond to the *Breard* Order. First, in its Judgment in the *Tehran Hostages* case, involving the United States as Applicant, the Court felt bound to observe, by way of *obiter dictum*, that the attempt by American military units on April 24-25, 1980, to free the hostages held at the U.S. Embassy in Tehran was an operation "of a kind calculated to undermine respect for the judicial process in international relations."[23] The Court recalled that in its Order on provisional measures of December 15, 1979, it had "indicated that no action was to be taken by either party which might aggravate the tension between the countries."[24] In that case, the Court stated that neither the question of the legality of the operation nor any possible question of responsibility flowing from it was before the Court, indicating that

---

21 ICJ Rules of Court, *supra* note 18, Art. 75, para. 1.

22 A good indication of this sentiment among the Members of the Court is found in the declaration of the late Judge Tarassov appended to the Court's 1993 Order indicating provisional measures in the *Genocide (Bosnia)* case. Judge Tarassov complained that certain passages in the operative paragraph of the 1993 Order "impose practically unlimited, ill-defined and vague requirements for the exercise of responsibility by the Respondent in fulfilment of the Order of the Court, and lay the Respondent open to unjustifiable blame for failing to comply with this interim measure." Application of the Convention on the Prevention and Punishment of the Crime of Genocide (Bosnia and Herzegovina v. Yugoslavia (Serbia and Montenegro)), Provisional Measures, 1993 ICJ REP. 3, at 26-27 (Order of April 8). Clearly, the reference to the responsibility of a state and the failure to comply with an interim measure indicate that such measures are binding legal obligations the breach of which triggers a state's responsibility under international law. Under international law, an international wrongful act is committed when conduct consisting of an action or omission is attributable to the state under international law and that conduct constitutes a breach of an international obligation of the state.

23 United States Diplomatic and Consular Staff in Tehran (U.S. v. Iran), Judgment, 1980 ICJ REP. 3, at 43, para. 93 (May 24).

24 United States Diplomatic and Consular Staff in Tehran (U.S. v. Iran), Provisional Measures, 1979 ICJ REP. 7, para. 47(1)(B) (Order of Dec. 15).

the violation of an Order indicating provisional measures may be the cause of a separate action before it.[25]

Second, the Judgment on the merits in the *Nicaragua* case refers to a request by Nicaragua for the indication of further measures dated June 25, 1984, triggered by the alleged failure of the United States to comply with the Court's Order of May 10, 1984. In response, the Court pointed out that when it "finds that the situation requires that measures of this kind should be taken, it is incumbent on each party to take the Court's indications seriously into account, and not to direct its conduct solely by reference to what it believes to be its rights."[26]

Clearly, in the light of the Court's jurisprudence referred to above, the failure of the United States to stay Breard's execution was of a kind that undermined respect for the judicial process in international relations, given that it frustrated the ability of the Court to grant the relief sought by Paraguay should it have upheld its jurisdiction and the applicant's claim. The U.S. response to the Order illustrates the perpetual ongoing conflict between domestic legal systems and their interaction with international obligations on the international plane. One of the main reasons underlying the Court's unanimous Order was the fact that Breard's "execution would render it impossible for the Court to order the relief that Paraguay seeks and thus cause irreparable harm to the rights it claims."[27] Consequently, the discontinuance of the case on November 10, 1998 should not have come as a surprise.[28] The *Tehran Hostages* precedent referred to above and the decision in the *LaGrand Case* discussed in Chapter 5 below indicate that Paraguay could have instituted separate proceedings arising from the U.S. violation of the Court's Order.

---

25 Presumably, such action would require an independent basis of jurisdiction, which may be difficult to establish.

26 Military and Paramilitary Activities in and against Nicaragua (Nicar. v. U.S.), Merits, Judgment, 1986 ICJ REP. 14, at 144, paras. 287-89 (June 27).

27 1998 ICJ REP. 248, at 257, para. 37.

28 *See* 1998 ICJ REP. 426.

◊

*ICJ compulsory jurisdiction – effective date of Optional Clause declara-
tions – existence of a dispute – effect of absent third states – diplomatic
negotiations as a precondition for recourse to ICJ – effect of negotiation
requirements of Law of the Sea Convention where jurisdiction is based on
Optional Clause*

LAND AND MARITIME BOUNDARY BETWEEN CAMEROON AND NIGERIA
(Cameroon v. Nigeria)

Preliminary Objections, Judgment
1998 ICJ REP. 275
International Court of Justice, June 11, 1998[1]

On March 29, 1994, Cameroon filed an Application[2] requesting that the Court
determine the question of sovereignty over the Bakassi Peninsula and a disputed
parcel of land in the area of Lake Chad (principally Darak and its region), and
to specify the course of the land and maritime boundary between Cameroon
and Nigeria. It also asked the Court to order an immediate and unconditional
withdrawal of Nigerian troops from alleged Cameroonian territory in the disputed areas.[3] As the basis of the Court's jurisdiction, Cameroon relied on the
declarations made by the parties under Article 36, paragraph 2 of the ICJ Statute.

On December 23, 1995, Nigeria filed eight preliminary objections alleging
that the Court lacked jurisdiction and that Cameroon's Application was inadmissible. Nigeria argued, inter alia, that Cameroon had acted prematurely and
in disregard of the relevant procedural rules, that Cameroon had accepted an
exclusive regional mechanism for dispute settlement, that there was no dispute
on the whole of the land boundary, that the absence of certain third states
blocked the proceedings, and that no maritime delimitation could be undertaken
by the Court without prior negotiations between the parties having taken place.

---

1   Reproduced with permission from 92 AJIL 751 (1998). © The American Society
    of International Law.
2   Amended without objection on June 6, 1994. *See* 1994 ICJ REP. 105 (Order of June
    16).
3   See also the Court's Order of March 15, 1996, by which it indicated certain provi-
    sional measures. 1996 ICJ REP. 13.

P.H.F. Bekker, World Court Decisions at the Turn of the Millennium (1997-2001), p. 103-110.
© 2002 *Kluwer Law International. Printed in the Netherlands.*

Hearings on the preliminary objections were held at the Peace Palace at The Hague on March 2-11, 1998.

On June 11, 1998, the Court ruled, by 14 votes to 3 (Vice President Weeramantry, Judge Koroma and Judge *ad hoc* Ajibola dissenting), that it has jurisdiction and that Cameroon's Application is admissible.

First, Nigeria argued that the Court lacked jurisdiction to entertain Cameroon's Application. Cameroon deposited its Optional Clause declaration with the UN Secretary-General on March 3, 1994, but Nigeria did not receive a copy of the document until almost one year after its deposit. On this basis, Nigeria, which deposited its declaration on September 3, 1965, claimed that it had no knowledge of Cameroon's declaration on the date Cameroon filed its Application with the Court, and that Cameroon had violated its obligation to act in good faith and abused the Optional Clause system.

The Court, seeing no reason to depart from the reasoning and conclusions of a previous line of cases,[4] explained that any state party to the ICJ Statute, in depositing a declaration under the Optional Clause, makes a standing offer to the other states parties to the Statute that have not yet deposited a declaration of acceptance. The very day that one of those states accepts that offer by depositing its own declaration, the consensual bond is established and no further condition needs to be fulfilled. Hence, the legal effect of a declaration does not depend upon subsequent action of the Secretary-General.[5] The Court noted that the regime for depositing and transmitting Optional Clause declarations laid down in Article 36, paragraph 4 of the Statute is distinct from that envisaged for treaties by the Vienna Convention on the Law of Treaties.[6] The notion of reciprocity in Optional Clause declarations "is concerned with the *scope* and *substance* of the commitments entered into, including reservations, and not with the formal conditions of their creation, duration or extinction."[7]

---

4   *See* 1998 ICJ REP. 275, at 292, paras. 26-27 (citing Right of Passage over Indian Territory (Port. v. India), Preliminary Objections, Judgment, 1957 ICJ REP. 125, at 146-47 (Nov. 26); Temple of Preah Vihear (Cambodia v. Thailand), Preliminary Objections, Judgment, 1961 ICJ REP. 17, at 31 (May 26), Military and Paramilitary Activities in and against Nicaragua (Nicar. v. US), Jurisdiction and Admissibility, Judgment, 1984 ICJ REP. 392 (Nov. 26) [hereinafter *Nicaragua*]).

5   *Id.*, paras. 25-27.

6   *Opened for signature* May 23, 1969, 1155 UNTS 331 (entered into force Jan. 27, 1980). *See id.* at 293, para. 30.

7   *Id.* at 298-300, paras. 41-45 (quoting *Nicaragua*, 1984 ICJ REP. 392, at 419 (emphasis added)).

The Court also rejected Nigeria's argument that Cameroon should have allowed a reasonable time to elapse between the deposit of its declaration with the UN Secretary-General and the filing of the Application with the Court. It explained that there is a fundamental difference between *withdrawal* of a declaration, which ends existing consensual bonds, and its *deposit*, which establishes such bonds. Given that the deposit of a declaration does not deprive any state of any accrued right, no time period is required for the establishment of a consensual bond following such a deposit.[8] Moreover, Cameroon did not violate the principle of good faith by failing to inform Nigeria of its intentions. The principle of good faith is not in itself a source of obligation where none otherwise exists. International law does not contain any specific rule obliging states to inform other states parties to the ICJ Statute that they intend to subscribe or have subscribed to the Optional Clause.[9] In any event, the Court agreed with Cameroon that, on the facts of the matter, Nigeria was not unaware of Cameroon's intentions, various public sources having documented those intentions in early March 1994.[10]

Second, Nigeria argued that for a period of at least twenty-four years prior to the filing of Cameroon's Application, the parties had in their regular dealings accepted a duty to settle all boundary questions exclusively through the existing bilateral machinery, instead of by recourse to the ICJ. The Court pointed out that neither in the UN Charter nor otherwise in international law is any general rule to be found that requires the exhaustion of diplomatic negotiations prior to having recourse to the Court.[11] Specifically, no such precondition is included in the ICJ Statute or the declarations of Cameroon or Nigeria. In the Court's view, the fact that the two states had attempted to solve some of the boundary issues between them during bilateral contacts does not imply that either one had excluded the possibility of bringing any boundary dispute before other fora, in particular the ICJ. The Court also rejected Nigeria's estoppel argument, observing that an estoppel would only arise if by its acts or declarations Cameroon had consistently made it clear that it had agreed to settle the boundary dispute submitted to the Court by bilateral avenues alone and, by relying on such attitude, Nigeria had changed its position to its detriment or had suffered some prejudice.[12]

---

8   *Id.* at 295, para. 34.
9   *Id.* at 296, para. 39.
10 *Id.* at 297, para. 40. The Court's vote rejecting the first objection was 14-3.
11 *Id.* at 302-03, para. 56.
12 *Id.* at 303, para. 57. The Court's vote rejecting the second objection was 16-1.

Third, Nigeria contended that the settlement of boundary disputes within the Lake Chad region is subject to the exclusive competence of the Lake Chad Basin Commission. In the Court's view, the commission does not have as its purpose the regional settlement of matters relating to the maintenance of international peace and security under Chapter VIII of the UN Charter. It is not a tribunal within the meaning of Article 95 of the Charter but an international organization exercising its powers within a specific geographic area. In any event, the existence of procedures for regional negotiation cannot prevent the Court from exercising the functions conferred upon it by the UN Charter and the ICJ Statute.[13]

Fourth, Nigeria contended that the Court should not determine the boundary in Lake Chad because it directly affects an absent third riparian state, the Republic of Chad. The Court pointed out that it has declined to exercise jurisdiction only when the interests of a third state not merely are affected by its judgment on the merits, but constitute the very subject matter of it. In this case, Cameroon's request to specify the Cameroon-Nigeria frontier, and that frontier alone, from Lake Chad to the sea does not imply that the tripoint (the northern end point) in Lake Chad where the frontiers of the three states meet could be moved away from the line constituting the Cameroon-Chad boundary. Any change in the location of the tripoint in Lake Chad following from the judgment on the merits of Cameroon's Application would have no legal consequence for Chad.[14]

In its fifth objection, Nigeria alleged that there is no dispute concerning "boundary delimitation as such" throughout the *whole* length of the boundary from the tripoint in Lake Chad to the sea–subject, within Chad, to the question of title over Darak and adjacent islands inhabited by Nigerians, and without prejudice to the title over the Bakassi Peninsula. Although the Court acknowledged that it cannot be said that the disputes over Darak and the Bakassi Peninsula in themselves concern so large a portion of the thousand-mile boundary that they would necessarily constitute a dispute concerning the entire boundary, it noted that Nigeria has constantly been reserved in the manner in which it has presented its own position on the matter. Because of Nigeria's

---

13 *Id.* at 306-07, paras. 67-68. The Court's vote rejecting the third objection was 15-2.

14 *Id.* at 311-13, paras. 79-81. The Court's vote rejecting the fourth objection was 13-4.

position, the exact scope of the dispute cannot be determined at this stage, but there does exist a dispute at least as regards the legal bases of the boundary.[15]

Sixth, Nigeria complained that the material that Cameroon presented to the Court did not give Nigeria adequate information to defend itself and did not enable the Court to carry out a fair and effective judicial determination of the issues of state responsibility and reparation raised by Cameroon. Cameroon argued that Article 38(2) of the Rules of Court, which requires that an application specify the precise nature of the claim, together with a succinct statement of the facts and grounds on which the claim is based, leaves the applicant free to develop the facts of the case presented in the application or to present them with more precision in the course of the proceedings. The Court agreed with Cameroon that "succinct" does not mean complete and that an applicant has some latitude to elaborate on the facts and grounds on which it relies after the filing of the application. In any event, it is the applicant, and not the respondent, that must suffer the consequences of an application that gives an inadequate presentation of the facts and grounds on which the claim is based.[16]

In its seventh objection, Nigeria contended that no determination of a maritime boundary is possible prior to the determination of title in respect of the Bakassi Peninsula. Moreover, even when there is a determination of that title, the issue of maritime delimitation will not be admissible in the absence of prior negotiations by the parties to effect a delimitation by agreement on the basis of international law, as the United Nations Convention on the Law of the Sea requires. The Court pointed out that it is within its discretion to arrange the order in which it addresses the issues before it in such a way that it can deal substantively with each of them. Moreover, it was not seised pursuant to Part XV of the UN Convention on the Law of the Sea, but on the basis of declarations made under the Statute's Optional Clause. The declarations of

---

15 *Id.* at 315-16, para. 91. The Court's vote rejecting the fifth objection was 13-4. During the oral proceedings, Judge Guillaume asked whether, apart from the parties' conflicting claims over the Bakassi Peninsula and the Darak region, there is agreement between Nigeria and Cameroon on the geographical coordinates of the boundary as presented by Cameroon. In reply to this question, Nigeria did not indicate whether or not it agreed with Cameroon on the course of the boundary or on its legal basis.

16 *Id.* at 318, para. 98, and 319, para. 101. The Court's vote rejecting the sixth objection was 15-2.

Cameroon and Nigeria do not contain any condition relating to prior negotiations to be conducted within a reasonable time period.[17]

Finally, Nigeria contended that the question of maritime delimitation
necessarily involves the rights and interests of third states and is to that extent
inadmissible. In particular, the Court needed to examine whether the prolongation of the maritime boundary seawards of a point that is some seventeen
nautical miles from the coast (Point *G*) would involve rights and interests of
third states. The Court acknowledged that it appears that rights and interests
of third states, in particular Equatorial Guinea and São Tomé and Principe,
will become involved if the Court accedes to Cameroon's request. However,
it would have to deal with the merits of Cameroon's request in order to determine where a prolonged maritime boundary beyond Point *G* would run, where
and to what extent it would meet possible claims of other states, and how its
judgment would affect the rights and interests of those states. In view of these
circumstances, the Court concluded that Nigeria's eighth objection did not
possess an exclusively preliminary character and should be settled during the
proceedings on the merits.[18]

* * * *

This case arose from a border dispute stemming from the division of two
African colonies once held by European powers, in this case France, Germany
and the United Kingdom. It is hardly surprising that the Court found that it
has jurisdiction in this particular case, given that both parties had made unreserved Optional Clause declarations. Since 1978, when the Court found that
it was without jurisdiction to entertain Greece's Application in *Aegean Sea
Continental Shelf*,[19] the Court has decided only once not to exercise its jurisdiction.[20]

---

17   *Id.* at 321-22, para. 109. The vote rejecting the seventh objection was 12-5.

18   *Id.* at 324-25, paras. 116-17. The vote rejecting the eighth objection was 12-5.

19   Aegean Sea Continental Shelf (Greece v. Turk.), Jurisdiction, 1978 ICJ REP. 3 (Dec.
     10).

20   *See* East Timor (Port. v. Austl.), Judgment, 1995 ICJ REP. 90 (June 30) *summarized
     in* 90 AJIL 94 (1996), *reprinted in* COMMENTARIES ON WORLD COURT DECISIONS
     (1987-1996) at 209 (P.H.F. Bekker ed., 1998). In that case, Australia's objections
     were heard and determined within the framework of the merits. Subsequent to this
     decision, the Court twice rejected jurisdiction in Initial Phase cases, namely, in
     Fisheries Jurisdiction (Sp. v. Can.) and Aerial Incident of 10 August 1999 (Pak.
     v. Ind.), discussed in Chapters 2 and 4, respectively.

The Court made it clear, in connection with Nigeria's fourth and eighth objections, that it believes that Article 59 of the Statute, incorporating the principle of *res inter alios acta* with regard to the Court's judgments, accords sufficient protection to third states in bilateral boundary delimitation cases. Although that provision also indicates the absence of a formal rule of *stare decisis* in the World Court, the Court's recent jurisprudence, including this case, evidences its desire to follow earlier precedents.

In their separate opinions, Judges Higgins and Kooijmans both addressed the Court's judicial function under Article 38 of the Statute in light of the majority's holding rejecting Nigeria's seventh preliminary objection concerning delimitation of the maritime boundary between Cameroon and Nigeria. The Court itself pointed out in connection with Nigeria's fifth objection that, for a dispute to exist, there must be a disagreement on a point of law or fact, a conflict of legal views or interests, and it must be shown that the claim of one party is positively opposed by the other.[21] Judges Higgins and Kooijmans argued that the Court, after observing that the parties had not raised this point,[22] should have addressed *proprio motu* whether a dispute exists relating to the line beyond Point *G* proposed by Cameroon. Both pointed to the absence of negotiations between the parties on that particular stretch of the maritime boundary. Judge Higgins found support for her conclusion that there is no dispute relating to the maritime boundary beyond Point *G* in the way Cameroon formulated the document instituting proceedings. In its Application, Cameroon asked for a delimitation of the maritime boundary "[i]n order to *prevent any dispute arising*."[23] Judge Kooijmans pointed out that Cameroon had not formulated a specific claim on that stretch of the maritime boundary until submitting the Memorial, so that at the date of the filing of the Application, there was no claim of Cameroon that was "positively opposed" by Nigeria.[24]

It is safe to assume that counsel for Nigeria chose not to argue this point precisely to avoid the appearance of a dispute. Because of this litigation strategy, and because the Court declined to address the issue *proprio motu* despite its observation that "Nigeria is entitled not to advance arguments that it considers are for the merits at the present stage of the proceedings,"[25] Nigeria's objection was rejected by a majority of the judges. The majority was satisfied

---

21 *See also* Land, Island and Maritime Frontier Dispute (El Sal./Hond.), Application to Intervene, Judgment, 1990 ICJ REP. 92 (Sept. 13).

22 1998 ICJ REP. 275, at 314, para. 87.

23 *Id*. at 322, para. 110.

24 *Id*. at 358, para. 10, separate opinion of Judge Kooijmans.

25 *Id*. at 316-17, para. 93.

that there is a dispute on the basis that Cameroon and Nigeria had not been able to agree on the continuation of the negotiations on the maritime boundary *beyond* Point *G*, when, in any event, they had set out to negotiate the whole of the maritime boundary.[26] The majority's holding will cause counsel in future similar cases to review their litigation strategy very carefully.

---

26 *Id.* at 322, para. 110.

Optional Clause declarations – reservation in declaration of respondent blocking Court's jurisdiction – no burden of proof on either party concerning Court's jurisdiction – rules of interpretation applicable to declarations as unilateral acts – natural and reasonable way of reading words – emphasis on intention of declarant

FISHERIES JURISDICTION (Spain v. Canada)

Jurisdiction, Judgment
1998 ICJ REP. 432
International Court of Justice, December 4, 1998

On March 28, 1995, the Kingdom of Spain filed an Application instituting proceedings against Canada. Spain requested the Court to declare that certain legislation of Canada, in particular the Coastal Fisheries Protection Act, as amended in 1994, and implementing regulations, is not opposable to Spain, insofar as it claims to exercise jurisdiction over ships flying a foreign flag on the high seas, outside Canada's 200-mile exclusive economic zone.[1] In addition, Spain asked the Court to declare that the boarding and seizure by the Canadian Navy in the NAFO Regulatory Area on the high seas, on March 9, 1995, of

---

1   According to Art. I(2) of the 1978 Convention on Future Multilateral Co-operation in the Northwest Atlantic Fisheries (NAFO Convention), to which both Canada and Spain are parties, the NAFO Regulatory Area "lies beyond the areas in which the coastal States exercise fisheries jurisdiction." For the text of the NAFO Convention, see United Kingdom Misc 9 (1979), United Kingdom Cmnd 78651, Canada Treaty Series 1979 no. 11. For a list of contracting parties, see 34 ILM 1452 (1995). The NAFO Regulatory Area is part of the NAFO Convention Area which includes also the 200-mile exclusive economic zone, i.e., the area that is under the jurisdiction of the respective coastal states. The effect of certain amendments to regulations adopted pursuant to the Coastal Fisheries Protection Act was that vessels registered in Spain were prohibited from fishing for Greenland halibut in the NAFO Regulatory Area and were subject to arrest and seizure. Pursuant to an agreement between the European Union and Canada signed in Brussels on April 20, 1995, Canada agreed not to include in its regulations vessels flying the flag of any E.U. member state and the domestic proceedings against the *ESTAI* and its master were discontinued by order of the attorney general of Canada. *See* 34 ILM 1260 (1995).

P.H.F. Bekker, World Court Decisions at the Turn of the Millennium (1997-2001), p. 111-120.
© 2002 *Kluwer Law International. Printed in the Netherlands.*

the Spanish flag fishing vessel *ESTAI* involving the use of force constituted a violation of international law for which Canada must make reparation.

As the basis of the Court's jurisdiction, Spain relied on the declarations made by the two parties accepting the Court's compulsory jurisdiction under the Optional Clause embodied in Article 36, paragraph 2 of the ICJ Statute. That provision provides that the states parties to the Statute may at any time file with the UN Secretary-General declarations stating that they recognize as compulsory, without special agreement, in relation to any other state accepting the same obligation, the Court's jurisdiction in all legal disputes concerning the interpretation of a treaty, any question of international law, the existence of any fact which, if established, would constitute a breach of an international obligation, or the nature or extent of the reparation to be made for the breach of an international obligation.

Canada argued that the Court manifestly lacked jurisdiction to deal with Spain's Application on the basis of a reservation contained in its declaration deposited on May 10, 1994. The Canadian reservation excludes from jurisdiction "disputes arising out of or concerning conservation and management measures taken by Canada with respect to vessels fishing in the NAFO Regulatory Area, as defined in the Convention on Future Multilateral Co-operation in the North-west Atlantic Fisheries, 1978, and the enforcement of such measures."[2]

On December 4, 1998, the Court ruled, by 12 votes to 5, that it lacked juris-diction to adjudicate the dispute submitted to it by Spain, on the basis of its interpretation of the facts of the dispute in relation to the Canadian reservation.[3]

The President's Order of May 2, 1995,[4] recorded the parties' agreement that the sole question to be decided by the Court at the initial phase of the proceedings was whether it had jurisdiction. Thus, the task of the Court essen-tially was to interpret the words of the Canadian reservation in order to deter-mine whether or not the acts of Canada of which Spain complained fell within the terms of the reservation, and hence whether or not the Court had juris-diction.

First, the Court had to identify the dispute submitted by Spain, given that each party characterized the dispute differently. In Spain's view, the dispute related mainly to Canada's lack of entitlement to exercise jurisdiction on the high seas against Spanish vessels pursuant to domestic legislation and to enforce that right by the use of force. According to Canada, the dispute concerned the

---

2   *See* 53 ICJ Y.B. 1998-1999, at 94.

3   1998 ICJ REP. 432.

4   1995 ICJ REP. 87.

adoption of measures for the conservation and management of fisheries stocks (Greenland halibut) with respect to vessels fishing in the NAFO Regulatory Area and their enforcement.

The Court disagreed with Spain that the applicant in a case determines the dispute that it wishes the Court to resolve. Although it is for the applicant to present the dispute it wishes to submit to the Court and to set out the related claims in the application, it is for the Court itself to determine on an objective basis the dispute dividing the parties, by examining the position of both applicant and respondent. The Court will look not only at the application, but also the parties' pleadings and final submissions, diplomatic exchanges, public statements and other pertinent evidence.[5] In the Court's view, the specific acts of which Spain's Application complained (i.e., the boarding and seizure of a Spanish vessel on the high seas involving the use of force and the arrest of its master) arose from Canada's amended Coastal Fisheries Protection Act and implementing regulations which Spain regards as contrary to international law and not opposable to it.[6] Hence, the essence of the dispute between the parties was whether these acts violated Spain's rights under international law and required reparation. The Court pointed out that, contrary to the parties' views, there is no burden of proof to be discharged by either party in the matter of the Court's jurisdiction; it is for the Court alone to determine the legal question of its jurisdiction, taking into account the facts and the arguments advanced by both parties.[7]

Canada and Spain differed on the rules of international law applicable to the interpretation of reservations to Optional Clause declarations. According to Spain, such reservations are not to be interpreted so as to allow reserving states to undermine the system of compulsory jurisdiction. Spain also argued that the principle of effectiveness dictates that a reservation must be interpreted by reference to the object and purpose of the declaration, i.e., the acceptance

---

5   1998 ICJ REP. 432, at 447-50, paras. 29-33.

6   *Id.* at 450, para. 35. Later in the Judgment, the Court stated that it had "no doubt that the said dispute is *very largely* concerned with these facts" (emphasis added). *Id.* at 467, para. 87. It is unclear whether the emphasized words were meant to be a qualification of the Court's concluding statement.

7   *Id.* at 450-51, paras. 36-38. In terms of litigation strategy, the Court's statement that there is no burden of proof on either party in the matter of the Court's jurisdiction is important given that Spain had accepted, at the outset of the proceedings, that it would submit a memorial addressing only the question of jurisdiction. Subsequently, Spain unsuccessfully complained of that particular sequence during the stage of the written and oral pleadings.

(as opposed to the exclusion) of the Court's compulsory jurisdiction. Stressing the unilateral nature of reservations, Canada argued that reservations are to be interpreted in a natural way, in context and with particular regard for the intention of the state making the reservation.

The Court pointed out that the interpretation of Optional Clause declarations serves to establish whether mutual consent has been given to the Court's jurisdiction and that it is for each state, in formulating its declaration, to determine the limits it places upon its acceptance of such jurisdiction. In the Court's view, conditions or reservations do not by their terms derogate from a wider acceptance already given, but operate to define the parameters of a state's acceptance of the Court's compulsory jurisdiction. Most importantly, an additional reservation contained in a new declaration of acceptance of the Court's jurisdiction, replacing an earlier declaration, is not to be interpreted as a derogation from a more comprehensive acceptance given in the earlier declaration. This means that there is no reason to interpret reservations restrictively. A declaration is a unilateral act of state sovereignty and, simultaneously, it establishes a consensual bond and the potential for a jurisdictional link with other states that have made similar declarations.

The Court noted that the regime established for the interpretation of treaties by the 1969 Vienna Convention on the Law of Treaties, in which the principle of effectiveness has an important role, may only apply by analogy to unilateral declarations to the extent compatible with the *sui generis* character of such declarations.[8] The relevant words of a declaration, including a reservation contained therein, are to be interpreted in a natural and reasonable way, having due regard to the intention of the state concerned at the time when it accepted the Court's compulsory jurisdiction. Such intention may be deduced not only from the text of the relevant clause, but also from the context in which the clause is to be read, and the circumstances of its preparation and the purposes intended to be served, including ministerial statements, parliamentary debates, legislative proposals and press communiqués.[9]

Spain contended that the Canadian reservation is invalid or inoperative by reason of its incompatibility with the Court's Statute, the United Nations Charter and international law. In Spain's view, such incompatibility dictates an interpretation of the reservation different from that advanced by Canada in conformity with the Statute, the Charter and international law; Canada's interpretation

---

8   *Id*. at 452-54, paras. 44-47. A reference to the principle of effectiveness is found later at the end of paragraph 66 of the Judgment.

9   *Id*. at 454, para. 49.

of the reservation did not come within the framework of an existing international agreement and could only result in the measures being directed at vessels flying the flags of other states, as opposed to stateless vessels.[10] However, the Court pointed out that its jurisprudence does not suggest that interpretation in accordance with the legality under international law of the matters that are exempted from the Court's jurisdiction under a reservation is a rule that governs the interpretation of reservations. Instead, that jurisprudence underscores that a state is absolutely free to make or not to make a unilateral declaration, including reservations.[11] The fact that a state lacks confidence or is uncertain as to the compatibility of certain of its actions with international law does not operate as an exception to its freedom to attach reservations to its consent to jurisdiction. The question of compatibility can only be reached when the Court deals with the merits *after* having concluded that it has jurisdiction.

Having identified the dispute brought before it and the rule governing the interpretation of reservations, the Court went on to interpret the words contained in the Canadian reservation. As regards the objectives that the reservation was intended to achieve, the Court noted the close links between Canada's 1994 declaration and its amended coastal fisheries protection legislation. Based on the parliamentary debates and official Canadian statements, the Court considered that it was evident that the purpose of the 1994 declaration was to prevent it from exercising jurisdiction over matters that might arise with regard to the international legality of the amended legislation and implementing regulations. However, Spain contended that, whatever Canada's intentions, they were not achieved by the words of the reservation for they do not cover the dispute submitted by Spain. In support of its view, Spain relied on four principal arguments.

First, Spain argued that the dispute brought before the Court fell outside the terms of the Canadian reservation by reason of its subject matter. However, the Court was satisfied that the words "disputes arising out of or concerning" exclude not only disputes whose immediate "subject-matter" is the measures

---

10 Spain relied on the rule of interpretation indicated by the Court in Right of Passage over Indian Territory (Portugal v. India), Preliminary Objections, Judgment, 1957 ICJ REP. 125, at 142 (Nov. 26). This rule is similar to U.S. jurisprudence which has held that federal statutes must be interpreted consistently with international law unless Congress has clearly indicated a contrary result. *See Murray v. The Schooner Charming Betsy*, 6 U.S. (2 Cranch) 64, at 118 (1804) and its prodigy.

11 1998 ICJ REP. 432, at 455-56, para. 54 (citing Military and Paramilitary Activities in and against Nicaragua (Nicar. v. U.S.), Jurisdiction and Admissibility, Judgment, 1984 ICJ REP. 392, at 418, para. 59 (Nov. 26)).

in question and their enforcement, but also those "concerning" such measures and those having their "origin" in those matters. In the Court's view, it had to determine whether the dispute had as its subject matter the measures mentioned in the reservation or their enforcement, or both, or concerned those measures or arose out of them.

The Court had to make this determination in the context of Spain's second argument, namely, that the Canadian legislation cannot, in international law, constitute "conservation and management measures" and excludes any unilateral measure by a state that adversely affects the rights of other states outside that state's own area of jurisdiction. By contrast, Canada argued that the word "measure" is a generic term used in international conventions to encompass statutes, regulations and administrative action.

The Court noted that "measure" covers any act, step or proceeding designed for the purpose of "conservation and management of fish," including the unity of a law and its implementing regulations. Moreover, "measure" imposes no particular limit on the material content or on the aim pursued by such laws and regulations. The Court was satisfied that the "measures" taken by Canada in amending its coastal fisheries protection legislation and regulations constituted "conservation and management measures." According to the Court, it is generally accepted in international law and the practice of states that, in order for a measure to be characterized as a "conservation and management measure," it is sufficient that its purpose it to conserve and manage living resources (in this case, Greenland halibut) and that, to this end, it satisfies various technical requirements.[12] To take the contrary view would be to disregard the intention of the declarant and to deprive the reservation of its effectiveness.

Third, Spain argued that the Canadian reservation covers only "vessels" that are stateless or flying a flag of convenience.[13] However, the Court found that the words "vessels fishing" referred to all vessels in the NAFO Regulatory Area, without exception. In the Court's view, Spain's interpretation ran contrary to a clear text expressing Canada's intention.[14]

Finally, Spain contended that the pursuit, boarding and seizure of the *ESTAI* cannot be regarded in international law as "the enforcement of " conservation and management "measures," because the use of force by one state against

---

12   *Id.* at 461-62, para. 70.

13   "Flag of convenience" refers to vessels registered under the laws of a jurisdiction that does not require the vessel's crew and master to have the nationality of the flag state and that imposes only mild restrictions, fees and taxes upon the shipowner. Examples are Liberia, the Marshall Islands, and Vanuatu.

14   *Id.* at 463-64, paras. 75-76.

a vessel of another state on the high seas necessarily is contrary to international law and the Canadian reservation, which must be interpreted in conformity with legality, may not be interpreted to subsume the use of force within the words "the enforcement of such measures." But according to the Court, Spain again confused the legality of acts with consent to jurisdiction. The Court was satisfied that the provisions of the Canadian legislation authorizing the use of force fall within the ambit of what is commonly understood as enforcement of fisheries conservation measures. According to a natural and reasonable interpretation, the boarding, inspection, arrest and minimum use of force are all contained within the concept of enforcement of conservation and management measures.

On the basis of the above analysis, the Court concluded that the dispute submitted by Spain constituted a dispute "arising out of" or "concerning" "conservation and management measures" taken by Canada with respect to "vessels fishing in the NAFO Regulatory Area" and "the enforcement of such measures." Consequently, the Court concluded that this dispute came within the terms of the Canadian reservation and held, by 12 votes to five, that it was without jurisdiction to adjudicate the dispute.

* * * *

The year 1998 is an important one in the history of the International Court given the Court's authoritative statements on Optional Clause jurisdiction in the decision of June 11 in *Land and Maritime Boundary between Cameroon and Nigeria*[15] and in this case. The June 11 Judgment having addressed primarily procedural requirements with which declarations must comply, the Court pointed out in this case that when a state replaces an existing declaration with one that contains additional reservations, such later declaration is not to be interpreted as a derogation from a more comprehensive acceptance given in the earlier declaration; the declaration that is *in existence* is the sole subject of interpretation. As to the applicability to declarations of the 1969 Vienna Convention on the Law of Treaties, the Court explained that the regime for depositing and transmitting declarations of acceptance of the Court's compulsory jurisdiction laid down in Article 36, paragraph 4 of the Statute is distinct from the regime envisaged for treaties by the Vienna Convention. In the Court's view, the provisions of the Vienna Convention governing interpretation may apply only analogously to the extent compatible with the *sui generis* character of an Optional Clause declaration as a unilateral act of state sovereignty.

---

15   1998 ICJ REP. 275.

The unilateral nature of a declaration in turn explains the emphasis that the Court places in interpreting reservations to its jurisdiction on the "bottom line" criterion of the intention of the depositing state.[16] However, it may be questioned whether the Court did so consistently in this Judgment. The Court indicated three levels for the interpretation of declarations, in order of relevance: (I) a declaration is to be interpreted in a natural and reasonable way; (II) due regard must be paid to the intention of the declarant at the time when it accepted the Court's compulsory jurisdiction; and (III) such intention may be deduced from (i) the text of the relevant clause; (ii) the context in which the clause is to be read; and (iii) an examination of the evidence regarding the circumstances of its preparation and the purposes intended to be served.[17] Thus, Level II supports Level I, expressing the paramount rule of interpretation ("in a natural and reasonable way"), and Level III, in turn, assists in identifying the declarant's intention referred to in Level II. However, in rejecting Spain's contention that interpretation must be in accordance with the legality under international law of the matters excluded, the Court seems to elevate the purpose element of Level III to Level II status.[18] It may even be argued that the Level II consideration of the intention of the declarant is elevated by the Court to Level I status, so that the paramount rule of interpretation that emerges from the Judgment is that of the intention of the declarant, instead of a natural and reasonable reading of the text. However, it should be pointed out that the Court does not examine the intention of the declarant in a subjective and isolated way, but ascertains such intention objectively in the exercise of its function under Article 36, paragraph 6 of the Statute.[19]

This decision also is significant in that it represents the first time since the Judgment in *Aegean Sea Continental Shelf* of 1978 that the Court has found, at a preliminary stage, that it is without jurisdiction to entertain an application.[20] The three Judgments upholding jurisdiction rendered earlier in 1998,

---

16 *See*, e.g., 1998 ICJ REP. 432, at 454, para. 49, 455-56, para. 54, 460, para. 66 (end), 462-63, para. 71 (end), and 463-64, para. 76 (end).

17 *Id.* at 454, para. 49.

18 *See id.* at 455, para. 54 ("a declaration ... is to be interpreted in a natural and reasonable way, with appropriate regard for the intentions of the reserving State and the purpose of the reservation.").

19 "In the event of a dispute as to whether the Court has jurisdiction, the matter shall be settled by the decision of the Court." *See also id.* at 467, para. 86.

20 The Court's refusal to entertain Portugal's Application in East Timor (Port. v. Austl.) in 1995, although technically a dismissal, was based on a finding at the merits stage that the Court should not exercise the jurisdiction conferred upon it to adjudicate the dispute referred by Portugal in the absence of Indonesia as a necessary third

equaling the total number of judgments upholding jurisdiction in the previous *decade*,[21] appeared to indicate that the Court's twenty-year record of upholding jurisdiction at the preliminary stage was going to extend into the 21st century. The December 4 Judgment sheds a different light on the chances of having the Court uphold jurisdiction in cases falling in the "probably hostile" category.

This Judgment represents a novelty in that, for the first time in the Court's jurisprudence, all opinions appended to the Judgment contain paragraph numbers and, with the exception of the opinions of Judge Oda and Judge *ad hoc* Torres Bernardez each of which contains a table of contents, they include concise italicized summaries describing the principal points made in the opinion. This format greatly assists commentators and counsel in citing to particular statements made by a Judge in an individual opinion.

In his separate opinion, Judge Kooijmans made the point that compulsory jurisdiction is more than just another method of settling legal disputes. He charged the Court with having limited its jurisdiction in an excessive way, thereby affecting the credibility of the Optional Clause system itself.[22] He did not explain what he meant by "excessive." It should be pointed out, however, that Optional Clause jurisdiction is only one of three principal ways in which the mutual consent of the parties may be construed. The Court's record indicates that, of all the cases that have been brought before the Court, only one-third were based on Optional Clause jurisdiction, the other two-thirds relying equally on special agreements and on jurisdictional clauses in bilateral or multilateral treaties. In other words, no matter how important the concept of compulsory jurisdiction represented by the Optional Clause may be, in reality this type of jurisdiction has not played a dominant role in establishing ICJ jurisdiction. This is evidenced by the place occupied by the United States in the Court's record: after the United States withdrew its acceptance of the Optional Clause during the *Nicaragua* case, its involvement in cases actually increased on the basis of jurisdictional clauses in treaties that applicant states successfully invoked against the United States.

---

party. *See* 1995 ICJ REP. 90 (June 30).
21   *See* COMMENTARIES ON WORLD COURT DECISIONS (1987-1996) at 278 (P.H.F. Bekker ed. 1998).
22   Separate opinion of Judge Kooijmans, 1998 ICJ REP. 432, at 492-93, para. 13.

3

THE YEAR 1999

THE 1999 JUDICIAL ACTIVITY OF
THE INTERNATIONAL COURT OF JUSTICE[*]

This introductory section summarizes the judicial work of the International Court of Justice during 1999,[1] using the updated General List, pleadings filed, Orders and Judgments/Advisory Opinions issued, and hearings held at the Peace Palace in The Hague to describe the Court's record in 1999.

THE WORK OF THE COURT

General List

During the calendar year 1999, the Court was seized of a record number of seventeen new contentious cases, in the following order of filing: *LaGrand Case (Germany v. United States);*[2] *Legality of Use of Force (Yugoslavia v. Belgium) (Yugoslavia v. Canada) (Yugoslavia v. France) (Yugoslavia v. Germany) (Yugoslavia v. Italy) (Yugoslavia v. the Netherlands) (Yugoslavia v. Portugal) (Yugoslavia v. Spain) (Yugoslavia v. United Kingdom) (Yugoslavia v. United States);*[3] *Armed Activities on the Territory of the Congo (Democratic*

---

[*]   Reproduced with permission from 94 AJIL 412 (2000). © The American Society of International Law.

[1]   Most of the information contained in this Note is available from the ICJ's Web site <www.icj-cij.org>.

[2]   Application of Germany filed in the ICJ Registry on March 2. *See* ICJ Communiqué 99/07 (Mar. 2, 1999).

[3]   Applications of Yugoslavia filed in the ICJ Registry on April 29. *See* ICJ Communiqué 99/17 (Apr. 29, 1999).

P.H.F. Bekker, World Court Decisions at the Turn of the Millennium (1997-2001), p. 123-128.
© *2002 Kluwer Law International. Printed in the Netherlands.*

Republic of the Congo v. Burundi)[4] (Democratic Republic of the Congo v. Rwanda)[5] and (Democratic Republic of the Congo v. Uganda);[6] Application of the Convention on the Prevention and Punishment of the Crime of Genocide (Croatia v. Yugoslavia) (hereinafter *Genocide (Croatia)* case);[7] *Aerial Incident of 10 August 1999 (Pakistan v. India)* (hereinafter *Aerial Incident* case);[8] and *Maritime Delimitation between Nicaragua and Honduras in the Caribbean Sea (Nicaragua v. Honduras).[9]* In addition, on February 16, Eritrea applied to the Court in a diplomatic dispute with Ethiopia concerning the alleged violation of the immunity of the premises and of the staff of Eritrea's embassy in Addis Ababa. Since Ethiopia has not in any way consented to the Court's jurisdiction, however, no action was taken by the Court on Eritrea's Application save for its transmission to Ethiopia in its capacity as the state named as respondent.[10] In 1999 a total of twenty-nine cases appeared on the General List at any particular time. In addition to the seventeen new cases (above), the contentious proceedings before the full Court were *Maritime Delimitation and Territorial Questions between Qatar and Bahrain (Qatar v. Bahrain)*; *Questions of Interpretation and Application of the 1971 Montreal Convention arising from the Aerial Incident at Lockerbie (Libya v. United Kingdom)* and *(Libya v. United States)* (hereinafter *Lockerbie Cases)*; *Oil Platforms (Iran v. United States)* (hereinafter *Oil Platforms* case); *Application of the Convention on the Prevention and Punishment of the Crime of Genocide (Bosnia-Herzegovina v. Yugoslavia)* (hereinafter *Genocide (Bosnia)* case); *Land and Maritime Boundary between Cameroon and Nigeria (Cameroon v. Nigeria; Equatorial Guinea intervening)*; *Gabčíkovo-Nagymaros Project (Hungary/Slovakia)*; *Kasikili/Sedudu Island (Botswana/Namibia)*; *Request for Interpretation of the Court's Judgment of June 11, 1998, in the Case Concerning the* Land and Maritime Boundary between Cameroon and Nigeria (Cameroon v. Nigeria), Preliminary Objections

---

4   Application of the Congo filed in the ICJ Registry on June 23. See ICJ Communiqué 99/34 (June 23, 1999).

5   *Id.*

6   *Id.*

7   Application of Croatia filed in the ICJ Registry on July 2. *See* ICJ Communiqué 99/38 (July 2, 1999).

8   Application of Pakistan filed in the ICJ Registry on September 21. *See* ICJ Communiqué 99/43 (Sept. 21, 1999).

9   Application of Nicaragua filed in the ICJ Registry on December 8. *See* ICJ Communiqué 99/52 (Dec. 8, 1999).

10 *See* ICJ Communiqué 99/04 (Feb. 16, 1999); ICJ Rules of Court, Art. 38, para. 5, *reprinted in* 73 AJIL 748, 761 (1979).

(*Nigeria v. Cameroon*) (hereinafter *Request for Interpretation*); *Sovereignty over Pulau Ligitan and Pulau Sipadan (Indonesia/Malaysia)*; and *Ahmadou Sadio Diallo (Republic of Guinea v. Democratic Republic of the Congo)*. In addition, one advisory proceeding was still pending, *Difference Relating to Immunity from Legal Process of a Special Rapporteur of the Commission on Human Rights* (hereinafter *Difference Relating to Immunity*). No cases were brought or pending before any chamber of the Court.

Pleadings

In 1999 pleadings were filed in the following instances. On February 22, Yugoslavia filed its Rejoinder in the *Genocide (Bosnia)* case. On March 10, Iran filed its Reply in the *Oil Platforms* case. The United Kingdom and the United States each filed a Counter-Memorial in the *Lockerbie Cases* on March 31. Qatar and Bahrain each filed a Reply in *Maritime Delimitation and Territorial Questions between Qatar and Bahrain* on May 30. On May 31, Nigeria filed a Counter-Memorial in *Land and Maritime Boundary between Cameroon and Nigeria*. On August 16, in the same case, Cameroon and Nigeria filed their written observations on Equatorial Guinea's application for permission to intervene, filed on June 30. On September 16, Germany filed a Memorial in the *LaGrand Case*. Finally, Indonesia and Malaysia each filed a Memorial in *Sovereignty over Pulau Ligitan and Pulau Sipadan* on November 2.

Orders

A record-breaking thirty-five Orders were made by the Court (but none by the president or the vice president) in 1999, most of which concerned time limits.[11]

---

11   Full Court Orders fixing time limits were issued in *LaGrand Case*, 1999 ICJ REP. 28 (Mar. 5), *Lockerbie Cases* (June 29, two separate Orders), *Land and Maritime Boundary between Cameroon and Nigeria* (June 30), *Legality of Use of Force* (June 30, eight separate Orders), *Genocide (Croatia)* case (Sept. 14), *Armed Activities on the Territory of the Congo* (Oct. 21, three separate Orders), *Aerial Incident* (Nov. 19) and *Ahmadou Sadio Diallo* (Nov. 25). Orders extending time limits were issued in the cases concerning *Maritime Delimitation and Territorial Questions between Qatar and Bahrain*, 1999 ICJ REP. 3 (Feb. 17 (also placing on record Qatar's decision to disregard 82 documents the authenticity of which was challenged by Bahrain)), *Land and Maritime Boundary between Cameroon and Nigeria*, 1999 ICJ REP. 24 (Mar. 3), and *Sovereignty over Pulau Ligitan and Pulau Sipadan* (Sept.

The Court indicated provisional measures against the United States in its unanimous Order of March 3 issued in the *LaGrand Case*.[12] On June 2, the Court issued similar Orders in the ten cases filed by Yugoslavia against certain NATO member states rejecting Yugoslavia's request for the indication of provisional measures in each instance due to lack of *prima facie* jurisdiction and ordering that the cases against Spain and the United States be removed from the General List.[13] The Court's Order of June 30 upheld the admissibility of the counterclaims filed by Nigeria in *Land and Maritime Boundary between Cameroon and Nigeria*.[14] On October 21, the Court issued a unanimous Order permitting Equatorial Guinea to intervene as a non-party in the same case.[15]

Hearings

In 1999 the full Court held public sittings (hearings) on the merits in *Kasikili/ Sedudu Island* (February 15 to March 5) and on Yugoslavia's requests for provisional measures in the ten cases concerning *Legality of Use of Force* involving various NATO member states (May 10-12).

Decisions

In 1999 the Court issued one Advisory Opinion and handed down one decision on a request for interpretation and another on the merits of a case. The Court's Judgment of March 25 declared inadmissible Nigeria's request for an interpretation of the Court's Judgment (preliminary objections) in *Land and Maritime Boundary between Cameroon and Nigeria (Cameroon v. Nigeria)*.[16] On April 29, the Court issued its Advisory Opinion in *Difference Relating to Immunity*.[17] Finally, on December 13, the Court handed down its Judgment on the merits of the *Kasikili/Sedudu Island (Botswana/Namibia)* case, finding, by eleven votes to four, that Kasikili/Sedudu Island forms part of the territory of Botswana.[18]

---

14).
12   1999 ICJ REP. 9. *See* ICJ Communiqué 99/09 (Mar. 3, 1999) and ICJ Communiqué 99/09*bis* (Mar. 5, 1999).
13   *See* ICJ Communiqués 99/23-33 (June 2, 1999).
14   *See* ICJ Communiqué 99/37 (July 2, 1999).
15   *See* ICJ Communiqué 99/44 (Oct. 22, 1999).
16   1999 ICJ REP. 31. *See also* ICJ Communiqués 99/14-14*bis* (Mar. 25, 1999).
17   1999 ICJ REP. 62. *See also* ICJ Communiqués 99/16-16*bis* (Apr. 29, 1999).
18   *See* ICJ Communiqués 99/53-53*bis* (Dec. 13, 1999).

TRIENNIAL ELECTIONS

During the regular triennial elections held at United Nations Headquarters in New York on November 3, the General Assembly and the Security Council elected Awn Shawkat Al-Khasawneh (Jordan) to occupy from February 6, 2000 the seat held for one nine-year term by Vice President Christopher Weeramantry (Sri Lanka), who was not reelected. Judges Gilbert Guillaume (France), Raymond Ranjeva (Madagascar), Rosalyn Higgins (United Kingdom) and Gonzalo Parra-Aranguren (Venezuela) were all reelected.[19] The following Judges also remained as Members of the Court (in order of seniority): Shigeru Oda (Japan); Mohammed Bedjaoui (Algeria); Géza Herczegh (Hungary); Shi Jiuyong (China); Carl-August Fleischhauer (Germany); Abdul Koroma (Sierra Leone); Vladlen Vereshchetin (Russian Federation); Pieter Kooijmans (the Netherlands); and Francisco Rezek (Brazil).

On September 20, it was announced that Registrar Eduardo Valencia-Ospina (Colombia), who had been the head of the Court's Registry since 1987, had informed President Schwebel of his decision to leave office on February 5, 2000, one day before the expiration of Judge Schwebel's term as president.[20] The decision of President Schwebel to resign effective February 29, 2000, was announced on December 15.[21] His regular term as a Member of the Court otherwise would have expired on February 5, 2006.

PRESIDENT'S ADDRESS

On October 26, on the occasion of the presentation of the Court's annual report, Judge Stephen M. Schwebel addressed the General Assembly of the United Nations for the last time as ICJ president.[22] Referring to the recent one

---

19 *See* ICJ Communiqué 99/47 (Nov. 3, 1999).

20 *See* ICJ Communiqué 99/42 (Sept. 20, 1999).

21 *See* ICJ Communiqué 99/54 (Dec. 15, 1999). The Security Council, by resolution 1278 adopted on November 30, 1999, decided that the election to fill the vacancy caused by President Schwebel's resignation would be held in New York on March 2, 2000.

22 The full text of the Address to the General Assembly of October 26, 1999, by the President of the International Court of Justice, Judge Stephen M. Schwebel, is available at the ICJ's Web site, *supra* note 1. *See also* ICJ Communiqué 99/46 (Oct. 26, 1999); UN Doc. A/54/PV.39 (1999).

hundredth anniversary of the first of the Hague Peace Conferences that laid the basis for the creation of a permanent court of international justice, he emphasized that the Court, as a body that is universal in its clientele and composition, can – and does, in practice – fundamentally foster peace through the adjudicated settlement of international disputes and the development of the body of international law. The steady increase of cases brought before the Court has raised the hope of wider adherence to the Court's compulsory jurisdiction through jurisdictional clauses in treaties and the Optional Clause contained in Article 36 of the Court's Statute – which, in President Schwebel's view, should be standard practice. He welcomed the recent proliferation of international courts and tribunals, as they make international law more effective by endowing legal obligations with the means of their determination and enforcement. In this context, he suggested that there might be virtue in enabling other international tribunals to request, through the Security Council or the General Assembly, advisory opinions of the Court on issues of international law arising before such tribunals that are important to the unity of international law. He proposed that a special committee be created within the United Nations to act as a medium for such requests.

President Schwebel announced that, as part of the Court's ongoing review of its work methods,[23] it has embarked on revision of the Rules of Court with a view to accelerating the judicial process. He suggested that parties be given less time for oral argument before the Court, following the practice introduced in advisory proceedings.

Finally, President Schwebel made a plea for what he called the repair of the financial fabric of the United Nations, which has been upset by the failure of member states to pay their assessments. He pointed out that the binding character of those assessments, which are determined by the General Assembly in the exercise of the authority expressly assigned to it by the UN Charter, in particular Article 17, paragraph 2, was affirmed by the Court in 1962.[24] In his view, the failure to comply with those terms transgresses the principles of free consent, good faith and *pacta sunt servanda* that are at the heart of international law and relations.

---

23   *See* ICJ Communiqué 98/14 (Apr. 6, 1998).

24   *See* Certain Expenses of the United Nations (Article 17, paragraph 2, of the Charter), 1962 ICJ REP. 151 (Advisory Opinion of July 20) (holding that assessments by General Assembly for expenditures authorized by it and incurred in connection with UN peacekeeping operations in the Congo were expenses of the organization and legally binding on member states). *See also World Court Chief Faults U.S. Over Its U.N. Dues*, N.Y. TIMES, Oct. 31, 1999, at A6.

Power to indicate provisional measures proprio motu – *absence of oral hearings* – prima facie *jurisdiction* – *U.S. failure of notification to detained German nationals under Vienna Convention on Consular Relations*

LaGrand Case (Germany v. United States)

Provisional Measures, Order
1999 icj Rep. 9
International Court of Justice, March 3, 1999

On Tuesday evening, March 2, 1999, Germany filed an Application in the Registry of the International Court of Justice instituting proceedings against the United States of America over a dispute concerning alleged violations by the U.S. of the Vienna Convention on Consular Relations (Vienna Convention)[1] with respect to the case of Karl and Walter LaGrand, two German nationals convicted of murder in Arizona. Germany simultaneously submitted a request for the indication of provisional measures pursuant to Article 41 of the Court's Statute, asking the Court to order the United States to take all measures at its disposal to ensure that Walter LaGrand, who at that time was scheduled for execution in Arizona on March 4, not be executed pending the final decision in the proceedings in The Hague.[2] Germany's request resulted in the Order discussed below.[3]

The violations of the Vienna Convention were said to arise out of the alleged failure by the state of Arizona, the U.S. state in which the LaGrand brothers were arrested, charged, tried, convicted for the murder of a bank

---

1   Convention on Consular Relations, done at Vienna, Apr. 24, 1963, 21 UST 77, 596 UNTS 261. Both Germany and the United States are parties to the Convention. The LaGrand brothers were born in Germany to a German mother and were later adopted by a U.S. serviceman who brought them to the United States at an early age.

2   Walter LaGrand's brother Karl Hinze was executed in Arizona on February 24, 1999, despite all appeals for clemency and diplomatic interventions by the German Government at the highest level.

3   *See also* William J. Aceves' summary in 93 AJIL 924 (1999). For a range of views and commentaries on the decisions of the ICJ and U.S. courts relating to the similar *Breard* case that was on the 1998 docket, see *"Agora: Breard,"* 92 AJIL 666-712 (1998) and William J. Aceves' summary in 92 AJIL 517 (1998).

129

P.H.F. Bekker, World Court Decisions at the Turn of the Millennium (1997-2001), p. 129-136.
© 2002 *Kluwer Law International. Printed in the Netherlands.*

manager during a robbery attempt in Arizona in 1982 and sentenced to death in 1984, to advise them of their right to communicate with, and receive assistance from, the consular officers of Germany and to advise such officers of their arrest and detention.[4] Germany, which did not learn of the detention of the LaGrand brothers until 1992,[5] asked the Court to declare that the criminal liability imposed upon the LaGrand brothers violated international legal obligations and was void and should be recognized as such by the U.S. legal authorities. Germany also asked the Court to hold that the United States must provide reparation in the form of compensation and satisfaction for the earlier execution of Karl Hinze LaGrand. It sought to have the conviction and death penalty imposed upon Walter LaGrand revoked by demanding the re-establishment of the situation that existed before the United States, as the country responsible for the acts or omissions of its federal states, failed to provide the notification required by the Vienna Convention. In this connection, Germany asked the Court to declare that the United States should provide Germany with a guarantee of the non-repetition of the alleged illegal acts.

During a meeting with the representatives of both parties convened by Vice President Weeramantry early on Wednesday morning, March 3, 1999, the representative of Germany informed the Court that, Arizona governor Jane Dee Hull having rejected a recommendation by her state's Mercy Committee for a stay of execution, Walter LaGrand would be executed that same day at 3:00 p.m. (Arizona time). In the light of the extreme urgency of the case, he requested that the Court indicate provisional measures *proprio motu* without holding any hearing. However, the U.S. objected to a procedure in which the two parties would not be duly heard following a very recent request. It also

---

4   Art. 36(1)(b) of the Vienna Convention, *supra* note 1, provides that the competent authorities of the receiving state have an active duty to inform a detained national of the sending state of his right to communicate with the consular officers of the sending state and must permit such detainee without delay to communicate with the relevant consular post.

5   Germany had accepted the contention of the authorities of the state of Arizona that they had been unaware of the German nationality of the LaGrand brothers until the Arizona State Attorney admitted during proceedings before the Arizona Mercy Committee held on February 23, 1999, that the authorities had been aware since 1982 that the two detainees were German nationals. *See* 1999 ICJ REP. 9, at 10, para. 3.

pointed out that the case had been the subject of lengthy state and federal court proceedings in the United States.[6]

At 7:00 p.m. local time on March 3, 1999, within 24 hours from having received Germany's request, the Court issued an Order ruling, unanimously, that, pending final judgment in the case, the U.S. should take all measures at its disposal to prevent Walter LaGrand's execution.[7]

At the outset, the Court had to determine whether Article I of the Vienna Convention's Optional Protocol concerning the Compulsory Settlement of Disputes of April 24, 1963,[8] on which Germany sought to base the Court's jurisdiction, appeared, *prima facie*, to afford a basis on which its jurisdiction might be founded. "In the light of the requests submitted by Germany in its Application and of the submissions made therein,"[9] the Court was satisfied that a dispute existed with regard to the application of the Convention within the meaning of Article I of the Optional Protocol. Consequently, the Court found that, *prima facie*, it had jurisdiction to decide the dispute brought by Germany.[10]

Addressing the issue of timing, the Court noted that the sound administration of justice dictates that a request for the indication of provisional measures be submitted "in good time." Given that Germany did not become fully aware of the facts of the case until February 24, 1999, and had pursued diplomatic action since that time, the Court was willing to make use, for the first time ever, of the power conferred upon it by Article 75, paragraph 1, of the Rules of Court to indicate provisional measures *proprio motu* and, in the light of the extreme urgency of the case, without holding oral hearings.[11]

---

6   *Id.* at 13, para. 12. *See also* Sean D. Murphy, *Contemporary Practice of the United States relating to International Law*, 93 AJIL 628, 644 (1999); Shabtai Rosenne, *Controlling Interlocutory Aspects of Proceedings in the International Court of Justice*, 94 AJIL 307, at 310 (2000).

7   *See* 1999 ICJ REP. 9. The Court's Order was followed by another one, issued on March 8, 1999, whereby it ordered Germany to file a Memorial by September 16, 1999, and the United States to file a Counter-Memorial by March 27, 2000. *See* 1999 ICJ REP. 28.

8   Art. I reads: "Disputes arising out of the interpretation or application of the Convention shall lie within the compulsory jurisdiction of the International Court of Justice and may accordingly be brought before the Court by an application made by the party to the dispute being a Party to the present Protocol."

9   1999 ICJ REP. 9, at 14, para. 17.

10 *Id.*, para. 18.

11 *Id.*, paras. 19-21.

The Court next considered that its power to indicate provisional measures of protection under Article 41 of the Statute in cases of urgency is intended to preserve the respective rights of the parties pending its decision. This power presupposes that irreparable prejudice is not caused to the rights that are the subject of the dispute in pending proceedings. The Court was satisfied that Walter LaGrand's execution scheduled for March 4, 1999, would cause irreparable harm to the rights claimed by Germany.[12]

Finally, the Court pointed out that the issues in this case did not concern the entitlement of the federal states of the United States, including Arizona, to resort to the death penalty "for the most heinous crimes."[13] The Court emphasized that its function is not to act as a universal supreme court of criminal appeal, but to resolve international legal disputes between sovereign states.

In the light of the above considerations, the Court found that the particular circumstances of the case required it to indicate, "as a matter of the greatest urgency and without any other proceedings," the provisional measures requested by Germany.[14] The Court thus ordered the United States to take all measures at its disposal to ensure that Walter LaGrand not be executed pending the final decision in these proceedings and to inform the Court of all the measures taken by the United States in implementation of the Court's Order.[15] In addition, the Court ordered the U.S. Government to transmit its Order to the governor of the state of Arizona, considering that she is obligated to act in conformity with the international undertakings of the United States and that the latter's international responsibility is triggered by the action of the competent organs and authorities acting in the United States, whatever they may be.[16]

* * * *

This is the second case related to alleged U.S. violations of the Vienna Convention on Consular Relations to reach the International Court within one year, the first such case having been filed by Paraguay against the same respondent

---

12   *Id.* at 14-15, paras. 22-24.
13   *Id.* at 15, para. 25.
14   *Id.*, para. 26.
15   *Id.* at 16, para. 29 (operative paragraph).
16   *Id.*, para. 28.

in April 1998.[17] Similar to the *Breard* case, the Court merely needed to satisfy itself that it had *prima facie* jurisdiction on the basis of (i) the existence of a dispute between Germany and the United States as to the application of the Vienna Convention within the meaning of Article I of the Optional Protocol; and (ii) there being urgency and a risk of irremediable harm to the subject matter of the case. An Order of this kind cannot be taken itself as establishing jurisdiction in a case; it does not preclude a subsequent finding that the Court lacks jurisdiction or that the application is inadmissible. In other words, the Court's Order left unaffected any future findings of the Court on its jurisdiction, the admissibility of Germany's Application or the merits.

The governor of Arizona ignored the Court's Order and Walter LaGrand was executed by lethal gas on March 4, 1999, after a last-minute appeal by Germany was rejected by the U.S. Supreme Court.[18] In his letter filed with the U.S. Supreme Court with regard to LaGrand's last-minute appeal, the U.S. solicitor general, who is the official representative of the U.S. Government before the high court, asserted that "an order of the International Court of Justice indicating provisional measures is not binding and does not furnish a basis for judicial relief."[19] LaGrand's execution triggered the non-compliance by the United States with the Court's Order of March 3, 1999. By not addressing the question of the legal ramifications of such non-compliance within the framework of the Court's Statute and the United Nations Charter of which it forms an integral part, a question which arose prominently in the aftermath of the Court's almost identical Order in the *Breard* case, the Court missed another opportunity to pronounce itself in explicit terms on whether or not provisional measures Orders are binding. From this perspective, the *LaGrand* Order must be considered disappointing notwithstanding the Court's concluding statements about the international responsibility of the United States being

---

17 *See* Application of Paraguay filed in the ICJ Registry on April 3, 1998 [hereinafter *Breard* case]. 1998 ICJ REP. 248 (Order of Apr. 9). The *Breard* case was discontinued by the Court's Order of November 10, 1998. *See* 1998 ICJ REP. 426.

18 *See* Germany v. United States, 119 S.Ct. 1016 (1999). Germany brought this action seeking a temporary restraining order to enforce the ICJ Order. Given that the German citizen involved was not an ambassador or consul, the Supreme Court found that Germany's ability to assert a claim against a U.S. state in the United States was without evident support in the Vienna Convention and in probable contravention of the Eleventh Amendment to the U.S. Constitution. The high court also cited the tardiness of the German pleas and the jurisdictional barriers that they implicated as grounds for its refusal to exercise jurisdiction over the case.

19 *See* Murphy, *supra* note 6, at 646.

engaged by "the action of the competent organs and authorities acting in that State."[20] Clearly, the actions, or inaction, of the U.S. solicitor general, the U.S. Supreme Court and, in the final resort, the governor of Arizona all fall within that category.

In the light of the Court's jurisprudence, the failure by the U.S. to stay Walter LaGrand's execution was of a kind that undermined respect for the judicial process in international relations given that it frustrated the ability of the ICJ to grant part of the relief sought by Germany should it later uphold its jurisdiction and the applicant's claim. One of the main reasons underlying the Court's unanimous Order was the fact that LaGrand's execution "would cause irreparable harm to the rights claimed by Germany in this particular case."[21] Given the precedent set by the *Breard* and *LaGrand* Orders, one may expect sovereign states to consider applying to the Hague Court in future circumstances similar to the ones prevailing in these two cases, even though the desired result has been consistently frustrated by the action, or inaction, of state and federal U.S. authorities and the U.S. Supreme Court. From this perspective, the Order issued in the *LaGrand Case* confirmed an important precedent introduced by the Court's Order of April 9, 1998 in the *Breard* case to which the Court likely will adhere, if only for reasons of judicial consistency.

The dual novelty represented by this case lies in the fact that the Court, for the first time in its history, employed the power assigned to it by Article 75, paragraph 1, of the Rules of Court to indicate provisional measures by its own motion (*proprio motu*) in response to a request for provisional measures *and* without offering both parties a hearing to state their views. In the Court's view, its power in this respect is clearly established and may be used irrespective of whether or not it has been seised by the parties of a request for

---

20 1999 ICJ REP. 9, at 16, para. 28. Obviously, this consideration was added by the Court in response to the aftermath of its similar unsuccessful Order in the *Breard* case one year earlier where the governor of the Commonwealth of Virginia and the U.S. Supreme Court went against the Court's Order of April 9, 1998.

21 *Id.* at 15, para. 24. In the comparable passage in the Court's Order in the *Breard* case, the Court considered that "execution would render it impossible for the Court to render the relief that Paraguay seeks and thus cause irreparable harm to the rights it claims." 1998 ICJ REP. 248, at 257, para. 37. In other words, whereas the Court in 1998 focused on the relief sought *and* the harm caused, in 1999 it relied only on the latter element. This difference in wording probably was caused by the absence of hearings in which the claims and arguments of the parties could be expressed.

the indication of provisional measures. In the event of extreme urgency, it may even be used without holding oral hearings.[22]

The case raises important procedural questions. Whereas in the *Breard* case the Court relied on the clearly opposing views of Paraguay and the United States, expressed during oral hearings, with regard to the question of what remedies are available under the Vienna Convention in concluding that it was confronted with a dispute with regard to the application of the Convention, in the instant case the Court reached this conclusion solely "in the light of the requests submitted by Germany in its Application and of the submissions made therein."[23] In other words, the Court relied entirely on Germany's initial written contentions without regard to the views of the respondent, which the full Court had not, and could not have, heard, given its decision to proceed without oral proceedings. This practice is questionable in the light of the Court's consistent jurisprudence requiring the existence of a legal dispute, traditionally defined as a conflict of legal views, between the parties involved. According to this jurisprudence, the mere contention by an applicant that a dispute exists has been held to be insufficient in order validly to establish the Court's jurisdiction, even *prima facie*.[24]

President Schwebel, who was disqualified from acting as president in this case due to the fact that he shares the nationality of the respondent in the case, gave expression of his "profound reservations about the procedures followed both by the Applicant and the Court" and to his hope that this Order will not form a precedent. His statements indicate that he might not have allowed the procedure followed in this Order to come into play had another respondent been before the Court and had he not been disqualified from exercising the function of the presidency in the case. Judge Schwebel found support in the literature for his view that only in the event that the Court is *not* confronted with a request for interim measures by one of the parties may it have resort to the power assigned to it in Article 75, paragraph 1, of the Rules of Court to indicate interim measures *proprio motu*.[25] In his view, once a party specifi-

---

22   1999 ICJ REP. 9, at 14, para. 21.

23   *Id.* at 14, para. 17.

24   *See*, e.g., East Timor (Port. v. Austl.), 1995 ICJ REP. 90, at 100, para. 22 (June 30) (citing South West Africa (Ethiopia v. South Africa; Liberia v. South Africa), Preliminary Objections, Judgment, 1962 ICJ REP. 319, at 328 (Dec. 21) and Interpretation of Peace Treaties with Bulgaria, Hungary and Romania, First Phase, 1950 ICJ REP. 65, at 74 (Advisory Opinion of Mar. 30)).

25   *See* separate opinion of President Schwebel, 1999 ICJ REP. 9, at 21-22 (citing JERZY SZTUCKI, INTERIM MEASURES IN THE HAGUE COURT 158 (1983)).

cally requests interim measures, Article 74 of the Rules is triggered, including its requirement for "a *hearing* which will afford *the parties* an opportunity of being represented at it."[26] But this Order indicates that this view is not supported by the majority of the Court.

The principal difference between this Order and the one issued in the *Breard* case is not only that no hearings were held in the *LaGrand Case* (due mainly to the fact of the extreme urgency in this case) and that it contained a statement on state responsibility,[27] but lies in the innovation contained in the *dispositif* of the Order in the *LaGrand Case*: the measures indicated in the latter Order not only contained the two familiar elements included in the *Breard* Order, according to which the respondent is to take all measures at its disposal to ensure that a certain event (here, the execution of a convicted foreigner) does not take place pending the final decision in the main proceedings and is to inform the Court of all the measures which it has taken in implementation of the Court's Order, the Court also ordered the respondent to transmit its Order to the authorities of the state concerned.[28] Thus, the United States can be said to have complied with at least the transmittal element of the provisional measures indicated by the Court's Order.

---

26   ICJ Rules of Court, Art. 74, para. 3, *reprinted in* 73 AJIL 748, 761 (1979) (emphasis added).
27   *See supra* note 21.
28   *Cf. Breard* Order, 1998 ICJ REP. 248, at 258, para. 41 (Apr. 9) and *LaGrand Case* Order, 1999 ICJ REP. 9, at 16, para. 29 (Mar. 3).

*Request by Nigeria for interpretation of judgment – jurisdiction to enter-
tain a request for interpretation of a judgment on preliminary objections –
conditions for admissibility – primacy of the principle of* res judicata *–
principle that each party bear its own costs*

REQUEST FOR INTERPRETATION OF THE JUDGMENT OF 11 JUNE 1998 IN
THE CASE CONCERNING THE *LAND AND MARITIME BOUNDARY BETWEEN
CAMEROON AND NIGERIA (CAMEROON V. NIGERIA)*, PRELIMINARY
OBJECTIONS (Nigeria v. Cameroon)

Judgment
1999 ICJ REP. 31
International Court of Justice, March 25, 1999

In a separate case filed by the Federal Republic of Nigeria (Nigeria) against
the Republic of Cameroon (Cameroon) on October 28, 1998, Nigeria requested
the Court to interpret the Judgment delivered by it on June 11, 1998, in the
case brought by Cameroon against Nigeria on March 29, 1994, concerning a
dispute over the land and maritime boundary between the two states.[1] The
Court's June 11, 1998 Judgment rejected Nigeria's preliminary objections
concerning the Court's jurisdiction and the admissibility of Cameroon's Application. Nigeria sought a declaration from the Court that, with regard to Nigeria's
international responsibility for certain alleged incursions by Nigerian groups
and armed forces into Cameroon's territory along the frontier between the two
countries referred to by Cameroon, the dispute before the Court is confined
to incidents specifically mentioned in Cameroon's Application of March 29,
1994, as amended on June 6, 1994 (Application), and that Cameroon could
present only additional facts and legal considerations relating to those specified
in its Application. In Nigeria's view, the June 11, 1998 Judgment was unclear
in that it failed to specify which of a number of incidents invoked by Cameroon
subsequent to the filing of its Application were to be considered properly as
falling within the scope of the merits of the case before the Court. Cameroon
asked the Court, primarily, to declare Nigeria's request for interpretation
inadmissible and, alternatively, to declare that Cameroon is entitled to rely on

---

1   *See* 1998 ICJ REP. 275 (June 11).

P.H.F. Bekker, World Court Decisions at the Turn of the Millennium (1997-2001), p. 137-143.
© 2002 *Kluwer Law International. Printed in the Netherlands.*

all facts, irrespective of their date, that go to establish the alleged continuing violation by Nigeria of its international obligations. In its Judgment of March 25, 1999, the Court, by 13 votes to three, declared inadmissible Nigeria's request for interpretation.[2]

The Court first had to determine whether it had jurisdiction over Nigeria's request for interpretation. Referring to Cameroon's allegations made in its Application and subsequently of Nigeria's responsibility for incursions by Nigerian groups and armed forces into Cameroon's territory at the Bakassi Peninsula and Lake Chad and along the frontier between the two countries, Nigeria claimed that the June 11, 1998 Judgment did not specify which of the incidents invoked by Cameroon were to be considered as part of the merits of the case before the Court. According to Nigeria, the Judgment did not make clear whether Cameroon could introduce into the proceedings new incidents subsequent to its Application, i.e., after June 6, 1994. In its view, Cameroon could invoke only additional *facts* in amplification of incidents averted to until June 6, 1994, and could not rely on entirely new *incidents*. Cameroon, on the other hand, pointed out that the Court already had rejected Nigeria's preliminary objections of lack of jurisdiction and admissibility and that the parties simply had to take note of the June 11, 1998 Judgment. In Cameroon's view, there also were serious doubts about the possibility of bringing a request for interpretation of a decision handed down following incidental proceedings (here, concerning preliminary objections).[3]

The Court confirmed that, by virtue of the second sentence of Article 60 of its Statute, it has jurisdiction to entertain requests for interpretation of any

---

2   *See* 1999 ICJ REP. 31, at 40, para. 19(1) (Mar. 25). Vice President Weeramantry and Judge Koroma dissented, as did Judge *ad hoc* Ajibola appointed by Nigeria. Cameroon filed its written observations on Nigeria's request on November 13, 1998. No hearings were held, constituting the first time in the history of the World Court that a Judgment was not preceded by hearings. *See* Shabtai Rosenne, *Controlling Interlocutory Aspects of Proceedings in the International Court of Justice*, 94 AJIL 307, 308 (2000). The Court considered that it had sufficient information on the positions of the parties and thus did not deem it necessary to invite them to furnish further explanations, at a hearing or in writing, as the Rules of Court empower it to do. *See* ICJ Rules of Court, Art. 98, para. 4, *reprinted in* 73 AJIL 748, 761 (1979). In Rosenne's view, *id.*, Article 98 of the Rules cannot derogate from the general rule embodied in the Statute according to which the procedure in a case shall consist of a written and an oral part. *See* ICJ STATUTE Art. 43, para. 1.
3   *See* 1999 ICJ REP. 31, at 34-35, paras. 8-9.

judgment rendered by it, irrespective of the type of judgment concerned.[4] Thus, a judgment on preliminary objections can be the object of a request for interpretation under Article 60. The Court was satisfied that Nigeria's request for interpretation concerned the operative part of the June 11, 1998 Judgment to which the request related and that, although the request also concerned the reasons underlying that Judgment set out in paragraphs 98 to 101, those reasons were inseparable from the operative part.[5]

Having upheld its jurisdiction, the Court next considered the admissibility of Nigeria's request for interpretation. It observed that the real purpose of such a request must be solely to obtain a clarification of the meaning and scope of what the Court has decided with binding force. In other words, the request must not seek to obtain an answer to questions not so decided lest it nullify the principle of the finality, the so-called *res judicata*, of the Court's Judgments. The Court's task is to maintain the primacy of this principle.[6] It noted that its decision of June 11, 1998, already clearly dealt with and rejected Nigeria's complaint that Cameroon had to confine itself, in relation to its submissions concerning alleged incidents involving Nigeria's international responsibility, to the facts presented in its Application and that additions presented subsequently by Cameroon had to be disregarded. The Court recalled that it was satisfied in 1998 that Cameroon had not transformed the dispute brought before it into another dispute which is different in character from the one introduced by Cameroon's Application. The subsequent introduction into the proceedings of additional incidents and facts, between which the June 11, 1998 decision did not distinguish, is governed by that principle.[7]

The Court concluded that it was unable in 1999 to entertain Nigeria's submission that the dispute brought before the Court did not include any alleged incidents other than (at most) those specified in Cameroon's Application,

---

4   According to the second sentence, "[i]n the event of dispute as to the meaning or scope of the judgment, the Court shall construe it upon the request of any party." Article 98, paragraph 1 of the Rules of Court, which supplements Article 60, provides that "[i]n the event of dispute as to the meaning or scope of a judgment any party may make a request for its interpretation." *Id.* at 35, para. 10.

5   *Id.* at 35-36, para. 11.

6   *Id.* at 36-37, para. 12 (citing the two earlier ICJ precedents, namely, Request for Interpretation of the Judgment of 20 November 1950 in the *Asylum Case* (Col. v. Peru), Judgment, 1950 ICJ REP. 395, at 402 (Nov. 27), and Application for Revision and Interpretation of the Judgment of 24 February 1982 in the Case concerning the Continental Shelf (Tunisia/Libyan Arab Jamahiriya) (Tun. v. Libya), Judgment, 1985 ICJ REP. 192, at 223, para. 56 (Dec. 10)).

7   *Id.* at 38, para. 15.

without calling into question the *res judicata* effect of its 1998 decision. For the same reason, the Court was unable to entertain Nigeria's other complaints seeking to remove from the Court's consideration elements of fact and law that it already had authorized Cameroon to present or that Cameroon had yet to put forward. On this basis, the Court, by 13 votes to three, declared inadmissible Nigeria's request for interpretation. In the light of this conclusion, the Court determined that there was no need for it to examine whether there existed a dispute as to the meaning or scope of the June 11, 1998 Judgment, as required by Article 60 of the Statute. Finally, the Court unanimously rejected Cameroon's submission requesting that Nigeria be charged with the additional costs caused to Cameroon by Nigeria's request, stating that it saw no reason to depart in this case from the basic principle laid down in Article 64 of the Statute according to which each party is to bear its own costs in contentious proceedings.[8]

* * * *

This was the first time in the Court's history that it was seised of a request for the interpretation of a judgment on preliminary objections while the related proceedings on the merits were still pending. Even though it could be said that Nigeria's request related to issues concerning her alleged international responsibility, which belong to the merits and can be answered only by the Court in its decision on the merits, the Court saw no objection in asserting jurisdiction over such a request.

In 1950, when the Court had its first encounter with a request for interpretation, it pointed out that Article 60 of the Statute lays down two conditions for the *admissibility* of such a request: (1) (a) the real purpose of the request must be to obtain an interpretation of the judgment to which the request relates, i.e., its object must be solely to obtain clarification of the meaning and scope of what the Court has decided with binding force and (b) the object of the request cannot be to obtain an answer to questions not so decided; and (2) a dispute must exist as to the meaning or scope of the judgment.[9] The present case turned on the first of these conditions.

---

8   *Id.* at 39-40, paras. 17-18 (citing Application for Review of Judgement No. 158 of the United Nations Administrative Tribunal, 1973 ICJ REP. 166, at 212, para. 98 (Advisory Opinion of July 12)).

9   *See* Request for Interpretation of the Judgment of 20 November 1950 in the *Asylum Case* (Col. v. Peru), Judgment, 1950 ICJ REP. 395 (Nov. 27).

Hudson has commented that the Permanent Court pointed out, in its Judgment on questions of interpretation relating to the *Chorzów Factory Case*, that the object of the provision in Article 60 of the Statute is "to enable the Court to make quite clear the points which had been settled with binding force in a judgment," and that it includes the question "whether a particular point has or has not been decided with binding force." In that case, the Court's predecessor stated that the interpretation adds nothing to the decision and only has "binding force within the limits of what was decided in the judgment construed."[10]

It has been clear from the first interpretation case in the World Court that interpretation cannot go beyond the limits of the judgment, just as the judgment cannot go beyond the submissions of the parties.[11] What were Nigeria's submissions? At the end of the hearings on Nigeria's preliminary objections, Nigeria added one paragraph asking the Court to declare that "any allegations by Cameroon as to State responsibility or reparation on the part of Nigeria in respect of matters referred to in paragraph 17(f) of Cameroon's amending Application of 6 June 1994 are inadmissible." Paragraph 17(f) referred to "repeated incursions of Nigerian groups and armed forces into Cameroonian territory, all along the frontier between the two countries."[12] Nigeria's entire

---

10   MANLEY O. HUDSON, THE PERMANENT COURT OF INTERNATIONAL JUSTICE 1920-1942 – A TREATISE 591 (1943) (citing Interpretation of Judgments Nos. 7 and 8 (Factory at Chorzów), 1927 PCIJ (ser. A), No. 13, 10, 88).

11   This principle, which derives from that of the consent of the parties, is expressed by the so-called *non ultra petita* or *infra petita* rule, according to which a tribunal in its pronouncements must stay within the *petitum* or claim submitted to it and must abstain from deciding points not included in the parties' submissions (see, especially, Corfu Channel (UK v. Alb.), Compensation, Judgment, 1949 ICJ REP. 244, at 249 (Dec. 15); Request for Interpretation of the Judgment of November 20th, 1950 in the *Asylum Case* (Col. v. Peru), Judgment, 1950 ICJ REP. 395, at 402-03 (Nov. 27); Right of Passage over Indian Territory (Port. v. India), Judgment, 1960 ICJ REP. 6, at 30 (Apr. 12); *see also* SHABTAI ROSENNE, 2 THE LAW AND PRACTICE OF THE INTERNATIONAL COURT (1920-1996), at 594-96 (1997); GERALD FITZMAURICE, 2 THE LAW AND PROCEDURE OF THE INTERNATIONAL COURT OF JUSTICE 524-33 (repr. 1995)). *See also* Treaty of Neuilly, Article 179, Annex, Paragraph 4 (Interpretation), Judgment No. 3, 1924 PCIJ (ser. A), No. 3.

12   *See also* ICJ Doc. CR 98/2 (Mar. 3), at 16 ("Nigeria is at this stage simply saying that it has not been told enough about the alleged incidents to be able to decide what its response should be. More importantly, the Court too has been left in ignorance of the facts: the Court is left without any judicial or manageable standards to apply in making a fair and effective judicial determination of the allegations of international responsibility raised by Cameroon. Further judicial pursuit of them

presentation of its sixth preliminary objection centered around the minimum level of particularity required for allegations made against a respondent state, which Nigeria claimed was not satisfied by Cameroon's Application. As Hudson has pointed out, however, "[i]n giving an interpretation, the Court considers no facts other than those *considered* in the judgment under interpretation."[13] Paragraph 99 of the June 11 Judgment, in particular its final words, indicates that the Court already had considered all the necessary facts on which to base its clear statement rejecting Nigeria's arguments relying on Article 38 of the Rules. The Court could not consider any additional facts introduced in Nigeria's request and not considered in the June 11, 1998 Judgment. Thus, it could be said, to paraphrase a statement made by the Court in 1950, that the real object of the questions submitted by Nigeria was to obtain, under the guise of a request for interpretation of jurisdictional issues, a decision on questions relating to its international responsibility. The Court was not called upon by the parties to answer such questions and, in any event, could not do so at the preliminary objections stage. In this respect, Nigeria's request hence might be said to seek a new decision, supplementing the June 11, 1998 Judgment rejecting Nigeria's preliminary objections, in advance of the Court's decision on issues belonging to the merits (i.e., issues of international responsibility).

Paragraph 5 of Nigeria's request stated that the June 11, 1998 Judgment "*does not specify* which of these alleged incidents are to be considered further as part of the merits of the case" (emphasis added). Paragraph 14 complained that the question that Nigeria sought to have answered "*is not resolved* by the Court's judgment on the Preliminary Objections" (emphasis added). Finally, in paragraph 16, Nigeria alleged that "the Court *did not deal expressly* with the question of which alleged incidents properly fall within the scope of the dispute before the Court" (emphasis added). It could be said that, through these statements, Nigeria acknowledged in fact that this question was not resolved, dealt with or answered by the Court and, therefore, according to the Court's jurisprudence, belongs to the category of "questions not so decided" – the answer of which cannot be obtained later through a request for interpretation.

The Court concluded that it did not need to examine whether there was a dispute as to the meaning or scope of the Judgment, as required by Article 60 of the Statute. It is doubtful that such a dispute existed. As the Court pointed out in 1950, "one cannot treat as a dispute ... the mere fact that one Party finds the judgment obscure when the other considers it to be perfectly clear;" instead,

---

would be futile.").

13   Hudson, *supra* note 10, at 591 (emphasis added).

a "dispute requires a divergence of views between the parties on definite points."[14] While the manifestation of the dispute in a specific manner is not required, there appears to be no divergence of views, no difference of opinion, no dispute as to the meaning and scope of the June 11, 1998 Judgment at the time of the filing of Nigeria's Application (October 28, 1998). Paragraph 4 of Nigeria's Application asserted that "Nigeria and Cameroon, either *expressis verbis* or by inference, hold differing views." Nigeria then jumped to the conclusion that "[t]here is accordingly a dispute between them as to the interpretation of the Judgment." But the problem for the applicant in interpretation cases is that the Court is not likely to jump to conclusions, given that it will not want to admit that its decision was unclear or that it contained gaps that are in need of being filled subsequently. It also is unclear on what basis Nigeria founded its statement, contained in paragraph 11 of its request, that "it is apparent from the reply of the Agent of Cameroon ... that Cameroon does not share Nigeria's understanding as to the meaning of the relevant parts of the Court's Judgment." Where are the opposing views? The "reply" referred to, contained in a letter of September 30, 1998, carefully avoided giving the impression that Cameroon agreed that a dispute concerning the meaning or scope of the June 11, 1998 Judgment existed, as opposed to a dispute concerning the admissibility of Nigeria's request. These are two entirely different matters.

If the objective of Nigeria's request for interpretation was to seek to further delay the proceedings instituted by Cameroon in 1994, the Court cannot be said to have cooperated. The Court disposed of Nigeria's request, which introduced a new case, in record time, i.e., within five months of the filing of the request. In his Order of March 3, 1999, President Schwebel was careful to point out, in reply to Nigeria's request for an extension of the time limit for the filing of its Counter-Memorial, that "such a request cannot in itself suffice to justify the extension of a time-limit."[15] In the circumstances of the case, that time limit nonetheless was extended from March 31 to May 31, 1999, conform Nigeria's request.

---

14   Request for Interpretation of the Judgment of 20 November 1950 in the *Asylum Case* (Col. v. Peru), Judgment, 1950 ICJ REP. 395, at 403 (Nov. 27).
15   1999 ICJ REP. 24, at 26 (Order of Mar. 3).

Advisory jurisdiction – Convention on the Privileges and Immunities of the United Nations – immunity from legal process of expert on mission appointed by UN Commission on Human Rights – effect of UN Secretary-General's assertion of immunity – procedural priority to be accorded assertion of immunity in municipal courts

DIFFERENCE RELATING TO IMMUNITY FROM LEGAL PROCESS OF A SPECIAL RAPPORTEUR OF THE COMMISSION ON HUMAN RIGHTS

Advisory Opinion
1999 ICJ Rep. 62
International Court of Justice, April 29, 1999[*]

On August 10, 1998, the United Nations Economic and Social Council (ECOSOC) requested an advisory opinion from the International Court of Justice on the applicability of Article VI, Section 22 of the 1946 Convention on the Privileges and Immunities of the United Nations (General Convention)[1] in

---

[*] Reproduced with permission from 93 AJIL 913 (1999). © The American Society of International Law.

[1] *See Resolutions Adopted by the General Assembly During the First Part of its First Session*, UN Doc. A/64 (1946), at 33. For the text of the Convention, see Convention on the Privileges and Immunities of the United Nations, February 13, 1946, 1 U.N.T.S. 15, UN Doc. ST/LEG/SER.B/10 (1959), at 184 *et seq.* At present, 137 UN member states are parties to the General Convention. Section 22 reads as follows: "Experts (other than officials coming within the scope of Article V) performing missions for the United Nations shall be accorded such privileges and immunities as are necessary for the independent exercise of their functions during the period of their missions, including time spent on journeys in connection with their missions. In particular they shall be accorded: ... *(b)* in respect of words spoken or written and acts done by them in the course of the performance of their mission, immunity from legal process of any kind."
The text of the General Convention was drafted, pursuant to Article 105 of the UN Charter, by the UN Preparatory Commission in 1945 and the initial draft did not contain anything corresponding to the present Article VI, of which Section 22 forms a part. Article VI was added by the Sub-Commission on Privileges and Immunities established by the Sixth Committee of the General Assembly to examine the draft. Consequently, no guidance on Section 22 may be found in the *travaux préparatoires* of the General Convention.

145

P.H.F. Bekker, World Court Decisions at the Turn of the Millennium (1997-2001), p. 145-173.
© 2002 *Kluwer Law International. Printed in the Netherlands.*

the case of Dato' Param Cumaraswamy, a lawyer of Malaysian nationality who lives in Kuala Lumpur and Special Rapporteur on the Independence of Judges and Lawyers of the UN Commission on Human Rights,[2] in connection with certain civil lawsuits instituted against him before Malaysian courts, and on the legal obligations of Malaysia in this case. ECOSOC's request was based on the dispute settlement mechanism laid down in Section 30 of the General Convention. In November 1995, *International Commercial Litigation*, a magazine published in the United Kingdom and circulated in Malaysia, published an interview with Cumaraswamy in which he commented on his investigation, for the Commission on Human Rights, into complaints that a number of corporations had influenced decisions rendered in favor of them by the Malaysian courts.[3] Some plaintiffs who received such favorable rulings sued Cumaraswamy for defamation, claiming total damages in excess of $100 million.[4] Three levels of Malaysian courts refused to uphold Cumaraswamy's immunity from legal process *in limine* in connection with the four defamation lawsuits.[5] They

---

2   Pursuant to Articles 55(c) and 68 of the UN Charter, ECOSOC, by resolution 5(I) of February 16, 1946, supplemented on February 18, 1946, created the Commission on Human Rights as one of ECOSOC's organs.

3   With regard to one specific Malaysian case (the *Ayer Molek* case), Cumaraswamy, who was repeatedly referred to in the article in his official capacity as Special Rapporteur, stated that it looked like "a very obvious, perhaps even glaring example of judge-choosing" and that complaints were rife that "certain highly placed personalities in the business and corporate sectors are able to manipulate the Malaysian system of justice." However, he also stressed that he had not completed his investigation and that it would be unfair to name any of the people involved. *See* Advisory Opinion, *infra* note 8, at 71, paras. 12-13.

4   Four separate law suits were filed on December 12, 1996, July 10, 1997, October 23, 1997, and November 21, 1997, respectively. The summary of the description of the Malaysian court proceedings given below relates only to the first of such suits.

5   On June 28, 1997, the High Court of Malaysia at Kuala Lumpur (Civil Division), the trial court of first instance, rejected Cumaraswamy's petition to set aside the suit on grounds that he is immune from legal process pursuant to Section 22(b) of the General Convention, concluding that it was "unable to hold that the Defendant is absolutely protected by the immunity he claims." *See* MBf Capital Berhard v. Dato' Param Cumaraswamy, Case No. S3-23-68-1996 (unpublished; text on file with the author), at 38 (H.C. Malaysia, Kuala Lumpur) (June 28, 1997) [hereinafter H.C. slip op.]. The court decided to postpone its determination of Cumaraswamy's immunity until after a full trial of the merits of the case and ordered him to file his defense within two weeks from the judgment. On July 8, 1997, the Malaysian Court of Appeal, per its President, heard and rejected the motion for a stay of execution on appeal. The substantive appeal was heard by a three-judge panel on

declined to give effect to various certificates, introduced into the proceedings by Cumaraswamy, in which the Secretary-General of the United Nations asserted immunity and certified that the alleged defamatory words were spoken in the course of the performance of Cumaraswamy's mission for the United Nations.[6]

With the exception of Malaysia, all of the states that participated in the proceedings before the Court strongly supported the Special Rapporteur's

---

August 20-21, 1997, and dismissed by unanimous judgment on October 20, 1997. *See* MBf Capital Berhard v. Dato' Param Cumaraswamy, Case No. W-02-323-1997 (Ct. of App. Malaysia) (Oct. 20, 1997) (unpublished; text on file with the author) [hereinafter C.A. slip op.]. The appeals court was presided over by a judge who also sat on one of the cases on which Cumaraswamy commented in the impugned interview. The judge refused to recuse himself. On February 19, 1998, the Federal Court of Malaysia summarily dismissed, by a unanimous decision, Cumaraswamy's application for leave to admit his appeal as one with merit for appeal. The Federal Court noted that it was not dealing with a sovereign or a full-fledged diplomat, but merely with someone who has to act with a mandate of an unpaid part-time provider of information. It agreed with the lower courts that the issue of immunity from legal process would be decided at the end of a full trial. Subsequently, the Malaysian courts did agree to stay the proceedings pending the outcome of proceedings in The Hague.

6   The High Court denied that the Secretary-General alone possesses the right to determine whether the Special Rapporteur's words were spoken in the course of a mission for the United Nations. In its view, the Secretary-General's certificate was merely an "opinion and has no more probative value than a document which appears wanting in material particulars" and has no binding force upon the court. *See* H.C. slip op., *supra* note 5, at 25. The court determined that neither the General Convention nor the Malaysian implementing legislation conferred any power or authority on the Secretary-General to determine or declare that the Special Rapporteur uttered the alleged defamatory statements in his official capacity. The High Court also found that a certificate filed by the Malaysian Minister for Foreign Affairs on March 12, 1997, which stated that immunity applies "only in respect of words spoken or written and acts done by [the Special Rapporteur] in the course of the performance of his mission" without referring to the Secretary-General's finding, "would appear to be no more than a bland statement as to a state of fact pertaining to the Defendant's status and mandate as a Special Rapporteur and appears to have room for interpretation." *See id.* at 29. The Court of Appeals agreed with the High Court. In its opinion, the General Convention and the Malaysian legislation merely confirm the Secretary-General's power to waive immunity, but they fail to grant him the authority to make the kind of determination of fact he made in his certificate. That factual determination was a question for the Malaysian courts to decide at a later stage. *See* C.A. slip op., *supra* note 5, at 28-30.

immunity.[7] On April 29, 1999, a nearly unanimous Court held that Article VI, Section 22, of the General Convention is applicable to the Special Rapporteur and that he was entitled to immunity from legal process of every kind for the words spoken by him during the impugned interview. Furthermore, the Court held that the Government of Malaysia had the obligation to inform the Malaysian courts of the Secretary-General's assertion of immunity, that such courts had the obligation to deal with the immunity question as a preliminary issue, and that Cumaraswamy must be held financially harmless for the costs imposed upon him by the Malaysian courts. Finally, the Court held that the Malaysian Government must communicate the Court's advisory opinion to the Malaysian courts in order that Malaysia's international obligations be given effect and Cumaraswamy's immunity be respected.[8]

The Court first observed that it had never before received a request for an advisory opinion referring to Article VIII, Section 30, of the General Convention.[9] It explained that Section 30 provides for the *exercise of* the Court's

---

7   In accordance with Article 66, para. 2 of the ICJ Statute, written statements were filed by the UN Secretary-General and by Costa Rica, Germany, Italy, Malaysia, Sweden, the United Kingdom and the United States. The filing of a written statement by Greece on October 12, 1998, and by Luxembourg on October 29, 1998, were also authorized. The Secretary-General and Costa Rica, Malaysia and the United States also filed written comments on the statements pursuant to Article 66, para. 4 of the Statute.

8   *See* Difference Relating to Immunity from Legal Process of a Special Rapporteur of the Commission on Human Rights, 1999 ICJ REP. 62, at 90, para. 67 (Advisory Opinion of Apr. 29) [hereinafter Advisory Opinion].

9   *See id.* at 76, para. 24. Section 30 provides as follows:
     "All differences arising out of the interpretation or application of the present convention shall be referred to the International Court of Justice, unless in any case it is agreed by the parties to have recourse to another mode of settlement. If a difference arises between the United Nations on the one hand and a Member on the other hand, a request shall be made for an advisory opinion on any legal question involved in accordance with Article 96 of the Charter and Article 65 of the Statute of the Court. The opinion given by the Court shall be accepted as decisive by the parties."

     Another case brought before the Court in 1989, representing the first time that ECOSOC requested the Court to give an advisory opinion concerning the applicability of Section 22 to a Special Rapporteur, namely one appointed by the Sub-Commission on Prevention of Discrimination and Protection of Minorities, was brought pursuant to Article 96(2) of the UN Charter and not on the basis of Section 30 of the General Convention. *See* Applicability of Article VI, Section 22, of the Convention on the Privileges and Immunities of the United Nations, 1989 ICJ REP. 177, at 194 para. 47 (Advisory Opinion of Dec. 15) [hereinafter Mazilu Opinion]. *See also* PETER H.F. BEKKER, THE LEGAL POSITION OF INTERGOVERN-

advisory function in the event of a difference between the United Nations and one of its member states. However, the fact that Section 30 stipulates that any opinion rendered pursuant to it "shall be accepted as decisive by the parties" must be distinguished from the advisory nature of the Court's function. The former relates to the particular *effects* to be given to an opinion issued pursuant to Section 30, whereas the latter deals with the Court's *power* to give advisory opinions regulated by Article 96 of the UN Charter and Article 65 of the ICJ Statute.[10] Consequently, the usual requirements for advisory opinions must still be complied with. First, the request must concern a "legal question." As all parties acknowledged in this case, the request related to the interpretation of the General Convention and to its application to the circumstances of Cumaraswamy's case. Second, the legal questions embodied in ECOSOC's request must arise within the scope of that body's activities. In this case, these questions related to the mandate of ECOSOC's Special Rapporteur and were pertinent to the functioning of one of its organs. Finally, in the circumstances of a particular case, the Court's inherent discretionary power may cause it to find compelling reasons not to give an opinion.[11] The Court found none to exist in the present case.

The Court then noted that the participants in the proceedings advanced differing views regarding the question to be answered by the Court. According to Malaysia, its difference with the United Nations related to the question of whether the Secretary-General has the exclusive authority to determine whether

---

MENTAL ORGANIZATIONS – A FUNCTIONAL NECESSITY ANALYSIS OF THEIR LEGAL STATUS AND IMMUNITIES 200 (1994). In 1989, ECOSOC invoked Article 96 of the Charter in a successful effort to circumvent Section 30, to which Romania had attached reservations. In the present case, ECOSOC had no such concerns, given that Malaysia ratified the General Convention without attaching any reservations.

10 *See* Advisory Opinion, *supra* note 8, at 76-77, paras. 25-26 (citing Application for Review of Judgment No. 158 of the United Nations Administrative Tribunal, 1973 ICJ REP. 166, at 171 para. 14 (July 12), Judgments of the Administrative Tribunal of the ILO upon Complaints Made against Unesco, 1956 ICJ REP. 77, at 84 (Oct. 23), and Interpretation of Peace Treaties with Bulgaria, Hungary and Romania, First Phase, 1950 ICJ REP. 65, at 71 (Mar. 30)). *See also* Roberto Ago, *Binding Advisory Opinions of the International Court of Justice*, 85 AJIL 439 (1991), and response by Derek Bowett, 86 AJIL 342 (1992).

11 According to Art. 65, para. 1 of the ICJ Statute: "The Court *may* give an advisory opinion on any legal question at the request of whatever body may be authorized by or in accordance with the Charter of the United Nations to make such a request" (emphasis added). ICJ STATUTE Art. 65, para. 1. *See also* GERALD FITZMAURICE, 2 THE LAW AND PROCEDURE OF THE INTERNATIONAL COURT OF JUSTICE 565-68 (Repr. 1995), calling this the Court's "power of appreciation."

acts of an expert were performed in the course of his or her mission. The arguments that the United Nations advanced centered around the same issue, as did those of the various participating states. However, the Court observed that it is for ECOSOC, and not for the Secretary-General or any member state, to formulate the terms of a question that ECOSOC wishes to ask and the Court is restricted to those terms.[12] In the Court's view, ECOSOC's request was not restricted, as Malaysia argued, to the threshold question whether the Special Rapporteur was and is an "expert on mission" in the sense of Section 22, but also pertained to the consequences of a positive finding in the circumstances of the case.[13]

As to the threshold question of the Special Rapporteur's status, the Court noted that Malaysia became a party to the General Convention on October 28, 1957, without attaching any reservation to Section 22 or any other provision. It recalled that it stated in an earlier case that Section 22 is designed to enable the United Nations to entrust missions to persons who do not have the status of an official of that organization and to guarantee them such privileges and immunities as are necessary for the independent exercise of their functions.[14] In the Mazilu Opinion, the Court concluded that a Special Rapporteur appointed by the Sub-Commission on Prevention of Discrimination and Protection of Minorities and entrusted with a research mission must be regarded as an expert on mission within the meaning of Article VI, Section 22, of the General Convention. The Court found the same to apply to Special Rapporteurs appointed by the Commission on Human Rights, of which the Sub-Commission is a subsidiary organ. What is essential is that these persons have been entrusted with a mission by the United Nations. This entitles them to Section 22 immunity designed to safeguard the independent exercise of their functions. On the basis of Cumaraswamy's mandate given to him by the Commission on

---

12 *See* Advisory Opinion, *supra* note 8, at 79-81, paras. 32-37.

13 *See id.* at 81, paras. 39 and 84, paras. 48-49. The Court was able to consider the circumstances of the Special Rapporteur's case because of a specific element of the question embodied in ECOSOC's request, namely "taking into account the circumstances set out in paragraphs 1 to 15 of the note by the Secretary-General." *See Note by the Secretary-General on Privileges and Immunities of the Special Rapporteur of the Commission on Human Rights on the Independence of Judges and Lawyers*, UN Doc. E/1998/94 and Add. 1 (July 28/Aug. 3, 1998), *reprinted in id.* at 66-71, para. 10.

14 *Id.* at 82, para. 42 (citing Mazilu Opinion, *supra* note 9, 1989 ICJ REP. 177, at 194, para. 47). For a summary of the 1989 opinion, see the case note by Terry Gill in 84 AJIL 742 (1990).

Human Rights in 1994 and extended in 1997,[15] the Court found that he must be regarded as an expert on mission within the meaning of Section 22, a fact acknowledged by Malaysia, and that by virtue of this capacity the immunity provisions of Section 22 were applicable to him when he gave the interview and remained applicable subsequently.[16]

The Court then considered whether the immunity provided for in Section 22(b) of the General Convention applied to Cumaraswamy in the specific circumstances of the case. This called for an examination whether the words used by him in the interview were spoken in the course of the performance of his mission, and whether he was therefore immune from legal process with respect to those words. The Court noted that the UN Secretary-General has a pivotal role to play in the process of determining whether a particular expert on mission is entitled, in the prevailing circumstances, to the immunity provided for in Section 22(b). As the organization's chief administrative officer, he has the authority and the responsibility to exercise the necessary functional protection where required.[17] The Court pointed out that Section 23 of the General Convention provides that "[p]rivileges and immunities are granted to experts in the interests of the United Nations and not for the personal benefit of the individuals themselves." Consequently, the Secretary-General, as the person with the primary responsibility and authority, is protecting the mission with which the expert is entrusted whenever he exercises protection of UN experts.

---

15 The Special Rapporteur's mandate is set forth in resolution 1994/41 adopted by the Commission on Human Rights on March 4, 1994, and endorsed by ECOSOC in its decision 1994/251 of July 22, 1994. By its resolution 1997/23 of April 11, 1997, the Commission on Human Rights renewed the Special Rapporteur's mandate for an additional three years. *See* Advisory Opinion, *supra* note 8, at 83, paras. 44-45. Under his mandate, the Special Rapporteur is expected to (a) inquire into any substantial allegations transmitted to him and report his conclusions thereon; (b) identify and record not only attacks on the independence of the judiciary, lawyers and court officials but also progress achieved in protecting and enhancing their independence; and (c) study important and topical questions of principle with a view to protecting and enhancing the independence of the judiciary and lawyers.

16 The vote on this part of the question was 14-1 (Judge Koroma dissenting). *See* Advisory Opinion, *supra* note 8, at 89, para. 67(1)(*a*). Even if the Special Rapporteur had ceased to be a special rapporteur, the second sentence of Section 22(b) of the General Convention provides that "immunity from legal process shall continue to be accorded notwithstanding that the persons concerned are no longer employed on missions for the United Nations."

17 *See id.* at 84-85, para. 50 (citing Reparation for Injuries Suffered in the Service of the United Nations, 1949 ICJ REP. 174, at 184 (Advisory Opinion of Apr. 11)).

The Court observed that the determination whether a UN agent has acted in the course of the performance of his mission depends upon the facts of a particular case. In this case, the Secretary-General was justified in asserting immunity before the Malaysian authorities for several reasons. First, it has become standard practice for Special Rapporteurs of the Commission on Human Rights to speak to the media about matters pertaining to their investigations, thereby keeping the general public informed of their work. Second, the article made several explicit references to the Special Rapporteur's official capacity.[18] Third, the Commission on Human Rights repeatedly approved of Cumaraswamy's working methods subsequent to the interview and extended his mandate in full awareness of the interview and the lawsuits to which it had given rise. Consequently, the Court was satisfied that Section 22 was applicable to Cumaraswamy not only as a threshold question, but also in the circumstances of the case, entitling him to immunity from legal process of every kind.[19]

Turning to the second part of ECOSOC's question, the Court addressed the legal obligations of Malaysia in this case. Malaysia argued that it was premature to deal with the question because its obligation under Section 22 is one of result and not of means to be employed in achieving that result. It asserted that it had complied with Section 34 of the General Convention[20] and it pointed out

---

18 *See id.* at 71, para. 13 and 85, para. 54. In the impugned article, wherever quoted remarks were attributed to the Special Rapporteur, it was expressly stated that the remarks were made in his capacity as Special Rapporteur and that he had not finished his investigations, and therefore that he had not yet made up his mind with regard to any conclusions to be drawn from such investigations. Thus, the statement of the Malaysian Court of Appeal that "the article in itself does not expressly declare that the defendant was interviewed and spoke the alleged defamatory words as Special Rapporteur" is manifestly incorrect. *See* C.A. slip op., *supra* note 5, at 20.

19 *See id.* at 86, para. 56. The vote on this part of the question was 14-1 (Judge Koroma dissenting). *See id.* at 89, para. 67(1)(*b*). Judge Koroma denied that there was in fact a dispute between Malaysia and the United Nations whether the General Convention applied to the Special Rapporteur as such. In his view, the real question was whether the Secretary-General is vested with exclusive authority in Section 22 matters. Judge Koroma believed that the Court should have exercised its judicial discretion and declined to answer the question put to it. Dissenting opinion by Judge Koroma, Advisory Opinion, *supra* note 8, at 111, paras. 15, 21 and 23.

20 Under Section 34 of the General Convention, Malaysia has undertaken to "be in a position under its own law to give effect to the terms of [the] Convention" through the enactment of appropriate legislation. It is not clear whether Malaysia in fact has complied with this provision, given that the Malaysian courts have interpreted Malaysia's legislation to be narrower in scope and meaning than the terms of the General Convention.

that the Malaysian courts had deferred a final decision as to Cumaraswamy's entitlement to immunity from legal process.

The Court noted that the difference between the United Nations and Malaysia originated in the failure of the Government of Malaysia to inform the competent Malaysian judicial authorities of the Secretary-General's finding that Cumaraswamy had spoken the words at issue in the course of the performance of his mission and was, therefore, entitled to immunity from legal process. Consequently, the question before the Court had to be answered from the time of this omission.[21]

In the Court's opinion, it is up to the Secretary-General to assess whether any UN agent has acted within the scope of his or her functions and, where he makes a positive finding, to protect such agent by asserting immunity. The Secretary-General has the authority and responsibility to inform the government of a member state of his particular finding and, where appropriate, to request it to act in conformity with such finding and, in particular, to request it to bring his finding to the attention of the local courts seized of a case in which the immunity of a UN agent is at issue. Such courts should immediately be notified of any immunity finding by the Secretary-General. That finding, together with its documentary expression, must be given the greatest weight by local courts and creates a presumption in favor of immunity. The presumption can be set aside only for the most compelling reasons. The proper application of the General Convention requires that the governmental authorities of a party to the Convention convey such information to the competent courts. Failure to comply with this obligation could lead to proceedings under Section 30 of the General Convention, as happened in this case.[22] Pursuant to Article 105 of the UN Charter and the General Convention, the Government of Malaysia should have informed its courts of the Secretary-General's finding. Instead, the Government failed to transmit his finding to the courts and the certificate of Malaysia's minister for foreign affairs filed in the proceedings failed to refer to it, triggering Malaysia's responsibility under international law.[23]

---

21 *See* Advisory Opinion, *supra* note 8, at 86-87, para. 59.
22 *See id.* at 87, paras. 60-61.
23 *See id.* at 87, para. 62. The vote on this part of the question was 13-2 (Judges Oda and Koroma dissenting). *See id.* at 89, para. 67(2)(*a*). In his separate opinion, Judge Rezek argued that the obligation incumbent upon Malaysia is not merely to notify the Malaysian courts of the finding of the Secretary-General, but to ensure that the immunity is respected. In his view, the Government can accomplish this by using all the means at its disposal in relation to the judiciary in order to have the immunity applied, in exactly the same way as it defends its own interests and positions before

Relying on "a generally-recognized principle of procedural law,"[24] the Court pointed out that questions of immunity are preliminary issues that must be expeditiously decided at the outset of any litigation. However, the Malaysian courts did not rule *in limine litis* on Cumaraswamy's immunity.[25] This meant that the essence of the immunity rule embodied in Section 22(b) was nullified by those courts, which are organs of the State of Malaysia for whose acts Malaysia is responsible. Consequently, Malaysia violated its obligations under international law in this respect as well.[26]

In addition, the Court decided unanimously that the immunity from legal process to which it found the Special Rapporteur entitled entails holding him financially harmless for any costs imposed upon him by the Malaysian courts. Having regard to the binding effect of Section 30 and the Court's findings concerning the Special Rapporteur's immunity under Section 22(b), the Court held that the Government of Malaysia must communicate its advisory opinion to the competent Malaysian courts, in order that Malaysia's international obligations be given effect and Cumaraswamy's immunity be respected.[27]

Finally, the Court pointed out, by way of *obiter dictum*, that the question of immunity is distinct from the issue of compensation for damages incurred as a result of acts performed by the United Nations or by its agents acting in their official capacity. The United Nations may have to bear responsibility for

---

the courts.

24 *Id.* at 88, para. 63.

25 Even though the Malaysian court rulings left open the question of Cumaraswamy's immunity, their consequence was that he was ordered to defend himself on the merits of the suits filed against him and that the courts arrogated to themselves the power to determine his capacity and the scope of his mission or mandate, in direct denial of the Secretary-General's assertions. *See* C.A. slip op., *supra* note 5, at 33, 44: "It is clear that the capacity in which the defendant spoke the impugned words is intertwined with his mandate. The former is, as we have earlier said, a matter for the courts to decide. It follows that the latter must also be resolved in like fashion. In our judgment the question whether the defendant exceeded the terms of his mandate is not a matter for the Secretary General to decide. It is a question that the court must determine according to the evidence presented at trial."
The Court of Appeal went so far as to say that "[i]t appears that the Secretary General has asserted the defendant's immunity in terms that clearly fall outside the scope of the General Convention and the [Malaysian implementing legislation.]" *Id.* at 34.

26 *See* Advisory Opinion, *supra* note 8, at 88, para. 63. The vote on this part of the question was 14-1 (Judge Koroma dissenting). *See id.* at 90, para. 67(2)(*b*).

27 The vote on the last part of the question was 13-2 (Judges Oda and Koroma dissenting). *See id.* at 90, para. 67(4).

such damages. However, the General Convention dictates that claims for compensation shall not be dealt with by national courts but shall be settled in accordance with the appropriate modes of settlement for which the United Nations is obliged to make provision pursuant to Section 29.[28] The Court finished with a reminder that all UN agents must take care not to exceed the scope of their functions and should so comport themselves as to avoid claims against the United Nations.

* * * *

Over the past decades, the United Nations has entrusted much of the responsibility for monitoring and enforcing human rights protection to "Special Rapporteurs" with specific mandates relating to particular countries. These individuals are not paid, although they receive expenses when they travel, together with research and administrative support from the Office of the United Nations High Commissioner for Human Rights in Geneva. An ever-increasing number of UN experts are being asked to conduct their investigations in countries whose authorities are suspected of being responsible for serious human rights violations and which may lack an independent judiciary. When states, or their organs or nationals, move against such experts, their only protection comes from the immunity provisions of the General Convention that safeguard, inter alia, the freedom of official speech and inquiry. The Cumaraswamy case underscores the importance of the General Convention in this respect.

This case represents the second time that ECOSOC asked the Court to give an advisory opinion on the status of a Special Rapporteur in connection with Section 22 of the General Convention. In the Mazilu Opinion, the Court concluded that a Special Rapporteur of the Sub-Commission on the Prevention of Discrimination and Protection of Minorities of the Commission on Human Rights was an "expert on mission" within the terms of Section 22, and that

---

28 In addition to the dispute settlement mechanism provided in Section 30 of the General Convention with regard to disputes between the United Nations and a member state, Section 29(a) provides that the United Nations shall make provision for appropriate modes of settlement of disputes arising out of contracts or other disputes of a private law character to which the United Nations is a party. Section 29 protects the interests of individuals or corporations that have a dispute with the United Nations. Pursuant to Section 29, the United Nations has regularly made provision in its contracts for recourse to binding arbitration in cases in which agreement cannot be reached by direct negotiations, which has resulted in arbitral proceedings in a limited number of cases. *See* BEKKER, *supra* note 9, at 196-98.

the privileges and immunities applicable in the case of such Special Rapporteur may be invoked as against the state of nationality, whether or not he travels. The Court also confirmed that "experts on mission enjoy the privileges and immunities provided for under the Convention in their relations with the States of which they are nationals or on the territory of which they reside," unless a reservation has been validly made in this respect by the state concerned.[29] But the Mazilu Opinion did not consider the question of the *application* of Section 22 in the case of Mr. Mazilu, the range of privileges and immunities he was entitled to in what circumstances, or who should determine whether a Special Rapporteur enjoys immunity in a given case.[30] Some of these questions, relating to the applicability and application of Section 22 *ratione materiae*, arose for the first time in the present proceedings. But the Court did not answer all of these questions completely, due mainly to its narrow interpretation of ECOSOC's request. As a consequence of the Court's approach, the issue that lay at the center of the difference between the United Nations and Malaysia, namely whether the Secretary-General has the exclusive authority to determine immunity issues with conclusive effect on national courts, was only given half-hearted treatment by the Court, perhaps in an effort to please all the parties.

By not endorsing the Secretary-General's view that it is for him alone to decide, with conclusive effect on national courts, whether a UN agent is entitled to immunity, the Court can hardly be said to have done a service to the United Nations, even though its opinion is, at first glance, favorable to the Special Rapporteur.[31] It is true that the Court found that the Secretary-General's find-

---

29 *See* Mazilu Opinion, *supra* note 9, at 195, para. 51.

30 In his written statement submitted in the Mazilu Case, the Secretary-General explained that the wording of ECOSOC's request meant that the Court was not asked about the consequences of the applicability of Section 22 to Mr. Mazilu, i.e., what immunity Mr. Mazilu might enjoy as a result of his status and whether or not such immunity had been violated by Romania. During the oral proceedings, the Legal Counsel of the United Nations observed that ECOSOC had merely addressed a preliminary legal question to the Court that was not designed to resolve the entire issue that separated the United Nations and the Government of Romania. *See id.* at 187, para. 27.

31 Although the Court held that Cumaraswamy should be held harmless for any costs imposed upon him by the Malaysian courts, it did not indicate whether this obligation fell upon the Government of Malaysia or the United Nations. Furthermore, it seems that he is still responsible for his considerable legal fees and for any collateral damage, such as lost income. As a direct consequence of the lawsuits, Cumaraswamy felt compelled to resign from Shook Lin & Bok, the Malaysian law

ing creates a presumption of immunity that can only be set aside by national courts for the most compelling reasons. But it is a presumption from which such courts can depart for good reason. In other words, the Court left the door open for national courts to disagree with the Secretary-General's finding. It would have been helpful if the Court had at least indicated what might constitute "most compelling reasons."[32] Some may argue that national courts should not necessarily be bound by the Secretary-General's finding because public charges of corruption or human rights abuses are a serious matter and the defamation action is a classic means under domestic law for clearing reputations and for deterring charges that are reckless and not made in good faith, especially if such charges are not uttered in an official report or during official proceedings but in a newspaper interview, as was the case here. However, this argument loses much weight in the instant case because the Malaysian judiciary was itself the object of the Special Rapporteur's investigation and statements. Allowing national courts to ignore the Secretary-General's findings is also inconsistent with the object and purpose of the General Convention and the UN Charter, as will be discussed below.

To answer the central question of the Secretary-General's authority when asserting immunity, which is not settled by the actual terms of the General Convention, the Court could have referred to several important sources that support the position of the Secretary-General. The latter's authority can be said to be based, expressly or implicitly, on the role assigned to him in the General Convention, his responsibilities under the UN Charter, international practice binding on UN member states, and international jurisprudence.

The second sentence of Section 23 of the General Convention assigns to the Secretary-General the right and duty to waive the immunity of an expert on mission in any case in which, in his opinion, immunity would impede the course of justice and can be waived without prejudice to the interests of the

---

firm where he had practiced for thirty years. At the time of his resignation, in January 1998, he was the senior partner and chief executive of that firm.

32　It is also not clear from the opinion whether the Secretary-General must explicitly request the local authorities concerned to bring his finding to the knowledge of the local courts or whether such authorities must do so on their own motion when faced with a positive immunity finding by the Secretary-General. Compare paragraph 60 of the opinion, referring to an explicit request from the Secretary-General, with paragraph 61, which appears to require the local authorities to act on their own motion. The separate opinion of the senior judge also seems to advocate the latter position. *See* separate opinion of Judge Oda, Advisory Opinion, *supra* note 8, at 106, para. 21.

United Nations.[33] Rather than deducing the Secretary-General's authority to exercise functional protection from the explicit authority accorded to him by the second sentence of Section 23, the Court opted for the first sentence and a statement in an advisory opinion rendered 50 years earlier on implied powers of the United Nations.[34] If national courts are given the power to determine immunity and decide that an expert on mission has no immunity in a given case because, in their view, the expert acted outside the scope of his mandate, such courts would in effect be usurping the responsibilities of the Secretary-General under Section 23, making a mockery out of that provision. In the case of the United Nations, it would mean that the courts of 137 states parties to the General Convention could effectively challenge the Secretary-General's assertion of immunity and replace their interpretation for the Secretary-General's. By denying an expert's immunity, national courts would thwart the right and duty incumbent upon the Secretary-General under Section 23 to waive immunity, should he decide, in the circumstances of a given case, that immunity is not in the interests of the United Nations. The fact that states parties to the General Convention assigned to the Secretary-General the right and duty to waive immunity implies that they wanted to prevent the domestic courts of the member states from rejecting immunity in individual cases. Leaving the ultimate decision with national courts would have the effect of having such courts create a multiplicity of standards applied to experts on mission. This could cripple the UN system of special rapporteurs and erode the uniform standard guaranteed by the General Convention. The object and purpose of Section 23 is to assign a central role to the Secretary-General in the case of

---

33 The logical consequence of the fundamental principle that a waiver of immunity must always be express and in a particular case is that the Secretary-General has the power and discretion *not* to waive, or to assert, immunity. What is there to waive for the Secretary-General if he cannot assert immunity?

34 *See* Advisory Opinion, *supra* note 8, at 84-85, para. 50 (citing Reparation for Injuries Suffered in the Service of the United Nations, 1949 ICJ REP. 174, at 184 (Advisory Opinion of Apr. 11)). However, the 1949 opinion did not concern the authority of the Secretary-General, but whether the United Nations, *as an organization*, had the capacity to espouse an international claim, by way of functional protection on behalf of an official, against the responsible government for damage caused to the organization and to the official. *See id.* at 175; *see also* BEKKER, *supra* note 9, at 58 *et seq.* According to the first sentence, "[p]rivileges and immunities are granted to experts in the interests of the United Nations and not for the personal benefit of the individuals themselves." If there was a role for the implied powers doctrine to be played in this case, it would be through the *second* sentence of Section 23.

immunity questions arising under the Convention.[35] The functions of special rapporteurs appointed by the Commission on Human Rights are of such a character that they could not be effectively and independently discharged if they were subject to challenge before, or interpretation by, the courts of the member states of the United Nations.[36] However, the determination (waiver or assertion) of immunity by the Secretary-General is not conclusive in the sense that it is non-appealable. His finding always remains subject to the possibility of review by the International Court pursuant to Section 30 of the General Convention, which provides for an objective international review mechanism.

Although the Court made reference to the Secretary-General's responsibilities under Articles 97 and 100 of the UN Charter, one will look in vain for explicit reliance on these provisions in the Court's analysis. The Court could have pointed out that the logical corollary to the undertaking by the UN member states in Article 100, paragraph 2, of the Charter, to respect the exclusively international character of the responsibilities of the Secretary-General and not to seek to influence him in the discharge of his responsibilities, is that it should be for the UN's chief administrative officer alone, free from interference by national authorities, to determine, with conclusive effect, whether words were spoken in the course of the performance of a mission for the United Nations

---

35 Employing the principle of *effet utile*, which dictates that a treaty instrument be interpreted in the manner which is most favorable to the fulfillment of the purposes of the organization concerned, the General Convention could be said to include the exclusive authority of the Secretary-General to determine immunity matters concerning experts on mission with a view to ensuring equality of treatment of experts on mission generally and uniformity in applying the standard of the Convention in individual cases.

36 *Cf.* the Court's statement in Reparation for Injuries Suffered in the Service of the United Nations, 1949 ICJ REP. 174, at 180 (Advisory Opinion of Apr. 11). Cumaraswamy was faced with four *civil* lawsuits in Malaysia. By the same token, if the decisions of the Malaysian courts were allowed to stand, a dangerous precedent would be created: a special rapporteur might face *criminal* prosecution in national courts for the words spoken by him or her in his or her official capacity if national courts were to dispute the Secretary-General's determination under Section 23 of the General Convention that he or she acted within his or her mandate. This could open the floodgates for civil and criminal lawsuits against special rapporteurs all over the world, seriously compromising the human rights mechanism of the United Nations. The determination of immunity by the Secretary-General alone is the only guarantee that such matters are resolved with the requisite speed and uniformity. *See also* dissenting opinion of Vice President Weeramantry, Advisory Opinion, *supra* note 8, paras. 2-3 of first chapter.

within the meaning of Section 22(b) of the General Convention, entitling an expert on mission to the immunity provided for in Section 22(b). This determination is subject only to the dispute settlement mechanism of Section 30. Given that experts on mission are often dispatched on dangerous or controversial missions for the United Nations, it is essential for the effective operation of Article 100, which establishes the international status of persons working for the United Nations, that those persons should be able to rely upon the protection of the organization and should not have to fear the interference of national authorities, especially not those of the states of which they are nationals.

There is no record of any opposition on the part of Malaysia relating to the customary practice followed under the General Convention with respect to the application of its provisions, in particular the Secretary-General's practice in giving effect to his responsibilities under Section 23 of the Convention and Article 100 of the UN Charter.[37]

The Court could also have deduced the Secretary-General's exclusive authority from the fundamental principle of the independence of the organization as an autonomous administrative body, or from a general rule according to which institutions of individual states may not review policy acts of international organizations.[38]

Surprisingly, no declarations or separate opinions were attached to the Court's opinion by judges with experience in the matter, including President

---

37 For recognition of the Secretary-General's prerogative in similar areas, *see, e.g., Note Verbale by the Secretary-General to the Permanent Representative of the United States*, Sept. 9, 1985, *reprinted in* 80 AJIL 440-41 (1986) (prerogative of Secretary-General to determine scope of official travel); *Personnel Questions: Respect for the Privileges and Immunities of Officials of the United Nations and the Specialized Agencies and Related Organizations*, Report of the Secretary-General, UN Doc. A/C.5/44/11 at 6, para. 19 (1989) (freedom to determine categories of personnel); *Report by the Secretary-General on Detention of Staff Members*, UN Doc. E/CN.4/Sub.2/1988/17 (prerogative of Secretary-General to determine whether act by staff member was performed in official capacity).

38 *See* BEKKER, *supra* note 9, at 173-74 & nn.767-70. Only Judge Rezek made reference to the fact of membership, requiring that every state, in its relations with the Organization and its agents, display an attitude at least as constructive as that which characterizes diplomatic relations between states. Separate opinion of Judge Rezek, Advisory Opinion, *supra* note 8.

Schwebel and Judges Higgins, Fleischhauer and Kooijmans.[39] Instead, it was Vice President Weeramantry who pointed to a broader problem represented by these Malaysian court decisions, namely that of the fundamental confusion between, on the one hand, the immunities traditionally enjoyed by sovereign states and their diplomatic representatives and, on the other hand, the immunities of intergovernmental organizations and persons connected with them.[40] Within the latter category, a special place is occupied by experts on

---

39 These judges were obvious candidates given their former expertise on the issue of immunity and the authority of the Secretary-General. President Schwebel served as research and drafting assistant to Secretary-General Trygve Lie and is the author of a book on the powers of the Secretary-General. *See* STEPHEN M. SCHWEBEL, THE SECRETARY-GENERAL OF THE UNITED NATIONS: HIS POLITICAL POWERS AND PRACTICE (1952). Judge Higgins acted as counsel for the International Tin Council in a series of landmark cases in the United Kingdom revolving around the issue of the immunities of an intergovernmental organization and persons connected with it. She is the author of a treatise that also deals with the immunity of intergovernmental organizations. *See* ROSALYN HIGGINS, PROBLEMS AND PROCESS: INTERNATIONAL LAW AND HOW WE USE IT (1994). Judge Fleischhauer was Under-Secretary-General for Legal Affairs of the United Nations between 1983 and 1994, in which capacity he argued the somewhat analogous Mazilu Opinion, *supra* note 9, in 1989. Finally, Judge Kooijmans was himself a Special Rapporteur of the UN Commission on Human Rights, namely on questions relevant to torture, between 1985 and 1992 and he chaired the Commission during 1984-85. Given the specific background of the above judges, one would have expected at least some of them to shed their authoritative light on the important issues raised in this case affecting the United Nations.

40 One of the key differences between sovereign and diplomatic immunity, on the one hand, and international organization immunity, on the other hand, is that international organizations, unlike states, do not have sovereignty. International organizations do not have their own territory but function within the territory of states. International organizations do not stand on a parity with states, and, consequently, cannot depend on reciprocity the way states can, nor are they in a position to retaliate against any violation of their integrity. Unlike states, international organizations are not in a position to grant to or withhold immunity from states. The immunities of international organizations are functional and reflect their needs requiring complete protection from national jurisdiction. *See* Brief submitted by the United Nations as *amicus curiae* in Broadbent v. Organization of American States, 628 F.2d 27 (D.C. Cir. 1980), *reprinted in* [1980] UN Jurid. Y.B. 224, at 229-30, UN Doc. ST/LEG/SER.C/18 (1983). As was noted in the preparatory documents of the United Nations in 1945: "In order to determine the nature of the privileges and immunities, the [drafting] Committee has seen fit to avoid the term diplomatic and has preferred to substitute a more appropriate standard, based, for the purposes of the Organization, on the necessity of realizing its purposes ... ." 13 United Nations Conference

mission whose status is neither that of a representative of a state nor that of a UN official.

The fundamental difference in the legal status of international organizations and sovereign states as subjects of international law, referred to by the Court in 1949,[41] dictates a basic difference in the approach that national courts should take with regard to the question of the immunities enjoyed by organizations and persons connected with them. An appreciation of this fundamental difference is critical in approaching the question of the status and immunity of experts on mission. Whereas it has been accepted, through the introduction of the restrictive concept of sovereign immunity, that domestic courts may determine whether a certain act qualifies as "sovereign" or instead as "commercial/non-sovereign," leaving it to such courts to uphold immunity in the former case or to deny immunity in the latter, no such distinction has been made in the case of the immunity of the United Nations and persons connected with it and no corresponding freedom to determine the acts of the United Nations has been assigned to domestic courts.[42] The decisions of the Malaysian courts failed to appreciate the necessary consequence to be drawn from their recognition that the immunities of experts on mission are based on functional needs, i.e., judicial deference on the part of domestic courts in favor of the procedure established by Sections 23 and 30 of the General Convention, as supplemented by practice. Deciding the question of immunity from legal process of an expert on mission involves a determination of whether the acts performed or the words spoken or written by the expert were made in the course of carrying out the expert's mandate derived from that of the organization itself.

---

on International Organization, Doc. 933, IV/2/42(2) 704 (1945).

41   *See* Reparation for Injuries Suffered in the Service of the United Nations, 1949 ICJ REP. 174, at 180 (Advisory Opinion of Apr. 11).

42   In RESTATEMENT (THIRD) OF THE FOREIGN RELATIONS LAW OF THE UNITED STATES, para. 467, under Comment (d), at 495, it was pointed out that it "appears that the restrictive theory that limits the immunity of a state from legal process ... does not apply to the United Nations." *See also id.* Reporters' Note 4, at 499-500. Judge Higgins has pointed out that "in reality there is no suggestion that ... any international organization is entitled to *sovereign* or *diplomatic* immunity. The issue is really quite different: it is whether international law requires that a different type of international person, an international organization, be accorded functional immunities." *See* Higgins, *supra* note 39, at 91. The Malaysian High Court erred in relying on the Court's observations in the Mazilu Opinion for its conclusion that contemporary thinking dictates that the doctrine of absolute immunity is passé and that the restrictive theory currently holds the field in matters of international organization immunity. *See* H.C. slip op., *supra* note 5, at 18.

Section 23 of the General Convention implies that the Secretary-General is to make such a determination. Section 30 of the General Convention makes it clear that any difference on the interpretation or application of the Convention is ultimately to be settled by the International Court of Justice as the principal judicial organ of the United Nations, and not by the courts of the member states. The General Convention sets forth a balanced regime providing for checks and balances with regard to the Secretary-General's determination that immunity applies and should not be waived in a given case. The national courts of member states cannot second-guess the Secretary-General's determination or provide their own interpretation of the terms of the Convention. Only the International Court has such power.[43]

In the light of the Court's findings in this case, it seems likely that it will be confronted with similar questions in future cases brought under its advisory jurisdiction, which, if framed correctly, might give the Court an opportunity to refine its views on the legal status and immunities of experts on missions and related questions.

---

43 Section 30 of the General Convention grants the Court *exclusive* authority over the settlement of any difference between the United Nations, on the one hand, and a member state, on the other hand, arising out of the interpretation or application of the Convention (i.e., Sections 22-23, in the case of a difference with respect to the Secretary-General's determination of an expert's immunity). Thus, it is for the International Court of Justice, and not the Malaysian courts, to resolve the Special Rapporteur's case with binding effect for the United Nations and Malaysia. When the Malaysian Court of Appeal stated that "[i]t appears that the Secretary General has asserted the [Special Rapporteur]'s immunity in terms that clearly fall outside the scope of the General Convention," (C.A. slip op., *supra* note 5, at 34) it entered the forbidden field of interpretation of the Convention. The Malaysian High Court obviously misunderstood the mechanism of the General Convention, when it stated that "[i]t would indeed be a naive supposition if [the Secretary-General's certificate] is to be construed as being conclusive, since can one be heard to say C'est fait and therefore, that is the end of the matter? Surely not." H.C. slip op., *supra* note 5, at 25. Apparently, what the court meant to say is that it would be arbitrary for the Secretary-General to end the matter through his certificate asserting immunity. But this statement neglects the dispute settlement mechanism of Section 30 of the General Convention, through which a difference between a member state and the United Nations arising from the application or interpretation of the Convention is to be submitted to the Court for a final determination. The Secretary-General's assertion does not necessarily end the matter, given that it is subject to the mechanism laid down in Section 30, as he acknowledged himself in paragraph 17 of his Note of July 28, 1998.

ADDENDUM: COMMENTARY ON THE AFTERMATH OF THE *CUMARASWAMY* OPINION

Malaysia's failure swiftly to comply with the Court's decision in the *Cumaraswamy* case calls for further comment, in the light of the statements made by Malaysian representatives both during and after the proceedings described above.

In advance of the advisory proceedings, Malaysia undertook, pursuant to Section 34 of the General Convention, "to give effect to the terms of this convention" when it acceded to the General Convention on October 28, 1957, without reservation. The undertaking to accept as decisive an advisory opinion of the Court issued in response to a request based on Section 30 of the General Convention forms an integral part of the terms of the Convention. However, during the first round of written pleadings, Malaysia argued that Section 34 merely obligates it to enact a law to give effect to the terms of the General Convention, which it has done.[1]

During the oral proceedings in the case, Malaysia gave several assurances of its intended compliance with the Court's process. First of all, the solicitor general of Malaysia emphasized at the beginning of her intervention that her country was not an unwilling or reluctant participant in the proceedings.[2] This statement was important, as it in essence established the "consent," or lack of opposition, to the Court's jurisdiction by the parties in relation to which

---

1   *See* Written Statement of Malaysia, at para. 7.21.

2   *See* ICJ Doc. CR 98/16, at 18, para. 2 (trans. 1998). However, the presentation of Malaysia's case by Sir Elihu Lauterpacht as Counsel for Malaysia later during the hearings moved away from the solicitor general's prior unequivalent assurance. Lauterpacht argued that Malaysia only accepted the prospect of recourse to the Court, acknowledged to be mandatory in the case of a difference arising out of the application of the General Convention, *after* the national courts of Malaysia had determined the question of whether certain words were spoken or written in the course of the performance of a mission for the United Nations. He sought to characterize this as a requirement of exhaustion of local remedies. *See id.* at 63, para. 115. In its Written Statement, Malaysia contended that it was futile to refer the dispute to the Court pursuant to Section 30 prior to adjudication by the Malaysian courts and that the invocation of "the provisions of section 30 is an expression of utter and complete disregard to [*sic*] the position not only of a private individual but also to the Courts in Malaysia." Written Statement of Malaysia, at para. 9.7. The Court clearly rejected Malaysia's arguments on this point, which are, however, of fundamental importance in understanding Malaysia's views regarding the subsequent implementation of the Court's Opinion.

the difference underlying ECOSOC's request had arisen. As the Court remarked in its Opinion, "no participant in these proceedings questioned the need for the Court to exercise its advisory function in this case."[3] This statement was made, not with regard to any consent requirement, but in the context of the condition, applicable to advisory proceedings generally, that there be no compelling reasons that should lead the Court to refuse to issue the opinion requested. Still, the Court's statement in the advisory opinion was odd and confusing in view of the fundamental difference between contentious cases and advisory proceedings. The latter distinguishes itself from the Court's other function ("to decide in accordance with international law such disputes as are submitted to it" by sovereign states)[4] by not requiring the consent of the parties involved, a requirement that is central to contentious jurisdiction.[5] As emerged from the *Mazilu* Opinion, the consent of the parties to the difference to which the Section 30 request relates is not a *condition sine qua non* for the exercise of the Court's advisory jurisdiction.

The solicitor general, as part of her concluding remarks during the oral proceedings, gave her Government's assurances by stating that "Malaysia fully recognizes the provisions of Section 30 of the General Convention, which accords binding quality to the advisory opinion of [the] Court."[6] In addition, Counsel for Malaysia assured the Court "that Malaysia has no intention of acting in a manner violative of its international duties."[7]

In the *Cumaraswamy* Opinion itself, the Court pointed out that the United Nations and Malaysia expressly acknowledged in advance the consequence of the binding effect of the Court's advisory opinion to be rendered in the case.[8] This binding effect represents the post-adjudicative aspect of Section 30 proceedings.[9]

---

3   1999 ICJ REP. 62, at 79, para. 30.
4   ICJ STATUTE Art. 38, para. 1.
5   *See*, e.g., Fisheries Jurisdiction (Spain v. Can.), Jurisdiction, Judgment, 1998 ICJ REP. 432 (Dec. 4).
6   ICJ Doc. CR 98/17, at 44 (trans. 1998).
7   ICJ Doc. CR 98/16, at 33, para. 22 sub (*f*) (trans. 1998).
8   *See* 1999 ICJ REP. 62, at 76-77, para. 25.
9   For an analysis of the referral (ante-adjudicative) and implementation (post-adjudicative) aspects of Section 30 proceedings, see Charles N. Brower & Pieter H.F. Bekker, *Understanding "Binding" Advisory Opinions of the International Court of Justice*, in LIBER AMICORUM JUDGE SHIGERU ODA (Ando/McWhinney/Wolfrum eds., 2001). *See also* Pieter H.F. Bekker, *The Independence of UN Special Rapporteurs: Dispute Resolution under the Convention on Privileges and Immunities*, in: INTERNATIONAL ADMINISTRATION – LAW AND MANAGEMENT PRACTICES IN INTER-

The situation in the aftermath of the Court's Opinion was as follows. Various Malaysian newspapers reported that the prime minister of Malaysia, Dr. Mahathir Mohamad, acknowledged that the Court decided that the Special Rapporteur was entitled to immunity from legal proceedings, that there was no way for Malaysia to overturn or appeal the Court's decision and that the Malaysian Government would "accept it."[10] However, in an interview with a Malaysian newspaper issued after the Court handed down the *Cumaraswamy* Opinion,[11] the solicitor general of Malaysia stated that, while her Government may need to officially convey to the competent Malaysian courts the text of the Court's opinion pursuant to one of the holdings contained therein, the mode of communication remained to be decided. She claimed that the advisory opinion stated that it is up to Malaysia how to implement the opinion and that it is for the national courts to decide whether the cases against the Special Rapporteur were closed without hearing any argument by the parties. The solicitor general complained that the Court had entered into an examination of the facts of the case instead of restricting itself to the legal question before it. She said she considered it "a victory of sorts" for Malaysia that the Court did not opine on the assertion by the Secretary-General that his certificate asserting immunity has conclusive effect on domestic courts. In her view, the implication of this is that the Court recognizes that the Secretary-General does *not* have exclusive jurisdiction to decide on immunity. She also maintained that the Court did not find that Malaysia had breached its obligations by not enforcing the Special Rapporteur's immunity. While she acknowledged that the Court was of the opinion that the Secretary-General correctly found that Cumaraswamy was acting in the course of his mission, she did not mention that the Court held that the Special Rapporteur was entitled to immunity in the specific circumstances of his case and that this immunity must be respected.

The statements made and assurances given by the solicitor general of Malaysia during the written and oral proceedings and by the prime minister of Malaysia in the aftermath of the *Cumaraswamy* Opinion had the effect of creating legal obligations under international law for Malaysia. In two parallel judgments rendered in 1974, the Court ruled that statements made by the president of the French Republic and by the French ministers of defense and

---

NATIONAL ORGANISATIONS III.2./1 (C. de Cooker ed., 2001).

10   *See* "PM: We accept decision on Param," NEW STRAITS TIMES, at 1 (May 1, 1999); "PM: Malaysia accepts World Court decision on Param," STAR, at 2 (May 1, 1999).

11   *See* "Elucidating the ICJ advisory opinion," NEW SUNDAY TIMES, at 12 (May 23, 1999).

of foreign affairs, made publicly and with an intent to be bound, created legal effects under international law and were binding on France, even though they were not made within the context of international negotiations. Interested parties may take cognizance of such unilateral declarations and place confidence in them. Such parties are entitled to require that the obligation thus created be respected and that a course of conduct is followed consistent with such declarations.[12] Having regard to their intention and to the circumstances in which they were made, the unequivocal statements made and assurances given by the prime minister and solicitor general of Malaysia during and after the proceedings in The Hague, which amounted to an acceptance of the binding effect that Section 30 attaches to advisory opinions issued pursuant to this provision, constituted an engagement of the state of Malaysia to respect the Special Rapporteur's immunity determined by the Court and to accept the other terms of the Court's Opinion. The language employed in the prime minister's public statements especially reveals a clear intention to abide by such terms. However, more than 24 months after the Court's Opinion was issued, the four lawsuits against the Special Rapporteur still were pending before the Malaysian courts. The first suit, instituted by MBf Capital Bhd and MBf Northern Securities Sdn Bhd on December 12, 1996, was scheduled for case management on September 29, 1999, which was later postponed several times, with a view to fixing a date for trial, despite the reminder by counsel for the Special Rapporteur that the action should be dismissed in view of the Court's Opinion. The Special Rapporteur's original applications to strike out the other three lawsuits filed against him, which were stayed pending the Court's decision on ECOSOC's request, initially were fixed for hearing in October 1999 but subsequently were postponed, after the competent Malaysian court acceded to requests by counsel for the plaintiffs that they needed more time to take instructions on the claim because they had not been notified of the Court's Opinion.

As part of its claim for relief, the United Nations submitted that "if the Court finds that Malaysia has breached her obligations under the General Convention, Malaysia must *immediately* take steps to restore the situation to what it would have been had the Secretary-General's assertion of immunity been given effect in Malaysia."[13] Such steps, in the organization's view, would

---

12 *See* Nuclear Tests (Aus. v. Fr.), Judgment, 1974 ICJ REP. 253, at 267-69, paras. 43-50 (Dec. 20); Nuclear Tests (NZ v. Fr.), Judgment, 1974 ICJ REP. 457, at 472-74, paras. 46-52 (Dec. 20).

13 *See* ICJ Doc. CR 98/15, at 32, para. 67 (trans. 1998) (emphasis added). According to the UN's Deputy Legal Counsel, this conclusion flows directly from the binding effect that Section 30 attributes to the Court's Opinion.

consist of a dismissal of all proceedings against the Special Rapporteur and reparations for damages caused by such proceedings. The United Nations argued that Malaysia, if found to be in breach of the General Convention, "must annul or dismiss the judgments and all on-going proceedings, against the Special Rapporteur and make reparations for damages caused by that breach *from the date of breach*, and not from the date of the Court's Advisory Opinion."[14] As to the reparation due by Malaysia, the United Nations maintained that the Special Rapporteur should be held harmless for any costs, expenses or damages incurred by, or assessed to, him in connection with the Malaysian lawsuits against him. The United Nations maintained also that, in the event it is compelled directly to assume such costs, damages and expenses, the Malaysian Government ultimately is responsible for any and all such costs, damages or expenses actually paid or incurred by the Special Rapporteur and/or by the United Nations directly or on his behalf.[15] Malaysia, on the other hand, appeared to regard the compensation issue as a separate question that would arise only *after* the Malaysian courts have ruled on the matter of the Special Rapporteur's immunity. While Malaysia agreed that the question of its liability is dependent upon the Court's Advisory Opinion, it argued that issues relating to its responsibility under international law should be resolved separately, because (1) if the Court upholds the assertion of immunity by the Secretary-General, it still is for the Government of Malaysia to determine how to give effect to that immunity and various stages have to be undertaken before Malaysia must assume responsibility, and (2) the damages sustained by the Special Rapporteur, which are not physical but are monetary arising out of civil actions instituted by Malaysian private parties, are not caused by the Government of Malaysia and do not result from a breach of a treaty provision but from a difference of opinion on the interpretation of a treaty.[16]

The above summary of the views of Malaysia and the United Nations begs the question: in the Court's view, what constituted the breach of obligations by Malaysia, when did such breach occur, and what are the consequences of such breach? The Court found that both the governmental and judicial authorities independently had caused Malaysia to breach its international obligations. First, the Court held that the governmental authorities of a party to the General Convention are under an obligation immediately to notify their national courts

---

14   *Id.*, at 40, para. 89 (emphasis in original).
15   *Id.*, at 24, para. 46.
16   *See* Written Statement of Malaysia, at para. 9.10; Written Comments of Malaysia, at paras. 3.1, 7.13, 7.14, 7.21, and 7.24.

of any finding by the Secretary-General concerning the immunity of a United Nations agent.[17] The failure of the governmental authorities of Malaysia to respect this obligation to "convey such information" to the national courts concerned, together with the failure by the Malaysian minister for foreign affairs to refer to the Secretary-General's finding in his own certificate submitted to the courts pursuant to domestic legislation implementing Article 34 of the General Convention, constituted Malaysia's breach of international law in this case.[18] The Court did not say that Malaysia had to "convey *its own views on, and support for,* such information." The Court merely concluded that the Malaysian Government had an obligation, under Article 105 of the Charter and the Convention, "to inform its courts of *the position taken by the Secretary-General.*"[19] Importantly, the Court did not say that Malaysia's governmental authorities at any stage had the obligation to inform the Malaysian courts of their *own* views on the Secretary-General's position. However, in the final item of the operative paragraph, the Court held, by 13 votes to two, that the Government of Malaysia had the obligation to communicate the Advisory Opinion to the Malaysian courts, "in order that Malaysia's international obligations be given effect and Dato' Param Cumaraswamy's *immunity be respected.*"[20] The latter words also make it abundantly clear that, in the Court's binding view, there was nothing for the Malaysian courts to determine anymore on the issue of immunity, these courts, in their capacity as organs of the state of Malaysia,

---

17 *See* 1999 ICJ REP. 62, at 87, para. 61.

18 *Id.* at para. 62.

19 *Id.* (emphasis added).

20 *Id.* at para. 67, sub (4) (emphasis added). The Court's senior judge, Judge Oda, voted against this paragraph, because he believed the final sentence of Section 30 made it unnecessary for the Court to make this statement. Separate opinion of Judge Oda, *id.* at 107-08, paras. 25-26. There is one recent precedent for this type of relief, whereby the Court orders a state to transmit its decision to the appropriate authorities within that state. In its Order on Germany's request for provisional measures issued on March 3, 1999, in the *LaGrand Case* between Germany and the United States, the Court held, unanimously, that the United States should transmit the Court's Order indicating provisional measures to the governor of one of the federal states of the United States. *See* LaGrand Case (Ger. v. U.S.) (Provisional Measures), 1999 ICJ REP. 9, at 16, para. 29(I)(*b*) (Order of March 3). The *LaGrand* Order also included an instruction to the United States to "inform the Court of all the measures which it has taken in implementation of this Order." *Id.* at 16, para. 29(I)(*a*). *See also* Case Concerning the Vienna Convention on Consular Relations (Par. v. U.S.), Provisional Measures, 1998 ICJ REP. 248, at 258, para. 41(I) (Order of April 9). Interestingly, this part of the instructions given in the *LaGrand Case* was not included in the *Cumaraswamy* Opinion.

being under an obligation to *respect* the immunity that the Court determined did exist in the Special Rapporteur's case. In other words, the Court did not leave room for an independent "second round" or a determination *de novo* by the Malaysian courts, except to *respect* the immunity asserted by the Secretary-General and found to exist by the Court.

In addition to the aforementioned breach committed by the *governmental* authorities of Malaysia, the Court found that Malaysia also was responsible for the breach committed by the *judicial* authorities of Malaysia, as organs of the state of Malaysia, in failing to rule *in limine litis* on the immunity of the Special Rapporteur.[21] When the judicial authorities failed to decide on the immunity issue in 1997, "Malaysia *did not* act in accordance with its obligations under international law."[22] At that point, and not later, the state of Malaysia incurred international responsibility, without the need for a separate and independent breach by the governmental authorities subsequent to the failure of the judicial authorities.

As to the issue of compensation, the Court held, unanimously, that the Special Rapporteur "shall be held financially harmless for any costs imposed upon him by the Malaysian courts, in particular taxed costs."[23] The Court failed to indicate who has to indemnify the Special Rapporteur, although it may be assumed that, following a fundamental principle of international law, the entity who commits a breach is the one owing reparation.[24] The Court

---

21 *See* 1999 ICJ REP. 62, at 88, para. 63. One month before the Court issued the *Cumaraswamy* Opinion, it stated in another case that "the international responsibility of a State is engaged by the action of the competent organs and authorities acting in that State, whatever they may be" and that such organs and authorities are obligated to act in conformity with the international undertakings of the state concerned. *See* LaGrand Case (Ger. v. U.S.) (Provisional Measures), 1999 ICJ REP. 9, at 16, para. 28 (Order of March 3). *See also* IAN BROWNLIE, SYSTEM OF THE LAW OF NATIONS: STATE RESPONSIBILITY, PART I, at 144 (1983); MARJORIE M. WHITEMAN, DAMAGES IN INTERNATIONAL LAW 7 (1937).

22 1999 ICJ REP. 62, at 88, para. 63 (emphasis added).

23 *Id.*, operative paragraph 67, sub (3).

24 *See* Factory at Chorzów (Ger. v. Pol.) (Claim for Indemnity), Jurisdiction, Judgment, 1927 PCIJ (ser. A) No. 9, at 21 (July 26) ("It is a principle of international law that the breach of an engagement involves an obligation to make reparation in an adequate form. Reparation therefore is the indispensable complement of a failure to apply a convention and there is no necessity for this to be stated in the convention itself."); Factory at Chorzów (Ger. v. Pol.), Judgment, Merits, 1928 PCIJ (ser. A) No. 17, at 4, 29 (Sept. 13) ("it is a principle of international law, and even a general conception of law, that any breach of an engagement involves an obligation to make reparation.").

did not rule, despite the specific claim of the United Nations, that the Special Rapporteur must be held financially harmless for any direct or indirect (consequential) costs, damages and expenses sustained by him in connection with, or arising from, the Malaysian lawsuits but not "imposed upon him by the Malaysian courts." The Court also did not rule on the claim of the United Nations that the Malaysian Government ultimately is responsible to hold the *United Nations* financially harmless for any costs, damages and expenses that it may be compelled to assume directly or on the Special Rapporteur's behalf.[25] Another hiatus in the Court's ruling is formed by its failure to indicate any time limit for Malaysia's compliance with the Advisory Opinion. Be that as it may, by its various holdings on Malaysia's responsibility and on compensation, the Court flatly rejected Malaysia's arguments summarized above as to the existence, content and timing of its responsibility under international law and the resulting compensation owed by it.

Based on the conduct and statements of Malaysia's governmental and judicial authorities in the aftermath of the *Cumaraswamy* Opinion, the question is: What next? As indicated above, the Court did not indicate any time limit for Malaysia to comply with its binding Advisory Opinion. However, the Court having held that Malaysia, as a state, is responsible for the actions of the Malaysian courts in allowing the proceedings against the Special Rapporteur to proceed, it follows that Malaysia also is responsible for such courts' continued failure, in the aftermath of the *Cumaraswamy* Opinion, to respect the Court's determination in favor of the Special Rapporteur's immunity.[26] This continued failure became manifest when the senior assistant registrar of Kuala Lumpur's High Court ruled, on October 18, 1999, in response to Cumaraswamy's motion to dismiss one of the lawsuits against him by reason of his immunity upheld by the International Court, that the General Convention is not a final and binding authority on the issue whether the Malaysian courts

---

25   Judge Oda complains in his separate opinion that the Court should have indicated whether the Government of Malaysia should make reparation to the United Nations as well as to the Special Rapporteur for its non-compliance and how that reparation for the damages caused to the United Nations and/or the Special Rapporteur should be effected. *See* separate opinion of Judge Oda, 1999 ICJ REP. 62, at 108, para. 26.

26   *See id.* at para. 24. Although the Court did not state that it was incumbent upon the Malaysian Government to further intervene in the proceedings before the Malaysian courts to ensure the respect for the Special Rapporteur's immunity, the continued inaction of those courts contributed to the international responsibility of Malaysia. *Cf.* ICJ Doc. CR 98/15, at 22, para. 39 (trans. 1998) (statement of the UN Legal Counsel).

should follow the Court's Advisory Opinion. The court determined that the issues, facts and laws governing Cumaraswamy's case should be decided upon in a final trial and ordered Cumaraswamy to file and serve his defense.[27] After that case finally was dismissed on July 7, 2000, the other three lawsuits remained on the docket of the Malaysian courts until notices of discontinuance were filed by the plaintiffs on May 22-23 and June 11, 2001, one day before a hearing on Cumaraswamy's motion to dismiss scheduled by Malaysia's Federal Court and more than two years after the ICJ issued its decision.[28] The withdrawals left unresolved the issue of costs and compensation of Special Rapporteur Cumaraswamy and/or the United Nations, despite the Secretary-General's strong protests.[29]

As the late Judge Ago wrote in 1991, a Section 30 opinion "would not bar a later request for a purely advisory opinion on a question subsequently arising in the same case, which might be interpretative in nature and upon which the parties wished to have the Court's advice."[30] ECOSOC, or another UN organ or agency, also could submit another Section 30 request relating to a difference between the United Nations and Malaysia concerning the exclusive question of the precise effect that is to be given to the Court's Opinion. However, as Rosenne has pointed out, this may raise the question of the Court's discretion.[31] It seems that a valid Section 30 request could also be made in relation to a dispute between the United Nations and Malaysia relating to reparation due[32] by reason of Malaysia's failure to comply with international law,

---

27   The text of this decision, which is unpublished, is on file with the author. Following Cumaraswamy's appeal, the judge in chambers finally upheld Cumaraswamy's immunity in a judgment delivered on July 7, 2000. *Id.*

28   *Id.*

29   *See*, e.g., UN Doc. E/1999/124 (Dec. 15, 1999), and a letter of August 2, 2000 from UN Secretary-General Kofi Annan addressed to the prime minister of Malaysia ("I hope that ... I will finally be in a position to report to the Economic and Social Council in the very near future that the advisory opinion of the International Court of Justice has been fully implemented with respect to all four cases *and the costs thereof*." (emphasis added)) (text on file with the author).

30   Ago, *supra* note 10, at 448.

31   *See* SHABTAI ROSENNE, 2 THE LAW AND PRACTICE OF THE INTERNATIONAL COURT, 1920-1996, at 1040 (1997).

32   *See* Factory at Chorzów (Ger. v. Pol.) (Claim for Indemnity), Jurisdiction, Judgment, 1927 PCIJ (ser. A) No. 9, at 32 (July 26) ("Differences relating to reparations which may be due by reason of failure to apply a convention, are consequently differences relating to its interpretation"). Malaysia's statement during the hearings seems to have invited such an Advisory Opinion on the issue of responsibility. *See* ICJ Doc.

as found by the Court in the *Cumaraswamy* Opinion, or even in relation to a dispute concerning Malaysia's timely implementation of the Advisory Opinion itself.

CR 98/16, at 33, para. 22 under (*f*).

NATO air campaign against Yugoslavia – provisional measures – juris-
dictional standard for provisional measures – Optional Clause jurisdiction
– effect of reservation ratione temporis *in declaration accepting*
compulsory jurisdiction – forum prorogatum *– effect of reservations to*
Article IX of Genocide Convention

LEGALITY OF USE OF FORCE (Yugoslavia v. Belgium) (Yugoslavia v.
Canada) (Yugoslavia v. France) (Yugoslavia v. Germany) (Yugoslavia v.
Italy) (Yugoslavia v. the Netherlands) (Yugoslavia v. Portugal)
(Yugoslavia v. Spain) (Yugoslavia v. United Kingdom) (Yugoslavia v.
United States)

Provisional Measures, Orders
ICJ REP. 124, 259, 363, 422, 481, 542, 656, 761, 826, 916
International Court of Justice, June 2, 1999[*]

After Yugoslavia refused to accept repeated demands by the United States and
other members of the North Atlantic Treaty Organization (NATO) to withdraw
Yugoslav military and paramilitary troops allegedly engaged in serious human
rights abuses against the local Kosovar-Albanian population in Kosovo, NATO
commenced an air campaign against Yugoslava on March 24, 1999. The
bombings continued for several months. In response, Yugoslavia instituted
proceedings before the International Court of Justice on April 29, 1999, against
Belgium, Canada, France, Germany, Italy, the Netherlands, Portugal, Spain,
the United Kingdom and the United States of America in their capacity as
member states of NATO. Yugoslavia asked the Court to hold each of the respondents individually responsible for certain breaches of international law arising
from their participation in the NATO air campaign against Yugoslavia in March
and April 1999, including the obligation not to violate the sovereignty of
another state and the obligation banning the use of force against another state
(by taking part in the bombing of Yugoslavia), the obligation not to intervene
in the internal affairs of another state (by assisting the "Kosovo Liberation
Army"), the obligation to protect the civilian population and civilian objects

---

[*] Reproduced with permission from 93 AJIL 928 (1999). © The American Society
of International Law.

175

in wartime (by taking part in the bombing of civilian objects, including histor-ical monuments), the obligation to protect the environment (by taking part in the bombing of oil refineries and chemical plants), the obligation relating to free navigation on international rivers (by taking part in destroying bridges), the obligation to respect fundamental human rights and freedoms (by taking part in killing civilians, destroying enterprises and health and cultural institu-tions), the obligation not to use prohibited weapons (by taking part in the use of cluster bombs and weapons containing depleted uranium), and the obligation not to deliberately inflict conditions of life calculated to cause the physical destruction of a national group.

Simultaneously, Yugoslavia submitted requests for the indication of pro-visional measures asking the Court to order each of the respondents to "cease immediately [their] acts of use of force" and to "refrain from any act of threat or use of force" against Yugoslavia. Yugoslavia invoked various bases of jurisdiction to establish the Court's jurisdiction in each of these cases, relying on (i) Article 36, paragraph 2 of the ICJ Statute in the cases against Belgium, Canada, the Netherlands, Portugal, Spain and the United Kingdom, (ii) Article 38, paragraph 5 of the Rules of Court in the cases against France, Germany, Italy and the United States, (iii) Article IX of the 1948 Convention on the Prevention and Punishment of the Crime of Genocide (Genocide Convention) in the cases against all ten respondents, and (iv) two treaties from the 1930s in the cases against Belgium and the Netherlands. Each of these bases of jurisdiction will be discussed separately below in relation to the respondents against which they were invoked. The Court, by clear majorities, issued ten Orders rejecting all of Yugoslavia's requests for the indication of provisional measures on the basis that it lacked jurisdiction *prima facie*.[1] In addition, the Court dismissed the cases against Spain and the United States and ordered their

---

[1]   *See* 1999 ICJ REP. 124, 259, 363, 422, 481, 542, 656, 761, 826, 916 (Orders of June 2). The vote was 14-2 in the case involving Spain, 13-3 in the case involving Italy, 12-3 in the cases involving France, Germany, the United Kingdom and the United States, 12-4 in the cases involving Belgium and Canada, and 11-4 in the cases involving the Netherlands and Portugal. Judges Shi and Vereshchetin and Judge *ad hoc* Kreća (appointed by Yugoslavia) voted against the main holding rejecting Yugoslavia's request in all ten Orders (except that Judge *ad hoc* Kreća did not dissent in the case involving Spain). Vice President Weeramantry dissented in the cases involving Belgium, Canada, Portugal and the Netherlands. The ten Orders contain similar language on common points; for practical purposes, except where expressly indicated otherwise, the reference is to the first of the ten Orders rendered in the case between Yugoslavia and Belgium, Legality of Use of Force (Yugo. v. Belg.), Order of June 2, 1999, [hereinafter Order].

removal from the General List on the ground that it was manifestly without jurisdiction in these two cases. The Court allowed the cases against the other eight NATO parties to remain on its docket, on the basis that the Court's findings on Yugoslavia's requests in no way prejudge the question of the Court's jurisdiction to deal with the merits of those cases and leave unaffected the rights of the parties to submit arguments in respect thereof.[2]

Yugoslavia invoked Article IX of the Genocide Convention in an effort to establish jurisdiction over all the respondents. Article IX provides that disputes relating to the interpretation, application or fulfillment of the Convention shall be submitted to the Court at the request of any party to the dispute. The respondents argued that Yugoslavia failed to make substantial allegations that the alleged actions of any of them fell within the ambit of the Genocide Convention. In their view, the Yugoslav complaint lacked any showing of the requisite intent on the part of any respondent to commit genocide, the intentional or subjective element being at the core of the definition of genocide in Article II of the Genocide Convention.[3] Moreover, the respondents argued that the relief that Yugoslavia asked for, pertaining to the use of force against a foreign state, was unrelated to the subject-matter regulated by the Genocide Convention, so that the jurisdictional clause contained in the Convention could not serve to establish jurisdiction to grant the relief requested by Yugoslavia. In addition, Spain and the United States pointed out that their instruments ratifying the Genocide Convention contain reservations in respect of Article IX so that their specific consent is required to establish jurisdiction in any case.

The Court determined that the threat or use of force against a state cannot in itself constitute an act of genocide within the meaning of Article II of the Genocide Convention. Article II establishes the intended destruction, in whole or in part, of a national, ethnic, racial or religious group as such as the essential characteristic of the crime of genocide. It did not appear to the Court at the

---

2   *See* Order, *supra* note 1, at 139 para. 46.
3   This definition reads as follows: "In the present Convention, genocide means any of the following acts committed with intent to destroy, in whole or in part, a national, ethnical, racial or religious group, as such:
    (a) Killing members of the group;
    (b) Causing serious bodily mental harm to members of the group;
    (c) Deliberately inflicting on the group conditions of life calculated to bring about its physical destruction in whole or in part;
    (d) Imposing measures intended to prevent births within the group;
    (e) Forcibly transferring children of the group to another group."
    See Order, *supra* note 1, at 138, para. 39.

present stage of the proceedings that the NATO bombings entailed the element of intent towards a group as such (i.e., the people of Yugoslavia). Consequently, it was not in a position to find, at this stage of the proceedings, that the imputed acts were capable of coming within the provisions of the Genocide Convention.[4] The jurisdictional clause of Article IX thus did not constitute a basis on which the Court's jurisdiction could *prima facie* be founded in the ten cases.

In relation to Spain and the United States, given their express reservations with respect to Article IX, the validity of which was upheld by the Court in previous proceedings[5] and which Yugoslavia did not object to, the Court found that it was manifestly without jurisdiction. Consequently, the Court dismissed the cases filed by Yugoslavia against Spain and the United States and ordered that they be removed from the General List of ICJ cases. The Court allowed the cases against the other eight NATO parties to remain on its docket, on the basis that the Court's findings on Yugoslavia's requests of April 29, 1999, in no way prejudge the question of the Court's jurisdiction to deal with the merits of those cases and leave unaffected the rights of the parties to submit arguments in respect thereof.

In relation to France, Germany, Italy and the United States, Yugoslavia invoked Article 38, paragraph 5, of the Rules of Court as a jurisdictional basis. According to that provision, when a state files an application against another state that has not accepted the Court's jurisdiction, the application is transmitted to the state named as respondent, but no action is taken in the proceedings unless and until that state has accepted the Court's jurisdiction for the purposes of the case (so-called *forum prorogatum*). However, none of the states involved expressed a willingness to accept the Court's jurisdiction for the purposes of these proceedings. Not surprisingly, the Court concluded that, in the absence of the requisite consent of France, Germany, Italy and the United States, it could not exercise prorogated jurisdiction on the basis of Article 38 of the Rules of Court in these cases, not even *prima facie*.

In relation to Belgium, Canada, the Netherlands, Portugal, Spain and the United Kingdom, Yugoslavia contended that the Court had jurisdiction based on the acceptance of Yugoslavia and each of those states of the compulsory jurisdiction of the Court under Article 36, paragraph 2, of the ICJ Statute (the Optional Clause). The respondents noted that Yugoslavia's declaration accepting the Court's compulsory jurisdiction, deposited with the UN Secretary-General

---

4   *See id.* at paras. 40-41.

5   *See* Reservations to the Convention on the Prevention and Punishment of the Crime of Genocide, 1951 ICJ REP. 15 (Advisory Opinion of May 28).

on April 26, 1999, three days before the institution of these proceedings, contains a reservation *ratione temporis* limiting recognition of the Court's jurisdiction to disputes arising after April 25, 1999, the date on which Yugoslavia signed its declaration, and concerning only situations or facts subsequent to that date. The NATO bombing began a month earlier. During the hearings, Yugoslavia sought to characterize each bombing attack as one of a number of separate disputes between the parties, even though Yugoslavia's Application speaks of the "subject of the dispute" as being the bombing of its territory.[6] Noting that the bombings began on March 24, 1999, the Court concluded that the legal dispute between Yugoslavia and the respondents arose well before April 25, 1999, and that each individual air attack did not give rise to a separate subsequent dispute. Consequently, the reservation *ratione temporis* contained in Yugoslavia's own declaration led the Court to conclude that the Optional Clause declarations of the parties in these proceedings did not constitute a basis on which its jurisdiction could *prima facie* be founded.[7]

In addition, Spain and the United Kingdom pointed to the reservations *ratione temporis* contained in their respective Optional Clause declarations excluding from the Court's jurisdiction disputes where the other party accepted jurisdiction less than twelve months prior to the filing of the application bringing the dispute before the Court. In light of these reservations, the Court concluded that it "manifestly" lacked *prima facie* jurisdiction over Spain and the United Kingdom under the Optional Clause.

---

6   For a discussion of the Yugoslav argument in the light of the concept of "continuing events" or a continuing breach of international law, see paragraphs 4-8 of the separate opinion of Judge Higgins appended to the Orders in the cases involving Belgium, Canada, the Netherlands, Portugal, Spain and the United Kingdom [hereinafter Sep. Op. Higgins].

7   *See* Order, *supra* note 1, at 134-35, paras. 27-30. The respondents were able to invoke the reservation *ratione temporis* contained in Yugoslavia's declaration because, by virtue of the principle of reciprocity laid down in Article 36, paragraph 2 of the Statute, the limitation contained in Yugoslavia's declaration "holds good as between the Parties." *See* Phosphates in Morocco (Italy v. Fr.), 1938 P.C.I.J. (ser. A/B) No. 74, at 10, 22 (Judgment of June 14). In 1957, the Court explained that "since two unilateral declarations are involved [reciprocal] jurisdiction is conferred upon the Court only to the extent to which the Declarations coincide in conferring it." Certain Norwegian Loans (Fr. v. Nor.), 1957 ICJ REP. 9, at 23 (July 6). In the case of Spain and the United Kingdom, the Court, recognizing the effect of the reservations *ratione temporis* contained in the Spanish and British Optional Clause declarations, concluded that it "manifestly" lacked *prima facie* jurisdiction under the Optional Clause.

Belgium, Canada, the Netherlands, Portugal, Spain and the United Kingdom also invoked resolutions of the Security Council and the General Assembly of the United Nations in support of their argument that the Federal Republic of Yugoslavia is not a member state of the United Nations or a party to the ICJ Statute as the successor state to the former Socialist Federal Republic of Yugoslavia, and that Yugoslavia cannot, therefore, rely on the Court's Statute in establishing jurisdiction in these cases.[8] Having decided on other grounds that the Optional Clause did not provide a *prima facie* basis for jurisdiction, the Court concluded that it did not need to consider at this stage the question of Yugoslavia's status.[9]

In relation to Belgium and the Netherlands, Yugoslavia introduced two additional grounds of jurisdiction during the second round of oral argument. It invoked Article 4 of the Convention of Conciliation, Judicial Settlement and Arbitration between Belgium and the Kingdom of Yugoslavia signed in Belgrade on March 25, 1930, and Article 4 of the Treaty of Judicial Settlement, Arbitration and Conciliation between the Netherlands and the Kingdom of Yugoslavia signed at The Hague on March 11, 1931. The Court observed that the invocation by a party of a new basis of jurisdiction in the second round of oral argument on a request for the indication of provisional measures had never before occurred in the Court's practice. Although Belgium and the Netherlands were given the opportunity to comment on these new contentions

---

8   In its Resolution 777, adopted on September 19, 1992, the Security Council considered that the Socialist Federal Republic of Yugoslavia had ceased to exist and recommended to the General Assembly that the latter decide that the Federal Republic of Yugoslavia (Serbia and Montenegro) should apply for membership in the United Nations and that it shall not participate in the work of the Assembly. The General Assembly, in Resolution 47/1 adopted on September 22, 1992, followed the Council's recommendation. However, Yugoslavia pointed to subsequent United Nations practice and to a letter that the UN Legal Counsel issued on September 29, 1992, stating that it was the UN Secretariat's view that Resolution 47/1 merely blocks Yugoslavia's participation in the work of the Assembly and neither terminates nor suspends Yugoslavia's membership in the United Nations. *See* UN Doc. A/47/485 (1992). On May 5, 1993, the General Assembly adopted Resolution 47/229, deciding that the Federal Republic of Yugoslavia would not participate in the work of the Economic and Social Council. However, no other action was taken pursuant to these resolutions. In particular, no admission procedure was completed, resulting in legal uncertainty as to Yugoslavia's status within the United Nations at the time.

9   *See* Order, *supra* note 1, at 135-36, paras. 31-33.

at the hearings and recorded their objections,[10] the Court found that such late introduction, when not accepted by the other party, seriously jeopardizes the principle of procedural fairness and the sound administration of justice. Consequently, the Court decided not to consider these new bases of jurisdiction in deciding on Yugoslavia's requests for provisional measures.[11]

The Court expressed its deep concern with the human tragedy in Kosovo[12] and with the loss of life and human suffering "in all parts of Yugoslavia." It also declared itself profoundly concerned with the use of force in Yugoslavia (it did not indicate by whom), which "under the present circumstances ... raises very serious issues of international law."[13] It emphasized that all parties before it must act in conformity with their obligations under the UN Charter and other rules of international law, including humanitarian law.[14] Finally, it reminded the parties that they should take care not to aggravate or extend the dispute between them and that, when such a dispute gives rise to a threat to the peace, breach of the peace or act of aggression, the UN Security Council has special responsibilities under Chapter VII of the UN Charter.[15]

Except for the cases involving Spain and the United States, the Court concluded that its findings in no way prejudge the questions of the Court's jurisdiction to deal with the merits of the case or of the admissibility of Yugoslavia's Application. Such findings leave unaffected the right of the governments involved to submit arguments in respect of those questions.

* * * *

This was the first time in the Court's history that it dismissed requests for the indication of provisional measures for lack of *prima facie* jurisdiction.[16] Over

---

10 Belgium and the Netherlands objected to the timing of the introduction by Yugoslavia of these supplemental bases of jurisdiction and pointed out that, in any event, Yugoslavia had not complied with the procedural requirements contained in the provisions invoked by it.

11 *See* Order, *supra* note 1, at 138-39, paras. 42-44.

12 *Id.* at 131, para. 16. This statement can be interpreted as a reference to the ethnic cleansing campaign carried out by the Serb military and police in Kosovo, a province of Serbia which, together with Montenegro, forms the Federal Republic of Yugoslavia.

13 *Id.* at 132, para. 17.

14 *See id.* at 132, para. 19 and 140, para. 48.

15 *See id.* at 137 paras. 37-38 (Belgium) and 557, paras. 49-50 (the Netherlands).

16 The traditional purpose of provisional measures of protection (comparable to an injunction under domestic law) is to preserve the respective rights of either party pending the Court's final decision.

the objection of the Court's senior judge, the Court nonetheless reserved the subsequent procedure for further decision in all but two cases.[17] According to well-established jurisprudence, although the Court need not, before deciding whether to indicate provisional measures, finally satisfy itself that it has jurisdiction over the merits of the case, it will indicate provisional measures only if the bases of jurisdiction invoked appear *prima facie* to afford a basis upon which the Court's jurisdiction over the case might be founded.[18] In addition, there must be urgency to the extent that, unless provisional measures are indicated, there will be a risk of irreparable injury pending final adjudication on the merits.

Had the Court addressed and upheld, at the provisional measures stage of the proceedings, the argument of the respondents that the Federal Republic of Yugoslavia is not a member state of the United Nations or a party to the ICJ Statute as the successor state to the former Socialist Republic of Yugoslavia, it would have had to declare inadmissible the Yugoslav applications and related requests and ordered all ten cases to be removed from the General List, as opposed to the ones involving Spain and the U.S. only. Only Judges Oda and Kooijmans were of the view that the question of Yugoslavia's status should have been addressed by the Court as a preliminary issue of standing. In the absence of special arrangements, only UN members may make declarations under the Optional Clause. Judge Kooijmans did not understand why the Court could say that there is no need to consider the question of the validity of Yugoslavia's declaration in light of this requirement and, at the same time, conclude that this declaration, by its terms, does not *prima facie* constitute a basis of jurisdiction. In his view, the proper order in which the Court must make its decisions is, first, to establish the existence or validity of an Optional Clause declaration that *prima facie* is capable of conferring jurisdiction upon the Court and, second, only after such existence has been established, to determine whether the declarations of the parties to the dispute contain reservations that manifestly exclude the Court's jurisdiction. In other words, the question of reservations arises only if the declaration containing the reservations is itself valid. In defense of the Court's approach, Judge Higgins noted that it is the Court's practice that weighty and complex issues relating to its jurisdiction

---

17 For a precedent, see Military and Paramilitary Activities in and against Nicaragua (Nicar. v. US), Provisional Measures, 1984 ICJ REP. 169, at 180 (Order of May 10).

18 For a discussion of the Court's jurisprudence on the jurisdictional pre-requisites for the issuance of provisional measures, *see* Sep. Op. Higgins, *supra* note 6, at paras. 10-17.

that are not the subject of comprehensive submissions by the parties during the oral hearings are not usually addressed at the provisional measures phase but rather will be treated as appropriate for resolution at the preliminary objections stage.[19] Judge Kooijmans, while he agreed that the factual and legal background of the membership question requires a more thorough analysis and a careful evaluation by the Court when it deals with its jurisdiction on the merits at a subsequent stage of the proceedings, believed the Court should have determined whether the doubts and uncertainties raised by the pertinent UN resolutions were serious enough to prevent the Court from assuming that it possesses *prima facie* jurisdiction necessary for the indication of provisional measures.

In circumstances such as those presented by these proceedings, the Court often has to walk a fine line in determining *prima facie* jurisdiction on an urgent basis. On the one hand, it cannot accept the mere invocation by an applicant of a jurisdictional clause, with nothing more, in an attempt to established *prima facie* jurisdiction, given the need for consent of both parties to the Court's jurisdiction. On the other hand, as these cases demonstrate, it must also determine whether the orderly administration of justice requires that the consideration of certain jurisdictional issues be deferred until a later stage, or, instead, requires that the case be dismissed *in limine* due to the manifest lack of jurisdiction. After having avoided the "thorny question" referred to by Judge Kooijmans in both the Court's 1993 Judgment rejecting preliminary objections in the Genocide Case[20] and these 1999 Orders, the Court will have the opportunity to present a thorough analysis and careful evaluation of the question at a later stage of the proceedings.

---

19 *See id.* at paras. 19 and 21-22.
20 *See* Peter H.F. Bekker & Paul C. Szasz, *Application of the Convention on the Prevention and Punishment of the Crime of Genocide (Bosnia-Herzegovina v. Yugoslavia)*, 91 AJIL 121, at 125-26 (1997), *reprinted in* COMMENTARIES ON WORLD COURT DECISIONS (1987-1996), at 253 (P.H.F. Bekker ed., 1998). In its Order of April 8, 1993, the Court merely stated that the solution adopted by the General Assembly in Resolution 47/1 was "not free from legal difficulties." 1993 ICJ REP. 3, at 14, para. 18.

◊

Counterclaims – absence of objections by applicant – proprio motu *exam-*
ination of requirements of Article 80 of Rules of Court – counterclaims
within the Court's jurisdiction and directly connected with the subject
matter of the applicant's claim

LAND AND MARITIME BOUNDARY BETWEEN CAMEROON AND NIGERIA
(Cameroon v. Nigeria)

Counterclaims, Order
Obtainable from <www.icj-cij.org>
International Court of Justice, June 30, 1999

On June 30, 1999, the Court issued a short Order upholding the admissibility
of the counterclaims filed by the Government of the Republic of Nigeria
(Nigeria) as part of its Counter-Memorial of May 31, 1999, and thereby allowed
these claims to form part of the proceedings on the merits of the case brought
by the Republic of Cameroon (Cameroon) on March 29, 1994. The Order
confirms the Court's jurisprudence concerning the admissibility of counterclaims
as part of the incidental jurisdiction conferred upon the Court by its Statute.[1]

Chapter 25 of Nigeria's Counter-Memorial, entitled "Particulars of the Nigerian counter-claims," referred to alleged incursions along the border from the
Cameroon side. Nigeria asked the Court to declare that Cameroon is internationally responsible for those border incursions and to determine compensation in the form of damages if the parties cannot agree on the amount of reparation within six months from the date of the Court's Judgment on the merits.

Cameroon did not challenge Nigeria's right to submit counterclaims, nor
did it otherwise object to the admissibility of such counterclaims. Hence, the
Court was called upon to examine their admissibility *proprio motu*. Thus, the

---

[1] The four earlier precedents are: Oil Platforms (Iran v. United States), 1998 ICJ REP.
190 (Mar. 10); Application of the Convention on the Prevention and Punishment
of the Crime of Genocide (Bosnia-Herzegovina v. Yugoslavia), 1997 ICJ REP. 243
(Dec. 17); Rights of Nationals of the United States of America in Morocco (France
v. United States), 1952 ICJ REP. 176 (Aug. 27); and Asylum (Peru v. Colombia),
1950 ICJ REP. 266 (Nov. 20). Judge Oda discusses the latter two precedents in
paras. 6-7 of part III of his separate opinion appended to the *Oil Platforms* Order.
See 1998 ICJ REP. 190, at 211-14.

185

P.H.F. Bekker, World Court Decisions at the Turn of the Millennium (1997-2001), p. 185-188.
© *2002 Kluwer Law International. Printed in the Netherlands.*

Court considered whether the Nigerian claims constituted "counterclaims" within the meaning of Article 80 of the Rules of Court and, if so, whether they satisfied the conditions embodied in Article 80.

The Court was satisfied that the Nigerian claims are counterclaims that come within the Court's jurisdiction as required by Article 80, paragraph 1, of the Rules of Court, without explaining further how the jurisdictional requirement was met in this case.

As to the condition *ratione temporis* contained in Article 80, paragraph 2, of the Rules, according to which the counterclaim must be made in the counter-memorial of the party presenting it and must appear as part of the submissions of that party, the Court was satisfied that Chapter 25 and the seventh submission of Nigeria's Counter-Memorial met this requirement.

Most important, the Court found that Nigeria's counterclaims are "directly connected" with the subject-matter of the claim of Cameroon, as required by Article 80, paragraph 1, of the Rules of Court. The Court agreed with Nigeria that its counterclaims rest on facts of the same nature as the corresponding claims of Cameroon, all of these facts allegedly having occurred along the frontier between Cameroon and Nigeria. In the Court's view, the claims of both parties pursue the same legal aim in that they seek to establish legal responsibility and determine the reparation due. Consequently, the Court found that the counterclaims submitted by Nigeria are admissible as such and form part of the proceedings in the case.[2]

Significantly, in its usual effort to ensure due process and strict equality between the parties, the Court reserved the applicant's right to present its views in an additional written document a second time on the respondent's counterclaims. As in previous cases, it also instructed the Registrar to transmit a copy of the Order to third states entitled to appear before the Court with a view to protecting any interests that they might have.

Finally, the Court fixed April 4, 2000, as the time limit for the filing by Cameroon of a Reply and it ordered Nigeria to file its Rejoinder by January 4, 2001.

* * * *

---

2   By contrast to the two earlier precedents, the June 30, 1999 Order does not indicate the voting on the Court's finding of admissibility. Apparently, the Members of the Court were all in agreement, so that a vote was not needed.

Reference has been made in Chapter 1 of this book to the recent increase of the instrument of counterclaims in "involuntary" cases in which the Court previously has rejected preliminary objections to its jurisdiction. This latest instance demonstrates that counterclaims have emerged as an important new tool for respondents whose preliminary objections have been rejected, as part of an effort to further delay the merits phase of a case involuntarily brought against them and to introduce independent claims similar to the applicant's.

The main difference between this Order and the ones issued in the *Genocide (Bosnia)* and *Oil Platforms* cases is that, by contrast to the latter two cases, the applicant did not object to the respondent's counterclaims. Consequently, the need to hear the parties was not at issue and the Court was able to issue its Order one month after the filing of the counterclaims.[3] The Court still was called upon to examine the requirements of Article 80 of its Rules *proprio motu* and the text of the Order indicates that the ICJ president heard the parties two days before the Order was issued in order to determine their views as to the time limits for a second round of written pleadings. Presumably, the meeting was restricted to timing issues and no substantive conversation concerning the counterclaims took place on that occasion.

The Court granted both parties some nine months to file their second round of written pleadings in the case. The Order indicates that the parties had asked for such time limits in a meeting with the ICJ president shortly before the issuance of the Order. This means that the case brought by Cameroon on March 29, 1994, will not be ready for hearing on the merits before Spring 2001, i.e., seven years after the commencement of proceedings. In the *Oil Platforms* case, such delay amounted to eight years. In the *Genocide* case, a delay of six years was encountered. Such delay has not been the subject of complaint by individual judges since the *Genocide (Bosnia)* case.[4]

The resemblance between this Order and the two previous Orders on counterclaims indicates that the Court is keen on developing a procedural jurisprudence on counterclaims that is to be applied consistently in other cases.

---

3   The Court took five months in the *Genocide (Bosnia)* case and some nine months in the *Oil Platforms* case to issue its Orders upholding the admissibility of the counterclaims submitted in those cases. However, the admissibility was heavily contested by the applicants in those cases. On the issue of the necessity or desirability to hear the parties in the context of counterclaims, see Shabtai Rosenne, *Controlling Interlocutory Aspects of Proceedings in the International Court of Justice*, 94 AJIL 307, 309 (2000).
4   Interestingly, Yugoslavia subsequently withdrew its counterclaims, as officially recorded in the president's Order of September 10, 2001.

The Order confirms that the Court prefers to settle the issue of the admissibility of counterclaims at a preliminary stage of the proceedings through a short Order.[5]

---

5   As described in Section 2.4.5 of the Introduction to this book, Art. 80 of the Rules of Court subsequently was amended with effect from February 1, 2001. *See* ICJ Communiqué 2001/1 (Jan. 12, 2001).

Application by Equatorial Guinea to intervene as a nonparty – proprio motu *examination of conditions of Article 62 of Statute and Article 81 of Rules of Court absent parties' objections – interest of a legal nature which may be affected by the decision – precise object of intervention – jurisdictional link not required for nonparty intervention*

LAND AND MARITIME BOUNDARY BETWEEN CAMEROON AND NIGERIA
(Cameroon v. Nigeria)

Application for permission to intervene, Order
Obtainable from <www.icj-cij.org>
International Court of Justice, October 21, 1999

In the case brought by the Republic of Cameroon (Cameroon) against the Federal Republic of Nigeria (Nigeria) on March 29, 1994, Equatorial Guinea filed an application for permission to intervene as a nonparty in the case on June 30, 1999, pursuant to Article 62 of the Court's Statute. Article 62 permits a third state to submit a request to the Court to be permitted to intervene if that state considers "that it has an interest of a legal nature which may be affected by the decision in the case."

Equatorial Guinea sought to inform the Court of its legal rights and interests in the Gulf of Guinea in order that these remain unaffected as the Court addresses the question of the maritime boundary between Cameroon and Nigeria. Equatorial Guinea made it clear in its application that it did not ask the Court to determine its maritime boundary with Cameroon and Nigeria and that the intervention did not concern the land boundary in dispute between the two parties. Neither Cameroon nor Nigeria opposed Equatorial Guinea's Application.[1] The Court decided, unanimously, that Equatorial Guinea was per-

---

1   As a consequence, no hearings were held on Equatorial Guinea's Application. *See* ICJ Rules of Court, Art. 84(2), *reprinted in* 73 AJIL 748, 761 (1979). *See also* Shabtai Rosenne, *Controlling Interlocutory Aspects of Proceedings in the International Court of Justice*, 94 AJIL 307, 311 (2000). However, Cameroon and Nigeria each submitted written observations within the time limit of August 16, 1999 fixed by the Court, as they were informed by the Deputy-Registrar's letters of June 30, 1999. While Cameroon stated that it had no objection in principle to Equatorial Guinea's intervention limited to the maritime boundary, it reserved its

P.H.F. Bekker, World Court Decisions at the Turn of the Millennium (1997-2001), p. 189-194.
© 2002 *Kluwer Law International. Printed in the Netherlands.*

mitted to intervene as a nonparty in the case "to the extent, in the manner and for the purposes set out in its Application of permission to intervene."[2] The Court fixed April 4, 2001, as the time limit for the filing of a written statement by Equatorial Guinea and July 4, 2001, as the time limit for the filing of written observations by Cameroon and Nigeria on Equatorial Guinea's statement.[3] This is the first time that the full Court, which hitherto had consistently rejected requests for intervention under Article 62, has accepted an application for permission to intervene as a nonparty in a case.

As part of its summary of the historical background of the proceedings between Cameroon and Nigeria, the Court referred to its decision of June 11, 1998, rejecting Nigeria's preliminary objections. In that decision, the Court itself envisaged the possibility of third states, including Equatorial Guinea and Sao Tome and Principe, intervening in the case.[4]

The Court next referred to excerpts from Equatorial Guinea's Application addressing each of the requirements that Article 81, paragraph 2 of the Rules of Court imposes on an application for permission to intervene. Apart from stating the name of the agent and containing a list of the documents in support of the application, it must (*a*) set out the interest of a legal nature which the state applying to intervene considers may be affected by the decision in the case; (*b*) describe the precise object of the intervention; and (*c*) set out any

---

position in relation to the validity and possible consequences of the unilateral delimitation undertaken by Equatorial Guinea. According to Cameroon, Equatorial Guinea's claims are based solely on the principle of equidistance and do not take into account the special geographical features of the area in dispute. In Nigeria's view, acceptance of Equatorial Guinea's Application to intervene makes no difference to Nigeria's legal position or the Court's jurisdiction. *See* slip opinion available from the ICJ Registry and from the ICJ Web site, <www.icj-cij.org>, at paras. 9-10 [hereinafter Order].

2   Order, *supra* note 1, at para. 18(1) (*dispositif*).

3   *Id.* at para. 18(2). *See* ICJ Rules of Court, Art. 85, *supra* note 1.

4   *Id.* at para. 2 (citing Land and Maritime Boundary between Cameroon and Nigeria (Cam. v. Nig.), Preliminary Objections, Judgment, 1998 ICJ REP. 275, at 324, para. 116 (June 11)). In its 1998 decision, the Court stated that "it is evident that the prolongation of the maritime boundary between the Parties ... will eventually run into maritime zones where the rights and interests of Cameroon and Nigeria will overlap those of third States. ... [T]he Court cannot rule out the possibility that the impact of the judgment required by Cameroon on the rights and interests of third States could be such that the Court would be prevented from rendering it in the absence of these States ... Whether such third States would choose to exercise their rights to intervene in these proceedings pursuant to the Statute remains to be seen."

basis of jurisdiction which is claimed to exist as between the state applying to intervene and the parties to the case.[5]

First, as to the existence of an interest of a legal nature, Equatorial Guinea explained in its Application that it was seeking to protect its sovereign rights and jurisdiction pertaining to it under international law up to the median line[6] between Equatorial Guinea and Nigeria, on the one hand, and between Equatorial Guinea and Cameroon, on the other hand. In its view, such protection requires that any Cameroon-Nigeria maritime boundary that may be determined by the Court should not cross over the median line with Equatorial Guinea. It pointed out that the general maritime area where the interests of Equatorial Guinea, Cameroon and Nigeria come together is active with oil and gas exploration. To extend the Cameroon-Nigeria boundary into Equatorial Guinea waters across the median line with Equatorial Guinea would in its view prejudice its rights and interests, especially *vis-à-vis* concessionaires who it fears will ignore Equatorial Guinea's protests and proceed to explore and exploit resources to the legal and economic detriment of Equatorial Guinea. In this respect, it was the Court's view, without further reasoning, that Equatorial Guinea had sufficiently established that it has an interest of a legal nature which could be affected by any judgment which the Court might hand down for the purpose of determining the maritime boundary between Cameroon and Nigeria.[7]

Addressing the second condition, Equatorial Guinea's Application stated that its precise object was twofold. First, it was meant to protect Equatorial Guinea's legal rights in the Gulf of Guinea by all legal means available. Second,

---

5   In addition, Article 81, paragraph 1 of the Rules requires that a request for intervention be filed "as soon as possible and not later than the closure of the written proceedings" (unless exceptional circumstances warrant a later submission). In the present case, Cameroon and Nigeria had completed a first round of written pleadings and were ordered, by an Order issued by the Court on the very day that Equatorial Guinea filed its Application, to engage in a second round of written pleadings consisting of a reply and a rejoinder. *See* Order, *supra* note 1.

6   I.e., the line dividing maritime zones between two states of which every point is equidistant from the coasts of each of those states.

7   Order, *supra* note 1, at para. 13. The Court did not address the standard of proof set forth by the *Gulf of Fonseca* Chamber in its 1990 Judgment, including that the applicant has the burden of proof to demonstrate convincingly what it asserts and that a general apprehension is not sufficient. *See* Land, Island and Maritime Frontier Dispute (El Salv./Hond.), Application by Nicaragua for permission to intervene, Judgment, 1990 ICJ REP. 92, at 117, paras. 61-62 (Sept. 13), *summarized in* 85 AJIL 680 (1991), *reprinted in* COMMENTARIES ON WORLD COURT DECISIONS (1987-1996), at 101 (P.H.F. Bekker ed., 1998).

the intervention was designed to inform the Court of the nature of the legal rights and interests of Equatorial Guinea that could be affected by the Court's decision in the light of the maritime boundary claims advanced by Cameroon and Nigeria. Equatorial Guinea emphasized that it was not seeking the Court's determination of its boundaries with Cameroon and Nigeria. The Court simply referred, without further reasoning, to the statement of the Chamber which dealt with Nicaragua's request to intervene in *Land, Island and Maritime Frontier Dispute* that to inform the Court of the nature of the legal rights of a state in issue in a dispute is not an improper object of an intervention.[8]

Third, although Equatorial Guinea acknowledged that there is no basis of jurisdiction in relation to Cameroon and Nigeria, it pointed out that it did not seek to be a party to the case before the Court and that it did not request the Court to determine Equatorial Guinea's maritime boundaries with Cameroon and Nigeria, which it prefers to do through negotiations. Equatorial Guinea made it clear that it had no intention of intervening in those aspects of the case that relate to the land boundary between Cameroon and Nigeria, including determination of sovereignty over the Bakassi Peninsula. The Court again referred, without further reasoning, to the 1990 statements of the *Gulf of Fonseca* Chamber pointing out that the existence of a valid link of jurisdiction between the state seeking to intervene and the parties is not a requirement for the success of an application to intervene; the procedure of intervention is to ensure that a state with possibly affected interests may be permitted to intervene even though there is no jurisdictional link and for that reason cannot become a party.[9]

On this basis, the Court decided, unanimously, that Equatorial Guinea was permitted to intervene in the case between Cameroon and Nigeria to the extent, in the manner and for the purposes set out in its application for permission to intervene.

* * * *

Prior to this precedent, the five-judge Chamber formed to deal with the case concerning the *Land, Island and Maritime Frontier Dispute* (El Salvador/

---

8   Order, *supra* note 1, at para. 14 (citing Land, Island and Maritime Frontier Dispute (El Salv./Hond.), Application by Nicaragua for permission to intervene, Judgment, 1990 ICJ REP. 92, at 130, para. 90 (Sept. 13)).

9   *Id.* at para. 15 (citing Land, Island and Maritime Frontier Dispute (El Salv./Hond.), Application by Nicaragua for permission to intervene, Judgment, 1990 ICJ REP. 92, at 135, para. 100 (Sept. 13)).

Honduras) allowed a limited intervention by Nicaragua in 1990.[10] But apart from that Chamber precedent, the full Court consistently had denied requests for intervention pursuant to Article 62 of its Statute.[11] The Court's decision, issued almost a decade after the precedent set by the Chamber, is, therefore, a significant one. However, due to its shortness and meager reasoning, this Order does not represent the landmark development in the Court's jurisprudence that the Chamber's decision of 1990 stands for. The Court's extensive and

---

10 *See* Land, Island and Maritime Frontier Dispute (El Salv./Hond.), Application by Nicaragua for permission to intervene, Judgment, 1990 ICJ REP. 92 (Sept. 13).

11 *See* Continental Shelf (Tun./Libya), Application by Malta for permission to intervene, Judgment, 1981 ICJ REP. 3 (Apr. 14); Continental Shelf (Libya/Malta), Application by Italy for permission to intervene, Judgment, 1984 ICJ REP. 3 (Mar. 21). In 1995, the Court dismissed, without consideration or hearings, the Article 62 applications of Australia, Samoa, the Solomon Islands, the Marshall Islands and the Federated States of Micronesia. *See* Request for an Examination of the Situation in Accordance with Paragraph 63 of the Court's Judgment of 20 December 1974 in the *Nuclear Tests (New Zealand v. France)* Case, 1995 ICJ REP. 288, at 306, para. 67 (Order of Sept. 22). For learned writings on intervention, *see,* e.g., W. FARAG, L'INTERVENTION DEVANT LA COUR PERMANENTE DE JUSTICE INTERNATIONALE (ARTICLES 62 ET 63 DU STATUT DE LA COUR) (1927); J.T. Miller, *Intervention in Proceedings before the International Court of Justice,* in 2 THE FUTURE OF THE INTERNATIONAL COURT OF JUSTICE 550 (L. Gross ed., 1976); Philip C. Jessup, *Intervention in the International Court,* 75 AJIL 903 (1981); Taslim O. Elias, *The Limits of the Right of Intervention in a Case before the International Court of Justice,* in: VÖLKERRECHT ALS RECHTSORDNUNG, INTERNATIONALE GERICHTSBARKEIT, MENSCHENRECHTE: FESTSCHRIFT FÜR HERMANN MOSLER 159 (1983); WOLFGANG W. FRITZEMEYER, INTERVENTION IN THE INTERNATIONAL COURT OF JUSTICE (1983); William D. Rogers *et al., Application of El Salvador to Intervene in the Jurisdiction and Admissibility Phase of* Nicaragua v. United States, 78 AJIL 929 (1984); Christine M. Chinkin, *Third-Party Intervention before the International Court of Justice,* 80 AJIL 495 (1986); Anna Madakou, *Intervention before the International Court of Justice* (Mémoire presenté en vue de l'obtention du diplôme, Institut Universitaire des Hautes Etudes Internationales, Geneva, 1988); Shigeru Oda, *The International Court of Justice viewed from the Bench (1976-1993),* 244 RdC 83-87 (1993-VII); SHABTAI ROSENNE, INTERVENTION IN THE INTERNATIONAL COURT (1993); Santiago Torres Bernárdez, *L'intervention dans la procédure de la Cour Internationale de Justice,* 256 RdC 193 (1995); José Maria Ruda, *Intervention before the International Court of Justice,* in: FIFTY YEARS OF THE INTERNATIONAL COURT OF JUSTICE 487 (Vaughan Lowe & Malgosia Fitzmaurice eds., 1996); SHABTAI ROSENNE, 3 THE LAW AND PRACTICE OF THE INTERNATIONAL COURT (1920-1996), at 1481-1555 (1997); Shabtai Rosenne, *Controlling Interlocutory Aspects of Proceedings in the International Court of Justice,* 94 AJIL 307, 310-11 (2000).

exclusive reliance on the Chamber's statements in the 1999 Order indicates that the Court likely will follow the 1990 precedent in all respects. Remarkably, the 1999 Order makes no reference whatsoever to the Court's earlier decisions issued in 1981 and 1984.

The format of the Court's decision is somewhat unusual in that, with the exception of its decisions on Fiji's Application for permission to intervene in the *Nuclear Tests* cases,[12] it usually decides on applications of this nature in the form of a Judgment.[13] Perhaps the form of an Order was used because the application in this case was unopposed by the parties and the decision was taken unanimously.

Article 85 of the Rules of Court provides that an applicant who has been permitted to intervene under Article 62 of the Statute will be supplied with copies of the pleadings and documents filed by the parties and may submit a written statement on the subject-matter of the intervention, on which the parties may submit written observations. The intervening state may also submit its observations orally during the hearings on the merits.

Due to its intervention as a nonparty in the case, Equatorial Guinea will not have the rights that parties to a case typically enjoy, including the right to appoint a judge *ad hoc*.[14] Most important, however, Equatorial Guinea will not have the obligation incumbent upon parties to accept the Court's Judgment as decisive, as expressed by the *res judicata* of Article 59 of the Statute.[15] In this respect, Equatorial Guinea's role in the case will be purely informative.

---

12 *See* 1973 ICJ REP. 320; 1973 ICJ REP. 324 (Orders of July 12).

13 *See* ROSENNE, *supra* note 11, at 1498 (III.359). Neither the Statute nor the Rules of Court require a judgment in an intervention proceeding or, for that matter, any interlocutory proceeding. *But see* ICJ Statute Art. 61, para. 2 ("The proceedings for revision shall be opened by a judgment of the Court") and ICJ Rules of Court, *supra* note 1, Art. 79, para. 7 ("After hearing the parties [on preliminary objections], the Court shall give its decision in the form of a judgment").

14 *See* ICJ STATUTE Art. 31, paras. 2-3.

15 In this respect, Cameroon's statement, contained in its written observations concerning Equatorial Guinea's Application, that "the intervention of Equatorial Guinea should allow the Court to decide on a delimitation of the boundary which will be stable and *final in relation to the States involved*" (emphasis added), failed to recognize the true nature of the application (i.e., one requesting nonparty intervention). *See* Order, *supra* note 1, at para. 9.

International law governing watercourses forming common boundaries of states – determination of disputed boundary around Kasikili/Sedudu Island in "main channel" and of island's legal status – interpretation of 1890 Anglo-German Treaty delimiting colonial spheres of influence – customary international law relating to treaty interpretation and application of 1969 Vienna Convention on Law of Treaties to non-parties – relevance of subsequent practice – evidentiary value of maps – doctrine of acquisitive prescription

KASIKILI/SEDUDU ISLAND (BOTSWANA/NAMIBIA)

Judgment
1999 ICJ REP. 1045
International Court of Justice, December 13, 1999

On May 29, 1996, the Republics of Botswana and Namibia jointly notified to the Registrar of the International Court of Justice the text of a Special Agreement between them that was signed at Gaborone (Botswana) on February 15, 1996, and entered into force on May 15, 1996. Through this Special Agreement, the parties submitted to the Court their dispute concerning the boundary around a 1.5 square mile island located in the Chobe River, known in Botswana as "Sedudu" and in Namibia as "Kasikili" (Island) and asked the Court to determine the boundary around the Island and its legal status. The Court was requested to do so mainly on the basis of a treaty, signed on July 1, 1890, between Great Britain and Germany (Anglo-German Treaty) whereby these colonial powers located the dividing line between their respective spheres of influence in this African region in the "main channel" of the Chobe River. A Joint Team of Experts on the Boundary around the Island appointed by the parties in May 1992 had been unable to determine the boundary and had recommended the peaceful settlement of the dispute.

Emphasizing different criteria, Botswana contended that the main channel constituting the boundary between Botswana and Namibia is the one running north and west of the Island and that the Island belongs exclusively to the territory of Botswana, whereas Namibia argued that the channel running south of the Island is governing and that the Island is part of Namibian territory. Two rounds of written pleadings were filed in 1997-98 and oral proceedings took place at the Peace Palace in The Hague between February 15 and March 5,

195

P.H.F. Bekker, World Court Decisions at the Turn of the Millennium (1997-2001), p. 195-209.
© 2002 *Kluwer Law International. Printed in the Netherlands.*

1999. On December 13, 1999, the Court, by 11 votes to four, found that the boundary around the Island follows the line of the deepest soundings in the northern channel of the Chobe River and that the Island forms part of the territory of Botswana. The Court also found, unanimously, that in the two channels around the Island, the nationals of, and vessels flying the flags of, both parties are to enjoy equal national treatment.[1]

The Court first addressed the issue of the law applicable to this case. In the Court's view, it was to perform a dual task under the parties' Special Agreement: (1) to determine the boundary between Botswana and Namibia around the Island; and (2) to determine the legal status of the Island. With regard to the interpretation of the Anglo-German Treaty, acknowledged by both parties to be binding on them, the Court determined that the rules reflected in Article 31 of the 1969 Vienna Convention on the Law of Treaties applied in this case.[2] Even though neither party has ratified the Vienna Convention, both considered, as confirmed by the Court's jurisprudence, that this provision is applicable inasmuch as it reflects customary international law.[3] The Special Agreement also referred to "the rules and principles of international law" as applicable law, which it described as "those set forth in the provisions of Article 38, paragraph 1" of the ICJ Statute. In addition, during the proceedings the parties invoked the principles set forth in the Charters of the United Nations and the Organization of African Unity (OAU) and referred to an OAU resolution

---

1   *See* Kasikili/Sedudu Island (Botswana/Namibia), Judgment, 1999 ICJ REP. 1045, at 1108, Para. 104 (Dec. 13) [hereinafter Judgment].

2   Vienna Convention on the Law of Treaties, signed May 23, 1969, entry into force Jan. 27, 1980, UN Doc. A/CONF.39/27, 4th Annex *reprinted in* 8 ILM 679 (1969) [hereinafter Vienna Convention]. Article 31 states:
    "1. A treaty shall be interpreted in good faith in accordance with the ordinary meaning to be given to the terms of the treaty in their context and in the light of its object and purpose.
    2. The context for the purpose of the interpretation of a treaty shall comprise, in addition to the text, including its preamble and annexes:
    (a) any agreement relating to the treaty which was made between all the parties in connection with the conclusion of the treaty;
    (b) any instrument which was made by one or more parties in connection with the conclusion of the treaty and accepted by the other parties as an instrument related to the treaty."

3   *See* Judgment, *supra* note 1, at para. 18 (citing Territorial Dispute (Libya/Chad), Judgment, 1994 ICJ REP. 6, at 21, para. 41 (Feb. 3); Oil Platforms (Iran v. U.S.), Preliminary Objection, Judgment, 1996 ICJ REP. 803, at 812, para. 23 (Dec. 12)).

expressing respect for the frontiers existing upon achievement of national independence in implementation of the principle of *uti possidetis juris*.[4]

The Court proceeded to interpret the provisions of the Anglo-German Treaty by applying the rules of interpretation contained in the Vienna Convention, giving priority to the text agreed upon at the time of the treaty's conclusion while taking into account the present-day state of scientific knowledge.[5] According to Article III of the Anglo-German Treaty, the boundary delimiting the respective spheres of influence of each contracting party "descends the centre of the main channel" of the Chobe River. However, neither Article III nor any other provision of the Anglo-German Treaty furnished criteria through which the "main channel" could be determined. Whereas the English treaty text locates the boundary in the "centre" of the main channel, the German version refers to the term "*thalweg*" of that channel ("Thalweg des Haupt-laufes"). The Court pointed out that the concepts of the "thalweg" of a watercourse and the "centre" of a watercourse are not equivalent but noted that these terms nonetheless were used interchangeably, i.e., as translations of each other, at the time of the conclusion of the Anglo-German Treaty. Accordingly, the Court, in analogous application of Article 33, paragraph 3 of the Vienna Convention, treated both words as having the same meaning.[6] Moreover, it employed the term "channel" in a broad sense as referring to each of the two branches of the Chobe River that ring the Island (as opposed to being restricted to the navigable passage of a river or of one of its branches).[7]

In the Court's view, the real dispute between the parties concerned the location of the main channel where the boundary lies. The parties disagreed on both the method to interpret the expressions "centre" and "thalweg" and on the location of the main channel. Whereas Botswana argued that the line

---

4   *See id.* at para. 19. For a description of the *uti possidetis juris* principle, see Frontier Dispute (Burkina Faso/Mali), Judgment, 1986 ICJ REP. 554, at 566, para. 23 (Dec. 22) ("The essence of the principle lies in its primary aim of securing respect for the territorial boundaries at the moment when independence is achieved ... [By this principle,] administrative boundaries [were] transformed into international frontiers in the full sense of the term.").

5   *See id.* at para. 20 (citing Territorial Dispute (Libya/Chad), Judgment, 1994 ICJ REP. 6, at 21-22, para. 41 (Feb. 3), and an *ad hoc* arbitration between Argentina and Chile concluded in 1994).

6   *See id.* at para. 25. Pursuant to Article 33(3), "the terms of the treaty are presumed to have the same meaning in each authentic text." From the Court's statement, it may be inferred that it regards Article 33 as forming part of the corpus of customary international law. *See also* LaGrand Case, *infra* Chapter 5.

7   *See id.* at para. 26.

of the boundary, and therefore the main channel, was to be found exclusively on the basis of a determination of the thalwegs in the northern and western channel of the Chobe River, Namibia claimed that the main channel had to be found first and in turn would identify the thalwegs constituting the boundary, which in its view was formed by the thalwegs of the southern channel of the river.[8]

Before the Court set out to determine, initially, the ordinary meaning of the words "main channel" by reference to the most commonly used criteria in international law and practice, it noted that the parties, while agreeing on many of the criteria for identifying the "main channel," disagreed on the relevance and applicability of several of those criteria. While both parties agreed that the greatest depth and width, flow velocity and annual volume of flow are among the criteria for identifying the main channel of a river with multiple channels, Namibia considered that the main channel of the Chobe was the one that carries the largest proportion of the annual flow of the river and is mostly used for river traffic and that neither width nor depth were suitable criteria in this case given the sharp variations in the level of the Chobe's waters. The Court found that it could not rely on one single criterion in carrying out its task, given that a river's natural features may vary markedly along its course and from one case to another. The Court instead took into account all of the criteria referred to by the parties and by scientific works.[9]

Noting that both parties agreed that the Island's hydrological situation had not radically changed since 1890, the Court first examined the criterion of depth. Namibia, while acknowledging that the northern channel has the greater mean depth, disagreed with Botswana that this criterion determined the main channel and argued instead that draught at the shallowest point of the channel has greater significance, without producing figures to prove that the minimum depth of the southern channel was the greatest. However, the Court concluded that the northern channel is deeper than the southern one as regards both mean depth and minimum depth.[10]

Considering the criterion of width, the Court observed that this often has been determined on the basis of the low water mark or the mean water level. Relying on a 1912 report and on aerial and satellite pictures taken since 1925,

---

8   *See id.* at paras. 22-23, 27.
9   *See id.* at para. 30.
10   *See id.* at paras. 31-32.

the Court concluded that, apart from the season of flooding, the northern channel of the Chobe River is wider than the southern one.[11]

In connection with the criterion of flow, i.e., the annual volume of water carried, to which both parties attached great importance, the parties submitted competing figures, maps and images from which they reached differing conclusions. In the Court's opinion, the main channel has to be determined according to the low water baseline and not the floodline. During the several months of flooding, the Island is submerged by flood water and the region turns into a giant lake, making it impossible to determine the main channel in relation to the other channel. The Court was unable to accept the channel described by Namibia as the main channel, given that its bed remains dry for most of the year, nor was such conclusion warranted in terms of visibility or general physical appearance, or even bed profile configuration as a criterion.[12]

Finally, the Court examined the criterion of the navigability of a watercourse, being the product of its depth, its width and the volume of water it carries and taking into account natural obstacles along its course. Whereas in Botswana's view this criterion was a primary consideration in 1890, Namibia considered that it was anomalous to apply this criterion to a river that is nonnavigable for most of its length, but it did point to the actual use of the southern channel for the purpose of navigation by tourist boats. The Court observed that the pertinent data proved that the navigability of both channels around the Island is limited due to their shallowness, leading it to conclude that the northern channel is the main channel as being that of the two channels which offers more favorable conditions for navigation. The Court noted that the economic importance of navigation and the use of flat-bottomed tourist boats in the southern channel do not alter its conditions of navigability.[13]

Having concluded that the ordinary meaning of Article III of the Anglo-German Treaty dictates that the northern channel of the Chobe River around the Island be regarded as its main channel, as supported by three on-site investigations conducted in 1912, 1948 and 1985 (the latter two resulting in joint reports),[14] the Court next considered how and to what extent the object and purpose of the Anglo-German Treaty could clarify the meaning to be given to its terms. Recognizing that this treaty is one delimiting spheres of influence and not a boundary treaty properly speaking, the Court observed that Great

---

11 *See id.* at para. 33.
12 *See id.* at paras. 34-39.
13 *See id.* at para. 40.
14 *See id.* at paras. 41-42.

Britain and Germany nonetheless intended it to establish a boundary between their territories separating their spheres of influence even in the case of a river with multiple channels. Their approach in doing so was that of describing a frontier line objectively and conveniently while possessing only rudimentary information about the Chobe's channels.[15] By choosing "the centre of the main channel" of the Chobe River as the mark separating their spheres of influences, the contracting parties ensured that there was a well-defined, recognizable boundary in a watercourse that they assumed was navigable. Although one of their objectives underlying this choice apparently was freedom of navigation, they also sought to delimit as precisely as possible their respective spheres of influence. The Court found support for its reasoning in the *travaux prépara-toires* (provisional agreement and subsequent correspondence) relating to the Anglo-German Treaty, demonstrating that the pertinent terms were synonymous in both the English and German versions and correctly and accurately expressed the will of the contracting parties.[16]

Botswana and Namibia also referred to the subsequent practice of Great Britain and Germany and their successors as an element relevant for the inter-pretation of the Anglo-German Treaty, but disagreed on the consequences to be drawn from such practice. According to the rule of customary international law embodied in Article 31, paragraph 3, of the Vienna Convention, any interpretation of a treaty must take into account, together with the treaty's context, "*(a)* any subsequent agreement between the parties regarding the interpretation of the treaty or the application of its provisions" (interpretative agreements), and also "*(b)* any subsequent practice in the application of the treaty which establishes the agreement of the parties regarding its interpreta-tion."[17] Botswana relied mainly on three sets of documents prepared in 1912, 1948 and 1985, respectively, and relating correspondence in support of its argument that these all pointed to the northern channel as constituting the main channel.[18] After examining each of these sources and both parties' views

---

15 *See id.* at para. 43 (referring to a similar approach identified by the Court in Temple of Preah Vihear (Cambodia v. Thailand), Merits, Judgment, 1962 ICJ REP. 6, at 34 (June 15)).

16 *See id.* at para. 46.

17 *See id.* at para. 50, listing examples from the Court's jurisprudence between 1949 and 1996.

18 These documents are: (a) a reconnaissance report by Captain H.E. Eason of the Bechuanaland Protectorate Police prepared in August 1912; (b) a 1951 understanding between Major L.F.W. Trollope, a Magistrate of the Eastern Caprivi Strip, and Mr. Dickinson, a District Commissioner in the Bechuanaland Protectorate; and (c) an

relating thereto,[19] together with certain other facts and incidents relied on by the parties,[20] the Court concluded that, while the subsequent practice of the parties to the Anglo-German Treaty referred to by Botswana and Namibia did not result in any interpretative agreement or in any understanding or practice in the treaty's application establishing the parties' agreement regarding its interpretation within the meaning of Article 31, paragraph 3 of the Vienna Convention, the factual findings made in 1912, 1948 and 1985 were not, as such, disputed at the time and, even though they do not constitute subsequent practice, they nevertheless support the Court's conclusions with regard to the ordinary meaning to be given to Article III of the Anglo-German Treaty.[21]

As part of its reliance on the subsequent practice of the parties to the Anglo-German Treaty, Namibia argued that such practice not only corroborated the treaty's interpretation but also gave rise to an independent alternative basis for its claim under the doctrines concerning acquisition of territory by prescription, acquiescence and recognition and the *uti possidetis juris* principle.[22] In Namibia's view, such subsequent practice consisted of the continued control and use of the Island by the Masubia tribe from the eastern part of the Caprivi Strip, the alleged exercise of jurisdiction over the Island by the governing authorities in the Caprivi Strip, and the silence, with full knowledge of the facts, by Botswana and its predecessors lasting nearly a century. For Namibia, this practice confirmed the interpretation of Article III as attributing the Island to Namibia. However, Botswana contended that Namibia's "subsequent conduct" argument really was one grounded in acquisitive prescription and that such concepts are irreconcilable: whereas the former relates to an existing legal instrument, the latter's purpose is to destroy and to supplant a pre-existing title. Botswana pointed out that the Island had been used for agricultural purposes only sporadically and it denied that there had ever been a permanent settlement or village on the Island.[23]

Deferring consideration of Namibia's prescription argument, the Court instead sought to ascertain whether the alleged long-standing, unopposed

---

agreement concluded in December 1984 between Botswana and South Africa for the conduct of a Joint Survey of the Chobe River, together with the resultant Survey Report of July 15, 1985. *See id.* at paras. 42, 52-70 and 74.

19   *See id.* at paras. 53-70.

20   *See id.* at paras. 76-78.

21   *See id.* at paras. 79-80.

22   I.e., Namibia claimed that it was in possession of the Island at the time of termination of colonial rule.

23   *See* Judgment, *supra* note 1, at paras. 71-72.

presence of members of the Masubia tribe on the Island constituted "subsequent practice" in the application of the Anglo-German Treaty establishing the parties' agreement regarding its interpretation, conform Article 31(3)*(b)* of the Vienna Convention. In the Court's view, this required that the occupation of the Island by the Masubia tribe was linked to a belief on the part of the Caprivi authorities that the boundary expressed by the Anglo-German Treaty followed the southern channel of the Chobe River. It also required that the Bechuanaland authorities associated with Great Britain were fully aware of and accepted this as a confirmation of the treaty boundary. However, the Court found that the Masubia's presence was intermittent and not linked to territorial claims by the Caprivi authorities. The Court observed that it is not uncommon for the inhabitants of African border regions to traverse such borders for purposes of agriculture and grazing, without raising concern on the part of the authorities on either side of the border. Moreover, even though reports drawn up in 1912, 1948 and 1985 mentioned the intermittent presence on the Island of members of the Masubia tribe and their livestock, this did not appear to be related to interpretation of the terms of the Anglo-German Treaty. The Court thus concluded that such presence did not constitute "subsequent practice" in the treaty's application as meant in Article 31(3)*(b)* of the Vienna Convention.[24]

The Court next considered the evidentiary value of the various maps that both parties had introduced into the proceedings in support of their respective positions. Namibia believed that the majority of these maps placed the boundary around the Island in the southern channel and it sought to rely on this as a specialized form of subsequent practice and as supporting its claim of sovereignty over the Island by virtue of the doctrine of prescriptive acquisition and the principle of *uti possidetis juris*. Botswana disputed Namibia's assertion that a preponderance of maps show the boundary to be located in the southern channel and contended that the only map evidencing agreement of the parties, drawn up in 1985, depicts the northern channel as containing the boundary.

The Court recalled that the Chamber formed to deal with the *Frontier Dispute* case had ruled in 1986 that maps cannot, merely by virtue of their existence, constitute a territorial title, i.e., they are not documents endowed by international law with intrinsic legal force to establish territorial rights. Maps constitute extrinsic evidence only and may be used, together with other circum-

---

24   *See id.* at paras. 73-75.

stantial evidence, to establish or reconstitute the real facts.[25] Even though Article III(2) of the Anglo-German Treaty refers to "a Map officially prepared for the British Government in 1889," in fact no map was appended to the Anglo-German Treaty that officially expresses the intentions of the contracting parties with regard to the course of the boundary. Given the absence of a map and the lack of agreement (express or tacit) concerning the validity or course of the boundary depicted in any map, coupled with the persistent uncertainty and inconsistency of the cartographic material submitted to it, the Court was unable to find that the authorities concerned had accepted any available maps as constituting subsequent practice in the application or interpretation of the Anglo-German Treaty or as recognition of the boundary shown on any map. Consequently, the cartographic evidence in this case did not alter the results of the Court's textual interpretation of the Anglo-German Treaty.[26]

Based on its interpretation of the Anglo-German Treaty, the Court concluded that the boundary between Botswana and Namibia around the Island provided for in the treaty lies in the northern channel of the Chobe River. Given that the text of the treaty specifies that the boundary follows the "centre" (English version) or "thalweg" (German version) of the main channel, using them as synonyms, and in the light of the treaty's *travaux préparatoires* indicating the parties' shared intention to exploit the possibility of navigation on the Chobe River, the Court considered that the term "thalweg" more accurately reflects this intention and is, therefore, determinative in Article III. The Court noted that the parties agreed that the thalweg is formed by the line of deepest soundings and concluded that the boundary in this case follows that line in the northern channel around the Island.[27]

Before the Court could hold that the Island forms part of the territory of Botswana, it had to deal with Namibia's alternative argument by which it claimed prescriptive title to the Island. For Namibia, this submission was grounded in general "rules and principles of international law" and was, in its view, sanctioned by the explicit terms of the Special Agreement. However, Botswana argued that Namibia's arguments relating to prescription and acquiescence were inadmissible because they were not included in the scope of the question submitted to the Court under the terms of the Special Agreement

---

25 *See* Frontier Dispute (Burkina Faso/Republic of Mali), Judgment, 1986 ICJ REP. 554, at 582, para. 54 (Dec. 22). The Chamber allowed an exception for maps that are annexed to an official text of which they form an integral part, such text being of intrinsic legal force as expressing the will of the states concerned.

26 *See* Judgment, *supra* note 1, at paras. 81-87.

27 *See id.* at paras. 88-89.

which, in its view, asked the Court to determine the boundary solely on the basis of the Anglo-German Treaty. The Court rejected Botswana's procedural objections and found that the general wording of the Special Agreement, and in particular its reference to Article 38(1) of the Court's Statute, showed that the parties had no intention of confining the rules and principles of law applicable in this case solely to the rules and principles of international law relating to treaty interpretation. It pointed out that, even if the Special Agreement had not referred to "the rules and principles of international law," the Court still would have been allowed to apply the general rules of treaty interpretation in order to interpret the Anglo-German Treaty. The Court concluded that the Special Agreement authorized it to interpret the treaty in the light of the rules and principles of international law and also to apply those rules and principles independently.[28]

In Namibia's view, all four conditions enabling possession of territory to mature into a prescriptive title were fulfilled in this case. First, it claimed that the possession of the Island by it and its predecessors dated back at least to the beginning of the 20th century and had, therefore, endured for a considerable length of time. Second, the possession and occupation and use of the Island by Germany and its successors were said to have been peaceful and uninterrupted. Third, Namibia contended that its possession of the Island was public and occurred with the full knowledge of Botswana and its predecessors, with Botswana remaining silent for almost two decades after gaining independence in 1966. Fourth and foremost, Namibia claimed that sovereign jurisdiction had been exercised over the Island.[29] Although Botswana accepted the criteria for acquiring prescriptive title cited by Namibia, it argued that those criteria were not satisfied in this case. In its view, even if peaceful, public and continuous possession of the Island by the people of Caprivi had been proven, there was no credible evidence that either Namibia or its predecessors had exercised state authority in respect of the Island.[30]

Without expressing itself on the status of, or conditions for, acquisitive prescription in international law, the Court agreed with Botswana that the conditions set out by Namibia were not satisfied in this case and, therefore, rejected Namibia's argument based on acquisitive prescription. In its view, since the Masubia tribe occupying the Island never exercised functions of state authority on behalf of the authorities of the Masubia and the Caprivi, Namibia

---

28   *See id.* at paras. 90-93.
29   *See id.* at para. 94.
30   *See id.* at para. 95

had failed to establish that this tribe had occupied the Island *à titre de souverain*. The evidence showed that the Masubia people used the Island intermittently and for exclusively agricultural purposes, without such use being linked to territorial claims by the authority administering the Caprivi. For Bechuanaland (the British Protectorate), the activities of the Masubia on the Island were independent from the issue of title to the Island. Finally, Bechuanaland's instant rejection of South Africa's official claim to title precluded acquiescence on its part.[31]

Having rejected Namibia's alternative argument, the Court found, by 11 votes to four, that Kasikili/Sedudu Island forms part of the territory of Botswana.[32]

Finally, the Court referred to a communiqué relating to the dispute concerning the Island signed by the presidents of Botswana and Namibia in Kasane (Botswana) on May 24, 1992, by which they agreed, *inter alia*, that "navigation should remain unimpeded including free movement of tourists." Recalling that the parties had empowered it to determine the legal status of the Island and having regard to statements made by Botswana during the proceedings, the Court concluded that Botswana and Namibia have undertaken to one another that there shall be unimpeded navigation for craft of their nationals and flags in the channels around the Island and found, unanimously, that in these channels the nationals of, and vessels flying the flags of, both parties are to enjoy equal national treatment.[33]

* * * *

As the Court notes in its Judgment, this dispute between Botswana and Namibia is set against the background of the 19th century race among the European colonial powers for the partition of Africa. The case demonstrates that such partition continues to strain the relations between several newly independent nations situated on the African continent, even if the object of the dispute does not represent huge economic or territorial interests. In this case, the dispute was about an island of modest size and economic importance. It is subject to flooding of several months' duration and serves modest local agricultural and

---

31 *See id.* at paras. 97-99.
32 *See id.* at paras. 101 and 104(2) (operative paragraph).
33 *See id.* at paras. 102-103 and 104(3).

tourist purposes only.[34] Still, it brought two sovereign nations to the great World Court for the first time since their independence.[35] Herein lies perhaps the greatest significance of this case: two young African nations deciding to conclude an agreement to submit their territorial dispute for peaceful settlement to the principal judicial organ of the United Nations. In the case of Namibia, the Court may be said to have contributed to the creation of that nation by its various pronouncements on the legal status of the territory formerly known as South West Africa.[36]

This case demonstrates, in a real sense, that international law, in all its different facets, can work. The same can be said about the process by which the ICJ contributes to the peaceful settlement of disputes and, in some cases, to the progressive development of international law, in this case by its contributions to the coming into being of a nation state and the determination of its borders. It is encouraging to see that such a state, in the early stages of its statehood, proceeded to employ the Court's process in resolving a sensitive dispute with one of its neighbors by jointly submitting it to the Hague Court through the conclusion of a special treaty. The trust of the parties in the Court is underscored by the fact that neither party exercised its right, under Article 31(3) of the Court's Statute and referred to in Article VIII(1) of the Special Agreement, to choose a judge *ad hoc* for purposes of this case.

---

34   However, as Prof. Abram Chayes, counsel and advocate for Namibia, reminded the Court in his opening remarks on February 15, 1999, "small places do not necessarily make small cases" and "the size of the place does not measure its meaning to those who may be affected by the judgment." ICJ Doc. CR 99/1, at para. 4 (1999).

35   The Republic of Botswana came into being on September 30, 1966, on the territory of the former British Bechuanaland Protectorate. The Republic of Namibia gained independence on March 21, 1990, after having been occupied by Germany (until 1914) and Great Britain (1914-1919). From 1919, South Africa first acted as administering authority of South West Africa under a mandate from the League of Nations, but was replaced by the United Nations Council for South West Africa/ Namibia after 1966. *See id.* at para. 14.

36   *See* International Status of South West Africa, 1950 ICJ REP. 128 (Advisory Opinion of July 11); Legal Consequences for States of the Continued Presence of South Africa in Namibia (South West Africa) notwithstanding Security Council Resolution 276 (1970), 1971 ICJ REP. 16 (Advisory Opinion of June 21) (finding South Africa's presence in Namibia to be illegal).

The case also confirms the Court's scant use of experts or assessors to assist it in cases, especially those that depend largely on scientific knowledge, despite the enabling clauses of Articles 30(2) and 50 of the ICJ Statute.[37]

The case once again demonstrates the necessity of drafting treaty provisions as clearly and carefully as possible, whether they are boundary treaties or treaties by which a dispute is submitted for peaceful resolution. In his separate opinion, Judge Oda alludes to the fact that the Special Agreement was not drafted with clarity in this case. In his view, the Court should have asked the parties to clarify their positions as to whether they regarded the determination of the boundary as a single issue, which would then result in the determination of the Island's legal status, or whether they regarded these as two separate issues. In this respect, the parties to this case were on notice through recent precedents involving two fellow African nations and by a case between two Arab countries pending at the time of these proceedings.[38]

The third part of the *dispositif* recognizing equal national treatment for the citizens and vessels of both parties in the two channels around the Island, although arguably not strictly forming a part of the question contained in the Special Agreement, has significance from the perspective of the law of international watercourses, especially the principle of the equitable utilization and treatment of shared water resources. This principle is embodied in the 1997 Convention on the Non-Navigational Uses of International Watercourses, although this instrument has not yet entered into force.[39] The Kasane Communiqué between Botswana and Namibia constitutes a further example of

---

37 *See* SHABTAI ROSENNE, 3 THE LAW AND PRACTICE OF THE INTERNATIONAL COURT, 1920-1996, at 1161-64 (3rd ed. 1997); Gillian White, *The use of experts by the International Court of Justice*, in: FIFTY YEARS OF THE INTERNATIONAL COURT OF JUSTICE 528 (Vaughan Lowe & Malgosia Fitzmaurice eds., 1996). Exceptions are the *Frontier Dispute (Burkina Faso/Mali) Case*, in which a Nomination of Experts phase was commenced but not concluded, the *Corfu Channel (United Kingdom v. Albania) Case*, in which experts were charged with carrying out an independent study of disputed facts in the merits phase and with giving an evaluation of damage sustained by the applicant in the compensation phase, and the *Gulf of Maine (Canada/United States) Case*, involving expert assistance in the preparation of a technical map concerning maritime delimitation.

38 *See* Arbitral Award of 31 July 1989 (Guinea-Bissau v. Senegal), Judgment, 1991 ICJ REP. 53 (Nov. 12); Maritime Delimitation and Territorial Questions between Qatar and Bahrain (Qatar v. Bahrain), Jurisdiction and Admissibility, Judgment, 1994 ICJ REP. 112 (July 1) and 1995 ICJ REP. 6 (Feb. 15).

39 *Opened for signature* May 21, 1997, UN Doc. A/51/869 (1997), text *reprinted in* 36 ILM 700 (1997).

relevant state practice followed as binding by the states concerned, as recognized by the Court. Thus, the Court's recognition of the parties' acceptance of this principle provides legitimacy to an essential principle of the law of international watercourses. This branch of international law is of increasing importance in international relations and is featured prominently on the agendas of recent peace negotiations involving neighboring nations and autonomous regions (e.g., 2000 Israel-Syria talks, 1999-2000 Israel-Palestinian Authority negotiations). It is no coincidence that the chairman of the Drafting Committee for this Judgment was President Schwebel, who submitted three reports as Special Rapporteur of the International Law Commission with regard to the topic "Law of the Non-Navigational Uses of International Watercourses" between 1979 and 1982.[40] This Judgment was also Judge Schwebel's final decision as President and Member of the Court.

Not since the Court's 1994 Judgment in *Territorial Dispute* (Libya/Chad),[41] another inter-African case brought by Special Agreement, has the Court so clearly ruled in favor of the submissions of one of the parties. The dissenting Members of the Court in this case, Vice President Weeramantry and Judges Fleischhauer, Parra-Aranguren and Rezek, all arrived at conclusions diametrically opposed to the result reached by the majority and would have placed the boundary in the southern channel of the Chobe River and accorded Namibia sovereignty over the Island. They all reached their conclusions based on different interpretations of various factors and criteria that were not all employed by the majority. Vice President Weeramantry, for whom this decision represented his last one as a Member of the Court, advocated the establishment of a joint international regime between Botswana and Namibia with a view

---

40 According to Article 6(ii) of the Resolution Concerning the Internal Judicial Practice of the Court, adopted on April 12, 1976, the "President shall ex officio be a member of the drafting committee [charged to prepare the Court's decision] unless he does not share the majority opinion of the Court." For the text of Schwebel's three reports, see UN Doc. A/CN.4/320 and Corr. 1 *reprinted in* [1979] 2(1) Y.B. INT'L L. COMM'N 143, UN Doc. A/CN.4/SER.A/1979/Add. 1 (Part 1); UN Doc. A/CN.4/ 332 and Corr. 1 and Add. 1 *reprinted in* [1980] 2(1) Y.B. INT'L L. COMM'N 159, UN Doc. A/CN.4/SER.A/1980/Add. 1 (Part 1); and UN Doc. A/CN.4/348 and Corr. 1 *reprinted in* [1982] 2(1) Y.B. INT'L L. COMM'N 65, UN Doc. A/CN.4/SER.A/ 1982/Add. 1 (Part 1), respectively.

41 *See* Territorial Dispute (Libya/Chad), Judgment, 1994 ICJ REP. 6 (Feb. 3).

to safeguarding the environmental interests of the Island, in keeping with his environmental advocacy during his tenure on the Court.[42]

---

42 Judge Weeramantry, who became a member of the Court's special Chamber for Environmental Matters at the time of its creation in 1993, once pointed out that the "Court, situated as it is at the apex of international tribunals, necessarily enjoys a position of special trust and responsibility in relation to the principles of environmental law." Dissenting opinion of Judge Weeramantry appended to Request for an Examination of the Situation in Accordance with Paragraph 63 of the Court's Judgment of 20 December 1974 in the *Nuclear Tests (New Zealand v. France)* Case, 1995 ICJ REP. 288, at 345 (Order of Sept. 22). *See also* his dissenting opinion in Legality of the Use by a State of Nuclear Weapons in Armed Conflict, 1996 ICJ REP. 66 (Advisory Opinion of July 8).

4

THE YEAR 2000

THE 2000 JUDICIAL ACTIVITY OF
THE INTERNATIONAL COURT OF JUSTICE

This introductory section summarizes the judicial work of the International Court of Justice during 2000, using the updated General List, pleadings filed, Orders and Judgments issued, and hearings held at the Peace Palace in The Hague to describe the Court's record in 2000.[1]

THE WORK OF THE COURT

General List

During the calendar year 2000, the Court was seised of one new contentious case: *Arrest Warrant of 11 April 2000 (Democratic Republic of the Congo v. Belgium).*[2] In 2000 a total of 25 cases appeared on the General List at any particular time. Besides the new case referred to, the contentious proceedings before the full Court were *Maritime Delimitation and Territorial Questions between Qatar and Bahrain (Qatar v. Bahrain); Questions of Interpretation and Application of the 1971 Montreal Convention arising from the Aerial Incident at Lockerbie (Libya v. United Kingdom) (Libya v. United States)* (hereinafter *Lockerbie Cases); Oil Platforms (Iran v. United States)* (hereinafter *Oil Platforms* case); *Application of the Convention on the Prevention and Punishment of the Crime of Genocide (Bosnia-Herzegovina v. Yugoslavia)* (hereinafter *Genocide (Bosnia)* case); *Land and Maritime Boundary between Cameroon and Nigeria (Cameroon v. Nigeria); Gabčíkovo-Nagymaros Project*

---

1   Most of the information contained in this Note is available from the ICJ's Web site <www.icj-cij.org>.

2   Application filed by the DRC in the ICJ Registry on October 17, 2000, accompanied by a request for the indication of provisional measures.

P.H.F. Bekker, World Court Decisions at the Turn of the Millennium (1997-2001), p. 213-218.
© 2002 *Kluwer Law International. Printed in the Netherlands.*

(Hungary/Slovakia); *Sovereignty over Pulau Ligitan and Pulau Sipadan (Indonesia/Malaysia)*; *Ahmadou Sadio Diallo (Republic of Guinea v. Democratic Republic of the Congo)*; *LaGrand Case (Germany v. United States)*; *Legality of Use of Force (Yugoslavia v. Belgium) (Yugoslavia v. Canada) (Yugoslavia v. France) (Yugoslavia v. Germany) (Yugoslavia v. Italy) (Yugoslavia v. the Netherlands) (Yugoslavia v. Portugal) (Yugoslavia v. United Kingdom)*; *Armed Activities on the Territory of the Congo (Democratic Republic of the Congo v. Burundi) (Democratic Republic of the Congo v. Rwanda) (Democratic Republic of the Congo v. Uganda)*; *Application of the Convention on the Prevention and Punishment of the Crime of Genocide (Croatia v. Yugoslavia)* (hereinafter *Genocide (Croatia)* case); *Aerial Incident of 10 August 1999 (Pakistan v. India)* (hereinafter *Aerial Incident* case) and *Maritime Delimitation between Nicaragua and Honduras in the Caribbean Sea (Nicaragua v. Honduras)* (hereinafter *Caribbean Sea* case). No advisory or chamber proceedings were brought or pending in 2000.

Pleadings

In 2000 pleadings were filed in the following instances. On January 5, Yugoslavia filed its Memorial in each of the *Legality of Use of Force* cases, followed, on July 5, by the preliminary objections of each of Belgium, Canada, France, Germany, Italy, the Netherlands, Portugal and the United Kingdom. On January 10, Pakistan filed its Memorial on jurisdiction in the *Aerial Incident* case, followed by India's Counter-Memorial on February 28. The United States filed a Counter-Memorial in the *LaGrand Case* on March 27. On April 4, Cameroon filed a Reply in *Land and Maritime Boundary between Cameroon and Nigeria*. On April 21, Burundi and Rwanda each filed a Memorial on jurisdiction and admissibility in the cases concerning *Armed Activities on the Territory of the Congo* brought against each of them by the Democratic Republic of the Congo (DRC). On October 23, the DRC filed its Counter-Memorial on jurisdiction and admissibility in these two cases. On June 19, the DRC filed a request for the indication of provisional measures in *Armed Activities on the Territory of the Congo (Dem. Rep. of the Congo v. Uganda)*, followed by its Memorial on July 21. Libya filed a Reply in each of the *Lockerbie* cases on June 29. On August 2, Indonesia and Malaysia each filed a Counter-Memorial in *Sovereignty over Pulau Ligitan and Pulau Sipadan*.

Orders

A total of 20 Orders were made by the Court, the president and the Vice President in 2000, most of which concerned time limits.[3] The Court indicated provisional measures in its Orders of July 1 issued in *Armed Activities on the Territory of the Congo (Dem. Rep. of the Congo v. Uganda)*[4] and of December 8 in *Arrest Warrant of 11 April 2000 (Dem. Rep. of the Congo v. Belgium)*.

Hearings

In 2000 the Court held public sittings (hearings) on jurisdiction in *Aerial Incident* (April 3-6), on the merits in *Maritime Delimitation and Territorial Questions between Qatar and Bahrain* (May 29-June 29) and *LaGrand Case (Germany v. U.S.)* (November 13-17), and on the DRC's requests for provisional measures in *Armed Activities on the Territory of the Congo (Dem. Rep. of the Congo v. Uganda)* (June 26 and 28) and *Arrest Warrant of 11 April 2000 (Dem Rep. of the Congo v. Belgium)* (November 20-21).

Decisions

In 2000 the Court handed down one decision. The Court's Judgment of June 21 rejected jurisdiction in the *Aerial Incident* case.[5]

---

3   The Court issued an Order fixing time limits in the *Caribbean Sea* case, 2000 ICJ REP. 6 (Mar. 21). An Order extending time limits was issued in the *Genocide (Croatia)* case (June 27). The President issued Orders fixing time limits in the *Lockerbie* cases (Sept. 6) and the *Sovereignty over Pulau Ligitan and Pulau Sipadan* case (Oct. 19) and extending time limits in the *Sovereignty over Pulau Ligitan and Pulau Sipadan* (May 11), 2000 ICJ REP. 9, *Genocide (Croatia)*, 2000 ICJ REP. 3 (Mar. 10), *Oil Platforms* (Sept. 4), *Ahmadou Sadio Diallo* (Sept. 8) and *Arrest Warrant* (Dec. 13) cases. The Vice President issued eight separate Orders fixing time limits in the *Legality of Use of Force* cases (Sept. 8).
4   *See* ICJ Communiqué 2000/24 (July 1, 2000) and 2000/24*bis* (July 4, 2000).
5   Slip opinion available from the ICJ Registry and the ICJ's Web site, *supra* note 1. *See also* ICJ Communiqués 2000/19-19*bis* (June 21, 2000).

ELECTIONS

At a private meeting held on February 7, the Court elected Judge Gilbert Guillaume (France) as president and Judge Shi Jiuyong (China) as Vice President for three-year terms. On February 10, the Court elected Philippe Couvreur (Belgium) as its new Registrar. On March 2, the UN General Assembly and Security Council elected Thomas Buergenthal (United States) to hold office for the remainder of Judge Stephen Schwebel's term expiring on February 5, 2006. This resulted in the following new composition of the Court (in order of seniority): Gilbert Guillaume (France), President; Shi Jiuyong (China), Vice President; Shigeru Oda (Japan); Mohammed Bedjaoui (Algeria); Raymond Ranjeva (Madagascar); Géza Herczegh (Hungary); Carl-August Fleischhauer (Germany); Abdul Koroma (Sierra Leone); Vladlen Vereshchetin (Russian Federation); Rosalyn Higgins (United Kingdom); Gonzalo Parra-Aranguren (Venezuela); Pieter Kooijmans (the Netherlands); Francisco Rezek (Brazil); Awn Shawkat Al-Khasawneh (Jordan); Thomas Buergenthal (United States).

PRESIDENT'S ADDRESS

On October 26, Judge Gilbert Guillaume addressed the General Assembly of the United Nations for the first time as ICJ president on the occasion of the presentation of the Court's annual report.[6]

Referring to the wide range of ICJ cases involving disputes from all corners of the world, and to the proliferation of written pleadings, preliminary objections, counterclaims and requests for the indication of provisional measures calling for a change in the Court's procedure in deciding cases, President Guillaume warned the General Assembly that the Court's financial and human resources no longer were sufficient for it properly to fulfill its task. If the lack of resources persisted, he predicted, the Court would be forced to delay passing judgment in a number of cases ready for decision in 2001-2002. According to the ICJ president, justice delayed is justice denied. The Court's annual budget being slightly over ten million U.S. dollars, representing less than one per cent

---

6   The full text of the Address by the President of the International Court of Justice, Judge Gilbert Guillaume, to the United Nations General Assembly, Oct. 26, 2000, is available on the ICJ's Web site, *supra* note 1. On October 31, Judge Guillaume also addressed the UN Security Council at a private session, the first time ever that a president of the ICJ has addressed the Council. *See* ICJ Communiqué 2000/37 (November 1, 2000).

of the UN's budget, he pointed out that the Court cannot adapt its programs to the resources available to it. He stated that he was obliged, therefore, to sound the alarm and announce that the Court would request supplementary credits and a budget increase of about three million U.S. dollars per year for the biennium 2002-2003. According to President Guillaume, the growth in ICJ cases required an increase in staff by some 38 posts, including law clerks, without which the judges will be unable to deliberate on more than two or three cases per year, as is currently the case. The president sought to justify the Court's requests by pointing to the situation prevailing at other international tribunals, especially the International Criminal Tribunal for the former Yugoslavia, also based in The Hague, whose budget and staff are roughly ten times the Court's. In President Guillaume's view, it was for the Assembly to decide whether the Court "is to die a slow death or whether [the Assembly] will give it the wherewithal to live."

He next addressed briefly "the problem raised for international law and the international community by the proliferation of international courts." In his view, proliferation leads to cases of overlapping jurisdiction and the resulting "forum shopping" by litigating states could generate unwanted confusion and distort the operation of justice. It also increases the risk of conflicting judgments: a given issue may be submitted to two courts simultaneously, which may render inconsistent judgments. In the president's view, proliferation of courts also gives rise to a serious risk of conflicting jurisprudence, as the same rule of law might receive different interpretations in different cases. Thus, proliferation runs the risk of affecting the cohesiveness of international law.

President Guillaume offered various solutions to combat the negative effects of the proliferation of international courts, particularly uncertainty regarding the content of the law in the minds of players on the international stage and a restriction of the role of international law in inter-state relations. In his view, the international legislator should ask itself whether the functions it intends to entrust to a new court could not properly be fulfilled by an existing court. Moreover, judges should realize the danger of fragmentation of the law, including conflicts of case law, caused by the proliferation of courts. This calls for a dialogue among judicial bodies, in which the Court will participate provided it receives the necessary resources. It also calls for a better structuring of the relationships among international courts. He admitted, however, that the strong political will of states required to make the ICJ the international court of appeal or review for judgments rendered by all other courts might not exist.

Finally, President Guillaume stated that he supported the idea, first raised by his predecessor from the same podium in 1999, of encouraging the various international courts (including the International Tribunal for the Law of the

Sea and the future International Criminal Court) to seek advisory opinions in some cases from the Court, by way of the Security Council or the General Assembly, with a view to reducing the risk of differing interpretations of international law. Such encouragement could take the form of a resolution of the General Assembly.

ICJ jurisdiction – General Act for Pacific Settlement of International Disputes – treaty succession – Commonwealth and multilateral-treaty reservations in Optional Clause declarations – UN Charter as basis of jurisdiction – effect of obligation to settle disputes by peaceful means

AERIAL INCIDENT OF 10 AUGUST 1999 (Pakistan v. India)

Judgment (Jurisdiction)
Obtainable from <www.icj-cij.org>
International Court of Justice, June 21, 2000[*]

On September 21, 1999, Pakistan filed an application requesting the ICJ to declare India responsible for the shooting down of an unarmed aircraft of the Pakistani navy by Indian air force planes on August 10, 1999.[1] Pakistan also maintained that Indian air force helicopters violated its territorial integrity by visiting the aircraft's crash site, which was inside Pakistan territory, in an attempt to collect items from the debris immediately after the incident. In Pakistan's view, India violated its sovereignty; breached its obligation to refrain from the threat or use of force under the United Nations Charter, other treaties and customary international law; and breached the 1991 bilateral Agreement on Prevention of Air Space Violations.[2] Pakistan requested U.S.$60 million in reparations for the loss of the aircraft and to compensate the heirs of the Pakistani servicemen.

As bases of jurisdiction, Pakistan invoked: under Article 37 of the ICJ Statute, Article 17 of the 1928 General Act for Pacific Settlement of Inter-

---

[*]   Reproduced with permission from 94 AJIL 707 (2000). © The American Society of International Law.

[1]   According to Pakistan, the aerial incident resulted in the death of all 16 personnel on board the aircraft, which was on a routine mission over Pakistani territory.

[2]   *See* Agreement on Prevention of Air Space Violations, Apr. 6, 1991, Pak.-India. Article 1 obligates both countries to ensure that violations of each other's air space do not take place, and provides that if any violation occurs inadvertently, the incident is to be investigated promptly, with the other side to be informed of the results without delay.

P.H.F. Bekker, World Court Decisions at the Turn of the Millennium (1997-2001), p. 219-230.
© 2002 *Kluwer Law International. Printed in the Netherlands.*

national Disputes[3] (General Act); under Article 36(2) of the Statute, the declarations made by each of the two states accepting the Court's compulsory jurisdiction; and under Article 36(1) of the Statute, the UN Charter. India contested all three bases.[4] On June 21, 2000, the Court found, by 14 votes to two, that it lacked jurisdiction to adjudicate the dispute.[5]

According to Article 37 of the ICJ Statute, "Whenever a treaty or convention in force provides for reference of a matter to ... the Permanent Court of International Justice, the matter shall, as between the parties to the present Statute, be referred to the International Court of Justice."[6] Article 17 of the General Act provides that all disputes with regard to which the parties to the General Act are in conflict as to their respective rights are to be submitted for decision to the Permanent Court of International Justice (PCIJ), which functioned between 1922 and 1940. Pakistan's view was that the General Act survived the demise of the League of Nations and is a treaty still in force, and that British India's obligations thereunder devolved upon India and Pakistan at the time of their independence in 1947.[7]

India argued that, with the demise of the League organs and the PCIJ,[8] to which the General Act refers, the act had lost its original efficacy. In support of this argument, India invoked the UN General Assembly's adoption of the

---

3   General Act for Pacific Settlement of International Disputes, Sept. 26, 1928, 93 LNTS 343 [hereinafter General Act].

4   By its Order of November 19, 1999, the Court decided that the initial phase of the proceedings would address solely the question of jurisdiction. Hearings were held on April 3-6, 2000.

5   *See* Aerial Incident of 10 August 1999 (Pak. v. India), Jurisdiction, Judgment of June 21, 2000, slip opinion available from the ICJ Registry and from the ICJ Web site at <www.icj-cij.org>, at para. 56 [hereinafter Judgment]. Judge Al-Khasawneh (Jordan) and Judge *ad hoc* Pirzada (appointed by Pakistan) voted against the judgment, and appended dissenting opinions.

6   *See* SHABTAI ROSENNE, 2 THE LAW AND PRACTICE OF THE INTERNATIONAL COURT, 1920-1996, at 677-91 (1997).

7   In support of its view that the General Act was organically and ideologically independent of the League of Nations, Pakistan cited the joint dissenting opinion of Judges Dillard, Jiménez de Aréchaga, Onyeama, and Waldock that was appended to a 1974 decision of the Court. *See* Nuclear Tests (Aus. v. Fr.), Judgment, 1974 ICJ REP. 253, 312, 327-41 (Dec. 20) [hereinafter Nuclear Tests]. This dissenting opinion is discussed by Fathi Kemicha, counsel for Pakistan, in ICJ Doc. CR 2000/1, at 33-37 (Apr. 3). *See* Judgment, *supra* note 5, at para. 15.

8   Although the PCIJ was created by the League of Nations and operated under its auspices, the PCIJ's Statute was not part of the League Covenant, and the Court was not a statutory organ of the League.

Revised General Act in 1949.[9] India also characterized the General Act as an agreement of a political character and, as such, not automatically binding on successor states like India and Pakistan. Noting that it had made no notification of succession as required by Articles 17 and 22 of the 1978 Vienna Convention on Succession of States in Respect of Treaties,[10] India referred to a communication of September 18, 1974, addressed to the UN Secretary-General, stating that India "never regarded [itself] as bound by the General Act of 1928 since [its] Independence in 1947, whether by succession or otherwise."[11] Pakistan argued that India's communication of September 1974 was a subjective statement devoid of objective validity and that the emergence of an independent India was not a case of state succession, but of continuity of the same state – namely, British India before 1947 and independent India thereafter. For its own status, Pakistan believed that it had succeeded automatically to the General Act in 1947 based on customary international law and, in any event, through its notification of succession addressed to the Secretary-General on May 30, 1974.[12]

---

9   *See* GA Res. 268A (III) (Apr. 28, 1949), at 10. For the text of the Revised General Act, see 71 UNTS 101. Article 17 is among the provisions that were amended by the new, 1949 Act. *See* Judgment, *supra* note 5, at para. 14.

10 Vienna Convention on Succession of States in Respect of Treaties, *opened for signature* Aug. 23, 1978, UN Doc. A/CONF 80/31, 17 ILM 1488 (1978).

11 Judgment, *supra* note 5, at paras. 17 and 23. India's communication was issued while different ICJ proceedings instituted against it by Pakistan were pending. *See infra* note 48.

12 *See id.*, at para. 18. In this connection, the parties also disagreed on the interpretation of a schedule to the Indian Independence (International Arrangements) Order issued by India's governor-general on August 14, 1947, which was stated to have the effect of an agreement between the two countries concerning treaty succession. According to Pakistan's interpretation, it had succeeded to the rights and obligations under all international agreements to which British India was a party. In India's view, however, Pakistan could not have succeeded, under the 1947 order and agreement, to British India's rights and obligations by virtue of British India's membership of the League of Nations; Pakistan needed to submit a new, independent application for membership in the United Nations. In support of its view, India referred to a judgment issued by the Supreme Court of Pakistan on June 6, 1961, which found, in considering Pakistan's status in relation to the 1927 Convention for the Execution of Foreign Arbital Awards, that Pakistan did not automatically become a member of the United Nations or succeed to the rights and obligations of British India deriving from its membership in the League of Nations or the United Nations. Pakistan claimed that this judgment could not be relied upon, because Pakistan had not had an opportunity in the case to express its views to the Supreme Court. *See id.*, at paras. 18-20; Yangtze (London) Ltd. v. Barlas Bros. (Karachi), Sup. Ct., Civ.

India and Pakistan also advanced differing interpretations of the practice of the two countries since 1947. Pakistan claimed that the General Act qualified as a "peaceful means [to settle their differences] mutually agreed upon between them" referred to in the so-called Simla Accord of July 2, 1972, which reaffirmed the General Act's procedure. India maintained, however, that the Simla Accord represented no more than an arrangement between the two countries to resort to negotiations before referring any difference to some other method of settlement through a further and specific agreement between the parties.[13]

The Court declined to address the question whether the General Act must be regarded as a convention in force for the purposes of Article 37 of the Statute. The Court found, instead, that India's communication of September 18, 1974, served the same legal ends as a notification of denunciation under Article 45 of the General Act. Exclusively on that basis,[14] the Court concluded that India cannot be regarded as having been a party to the General Act on the date on which Pakistan filed its application.[15]

With respect to Article 36, paragraph 2, of the ICJ Statute (the Optional Clause), India noted that its declaration accepting the Court's jurisdiction excludes "disputes with the government of any State which is or has been a Member of the Commonwealth of Nations,"[16] including Pakistan. Pakistan argued, however, that India's Commonwealth reservation was made in bad faith and was extrastatutory and illicit because it lay outside the range of reservations permitted by the Court's Statute.[17] In Pakistan's view, the permissible conditions to which an Optional Clause declaration may be made subject are listed exhaustively in Article 36(3) of the Statute. Thus, India's declaration was valid

---

Appeal No. 139, Judgment of June 6, 1961 (Pak.); *see also* Materials on Succession of States, UN Doc. ST/LEG/SER.B/14, at 133-41 (1967).

13 *See id.*, at paras. 22-23.

14 The Court justified its approach by pointing out that it "is free to base its decision on the ground which in its judgment is more direct and conclusive." *Id.*, para. 26 (citing Certain Norwegian Loans (Fr. v. Nor.), Judgment, 1957 ICJ REP. 9, 25 (July 6) [hereinafter Certain Norwegian Loans]; Aegean Sea Continental Shelf (Greece v. Turk.), 1978 ICJ REP. 3, 16-17 (Dec. 19) [hereinafter Aegean Sea Continental Shelf]).

15 Consequently, Article 17 of the General Act, read in conjunction with Article 37 of the ICJ Statute, did not form a basis of jurisdiction in this case. *See* Judgment, *supra* note 5, at paras. 27-28.

16 *Id.*, at para. 29.

17 *See id.*, at para. 30. Pakistan relied on a similar argument in an attempt to dismiss India's reliance on British India's reservations attached to its May 21, 1931, instrument of accession to the General Act. *See id.*, at paras. 24-25.

except for its Commonwealth reservation, which was unopposable to Pakistan absent its acceptance by that state. India, by contrast, argued that a reservation cannot be severed from the declaration and forms an integral part of it.

Pakistan further claimed that India's reservation was, in any event, obsolete and lacked any contemporary justification: the members of the Commonwealth are no longer united by a common allegiance to the British Crown, and the modes of dispute settlement originally contemplated (that is, special Commonwealth tribunals) never materialized. In reply, India pointed out that there is no support for the applicability of the doctrine of obsolescence to unilateral acts and that the doctrine certainly could not apply, in any case, to a reservation that had been a part of practice since 1974.[18]

Pakistan also argued that India's Commonwealth reservation amounted, as a practical matter, to discrimination and an abuse of right vis-à-vis Pakistan. Finally, Pakistan argued, by way of alternative, that Article 1(ii) of the 1972 Simla Accord, through which both parties agreed "to settle their differences by peaceful means through bilateral negotiations or by any other peaceful means mutually agreed upon between them," had the effect of an estoppel preventing India from invoking its reservation in an attempt to block the Court's jurisdiction. In reply, India simply pointed out that the Simla Accord does not contain a compromissory clause.

For its part, India stressed the importance of a state's intention in making its declaration accepting the Court's Optional Clause jurisdiction, and pointed out that it has long been recognized that a state is allowed to select its partners in regard to which it is prepared to accept such jurisdiction. India characterized its Commonwealth reservation as an unambiguous statement of a classical reservation *ratione personae*. To accept Pakistan's theory of extrastatutory reservations as valid would allow any party to escape the effect of a reservation by merely stating that it was extrastatutory in character.[19]

The Court rejected all of Pakistan's arguments relating to Optional Clause jurisdiction. With regard to Pakistan's contention that India's Commonwealth reservation is extrastatutory, the Court affirmed a prior decision in which it observed that declarations accepting the Court's compulsory jurisdiction are facultative, unilateral engagements that states are absolutely free to make or not to make – either unconditionally and without temporal restrictions, or by

---

18 *See id.*, at para. 31.
19 *See id.*

qualifying the acceptance through conditions or reservations.[20] The Court noted that Article 36(3) of the Statute has never been regarded as laying down exhaustively the conditions under which declarations might validly be made, and also noted that practice has recognized the right of states to attach reservations to their Optional Clause acceptance, thus enabling them to define the parameters of that acceptance.[21]

In reply to Pakistan's argument that India's Commonwealth reservation is a discriminatory act constituting an abuse of right, the Court noted that the reservation refers generally to states that are or have been members of the Commonwealth, and that states are, in any event, free to limit the scope *ratione personae* of their acceptance of the Court's compulsory jurisdiction.[22] As to Pakistan's obsolescence argument, the Court confirmed that an Optional Clause declaration must be interpreted and given effect as it stands, based on the words actually used and having due regard to the intention of the state concerned when it made the declaration.[23] Whatever reasons India may have had for limiting as it did the scope of its acceptance of the Court's compulsory jurisdiction, the Court must abide by this limitation expressing the intention of India as the state making the declaration.[24] The Court disagreed with Pakistan that Article 1(ii) of the Simla Accord estopped India from invoking its Commonwealth reservation; this provision imposed only a general obligation on the parties to settle their differences by peaceful means, to be further determined by mutual agreement. Thus, the Simla Accord does not as such require India and Pakistan to submit their disputes to the Court.[25] Given that Pakistan and India are both members of the Commonwealth of Nations, the Court concluded that their Optional Clause declarations provided no basis of jurisdiction in this case.

India also pointed to another reservation in its declaration, which excludes disputes concerning the interpretation or application of a multilateral treaty

---

20 *See id.*, at para. 36 (citing Military and Paramilitary Activities in and against Nicaragua (Nicar. v. U.S.), Jurisdiction and Admissibility, Judgment, 1984 ICJ REP. 392, 418 (Nov. 26)).

21 *See id.*, at paras. 37-38 (citing Fisheries Jurisdiction (Spain v. Can.), Jurisdiction, Judgment, 1998 ICJ REP. 432, at 453, para. 44 (Dec. 4) [hereinafter Fisheries Jurisdiction]); *see also* Barbara Kwiatkowska, Case Report: Fisheries Jurisdiction (Spain v. Canada), Jurisdiction, 93 AJIL 502 (1999).

22 *See id.*, at para. 40.

23 *See id.*, at para. 42 (citing Anglo-American Oil Co. (U.K. v. Iran), Preliminary Objection, Judgment, 1952 ICJ REP. 93, 105 (July 22); Certain Norwegian Loans, *supra* note 14, at 27; Fisheries Jurisdiction, *supra* note 21, at 454, para. 49).

24 *See id.*, at para. 44.

25 *See id.*, para. 45.

(here, the UN Charter), unless India specially agrees to jurisdiction or all the parties to the treaty are also parties to the case before the Court.[26] Relying on the *Nicaragua* precedent,[27] Pakistan pointed out that, because its case against India ultimately rested on considerations of customary international law, the case was not affected by India's multilateral-treaty reservation. India, by contrast, argued that the reservation would still apply wherever an application relies upon a cause of action that, in the final analysis, is based on the UN Charter.[28] Given that it had already concluded that India's Commonwealth reservation blocked its jurisdiction in the case, the Court found it unnecessary to consider India's objection based on its multilateral-treaty reservation.[29]

According to Article 36, paragraph 1, of the ICJ Statute, the Court's jurisdiction comprises all matters specially provided for in the UN Charter or in treaties and conventions in force. In Pakistan's view,[30] Article 36(1) should be read in conjunction with Articles 1(1), 2(3)-(4), 33, 36(3) and 92 of the Charter as establishing a basis for jurisdiction. Moreover, Pakistan argued that the parties had reaffirmed such jurisdiction under Article 36(1) in the 1972 Simla Accord, which provides that "[t]he principles and purposes of the United Nations Charter shall govern the relations between the two countries." The Court observed, however, that neither the UN Charter nor the Simla Accord contains any specific provision conferring compulsory jurisdiction on the Court

---

26 For a discussion of this type of reservation, see STANIMIR A. ALEXANDROV, RE-SERVATIONS IN UNILATERAL DECLARATIONS ACCEPTING THE COMPULSORY JURIS-DICTION OF THE INTERNATIONAL COURT OF JUSTICE 112-19 (1995); ROSENNE, *supra* note 6, at 803-04.

27 *See* Military and Paramilitary Activities in and against Nicaragua (Nicar. v. U.S.), Jurisdiction and Admissibility, Judgment, 1984 ICJ REP. 392, 424 (Nov. 26) (in considering claims alleging violation of principles of customary and general international law, the Court cannot dismiss the claims simply because such principles also have been enshrined in the texts of multilateral conventions relied upon by the applicant; therefore, if the claim before the Court is not confined to violation of the multilateral conventional provisions invoked, its adjudication is not barred by the multilateral-treaty reservation).

28 *See* Judgment, *supra* note 5, at paras. 32-33.

29 *See id.*, para. 46. Since the case concerned an incident between the armed forces of the two countries, it is unclear why India did not, in addition, invoke the reservation contained in its Optional Clause declaration excluding "disputes relating to or connected with facts or situations of hostilities, armed conflicts, individual or collective actions taken in self-defence, resistance to aggression, fulfilment of obligations imposed by international bodies, and other similar or related acts, measures or situations in which India is, has been or may in future be involved."

30 Pakistan did not pursue this argument during the hearings.

in relation to disputes between India and Pakistan. Consequently, the Court concluded that it did not have jurisdiction to entertain Pakistan's application on the basis of Article 36(1) of the Statute.[31]

By way of *obiter dictum*, the Court noted the fundamental distinction between a state's acceptance of its jurisdiction and the question of whether particular acts violate international law. Independent of states' acceptance (or not) of the Court's jurisdiction, "they remain in all cases responsible for acts attributable to them that violate the rights of other States."[32] The Court re-affirmed its view that the judicial settlement of international disputes is simply an alternative to the direct and friendly settlement of such disputes between states, which the Court is to facilitate.[33] It reminded both parties that its lack of jurisdiction did not relieve them of the international obligations undertaken by them, which require that they act in good faith in seeking a peaceful settle-ment of their disputes, including, in particular, the dispute arising out of the aerial incident of August 10, 1999.[34]

* * * *

This judgment, the first issued under the presidency of Gilbert Guillaume,[35] represents the second time since the Court's decision in *Aegean Sea Continental Shelf*,[36] rendered in 1978, that the Court has found at a preliminary stage that it is without jurisdiction to entertain an application.[37] On December 4, 1998,

---

31   *See* Judgment, *supra* note 5, at paras. 47-50. For a discussion of Article 36(1), see ROSENNE, *supra* note 6, at 692-95.

32   *See* Judgment, *supra* note 5, at para. 51 (quoting Fisheries Jurisdiction, *supra* note 21, at 456, paras. 55-56).

33   *See id.*, at para. 52 (citing Free Zones of Upper Savoy and the District of Gex, Order, 1929 PCIJ (ser. A) No. 22, at 13 (Aug. 19); Frontier Dispute (Burk. Fas./Mali), Judgment, 1986 ICJ REP. 554, 577, para. 46 (Dec. 22); Passage Through the Great Belt (Fin. v. Den.), Order, 1991 ICJ REP. 12, 20 (July 29)).

34   *See id.*, at paras. 53-55 (citing Fisheries Jurisdiction, *supra* note 21, at 456, para. 56; invoking the Simla Accord of July 2, 1972, and the Lahore Declaration of February 21, 1999).

35   Interestingly, the authoritative language of the judgment, signed by a French pres-ident and a French-speaking registrar, is English and not French.

36   Aegean Sea Continental Shelf, *supra* note 14.

37   The Court's refusal to entertain Portugal's application in *East Timor* (Port. v. Austl.) in 1995, although technically a dismissal, was based on a finding at the merits stage that the Court could not, in the absence of Indonesia as a necessary third party, exercise the jurisdiction conferred upon it to adjudicate the dispute referred by

the Court rejected jurisdiction over a dispute concerning fisheries jurisdiction in the initial phase of the proceedings.[38]

The remarkable speed with which the Court disposed of this case is evidence of its recent attempts to accelerate the judicial process:[39] the Court handed down its decision on jurisdiction nine months after the application was filed and less than three months after the close of the oral proceedings.

Many international lawyers will be disappointed that the Court decided not to address the question whether the General Act must be regarded as a convention in force for the purposes of Article 37 of the Statute. On two prior occasions, the Court similarly shied away from tackling this question.[40] In explanation, the Court has noted – in deference to Article 59 of the Statute, which states that a decision "has no binding force except between the parties and in respect of that particular case" – that any pronouncement concerning the status of the General Act may have implications for relations between states that are not parties to the case before it.[41]

The Court also left unanswered the question of India's reliance on the 1978 Vienna Convention on Succession of States in Respect of Treaties, which was invoked in support of India's argument that the parties did not succeed to the General Act.[42] In the end, the Court concluded only that India was not a party to the General Act when Pakistan filed its application. The Court did not address Pakistan's status in relation to that act.

Although the Court's statements concerning reservations contained in Optional Clause declarations are important in that they affirm prior pronounce-

---

Portugal. *See* East Timor (Port. v. Austl.), 1995 ICJ REP. 90 (June 30); Peter H.F. Bekker, Case Report: East Timor (Port. v. Austl.), 90 AJIL 94 (1996), *reprinted in* COMMENTARIES ON WORLD COURT DECISIONS (1987-1996), at 209 (P.H.F. Bekker ed., 1998).

38 Fisheries Jurisdiction, *supra* note 21.

39 *See* ICJ Communiqué 98/14 (Apr. 6, 1998). The fact that only four days were devoted to hearing the parties' arguments on jurisdiction is further evidence of this trend.

40 *See* Nuclear Tests, *supra* note 7; Aegean Sea Continental Shelf, *supra* note 14.

41 *See* Aegean Sea Continental Shelf, *supra* note 14, at 16-17, para. 39. If this approach were to be followed consistently, however, the Court could *never* say anything useful in a case involving a multilateral treaty, out of fear that its statements might reach beyond the rights and obligations of the parties to the case.

42 In the light of the increasing significance of domestic court decisions in international responsibility cases, it also would have been interesting to see how the Court might have treated the judgment of the Supreme Court of Pakistan, on which both parties relied. *See supra* note 12.

ments, they add little to the relevant body of law.[43] In this context, the most significant contribution is that the Court confirmed that Article 36(3) of the Statute does not contain an exhaustive list of conditions under which such declarations may be made. What is particularly disappointing, however, is that the Court found it unnecessary to consider India's reservation purporting to exclude multilateral treaties from the Court's consideration. This question is of great importance to potential claimants who rely on Optional Clause declarations as the sole basis of jurisdiction in disputes arising under an increasing number of multilateral treaties. The Optional Clause declarations of India, Malta, Pakistan, and the Philippines all contain multilateral-treaty reservations. The *Nicaragua* precedent on which Pakistan relied is in dire need of clarification and expansion in many respects.[44] The Court also failed to comment on India's contention that because a reservation forms an integral part of the declaration in which it appears, the reservation cannot be severed from the declaration. In connection with Canada's similar contention advanced in recent proceedings,[45] the Court stated that "declarations and reservations are to be read as a whole."[46]

In the 1970s India and Pakistan were also unsuccessfully involved in proceedings before the Court, namely, in *Appeal Relating to the Jurisdiction*

---

43 Inasmuch as two 1998 decisions dealt extensively with Article 36(2), the absence of significant new developments regarding that provision was perhaps to be expected. *See* Land and Maritime Boundary between Cameroon and Nigeria (Cam. v. Nig.), Preliminary Objections, Judgment, 1998 ICJ REP. 275 (June 11); Peter H.F. Bekker, Case Report, Land and Maritime Boundary between Cameroon and Nigeria (Cameroon v. Nigeria), 92 AJIL 751 (1998); Fisheries Jurisdiction, *supra* note 21. The Optional Clause declarations of Barbados, Canada, Gambia, Kenya, Malta, Mauritius, and the United Kingdom all include versions of the Commonwealth reservation. No state in the Court's history had previously challenged the validity of the Commonwealth reservation.

44 *See supra* note 27.

45 *See* Counter-Memorial (Jurisdiction) of Canada at 32-35, paras. 72-75, Fisheries Jurisdiction, *supra* note 21.

46 Fisheries Jurisdiction, *supra* note 21, at 454, para. 47. The Court's subsequent statement in paragraph 59 of that judgment, however, appears to make a finding that a reservation is an integral part of a declaration dependent upon the specific circumstances of a case ("It follows that *this* reservation is not only an integral part of *the current* declaration but also an essential component *of it*, and hence of the acceptance by Canada of the Court's compulsory jurisdiction." (emphasis added)).

of the ICAO Council (India v. Pakistan)[47] and *Trial of Pakistani Prisoners of War* (Pakistan v. India).[48] Given the Court's approach to the Optional Clause and the extremely broad reservations contained in India's Optional Clause declaration, it is unlikely that the Court will be able to entertain any dispute involving that country, whether as applicant or as respondent, based on the Optional Clause.

---

47 1972 ICJ REP. 46 (Aug. 18) (dismissing India's appeal of an International Civil Aviation Organization Council decision, the Council being found to be competent to deal with India's application and complaint).

48 1978 ICJ REP. 347 (Order removing the case from the General List upon discontinuance of the proceedings).

Provisional measures – prima facie jurisdiction based on unconditional Optional Clause declarations – indication of provisional measures in face of Security Council resolution under Chapter VII of UN Charter addressing similar subject matter – effect of timing of request on condition of urgency – effect of other similar cases involving one common applicant and different respondents on request for provisional measures against one particular respondent

ARMED ACTIVITIES ON THE TERRITORY OF THE CONGO (Dem. Rep. of the Congo v. Uganda)

Provisional Measures, Order
Obtainable from <www.icj-cij.org>
International Court of Justice, July 1, 2000

On June 23, 1999, the Democratic Republic of the Congo (DRC) filed an Application in the Registry of the International Court of Justice instituting proceedings against the Republic of Uganda (Uganda) in respect of a dispute over alleged acts of armed aggression, plundering and oppression perpetrated by Ugandan troops on Congolese territory since August 1998, including looting of property, deportation of Congolese civilians and the exploitation and destruction of natural resources belonging to the DRC. Almost a year later, on June 19, 2000, the DRC submitted a request for the indication of provisional measures pursuant to Article 41 of the Court's Statute and Articles 73-75 of the Rules of Court, asking the Court to order Uganda immediately to cease all military action on, and withdraw its army from, Congolese territory; to take all measures to ensure that any persons under Uganda's control or authority desist from committing or inciting the commission of war crimes on Congolese territory; to discontinue any act interfering with the fundamental human rights of the Congolese people; to cease all illegal exploitation of the natural resources of the DRC; and to respect the DRC's right to sovereignty, political independence and territorial integrity and the fundamental rights and freedoms of all persons on Congolese territory.[1] The request was triggered by heavy fighting between the armies of Uganda and Rwanda on Congolese territory, the aim of which,

---

1   *See* Order of July 1, 2000, at para. 13 [hereinafter Order].

P.H.F. Bekker, World Court Decisions at the Turn of the Millennium (1997-2001), p. 231-240.
© 2002 *Kluwer Law International. Printed in the Netherlands.*

the DRC contended, was the seizure of its natural resources.[2] In response, Uganda argued that the request was inadmissible and moot, in view of Uganda's full acceptance of, and compliance with, Security Council Resolution 1304 adopted, on June 16, 2000, under Chapter VII of the United Nations Charter, which addressed the situation in the DRC.[3]

On July 1, 2000, the Court issued an Order ruling, unanimously, that, pending final judgment in the case, both parties are to refrain from any armed action which might aggravate their dispute, and enjoining them to ensure full respect within the zone of conflict for fundamental human rights and applicable provisions of humanitarian law.

At the initial hearing in The Hague on June 26, 2000, the DRC focused its argument on four main areas: (1) Uganda's permanent military and paramilitary presence on Congolese territory since August 2, 1998; (2) the repeated armed confrontations between the armies of Uganda and Rwanda, two foreign nations, in Kisangani, the third largest city in the DRC; (3) the plundering and illegal exploitation of the wealth and resources of the DRC; and (4) the persistence and aggravation of acts of oppression directly affecting Congolese civilians. According to the DRC, Uganda's actions in respect of these four areas resulted in seven groups of violations of international law: (1) the respect for the sovereignty, territorial integrity and political independence of the DRC required by Article 2, paragraph 1, of the United Nations Charter, General Assembly Resolution 2625 and the Court's jurisprudence;[4] (2) the prohibition of the use of force embodied in Article 2, paragraph 4, of the United Nations Charter and confirmed in the Court's jurisprudence;[5] (3) the prohibition of interference

---

2   Although the facts (armed action, plundering and acts of oppression) and applicable rules of law (non-use of force, non-intervention and protection of the rights of the individual) referred to in the 1999 application and 2000 request are similar, the DRC emphasized during the initial hearing on June 26, 2000, that it was not asking the Court to condemn Uganda, nor to declare that Uganda must pay an indemnity to the DRC or that it has violated international law. Instead, the request's sole aim was to have the Court order Uganda to withdraw its troops from Congolese territory and to end support for military and paramilitary groups active on such territory. *See* Order, *supra* note 1, at para. 21; ICJ Doc. CR 2000/20, at 23 (June 26).

3   For the text of the substantive part of this resolution, *see* Order, *supra* note 1, at para. 35. It also is available from the UN's Web site, <www.un.org/Docs/scres/2000/sc2000.htm>.

4   The DRC referred to Military and Paramilitary Activities in and against Nicaragua (Nicar. v. U.S.), Merits, Judgment, 1986 ICJ REP. 14, 133, para. 263 (June 27) [hereinafter *Nicaragua*].

5   *Nicaragua*, *supra* note 4, at 100, para. 190.

in matters within the domestic jurisdiction of states, a principle set forth in General Assembly Resolution 2625 and confirmed in the Court's jurisprudence;[6] (4) the right of peoples to self-determination guaranteed by Article 1, paragraph 2, of the United Nations Charter and referred to in General Assembly Resolution 2625; (5) the obligation to settle international disputes peacefully set forth in Article 2, paragraph 3, of the United Nations Charter; (6) the obligation to respect international human rights and humanitarian law, embodied in the Geneva Conventions of 1949 and the Court's jurisprudence;[7] and (7) the obligation to apply the resolutions adopted by the UN Security Council in accordance with Article 25 of the United Nations Charter and the Court's jurisprudence.[8]

In support of the conditions imposed on requests for the indication of provisional measures by Article 41 of the Court's Statute and its jurisprudence, especially that the measures requested be urgent and the harm irreparable and that there be a sufficient connection between the measures requested and the rights to be protected, the DRC pointed out that its resources and assets were being systematically plundered and its inhabitants wounded or killed, for which no compensation or restitution could wholly make amends. Finally, the DRC submitted that there was no particular circumstance specific to the political and diplomatic context of this case preventing the Court from indicating the measures requested by the DRC. In its view, such circumstance did not lie in Security Council Resolution 1304, demanding that Uganda withdraw its troops from the whole of Congolese territory without further delay, given that it was requesting the Court to order such withdrawal, not as a political measure designed to maintain international peace and security, but as a purely judicial measure, which, in any event, would be in support of Resolution 1304. Nor did the absence of any other countries, especially Burundi and Rwanda against which the DRC had filed separate proceedings on June 23, 1999, impede the indication of provisional measures specifically and exclusively against Uganda, given that the DRC was not asking the Court at this stage to rule on the rights of any nonparty state.[9]

---

6   *Nicaragua*, *supra* note 4, at 108, para. 205, and Corfu Channel (UK v. Albania), Judgment, 1949 ICJ REP. 4, 35 (Apr. 9) [hereinafter *Corfu Channel*].

7   *Nicaragua*, *supra* note 4, at 114, para. 218, and *Corfu Channel*, *supra* note 6, at 22.

8   The DRC referred to Questions of Interpretation and Application of the 1971 Montreal Convention Arising from the Aerial Incident at Lockerbie (Libya v. UK), Provisional Measures, 1992 ICJ REP. 3, at 15, para. 39 (Order of Apr. 14).

9   *See* Order, *supra* note 1, at para. 23.

At the hearing on June 28, 2000, which was convened in the late afternoon after the Court heard the oral statement of the respondent in another unrelated case,[10] Uganda submitted that there was neither a legal nor a factual basis for any of the provisional measures requested. It explained that its security forces found themselves on Congolese soil pursuant to a protocol, signed by the DRC and Uganda, providing for joint operations to improve security in the border areas of the two countries in which central governmental authority was lacking. Such security was threatened by foreign-sponsored rebel groups operating against Uganda from bases inside the DRC. Thus, in Uganda's view, the DRC was facing an internal rebellion, as opposed to a foreign invasion. It stated that it had no territorial interests in the DRC. According to Uganda, the filing of an application with the Court on June 23, 1999, was tantamount to an act of bad faith by the DRC, given that the parties already were actively involved in direct negotiations aimed at resolving their conflict. The Lusaka Agreement, signed by all the major parties to the conflict on July 10, 1999, together with the Kampala Disengagement Plan of April 8, 2000, established a comprehensive public order and framework for peace in the Great Lakes Region, in the implementation of which Uganda had fully cooperated.[11] Uganda rejected all allegations by the DRC and blamed the DRC for hampering the proper implementation of the peace process. It pointed out that the DRC and its neighbors had agreed in the Lusaka Agreement that foreign forces would not leave Congolese territory immediately or unilaterally, but would remain in the DRC pending the disarmament of certain armed groups. The eventual withdrawal was made subject to the timetable set forth in Annex B to the Lusaka Agreement and the Kampala Disengagement Plan, as confirmed by paragraph 4(a) of Resolution 1304.[12]

In respect of the request itself, Uganda argued that it was inadmissible, given that, as a matter of law, the Court is prevented from exercising its powers under Article 41 of the Statute when faced with a Security Council resolution under Chapter VII. It found support for this argument in the Court's rejection

---

10 Maritime Delimitation and Territorial Questions between Qatar and Bahrain (Qatar v. Bahrain) (merits). After Uganda was assigned two hours of speaking time, the Court allowed 20 minutes for the DRC's rebuttal and 30 minutes for Uganda's surrebuttal during the second hearing held on June 28, 2000. Believing that there was no need to respond to the arguments made by the applicant in rebuttal, Uganda did not use the 30 minutes allocated to it. *See* ICJ Doc. CR 2000/24, at 3, 7 (June 28).

11 *See* Order, *supra* note 1, at para. 24.

12 *See* ICJ Doc. CR 2000/23, at 18-19 (June 28).

of Libya's requests for provisional measures in the *Lockerbie* cases.[13] In Uganda's view, the subject matter of the DRC's request was essentially the same as the matters addressed already by Security Council Resolution 1304, so that the principles invoked by the Court in 1992 had to apply also in this case.[14]

By way of alternative argument, Uganda submitted that, even if the Court were to accept that it had *prima facie* jurisdiction under Article 41 of the Statute, considerations of judicial prudence and propriety militated against the indication of provisional measures in this case. The request in practical terms had been rendered redundant and had become moot in view of the complete withdrawal of Ugandan troops from Kisangani in accordance with the wishes of the Security Council. Moreover, the measures requested were in direct conflict with the Lusaka Agreement, providing for an exclusive framework binding on the parties, and Resolution 1304. Such measures also were prejudicial to Uganda, because, apart from that state, they would not apply to any other party to the Lusaka or Kampala Agreements. Uganda also claimed that the DRC had not complied with the normal and necessary standards of procedural fairness, the request being deficient in substance, unsupported by any evidence and submitted without adequate notice to the respondent state,[15] and, in any event, Uganda had acted in accordance with the principles embodied in the United Nations Charter, including the right of self-defense set forth in Article 51. Finally, the fact that the DRC had waited almost a year before filing the request was seen as proof of the lack of urgency of the request.[16]

The Court first satisfied itself that the declarations by which each of the parties recognized the Court's compulsory jurisdiction under Article 36, paragraph 2, of the Statute, neither of which contains any reservation, constitute a *prima facie* basis on which its jurisdiction in this case might be founded.[17]

With regard to Uganda's argument that the request was inadmissible and moot, in view of its alleged compliance in full with Security Council Resolution 1304 adopted under Chapter VII of the United Nations Charter, the Court stated

---

13 *See* Questions of Interpretation and Application of the 1971 Montreal Convention arising from the Aerial Incident at Lockerbie (Libya v. UK) and (Libya v. U.S.), Provisional Measures, 1992 ICJ REP. 3, 15, paras. 39-40, and 114, 126-27, paras. 42-43 (Orders of Apr. 14). *See* ICJ Doc. CR 2000/23, at 8 (June 28).

14 *See* Order, *supra* note 1, at para. 26.

15 *See* ICJ Doc. CR 2000/23, at 10 (June 28). On recent developments relating to the scheduling of oral proceedings, see Shabtai Rosenne, *Controlling Interlocutory Aspects of Proceedings in the International Court of Justice*, 94 AJIL 307 (2000).

16 *See* Order, *supra* note 1, at paras. 27-31; ICJ Doc. CR 2000/23, at 12 (June 28).

17 *See id.* at paras. 32-34.

that neither this resolution and the measures taken in its implementation nor the Lusaka Agreement precluded the Court from acting in accordance with its Statute and the Rules of Court. The Court confirmed its earlier jurisprudence according to which the Security Council and the Court can perform their separate (political versus judicial) but complementary functions with respect to the same events, absent a Charter provision clearly demarcating the functions between the two organs in respect of any dispute or situation.[18] In the Court's view, the Security Council had taken no decision that *prima facie* would preclude the rights claimed by the DRC from "be[ing] regarded as appropriate for protection by the indication of provisional measures."[19] Moreover, the Court noted that it is not precluded from indicating provisional measures in a case merely because an applicant which simultaneously has brought a number of similar cases before the Court seeks such measures in only one of them.[20]

The Court next pointed out that its power to indicate provisional measures of protection under Article 41 of the Statute is intended to preserve the respective rights of the parties pending its decision and presupposes that irreparable prejudice shall not be caused to the rights that are the subject of dispute in pending proceedings. Moreover, such measures are justified only if there is urgency.[21] Such rights were identified as the applicant's rights to sovereignty and territorial integrity, to the integrity of its assets and natural resources, and to respect for the rules of international humanitarian law and for the instruments relating to the protection of human rights. In this context, the Court was satisfied that persons, assets and resources present on Congolese territory, particularly in the area of conflict, remained extremely vulnerable and that there was a serious risk that the rights at issue in the case might suffer irreparable prejudice. In the Court's view, even though it could not make definitive findings of fact or imputability, it was undisputed that Ugandan forces present on Congolese territory had been involved in fighting which had caused substantial

---

18 *See id.*, at para. 36 (citing Military and Paramilitary Activities in and against Nicaragua (Nicar. v. U.S.), Jurisdiction and Admissibility, Judgment, 1984 ICJ REP. 392, at 434-35, para. 95 (Nov. 26); and Application of the Convention on the Prevention and Punishment of the Crime of Genocide (Bos.-Herz. v. Yugo.), Provisional Measures, 1993 ICJ REP. 3, at 15, para. 40 (Order of Apr. 8)).

19 *Id.* (citing Questions of Interpretation and Application of the 1971 Montreal Convention arising from the Aerial Incident at Lockerbie (Libya v. UK), Provisional Measures, 1992 ICJ REP. 3, at 15, para. 40 (Order of Apr. 14)).

20 *Id.* at para. 38.

21 *Id.* at para. 39.

civilian casualties and material damage.[22] The urgency in the situation with which the Court was confronted could not in any way be affected by the fact that the applicant had not presented its request for provisional measures at the same time as its application.[23]

On the basis of the general power that the Court possesses by virtue of Article 41 of the Statute and the information at its disposal, and having regard "in particular [to] the fact that the Security Council has determined, in its resolution 1304 (2000), that the situation in the Congo 'continues to constitute a threat to international peace and security in the region,'" the Court concluded that there existed a serious risk of events occurring which might aggravate or extend the dispute between the DRC and Uganda or make it more difficult to resolve.[24]

By virtue of Article 75, paragraph 2, of the Rules of Court, empowering the Court to indicate measures that are, in whole or in part, different from those requested, the Court, by unanimous votes, ruled that, pending a decision in the main proceedings, both parties must, forthwith, (1) prevent and refrain from any action, and in particular any armed action, which might prejudice the rights of the other party in respect of whatever judgment the Court may render in the case, or which might aggravate or extend the dispute before the Court or make it more difficult to resolve; (2) take all measures necessary to comply with all of their obligations under international law, in particular those under the Charters of the United Nations and the Organization of African Unity, and with UN Security Council Resolution 1304 (2000); and (3) take all measures necessary to ensure full respect within the zone of conflict for fundamental human rights and for the applicable provisions of humanitarian law.[25]

* * * *

During the hearings, Uganda complained that the DRC, having failed to obtain the resolution it requested from the Security Council on June 16, 2000, came to the Court on the first business day following the Council's adoption of Resolution 1304, and asked the Court to order the same measure that the Council had rejected.[26] Judging from the text of the request and the DRC's

---

22   *Id.* at para. 41.
23   *Id.* at paras. 39-43.
24   *Id.* at para. 44.
25   *Id.* at para. 47 (*dispositif*).
26   *See* ICJ Doc. CR 2000/23, at 19 (June 28).

oral submissions, Uganda's explanation for the DRC's procedural move seems plausible. However, it cannot be said that the DRC achieved its objective through this Court action, given that the Court did not order the immediate withdrawal of Ugandan troops that the DRC requested or, for that matter, any of the specific measures requested by the DRC. Instead, the measures indicated are general in scope and nature and apply to *both* parties.

A comparison of the provisional measures indicated by the Court in this case with those contained in its Orders in the *Genocide* case in 1993[27] and in *Land and Maritime Boundary between Cameroon and Nigeria* in 1996[28] results in the following observations. Instead of using the word "should" as employed in the operative paragraphs of the 1993 and 1996 Orders, the current Order prominently features the word "must" in the *dispositif*, which perhaps indicates that the Court was desirous to emphasize the binding effect of the provisional measures indicated in this case, which is understandable when viewed in the light of the *Breard* precedent discussed in Chapter 2 above. By contrast to the first measure indicated in the *Genocide* case,[29] the Court in this case did not specifically order the respondent to take all measures within its powers to prevent the commission of war crimes to which the DRC referred in the third measure requested. Instead, it indicated, in more general terms, that the parties were to take all measures necessary to ensure full respect within the zone of conflict for fundamental human rights. Although the Court in the *Genocide* case indicated that the respondent was to ensure "that any military, paramilitary or irregular armed units which may be directed or supported by it, as well as any organizations and persons which may be subject to its control, direction or influence, do not commit any acts of genocide," it did not grant the DRC's similar request to indicate that Uganda "desist from providing any direct or indirect support to any State, group, organization, movement or individual engaged or preparing to engage in military activities" on Congolese territory and that it "take all measures in its power to ensure that units, forces or agents which are or could be under its authority, or which enjoy or could enjoy its support, together with organizations or persons which could be under

---

27 *See* Application of the Convention on the Prevention and Punishment of the Crime of Genocide (Bos.-Herz. v. Yugo.), Provisional Measures, 1993 ICJ REP. 3 (Order of Apr. 8).

28 *See* Land and Maritime Boundary between Cameroon and Nigeria (Cam. v. Nig.), Provisional Measures, 1996 ICJ REP. 13 (Order of Mar. 15).

29 *See* Application of the Convention on the Prevention and Punishment of the Crime of Genocide (Bos.-Herz. v. Yugo.), Provisional Measures, 1993 ICJ REP. 3, at 24, para. 52 sub (A)(1) (*dispositif*) (Order of Apr. 8).

its control, authority or influence, desist forthwith from committing or inciting the commission of war crimes or any other oppressive or unlawful act against all persons" on Congolese territory. Only the second part of the first measure indicated by the Court resembles the third and final measure indicated in the *Genocide* case,[30] whereas the first measure as a whole is almost identical to the first measure indicated in the *Land and Maritime Boundary* case.[31]

In the light of the resort by the Court to its general power under Article 75, paragraph 2, of the Rules of Court, it is somewhat surprising that the Court did not indicate some of the measures featured in the *Land and Maritime Boundary* case, such as that both parties were to take all necessary steps to conserve evidence relevant to the case within the area of conflict[32] and that they should lend every assistance to the United Nations mission in the region.[33] This indicates that the Court uses its powers conservatively in cases where it relies on Article 75, paragraph 2. In further comparison to the measures indicated in the *Land and Maritime Boundary* case, it also is unclear why the Court did not make specific reference, in the second measure indicated in the present case, to the Lusaka and Kampala Agreements, but this may be because the Security Council's binding resolution already covered that ground.[34] During the hearings, the DRC made explicit reference to the *Genocide* and *Land and Maritime Boundary* precedents, albeit in a different context.[35]

It is interesting to note that Greece requested the Court in *Aegean Sea Continental Shelf* to indicate provisional measures aimed at preserving certain rights claimed by it in somewhat similar circumstances.[36] In its Order of September 11, 1976, the Court found that the circumstances in that case were not

---

30   *Id.*, at para. 52 sub (B).
31   *See* Land and Maritime Boundary between Cameroon and Nigeria (Cam. v. Nig.), Provisional Measures, 1996 ICJ REP. 13, at para. 49 sub (1) (*dispositif*) (Order of Mar. 15).
32   *Cf. id.*, at para. 49 sub (4).
33   *Cf. id.*, at para. 49 sub (5).
34   *Cf. id.*, at para. 49 sub (2) (ordering both parties to observe an agreement reached by their ministers for foreign affairs on February 17, 1996, providing for the cessation of all hostilities in the disputed area).
35   *See* ICJ Doc. CR 2000/20, at 21 (June 26, 2000).
36   This precedent was invoked by Uganda during the hearing of June 28, 2000, in support of the proposition that the Court is prevented from exercising its powers under Article 41 as a consequence of Security Council action. *See* ICJ Doc. CR 2000/23, at 11-12 (June 28).

such as to require the indication of such measures.[37] As part of the measures requested, Greece asked the Court to order Turkey "to abstain from any sort of action whatsoever which may aggravate or extend the present dispute between Greece and Turkey."[38] Noting that Security Council Resolution 395 of August 25, 1976 recalled the need for the parties "to respect each other's international rights and obligations and to avoid any incident which might lead to the aggravation of the situation and which, consequently, might compromise their efforts towards a peaceful situation," the Court observed that official statements made by both parties in the aftermath of the resolution indicated that, presumably, they would comply with the Council's recommendations and their obligations under the Charter. Consequently, the Court did not deem it necessary to decide whether Article 41 of the Statute confers upon it the power to indicate provisional measures for the sole purpose of preventing the aggravation or extension of a dispute.[39] By contrast to Resolution 395 (1976), which was adopted under Chapter VI of the Charter, Resolution 1304 (2000), a binding resolution made pursuant to Chapter VII, did not contain words similar to those quoted in the *Aegean Sea Continental Shelf* case. In cases where there is potential overlap between the functions of the Court and the Council, the Court must walk a fine line, which is defined by the fact that "[t]he Court's specific power under Article 41 of the Statute is directed to the preservation of rights 'sub judice' and does not consist in a police power over the maintenance of international peace nor in a general competence to make recommendations relating to peaceful settlement of disputes."[40]

---

37   *See* Aegean Sea Continental Shelf (Greece v. Turk.), Provisional Measures, 1976 ICJ REP. 3, at 6, para. 15, 14 (Order of Sept. 11).

38   *Id.*, at 7, para. 15.

39   *See id.* at 12-13, paras. 36-42.

40   *Id.* at 16 (separate opinion of ICJ President Eduardo Jiménez de Aréchaga).

Request for immediate discharge of one state's international arrest warrant indicting foreign minister of another state – effect of fundamental change of circumstances disclosed at opening of hearings on conditions of urgency and irreparable prejudice – prima facie *jurisdiction based on Optional Clause declarations invoked only in second round of hearings-separateness of questions of mootness affecting application instituting proceedings and request for provisional measures*

ARREST WARRANT OF 11 APRIL 2000 (Dem. Rep. of the Congo v. Belgium),

Provisional Measures, Order
Obtainable from <www.icj-cij.org>
International Court of Justice, December 8, 2000

On October 17, 2000, the Democratic Republic of the Congo (DRC) filed an Application in the Registry of the International Court of Justice instituting proceedings against the Kingdom of Belgium (Belgium) in respect of an alleged dispute concerning an international arrest warrant issued on April 11, 2000 by judge Damien Vandermeersch of the Brussels court of first instance against the DRC's acting foreign minister, Mr. Abdulaye Yerodia Ndombasi (Yerodia). The arrest warrant, which was transmitted to all states (including the DRC) sought Yerodia's provisional detention pending a request for extradition to Belgium for alleged "crimes of international law committed by action or omission against persons or property protected by the Geneva Conventions of 12 August 1949 and the Additional Protocols I and II to those Conventions" (Geneva Conventions) and crimes against humanity by making various public speeches inciting racial hatred and thereby contributing to the massacre of Tutsi people by the Congolese population at the beginning of the rebellion against the late Congolese president Laurent-Désiré Kabila in August 1998. At the time of the speeches, Yerodia was Kabila's principal private secretary.[1] The DRC's Application requested the Court to declare that Belgium must annul the international warrant issued against Yerodia. Simultaneously with the filing of the Application, the DRC submitted a request for the indication of provisional

---

1   *See* Order of December 8, 2000, at para. 26 [hereinafter Order].

P.H.F. Bekker, World Court Decisions at the Turn of the Millennium (1997-2001), p. 241-254.
© 2002 *Kluwer Law International. Printed in the Netherlands.*

measures pursuant to Article 41, paragraph 1 of the Court's Statute and Articles 73-74 of the Rules of Court, asking the Court to order Belgium immediately to withdraw the disputed arrest warrant.[2] The DRC pointed out that the Belgian arrest warrant in effect prevented its foreign minister from leaving the DRC, thereby hampering him in carrying out his official duties. In response, Belgium argued that the DRC's request should be dismissed and the case should be removed from the General List as being without object, especially in view of an internal cabinet reshuffle that saw Yerodia moved to the education portfolio on the first day of the hearings in The Hague.

The Court's Order issued on December 8, 2000 unanimously rejected Belgium's request to remove the case from the General List and, by 15 votes to two, found that the circumstances, as they presented themselves to the Court, were not such as to require the exercise of its power under Article 41 of the Statute to indicate provisional measures.[3]

The DRC's Application directly challenged the legality of a Belgian statute of June 16, 1993 (amended on February 10, 1999) pertaining to the punishment of "serious violations of international humanitarian law" to which the arrest warrant refers. Article 5 of the Belgian statute prescribes that "the immunity conferred by a person's official capacity does not prevent application of this Law." In the DRC's view, this provision and the arrest warrant contravene international law *inter alia* by derogating from the diplomatic immunity of the minister for foreign affairs of a sovereign state based on the Court's jurisprudence[4] and Article 41, paragraph 2 of the 1961 Vienna Convention on Diplomatic Relations.[5] Article 41 provides that "[a]ll official business with the receiving State entrusted to the mission by the sending State shall be conducted with or through the Ministry for Foreign Affairs of the receiving State or such other ministry as may be agreed."

According to Belgium, however, the rule introduced by the 1999 amendments refusing immunity for state representatives, regardless of rank, implicated

---

2 *Id.* at paras. 43-44.

3 For the text of the *dispositif, see id.* at para. 78. Judge Rezek and Judge *ad hoc* Bula-Bula (appointed by the DRC) voted against the latter decision and appended dissenting opinions to the Order.

4 The DRC relied explicitly on an Order issued by the Court on December 15, 1979, holding that the violation of diplomatic immunity justified the indication of provisional measures. *Id.*, at para. 20 (citing United States Diplomatic and Consular Staff in Tehran (U.S. v. Iran), Provisional Measures, Order, 1979 ICJ REP. 3 (Dec. 15)).

5 Signed on April 18, 1961, entry into force April 24, 1964, 500 UNTS 95.

in one of the crimes provided for in the Belgian law, merely transcribed into domestic legislation a rule of international law.[6] Belgium pointed out that the disputed arrest warrant took account of the immunity issues arising from the indictment of a foreign minister by dispelling any notion that Yerodia would be arrested immediately upon entering Belgian territory at the official invitation of the Belgian Government, or while visiting or passing through Belgium in response to an invitation received from an international organization of which Belgium is a member. Such an invitation would constitute an implied waiver preventing Belgian courts from enforcing the warrant for the duration of the official stay, which the Belgian judicial authorities could not disregard without incurring the international responsibility of the Belgian state.[7] Besides, Yerodia's status as foreign minister or representative of a state did not entitle him to violate domestic or international law. Belgium claimed that Yerodia's arrest would occur in the course of ordinary criminal proceedings, in accordance with an exception to the right to personal liberty recognized by international instruments for the safeguard of the rights of the individual. Since no right had been violated, however, the DRC could not claim that the infringement of Yerodia's liberty was a breach of international law directly affecting the DRC.[8]

The DRC's Application also asserted that Article 7 of the Belgian statute, which establishes its universal applicability and the universal jurisdiction of the Belgian courts in relation to "serious violations of international humanitarian law," without the accused having to be present on Belgian territory,[9] and the arrest warrant violate international law, including the principle that a state may not exercise its authority on the territory of another state and the principle of the territorial integrity and sovereign equality of all member states of the United

---

6   Order, *supra* note 1, at para. 24 (referring *inter alia* to the statute and 1946 judgment
     of the Nuremberg Tribunal, the Treaty of Versailles, and the statutes of the Tokyo
     Tribunal, the Yugoslav and Rwandan war crimes tribunals, the International Criminal
     Court and the Special Court for Sierra Leone).
7   *Id.*, at para. 27.
8   *Id.*, at para. 28.
9   The DRC also pointed out that the Belgian judge who issued the disputed arrest
     warrant had considered in an unrelated case that Article 7 derogated from Article
     12 of the Preliminary Title of the Belgian Code of Criminal Procedure, according
     to which prosecutions dealt with therein are to take place only if the accused is
     found in Belgium, and thus did not make Belgian jurisdiction dependent on the
     accused's presence on Belgian territory. In the DRC's view, this interpretation,
     which Belgium had not disavowed, meant that the Belgian state conferred unlimited
     jurisdiction upon itself without any basis of territorial or *in personam* jurisdiction,
     as Yerodia's case demonstrated. *Id.*, at para. 18.

Nations laid down in Article 2, paragraph 1, of the UN Charter.[10] The Application pointed out that the arrest warrant affirmed the Belgian judge's competence
to deal with facts allegedly committed on the territory of the DRC by a national
of that state, without it being alleged that the victims are of Belgian nationality,
or that the facts constitute violations of the security or dignity of the Kingdom
of Belgium.

Referring to the various multilateral conventions for the suppression of
specifically defined offences that provide for universal jurisdiction of the states
parties to them, the DRC argued that these instruments, which make universal
jurisdiction conditional on the perpetrator's presence on the territory of the
prosecuting state, are not part of general international law.[11] In the DRC's view,
general international law currently does not recognize a further exception in
favor of universal jurisdiction regarding war crimes or crimes against humanity.
The UN Security Council resolutions that established international tribunals for
crimes in the former Yugoslavia and Rwanda[12] may have inspired states to
adopt laws designed to bring their legislation into line with these resolutions,
but they in no way are materially comparable to Article 7 of the Belgian law.[13]

Belgium argued that the Belgian judge acted within the framework of action
urged on the international community by the UN Security Council, referring
to Resolution 1291 of February 24, 2000. Resolution 1291 urged that an international investigation be carried out into all massacres that had occurred in
and around the territory of the DRC aimed at bringing to justice those responsible. It called on "all parties to the conflict in the Democratic Republic of the
Congo" to bring to justice those responsible for the massacres.[14] In Belgium's
view, its 1993 law and 1999 amendments merely adapted Belgian domestic
law to Belgium's international obligations, and Article 7 is consistent with the
second paragraph of the Article common to the four 1949 Geneva Conventions
(Articles 49, 50, 129 and 146, respectively). According to Belgium, the 1999
extension to crimes against humanity and genocide of the universal jurisdiction
provided for in Article 7 of the 1993 law merely represented "the incorporation

---

10 *Id.* at para. 1.
11 *Id.*, at para. 5.
12 UN Res. SC 827 of May 25, 1993 and SC 955 of Nov. 8, 1994, respectively.
13 *Id.*, at para. 6. The DRC pointed out that these resolutions could interfere only in
    the affairs of sovereign states in view of the United Nations' mission to maintain
    peace and international security, which no individual state may usurp.
14 *Id.*, at para. 23. It is unclear whether the Security Council considered Belgium to
    be among the "parties to the conflict," even though Belgium is the former colonial
    power of the DRC (called Zaire under Belgian rule).

into domestic law of an obligation long recognized in general international law."[15] Belgium argued that there exist clear and reasonable links between the acts referred to in the arrest warrant and Belgium, given that the Belgian judge acted *inter alia* on the complaints from a dozen private individuals, including five of Belgian nationality and seven of Congolese nationality.[16] Finally, Belgium pointed out that the disputed arrest warrant was no more enforceable directly on the territory of a third state than it was on Congolese territory, given that an international arrest warrant can produce compulsory effects only on the territory of a foreign state if that state agrees to assist in its enforcement and execute it. In other words, the extraterritorial effects of the warrant are entirely conditional on the willingness of the DRC as the requested state to act upon it or not.[17]

At the hearings, the DRC also argued that the disputed arrest warrant contravened the principle of non-retroactivity, citing Article 2, paragraph 1, of the Belgian Penal Code and the 1966 International Covenant on Civil and Political Rights and the 1950 European Convention for the Protection of Human Rights and Fundamental Freedoms in support.[18]

During the first round of oral argument held in The Hague on November 21, 2000, Belgium argued that the Court should refuse the DRC's request for provisional measures based on information, obtained by it at the opening of the hearings, that Yerodia had ceased to be minister for foreign affairs following a Congolese cabinet reshuffle on November 20, 2000, resulting in his reassignment as minister of education.[19] This information was confirmed by the DRC during the hearings. In Belgium's view, this fact rendered the request, which was premised on the impossibility for the DRC's foreign minister to leave his country to visit another state that his duties require him to visit, without object. Moreover, the ministerial reshuffle was a fundamental change of circumstances that affected the application in such a way that it should lead the Court to remove the case from the General List.[20] According to the DRC, however, Belgium had violated the immunities of its minister for foreign affairs at the time of the issuance of the arrest warrant and "any minister sent by his or her

---

15 *Id.*, at para. 24.
16 *Id.*, at para. 25.
17 *Id.*, at para. 29-30.
18 *Id.*, at para. 41. Of these two treaties, the International Covenant is the only one that has been ratified by both parties.
19 *Id.*, at paras. 22, 34, and 51.
20 *Id.*, at paras. 48 and 52.

State to represent it abroad … enjoy[ed], *sensu lato*, … [such] immunities."[21] The DRC emphasized that it was not exercising any right of diplomatic protection of a Congolese citizen, but instead was seeking to make good the alleged international law breaches "affecting the Congolese State in the exercise of its sovereign prerogatives in diplomatic matters."[22] In the DRC's view, the disputed arrest warrant was not directed at Yerodia in his personal capacity, but at the office of minister for foreign affairs.[23]

In the light of Belgium's arguments, the Court first addressed the question whether, as a result of the ministerial reshuffle, the DRC's *Application* had been deprived of its object and had to be removed from the General List as a result. The Court confirmed that it has the power to remove a case *in limine* without consideration if it is unable of being adjudicated on the merits (e.g., because of mootness of the application) and that events subsequent to the filing of an application may render the application without object.[24] The Court must ascertain the claim contained in the application in order to determine whether an application has been rendered without object. The DRC's Application requested the Court to declare that Belgium was to annul the arrest warrant issued on April 11, 2000 against Yerodia, the DRC's minister for foreign affairs then in office. Given that the disputed arrest warrant had not been withdrawn

---

21 *Id.*, at paras. 40 and 53. The DRC claimed that, as the plenipotentiary personal representative of the DRC Head of State, Yerodia was entitled to benefit from the principle of assimilation to the Head of State, the Head of Government, or the minister for foreign affairs, support for which it found in Art. 7, para. 2(*c*) of the 1969 Vienna Convention on the Law of Treaties, *opened for agreement* May 23, 1969, *entry into force* Jan. 27, 1980, 1155 UNTS 331.

22 *Id.*, at para. 19. Interestingly, ICJ President Guillaume, in his first address to the UN General Assembly on the occasion of the Assembly's examination of the Court's annual report, explicitly referred to this case as one "in which a State complains before the Court of the manner in which one of its nationals has been treated by another State," implying that this is after all a case brought through the exercise of diplomatic protection. President Guillaume made his remarks almost one month before the hearings in this case. Address by the President of the International Court of Justice, Judge Gilbert Guillaume, to the United Nations General Assembly, Oct. 26, 2000, available on the ICJ's Web site, <www.icj-cij.org>.

23 Even though the Court did not specifically address this argument, it did refer to Yerodia as "the subject of the arrest warrant of 11 April 2000." *Id* , at para. 51.

24 *Id.*, at para. 55 (citing *inter alia* Legality of Use of Force (Yugo. v. Sp.), Provisional Measures, Order, at para. 35 (June 2); Border and Transborder Armed Actions (Nica. v. Hond.), Jurisdiction and Admissibility, Judgment, 1988 ICJ REP. 69, 95, para. 66 (Dec. 20); Nuclear Tests (Austl. v. Fr.), Judgment, 1974 ICJ REP. 253, 272, para. 62 (Dec. 20)).

and continued to relate to the same individual, notwithstanding his new ministerial duties, and in the light of the fact that the DRC maintained its claim on
the merits and various supporting grounds during the hearings, the Court
concluded that the application had not been deprived of its object.[25]

The Court next addressed the separate question whether or not the *request*
for the indication of provisional measures had been deprived of its object after
the cabinet reshuffle of November 20, 2000 and had to be rejected as a result.
The Court observed that the request sought an order for the immediate discharge
of the disputed arrest warrant, which continued to be in Yerodia's name.
Moreover, the DRC considered that Yerodia continued to enjoy immunities
rendering the arrest warrant unlawful and it maintained both its original request
and the arguments advanced in support of its request at the hearings. In view
of these considerations, the Court concluded that the DRC's request had not
been deprived of its object by reason of Yerodia's appointment as minister
of education on November 20, 2000.[26]

The Court was satisfied that there was a *prima facie* basis on which its
jurisdiction in this case might be founded.[27] The application simply stated
that "Belgium has accepted the jurisdiction of the Court and, in so far as may
be required, the present Application signifies acceptance of that jurisdiction
by the Democratic Republic of the Congo."[28] During the second round of
oral argument, on November 22, 2000, the DRC argued that, *prima facie*, the
Court's jurisdiction derived from the declarations by which each of the parties
recognized the Court's compulsory jurisdiction under Article 36, paragraph
2, of the Statute (the "Optional Clause"). In the DRC's view, the parties' declarations "appear to contain no reservation."[29] Belgium, on the other hand, pointed
out that the DRC's Application made no reference to any specific basis of jurisdiction. Relying on an earlier precedent in which it was involved as respondent,
Belgium argued that the invocation by the DRC of the Optional Clause declarations of the parties during the second round of oral argument "seriously jeopardizes the principle of procedural fairness and the sound administration of justice."[30] Belgium also pointed to a clause in its declaration of April 3, 1958

---

25 *Id.*, at paras. 56-57.
26 *Id.*, at paras. 59-60.
27 *See id.*, at paras. 32-34.
28 *Id.*, at para. 2.
29 *Id.*, at para. 42. The substantive part of the text of the declarations is set forth in
    para. 61.
30 *Id.*, at paras. 32, 46, and 62 (citing Legality of Use of Force (Yugo. v. Belg.), Provi-
    sional Measures, Order, 1999 ICJ REP. 124 at 139 para. 44 (June 2)).

excluding disputes "to which the parties have agreed or may agree to have recourse to another method of pacific settlement." It argued that this clause blocked the Court's jurisdiction in the present case given that high-level discussions between the parties on the issue of the arrest warrant were pending at the time of the filing of the application.[31]

The Court noted that, even though the DRC's Application suffered from a certain lack of precision in setting out the jurisdictional grounds, it did refer to Belgium's acceptance of the Court's jurisdiction. Article 38, paragraph 2, of the Rules of Court requires only that the application specify "as far as possible" the legal grounds upon which the Court's jurisdiction is said to be based. In any event, it is for the Court itself to ascertain in each case whether it has jurisdiction. The Court observed that the declarations of both parties were duly deposited with the UN Secretary-General. In view of the fact that the Secretary-General had transmitted copies of the declarations to all the parties to the Court's Statute and their reproduction in the Court's Yearbook, the Court concluded that the declarations were within the knowledge both of the Court and of the parties, who cannot but be aware of the Court's compulsory jurisdiction.[32] Based on the terms of the application and the submissions of the applicant in this case, the Court concluded that Belgium "could readily expect that the declarations made by the two Parties would be taken into consideration as a basis for the jurisdiction of the Court in the present case" and that Belgium was, therefore, in a position "to prepare and put forward any such argument as it thought fit in this regard."[33] Consequently, it could not be said that the timing of the invocation of the declarations was likely to seriously jeopardize the principle of procedural fairness and the sound administration of justice, as Belgium had argued, and there was nothing to prevent the Court from taking into account the parties' Optional Clause declarations.

The high-level negotiations to which Belgium had referred did not affect the Court's conclusion, since Belgium had not supplied any details on the nature, duration, scope, state of progress or precise consequences of those negotiations. Noting that, when confronted with a request for the indication of provisional measures, the Court need not satisfy itself beyond any doubt that it has jurisdiction on the merits of the case, but may indicate such measures

---

31 *Id.*, at para. 46.

32 *See id.*, at para. 63 (citing Military and Paramilitary Activities in and against Nicaragua (Nicar. v. U.S.), Merits, Judgment, 1986 ICJ REP. 14, at 32, para. 44 (June 27)).

33 *Id.*

when the jurisdictional bases invoked appear *prima facie* to constitute a basis on which the Court's jurisdiction could be founded, the Court concluded that its jurisdiction in the provisional measures stage could not be excluded solely by reason of the negotiations to which Belgium referred.[34]

The Court next pointed out that its power to indicate provisional measures of protection under Article 41 of the Statute is intended to preserve the respective rights of the parties pending its decision and presupposes that irreparable prejudice should not be caused to rights that are the subject of dispute in pending proceedings. Moreover, such measures are justified only if there is urgency.[35]

In support of these requirements, the DRC pointed out that, as a result of the Belgian arrest warrant, its foreign minister could not visit any state to which his duties might call him. Moreover, it viewed the consequences of excluding the DRC's representative from the international arena as irreparable by their very nature.[36] As described above, Belgium argued that the DRC's Application, and hence the request, was rendered without object following the cabinet reshuffle and should be dismissed on this ground. The reshuffle indicated that there was no "real risk" of irreparable prejudice to the DRC's rights. In Belgium's view, there also was a lack of urgency even before the cabinet reshuffle when Yerodia was still the DRC foreign minister, given that the DRC had known about the arrest warrant, which was issued on April 11, 2000, since at least July 12, 2000 and had made no suggestion of any urgency prior to the filing of the case on October 17, 2000. In particular, Belgium argued that the alleged right claimed to be in need of preservation, namely, that of the DRC's foreign minister to travel abroad on government business, was not a right at all, but a function of diplomatic discourse requiring the consent of the receiving state.[37] Finally, Belgium argued that there was no risk of a significant deterioration in relations between Belgium and the DRC sufficient to warrant the indication of provisional measures and that the long history of United Nations involvement in the Great Lakes regional conflict militated against the requested measures.[38]

The Court observed that the DRC's claim essentially was that the Belgian arrest warrant, the discharge of which was sought by the DRC's request, violated

---

34 *Id.*, at paras. 65-68.
35 *Id.*, at para. 69.
36 *Id.*, at paras. 20 and. 71. In support of its request, the DRC also referred to the "seriousness of the substantive legal grounds of the Application." *Id.*, at para. 21.
37 *Id.*, at paras. 33-35.
38 *Id.*, at paras. 37-38 and 49.

international law regarding the jurisdiction of national criminal courts and the immunity of heads of state and members of governments. In the light of the cabinet reshuffle leading to Yerodia's re-assignment as minister of education, involving less frequent foreign travel than the post of foreign minister calls for, the Court found that the DRC had not established that irreparable prejudice might be caused in the immediate future to the DRC's rights. On the same ground, the Court concluded that the degree of urgency was not such that the DRC's rights needed to be protected through the indication of provisional measures.[39]

The Court did not entertain the suggestions made by both parties individually to consider the indication of alternative measures of protection. Belgium stated during both rounds of its oral argument that it would not object to provisional measures calling upon the parties "jointly, in good faith, to address the difficulties caused by the issuance of the arrest warrant with a view to achieving a resolution to the dispute in a manner that is consistent with their obligations under international law, including Security Council resolutions 1234 (1999) and 1291 (2000)."[40] Similarly, the DRC, referring to "the readiness of both Parties to seek a friendly settlement by diplomatic means," during its second round of oral argument submitted a general request for the indication of measures consisting "*inter alia*, in urging both Parties – Belgium in particular, and the Democratic Republic of the Congo – to adopt a course of conduct which will prevent the continuation, aggravation and extension of the dispute, in particular by eliminating the main cause of this dispute."[41] Notwithstanding these requests and Belgium's assertion that there was no risk of a deterioration of relations between Belgium and the DRC, the Court pointed out that the positions regarding the parties' respective rights set out before it during the hearings still were a long way apart. While the Court stated that it continued to welcome any bilateral negotiations with a view to achieving a direct and friendly settlement, the outcome of such negotiations could not be foreseen. In the Court's view, it was desirable that the issues before it should be determined as soon as possible, making it appropriate to ensure that a decision on the DRC's Application be reached expeditiously.[42]

---

39 *Id.*, at paras. 70-72.
40 *Id.*, at paras. 39, 49, and 75. Under Art. 75, paras. 1 and 2, of the Rules of Court, the Court has the power to indicate provisional measures that deviate in whole or in part from those requested.
41 *Id.*, at paras. 43-44 and 74.
42 *Id.*, at para. 76.

In view of the conclusions reached by it, the Court also found it unnecessary to address Belgium's argument that the Court's jurisprudence prevented it from granting the DRC's request for a provisional measure relating to the immediate discharge of the arrest warrant, as such request was identical to the relief sought by the applicant on the merits of its claim.[43]

Finally, the Court pointed out that its decision in no way prejudged the question of its jurisdiction to deal with the merits of the case or any questions relating to the admissibility of the DRC's Application, or relating to the merits themselves, in respect of which both parties are entitled to submit arguments.[44]

* * * *

The outcome of these interim proceedings clearly depended on the effect that the Court would assign to the Congolese cabinet reshuffle coinciding with the opening of the hearings relating to the DRC's request for provisional measures. The reassignment of the foreign minister to the education portfolio essentially led to the dismissal of the request for lack of irreparable prejudice and urgency. The event was, therefore, poorly timed on the applicant's part from the perspective of these proceedings. It is unclear how the Court would have ruled had the reshuffle not taken place. Assuming that the Court would have been satisfied that irreparable prejudice and urgency were present, this, in combination with its finding of *prima facie* jurisdiction, would have made the indication of provisional measures more likely. The Court's principal reason for dismissing the DRC's request was that the post of minister of education involves "less foreign travel" than that of foreign minister; but "less foreign travel" still implies "some" foreign travel.[45] Apparently, it is the level of foreign travel

---

43 *Id.*, at para. 73 and 36 (Belgium invoked a 1927 PCIJ case in support of its argument that "[t]he exceptional nature of the provisional measures procedure [did] not admit of an interim judgment granting the relief requested in the Application," citing Factory at Chorzów (Ger. v. Pol.), Provisional Measures, Order, 1927 PCIJ (ser. A) No. 12, at 10 (Nov. 21)). Although the DRC reiterated the arguments advanced in its Application, it also explained that its request did not ask the Court to determine the merits of the legal grounds on which the application relied, but that the Court should note that these grounds were serious and justified "steps to ensure that the *capitis deminutio* which a Belgian judge ha[d] sought to inflict on" the DRC should cease. *Id.*, at para. 21.

44 *Id.*, at para. 77.

45 The DRC in fact pointed out during the hearings that "Mr. Yerodia, yesterday Minister for Foreign Affairs, today Minister of Education in the new Congolese Government ... [would] be called upon to travel, to respond to invitations from

that determines whether the conditions of irreparable prejudice and urgency are satisfied in circumstances such as these.

The reshuffle resulted in the Court being able to avoid having to tackle thorny international law issues touching upon the merits of this case, including those of international criminal jurisdiction and diplomatic and sovereign immunity.

The question of universal jurisdiction over the most heinous crimes has come into the international spotlight in connection with the arrest and detention by the United Kingdom of the former Chilean leader General Augusto Pinochet. After judge Vandermeersch unsuccessfully demanded Pinochet's extradition from the United Kingdom to Belgium, he relied on the Belgian statute challenged by the DRC in this case to probe human rights charges against former Iranian president Akbar Hashemi Rafsanjani, which strained diplomatic relations between Iran and Belgium in March 2000. Similar indictments have also been issued in Belgium against Prime Minister Ariel Sharon of Israel, President Fidel Castro of Cuba, President Laurent Gbabo of Ivory Coast, and President Denis Sassou Nguesso of the Congo.

Under present international law, only certain universally-condemned acts may be prosecuted without regard to where they were committed or to the nationality of the perpetrator or the victim. In connection with a dispute between Turkey and France arising from the collision on the open sea between a French steamship and a Turkish steamship and the subsequent exercise by Turkey of criminal jurisdiction over the Turkish vessel and the officer of the watch on board the French vessel, the Permanent Court of International Justice ruled in 1927, by the president's casting vote, that Turkey had not acted in conflict with the principles of international law and found that there is no international law rule prohibiting a state from exercising jurisdiction over a foreigner in respect of an offense committed outside its territory, especially where the offense involved produced effects on the territory of the state asserting jurisdiction.[46] Several U.S. courts have held that there is universal jurisdiction over such acts permitting the United States to provide a remedy for violations

---

abroad, to attend international meetings" and that he would "often be called upon to be sent as the plenipotentiary personal representative of the Head of State to represent him abroad." *Id.*, at para. 40.

46 *See* S.S. "Lotus" (Turkey v. France), Judgment, 1927 PCIJ (ser. A) No. 10, at 20 ("The territoriality of criminal law ... is not an absolute principle of international law and by no means coincides with territorial sovereignty."); *see also* OPPENHEIM'S INTERNATIONAL LAW, Vol. 1, at 469-79 (R. Jennings & R. Watts eds., 9th ed. 1996).

of international law through its domestic courts, even where the conduct complained of took place entirely outside the United States.[47]

Even though international tribunals have been established to deal with crimes in the former Yugoslavia and Rwanda, no criminal court with general jurisdiction currently exists at the international level. The 1998 Rome Statute providing for the creation of the International Criminal Court (ICC), which would fill this gap for future crimes, had not yet entered into force in 2000.[48] The former prime minister of Rwanda, Jean Kambanda, was found guilty by an international court, the International Criminal Tribunal for Rwanda in Arusha (Tanzania), on September 4, 1998, on counts of genocide and crimes against humanity arising from the murder and extermination of Rwandan civilians in 1994. Kambanda's life sentence was upheld on appeal on October 19, 2000.[49]

In support of the Belgian law at issue in this case, Article 27 of the Statute of the International Criminal Court provides that official capacity as a member of a government does not exempt a person from criminal responsibility under the ICC Statute. It also provides that immunities which may attach to the official capacity of a person do not bar the ICC, once it is in existence, from exercising its jurisdiction over such a person for genocide, crimes against humanity, or war crimes. Although the Brussels court is not an international court to which the ICC Statute will apply once it enters into force, it might adopt a similar approach to an official's asserted immunity when the charges involve crimes against humanity and war crimes.

The Vienna Convention on Diplomatic Relations invoked by the DRC in this case shields "diplomatic agents" with immunity from criminal prosecution and, with limited exceptions, immunity from civil suit. Based on the express provisions of the Vienna Convention, however, and absent fulfillment of certain procedural rules (including official accreditation of the diplomat concerned with the receiving state), cabinet ministers cannot automatically be categorized as immunized "diplomatic agents." By its terms, "the purpose of [the immunities

---

47 For a recent overview of U.S. precedents under the Alien Tort Claims Act, which grants U.S. federal district courts jurisdiction to hear "any civil action by an alien for a tort only, committed in violation of the law of nations or a treaty of the United States" (28 U.S.C. §1350 (1994)), see Richard L. Herz, *Litigating Environmental Abuses Under the Alien Tort Claims Act: A Practical Assessment*, 40 VA.J.INT'L L. 545 (2000).

48 Signed on July 17, 1998, *reprinted in* 37 ILM 999 (1998).

49 *Kambanda v. Prosecutor*, Judgment, Case No. ICTR-97-23-A, ICTR Appeals Chamber. *See* Olivia Swaak-Goldman, Case Report: Kambanda v. Prosecutor, 95 AJIL 656 (2001).

provided in the Vienna Convention] is not to benefit individuals but to ensure the efficient performance of the functions of diplomatic missions as representing States."

This Order, the first decision counter-signed by the Court's new Belgian Registrar,[50] incorporates a procedural novelty recently decided upon by the Court whereby the declarations and separate and dissenting opinions appended to the decision are no longer presented sequentially, but feature in the order of precedence of their authors.[51]

---

50 By contrast to the ICJ President, the ICJ Registrar is not disqualified from exercising his functions in a case in which the state of his nationality is a party.

51 *See* ICJ Communiqué 2000/40 (Dec. 8, 2000).

◊

*"International Law in Ferment and the World Court: A Discussion on the Role and Record of the International Court of Justice"** *
94th Annual Meeting, American Society of International Law
Washington, D.C., Friday, April 7, 2000

Participants: Stephen Schwebel, retired Judge and immediate past President of the ICJ (1981-2000); Eduardo Valencia-Ospina, former Registrar of the ICJ (1987-2000); Keith Highet, McDermott, Will & Emery, Washington, D.C.; and Thomas Franck, ASIL President and professor of law, New York University. Interlocutor: Pieter H.F. Bekker, White & Case LLP, New York City, and Co-Chair, 94th Annual Meeting.

PIETER BEKKER

We are honored by the presence today of what I consider to be my "ICJ Dream Team." I will turn first to developments relating to the General List of cases. Much has been said lately about the Court's docket, which currently consists of not less than 24 cases. Recalling past decades, there have been periods, however, where the Court was confronted with cases that really never materialized. One recalls the *Aerial Incident* cases involving Bulgaria in the 1950s. So the question arises: How real is this number, 24? I should point out that in eight cases brought by Yugoslavia against various NATO member States in April 1999, the Court already has held at the provisional measures stage that it has no *prima facie* jurisdiction. In the two *Lockerbie* cases, brought by Libya against the United States and the United Kingdom, the Court has not fixed any time limits for the Rejoinder by the UK and the US. In this light, the question is: What developments can we expect for the future based on the current docket and perhaps the Court's recent decisions, especially on provisional measures and jurisdiction?

---

*   Reproduced, in unedited and unabridged form, with permission from 94 ASIL Proc. 172 (2000). © The American Society of International Law.

P.H.F. Bekker, World Court Decisions at the Turn of the Millennium (1997-2001), p. 255-275.
© 2002 *Kluwer Law International. Printed in the Netherlands.*

JUDGE SCHWEBEL

I would say that the docket is a real docket. The fact that cases at times are settled is unexceptionable. Peter Trooboff remarked to me the other day that in U.S. litigation, 99% of the cases brought are settled and it is his impression that in arbitration about two thirds of the claims brought are settled. Far fewer are settled in the International Court of Justice, but if there is a settlement satisfactory to the parties, I do not think that suggests that the Court's docket in respect to that case has been unreal and the settlement in principle is to be welcomed. You are right, Pieter, in indicating that eight of the cases of the docket, those brought by Yugoslavia against members of NATO, indeed are closely connected on the merits. That is not true for the first stage of the case that the court surmounted, namely that on provisional measures, because the jurisdictional bases of the cases vary distinctly one to another, and it will not be true at the stage of jurisdiction which remains.

EDUARDO VALENCIA-OSPINA

I would agree with Steve that these are real cases in a formal, legal way. They have been submitted by States parties as distinct cases and the Court has treated them as such and has not joined them – either because the parties have not requested it or because it itself has found it inappropriate. So as long as they are not joined, they remain to be treated independently. And statistically, of course, there are 24 cases. But statistics can always be manipulated and I might perhaps be guilty of manipulating them now. While these cases are real and legally distinct, one has to see beyond. It is not unconnected with subsequent discussion on the future of the Court and the volume of cases that we may expect. Among these 24 cases, there are at least four that, for all practical purposes, are suspended at the stage of going into hearings on the merits. One such case, *Gabčíkovo-Nagymaros Project*, in fact is rather exceptional in that the judgment on the merits already was handed down by the Court and what the Court is presented with – the case is, as it were, suspended pending negotiations among the parties – is a judgment on implementation of the Court's judgment on the merits. The other three cases, the *Lockerbie* cases and the *Genocide* case (Bosnia against Yugoslavia), are presently not active. So this brings down the number to twenty and among these cases, there are, in reality, only three that are ready to go into the merits phase and on which hearings should be programmed. In the *Qatar-Bahrain* Case, the Court will be commencing hearings at the beginning of June. The other cases, except for one which was brought by a special agreement (Indonesia/Malaysia), are susceptible of having preliminary objections raised either on jurisdiction or on admissibility.

Of course, it is anybody's guess how the Court will go in deciding these preliminary objections. The worst scenario could be that in all 16 cases the preliminary objections would be upheld, in which case, of course, the docket would be reduced to four cases. This is one way of looking at it. You have alluded to what is an interesting development in the last years in the Court. It is the submission of cases that are so similar that they could be considered as a group of cases. It may be exemplified with the Nicaragua action against the United States. Nicaragua also brought actions against Honduras and Costa Rica. These are cases that emerged from a similar complex of legal/political situations where the legal issues may be fundamentally similar and even the factual issues not dissimilar. Even in cases of advisory opinions, we have had two advisory opinions requested fundamentally on the legality of nuclear weapons. We have had a *Breard* case and a *LaGrand* case. We have the ten cases that Yugoslavia brought to the Court against NATO member states, eight of which remain. There are three cases brought by the Congo against Uganda, Burundi and Rwanda, two of which will be dealt with at the jurisdictional stage first. But still, the fundamental cause of action remains the same: they are genocide cases. So if we look at it in terms of the legal issues, even if they are not joined, the intellectual effort that is required and even the material requirements of such cases, then the reality is a little different. Not just by way of the precedential force of decisions in previous cases. Let's say *LaGrand* would be in a way a repetition of the *Breard* case or Croatia/Yugoslavia would raise issues similar to Bosnia/Yugoslavia. The Court has the power, even if it does not join these cases, to treat them in common so that the applicant would file only one pleading, would plead only orally once against all the respondents, even if the cases are all separate. Judges would write one note for all of these cases, judgments would be separate but similar, even fairly identical, if you compared judgments in *Lockerbie* or, even on provisional measures, the ten Orders in the NATO cases. I am not trying to minimize, of course, the unprecedented number. I think this a great tribute to Judge Schwebel's presidency, that the largest number of cases in the history of the Court was brought to the Court during his presidency. But the considerations that I have made should be taken into account to establish the real state of the situation of the docket.

PIETER BEKKER
Thank you, Mr. Former Registrar. What do my fellow Court commentators think about the current docket of the Court?

THOMAS FRANCK

Well, there is no real reason for me to think anything about the current docket of the Court. It is the docket of the Court and if the judges feel overworked or underappreciated or feel that some of the cases are bogus cases, they have ways they can deal with that, but it is a judgment that I think this side of the process cannot really assist in. I do think, more generally, that there is a legitimate function for bringing a case with a view that earlier stages of the case, whether it be provisional measures or jurisdiction, will be straws in the wind as to how the Court would decide the case on the merits and that that may be an important factor in prodding the parties to negotiate. It seems to me a perfectly useful and legitimate use of the Court's time to employ them in that kind of process of accelerating negotiations. The classic case of that is the *Great Belt* Case and I do not think anyone feels disappointed – not the counsel, not the parties, and certainly not the judges – if that is the function that the Court fulfills. There is a somewhat different version of that, which is the use of the Court simply to publicize an issue. That is a well-known practice in the U.S. and may be considered to be a legitimate use of the courts in this country, but many of the judges on the Court are not from this country and have not been trained to regard themselves as megaphones for the promotion of agendas, or solely for that purpose, and may feel themselves ill-used. But that is not for me to say.

KEITH HIGHET

I just want to add a couple of obvious points as reminders. We must remember that a case before the International Court of Justice, as a case before an international arbitration tribunal, is a case tried on the trial level, essentially, and that it involves a vast panoply. Every single one of these cases involves vast amounts of documentation: proof in the first instance, documents, testimonies, opinions, views, maps, charts, everything – so each case is an enormous case. I do not think that you can talk about "the docket" of the Court. I get very cross with my colleagues who say that the Court has nothing to do, that it only has 12 cases or 14 cases. That would break the back of the Supreme Court of the United States! If you just look at the Supreme Court, or the appellate divisions of the courts of New York, and I have sat with them and watched how they function, or the circuit courts of appeals, they have tiny little, narrow issues. They are deep, but they are narrow and they are issues of law. And they are briefed, clerked and prepared. When you deal with these international cases, it is very different. So when you talk about the docket of the Court, you have got to keep that in mind. Point two, historical reflection. The *S.S. "Wim-*

bledon" Case was brought in 1923 by four applicants against one respondent and it was joined essentially as one. The *South West Africa* Cases, which I always refer to for Tom Franck's benefit in any meeting of any kind, my first case, actually was called the South West Africa *cases* – it was two cases joined. They were identical, but there was a memorial of Ethiopia and a memorial of Liberia. I prepared both of them and they were joined. Arthur Rovine helped me. In the *North Sea Continental Shelf* Cases, plural, there were two. Also, the *Fisheries Jurisdiction* Cases and other examples share a common parentage or fact situation referred to by Eduardo. They are nonetheless very real. I think that in 20 years, you will find people referring to the NATO *cases* probably. Even the *Continental Shelf* Cases can, for those of us who practice in the field, become a happy blur.

PIETER BEKKER
Keith, I am going to stay with you for my next question, which is related to the docket. The *East Timor* Case between Portugal and Australia (1995) and the *Fisheries Jurisdiction* Case in which you represented Spain against Canada, dismissed in 1998, are the only two cases, since the Court's 1978 decision in the *Aegean Sea* Case, that have been dismissed for lack of jurisdiction. Until a few years ago, some commentators were charging the Court with judicial activism, especially in the aftermath of its decisions upholding jurisdiction in the case between Nicaragua and the United States (1984), and again in the case in which you were involved, *Qatar-Bahrain* (1994 and 1995). Others believed that the Court was reluctant to dismiss cases because it used to have so few cases on its docket. Does the Court's full caseload and also its decision of December 4, 1998 in the Spanish *Fisheries Jurisdiction* Case, now suggest the opposite or was that decision perhaps an isolated incident?

KEITH HIGHET
That is a very interesting question. It is hard to answer and I certainly would not dream of answering it from the point of view of judges. The *Qatar-Bahrain* cases – there were two decisions by the Court – are very interesting. They should be read, I think, and of course I am partisan as having represented Bahrain, in close conjunction with the *Aegean Sea* Case because I think, basically, that they came out exactly the opposite way. Now you could, if you wished, say that this is the result of perhaps judicial activism of the Court; but I find these descriptors really basically unhelpful. The judges have a job to do. They have texts to work with, they have documents to look at. Of course, there may be a tilt one way or another. Counsel's arguments may even help

tilt the Court one way or another. But basically it comes down to a question of treaty interpretation, the interpretation of texts and, even more subtly, the interpretation of facts. I cannot really say that the Court suddenly finds an appetite to inhale cases and to take jurisdiction where twenty years before the judges might have resisted it just because they fear that their docket be empty. I cannot imagine that and I would love to hear some other comment, if that is possible.

PIETER BEKKER
Perhaps from the Peace Palace?

JUDGE SCHWEBEL
I would agree with Keith that one cannot plausibly speak of judicial activism or inactivism. At the time that the Court very controversially dismissed the cases brought by Ethiopia and Liberia it had rather little on its docket, so that suggests the inaccuracy of such a speculation. In this, as in so many other matters in the judicial process – national, local, international – there is room for difference of opinion. It is difficult to maintain that there is a sole truth. Judges can reasonably differ on matters of jurisdiction and they have in the World Court since its inception, and built up what may be a most intricate and recondite body of jurisprudence anywhere on jurisdiction, because of the peculiarities, the very limited nature of the Court's jurisdiction, which differs very much, quite obviously, from that obtaining in national courts. A digression, by the way, with reference to national courts: we speak of the size of the docket of the Court and say 24 is a lot and 12 may be little. But obviously one has to bear in mind that the number of parties that can have contentious access to the Court are less than 200. If there were only 200 potential parties in New York City to the courts there, you could not have tens of thousands of cases. It would be impossible, and it is impossible to have before the International Court of Justice thousands of cases. There are few litigants with the capacity to generate cases. Considering the number of entities that can have recourse to the Court, the Court's docket is currently a remarkably full one, even taking account of the well-taken points that Eduardo advanced. As to whether the Court has been activist or not, a final word. In my view, the Court has more than once asserted a jurisdiction which was unfounded. But I do not say, quite obviously, that my view was the final word. Indeed, it was not the final word. I dissented on these matters rather often.

PIETER BEKKER

Did I mention the *Nicaragua* case?

JUDGE SCHWEBEL

You might have mentioned it! But if you did not, I do not think it is entirely forgotten. I dissented as well in *Qatar-Bahrain*. I did not dissent in the two cases where the Court declined jurisdiction. I was with the majority there. And I guess if one wants to attach labels, one could say that in matters of jurisdiction I have been rather minimalist or conservative and I would acknowledge that. I think that that is the correct approach in a Court whose jurisdiction is fundamentally and loudly consensual. We all know perfectly well that the Court only has jurisdiction if States have agreed to give it jurisdiction, and there is a grave danger, in my view, in taking an expansive view of that consent because it can cut off future consent. That is one side of the picture. But on the other side is another substantial view which is that if the parties have given the Court jurisdiction, then it is the duty of the Court to fulfill that grant and render judgment. And whether they have or have not, is, as I have said at the outset, a question on which minds can reasonably differ.

PIETER BEKKER

I would also point out that although there may be only 24 cases, of course, they involve over 40 states and there are only some 190 constituents of the world community that can be involved in ICJ litigation, so the number is actually quite high if you look at it from that perspective.

EDUARDO VALENCIA-OSPINA

The impression I had initially when I came to the Court in 1984 was that it appeared as if the intellectual effort was being made to dismiss cases on the ground of lack of jurisdiction in the period before 1984, and that this effort had turned, rather, to try to find ways to assert jurisdiction, and the Court went to some lengths to do that. I would not dispute whether it was right or wrong, but it resurrected the Optional Clause declaration of Nicaragua from the time of the League of Nations. It resurrected the Pact of Bogotá, it delivered two judgments on jurisdiction in *Qatar-Bahrain*, and so on and so forth. I agree that, fundamentally, the main point here is the consensual aspect of the jurisdiction of the Court and, if there is a *prima facie* grant of jurisdiction, the Court should make every effort to try to ascertain if, indeed, there is jurisdiction on the basis of which it can continue a case. I have not made such a study, but one could look at challenges to jurisdiction or objections to the admissibility of applications, in particular challenges to jurisdiction based on the assertion of very specific provisions of reservations, either reservations to the Optional Clause or reservations to jurisdictional clauses in bilateral and multilateral treaties. An impression might be, *prima facie*, that the Court is particularly careful when it comes to dealing with a challenge to jurisdiction based on the text of a reservation. It could be a question of the validity of the reservation or it could be a question of the applicability of a valid reservation. In cases like the *Nicaragua* Case, where the Court was confronted with such a challenge regarding the United States' multilateral treaty reservation, the Court avoided the issue and declared that this reservation was not, in the circumstances of the case, of a preliminary character and sent it to the merits. The Court was presented with a reservation in the *Nauru* Case and upheld its jurisdiction. At the same time, in the recent NATO cases, the Court, at the stage of provisional measures, almost *in limine litis* on jurisdictional grounds dismissed two applications by Yugoslavia against Spain and the United States without even giving a chance to the applicant to debate the jurisdictional question at a further stage than the *prima facie* stage. Of course, the cases that I mentioned before on which challenges are possible are *sub judice* and it is very difficult to speculate on them. But one could imagine, as the precedent shows, that in every case brought by application, the respondents will avail themselves of the right to raise objections to jurisdiction. Of all these 24 cases that are before the Court, there is only one case brought by special agreement, all the others having been brought unilaterally by application. They are all before the plenary Court, not before a chamber. I would not think that the Canada/Spain case necessarily is an isolated case – one then could point to the two NATO cases. Of course, one cannot say that there is a trend. The Court will deal with each case on its own merits, except that I think it will look at specific reservations much more closely than if it is a question of objections to jurisdiction based sometimes on very far-fetched interpretations or other legal grounds.

KEITH HIGHET

I just wanted to add very briefly to what Eduardo has just said. I am counsel to Cameroon in the case brought by Cameroon against Nigeria, which is a case that has been proceeding for some six or seven years and has gone through practically every single procedural form known. It is like a caterpillar becoming a butterfly becoming a moth becoming a monkey becoming a fish ... But this is a very interesting and complicated case and there we are dealing with two Optional Clause declarations, as I recall, without reservations, and this will show what good counsel can do. Good counsel, in this case, of course, on both sides ... But good counsel for Nigeria filed at the last moment eight – not one, not three, not seven but *eight* – preliminary objections to admissibility and jurisdiction based on a declaration with no reservation to be interpreted. That tied up the Court for it was very difficult, and fortunately the Court retained jurisdiction and the case is still on the docket.

PIETER BEKKER

That leads me to my next question. We have spent a lot of time so far on the jurisdiction of the Court, and rightly so, because that is in reality the most important element of litigation before the Court. But let us move on to assess some of the consequences of what we have discussed with respect to the docket – the question of working methods and case management. It has been reported that the Court's Rules Committee has embarked on revision of the Rules of Court with a view to accelerating the judicial process. An overhaul of the Court's working methods was first announced in the Court's press communiqué of April 6, 1998. The slowness of the Court's process continues to attract widespread criticism from outside the Peace Palace. Several cases have been pending for more than seven years: *Qatar-Bahrain* has been on the docket since 1991, *Oil Platforms* between Iran and the United States has been around since 1992, the *Lockerbie* Cases since 1992, the Bosnian *Genocide* Case since 1993 and Keith mentioned the *Cameroon-Nigeria* Case that has been pending since 1994. In apparent recognition of this criticism, newly-elect President Gilbert Guillaume in his press conference of February 15, 2000, emphasized that "in most, if not all, cases the delays have resulted from the parties' wishes." But he also admitted that it is for the Court to determine time limits for filing written pleadings. He failed to mention the scheduling of oral proceedings in cases that are ready for hearing. The Court's press communiqué of February 24, 2000, announcing the opening of hearings in the case between Pakistan and India, contained the following unprecedented statement: "The Court had wished to hold hearings in March, but at the pressing request of the parties it has exceptionally agreed to open them later." Of the 18 or so cases that were brought between 1987 and 1997, only three were filed jointly by way of a special agreement. That means that 85% or so of all cases may be characterized, to borrow from Keith Highet, as possibly or probably hostile or unfriendly – involving unwilling respondents who are haled into the World Court. It raises the question: Should the Court defer to the wishes of the sovereign parties, thereby accepting that it cannot avoid any delay in unfriendly cases, or should it perhaps be more independent and aggressive in its case management?

JUDGE SCHWEBEL

The remark by Judge Guillaume which you quoted is correct. Fundamentally, the protracted nature of some cases, by no means all, in the Court stems from either the wishes of both parties or one of them and the Court traditionally has been deferential to the wishes of parties in matters of time scheduling. It is not in the position of ordering them about as a national court can order private individuals. That said, it is nevertheless recognized that there has been too much of what some might see as a good or reasonable thing. Not so much in terms of the years mentioned by you, Pieter, which are not extraordinary when compared with the duration of litigation in other fora, but, first, because the Court's Rules have lent themselves to delay over jurisdictional matters and, second, because some parties clearly have abused the process as litigants will often tend to do. On the first point, the Rules have provided, and still do provide though they are in the process of revision, that a respondent can put in its objection to jurisdiction as late as the day on which its counter-memorial on the merits is due. The Court will typically agree with the parties that they each have nine months for the filing of the memorial and nine for the counter-memorial, or a year or possibly six months, which would be unusually short. As Keith points out, the pleadings are voluminous. They are not pleadings that can be turned out very quickly in the nature of things. First, because they are voluminous and, second, because no government of which I am informed in the world has a staff particularly and peculiarly devoted to litigation before the World Court. When a State has a case before the Court, the same lawyers who are doing many other things, have that as an additional item of work and have to fit it in among other responsibilities, so naturally it takes time. But the result of that rule is that the respondent typically waits until that last day – so 18 months have transpired since the filing of the case or a bit more when you add the time of the application until the president has met with the parties and set the time for the filing of the memorial and counter-memorial. Maybe all that is 20 months, and at the end of that 20 months the respondent for the first time raises a jurisdictional objection. At that point, proceedings on the merits are suspended. We have a memorial and counter-memorial on jurisdiction. That of itself can take another six months, nine months. Then the hearings on jurisdiction. It will take some months for the result in judgment to emerge. So the whole process is a slow one and the Rules are in process of revision to give a shorter trigger to the making of an objection to jurisdiction, as indeed the International Tribunal on the Law of the Sea constructively does in the drafting of its rules which it has drafted, modeling them on those of the World Court, but making some improvements in the light of the history of the

Court. It is not unusual for the defendant state to seek delay and for the applicant to be somewhat, I only say somewhat in the International Court of Justice, in a hurry. That is just standard. The Court tries to deal with that. It does not always accept what the parties want and particularly if they differ, it will strike its own position, often down the middle.

EDUARDO VALENCIA-OSPINA

I agree completely with what Steve has said, but I would like to make two or three brief comments. First, you have mentioned that it is reported that the Court is engaged in a revision of its Rules. We should be careful: it is not a revision of the kind the Court undertook in 1978. This is a revision that touches on various specific provisions of the Rules, and has only to do with accelerating the process, but it does not touch on any of the fundamental premises on which the rules of procedure of the Court have been framed. There seems to be an assumption that perhaps delays are related to the fact that cases are brought by application or by special agreement. I would disagree with that. If one looks at the record of the Court, one can see that perhaps it were cases brought by special agreement that were the ones that lasted longest. The *El Salvador/ Honduras* Chamber Case led to the longest hearings on record, and yet it was a chamber case and was brought by special agreement. So I do not think, really, there is a correlation between having a case brought jointly or not, in terms of length of the proceedings. A lot has been made of delays and we should not be over-impressed by the arguments in this respect. What is fundamental is to give states litigants every opportunity to make their cases – and there is no small case before the Court. When litigants come to the Court, there are fundamental interests at stake and they should be given every opportunity at the written and at the oral stages. There may be a trend emerging towards limiting the opportunity to express views at hearings. I would deplore it if that trend were to become, indeed, the general rule. Hearings do have an important role to play and it is not saving one week or two in a hearing that is going to make such a difference in the final resolution of the case in terms of having states apply the judgment. But this may make a difference in terms of the legal quality of the judgment. So, this is an issue on which the Court has taken certain measures. It has dispensed, in principle, with notes in cases dealing with jurisdiction, although it is not a general rule, and this can be applied with certain circumspection on a case-by-case basis. But on the whole, one can say that the Court is doing its best. In the light of the wishes of the parties, the Court found itself this year with only one case in which it could have had hearings on the merits, the *Qatar-Bahrain* Case, even though it has 24 cases on its docket. Given the time limits that have been imposed for written pleadings in various other cases, there was no other case that could have been taken up. Pakistan came at the last moment. The reference in the press communiqué that you consider unusual, is more than unusual. I think it is a little over-killing in that the Court could not have taken up the Pakistan/India hearings before the end of March, and it only postponed them for a week.

PIETER BEKKER
Having heard from the two ICJ representatives, what does the ICJ practitioner and commentator have to say about this?

THOMAS FRANCK
I do not have a cause here. I simply, as a matter of clarification, want to note that there are various reasons that are quite different for delays and, specifically, I think they fall into three categories. That is, delays caused by counsel; delays caused by a state; and delays caused by the Court. Delays caused by counsel range from genuine inability to meet deadlines to something as little-mentioned, and obviously inapplicable to anyone on this stage, as incompetence. The missing of deadlines, the asking for postponements in a case that obviously proceeds in part on the basis of the extreme urgency of arriving at a solution can have a very big impact on the case. So there are some problems that might be put under the general heading of counsel and those raise questions about whether there should be an international bar, whether the international bar should be subject to discipline, if there is going to be discipline who is going to exercise it, whether there are going to be qualifications for counsel, and so on and so forth, but a very big topic overlapping the issue of delays only in practical terms, because occasionally delays are caused by less than totally competent counsel. Then, of course, there are the tactical delays. Usually, as has been noted, delays are moved by the respondent state for strategic reasons and those have to be addressed by the Court, but I do not think it is an illegitimate tactic by a party. But it may be a legitimate tactic the Court has to recognize as a tactic and weigh, on the one hand, the need to try to keep the respondent party litigating and give it no excuse for pulling out of the litigation, or no easy excuse for pulling out of the litigation. On the other hand, there is the concern for doing justice and letting the applicant have a say in court. I think on the whole the Court has managed that well. It is not true, I think, to take the question of acceleration of justice into account in discussing the issue of scheduling because, in many instances, the parties are not in a tremendous hurry and the Court is able, by stretching out its calendar somewhat, to accommodate more parties that want to be heard and sometimes to move

a more urgent case ahead of a less urgent case. I think that has been done on the whole quite well. Then there are the questions of the pace-making function of the Court itself and there I think there are a couple things at play, some of which are related. As I said, on the whole I think the Court itself is not the main engine of the speed with which cases move, but there are two factors which do thrust the Court forward and that is that there are some judges who are simply not very interested in a case and not being very interested in a case, for various reasons – sometimes because they think the case is unmanageable; sometimes because they think the case is boring; sometimes because they think the case raises evidentiary issues for which the Court is not suited – may be in favor of slowing things down in the hope that the parties will resolve the conflict. That brings us to the second reason why judges may put on the brakes in their scheduling of cases. That is that they do have a, perhaps well-founded, hope, perhaps simply the aspiration of a facilitator of peaceful settlement, that the parties are just going to go away and solve the problem. I think the *Lockerbie* Case certainly fitted into that category and it turned out to be the right thing to do because the parties eventually did sort of go away and settle the subject matter, although not everything about the case has been totally resolved to the satisfaction of the parties. So the instincts of the judges I think do play a role. The judges get a lot of trivia, at least what some of the judges think is trivia – tiny rocks and straits that do not cause the judges' hearts to quicken. There are some judges who wish those cases would just go away. On the other hand, I think a more defensible position is that those are precisely the kinds of cases that strengthen the role of the Court. That it is the big cases that make the Court have legitimacy deficits in the international system. It is the little cases that allow them to build up legitimacy surpluses and from those surpluses they can from time to time draw on the big cases. But those are simply observations of an outsider from discussions with some of the judges.

PIETER BEKKER
Tom, you referred to big cases. I would also like to bring Keith into this discussion, from your perspectives as counsel in two cases, Keith as counsel for Cameroon and Tom as counsel for Bosnia. This is a question of fundamental importance to the role of the Court. We have talked about the record of the Court so far, so let us turn to its role. There have been recent admissions of counterclaims in the cases I have referred to, and the question is: How do they affect the management of pending cases? In his separate opinion appended to the Court's Order of December 17, 1997, upholding the admissibility of Yugoslavia's counterclaims against Bosnia in the *Genocide* Case, Judge *ad hoc* Lauterpacht pointed to the immense, additional complexity to which treatments

of counterclaims simultaneously with the principal claims is bound to give rise. He said it could easily take months of hearings and deliberation. In his dissenting opinion, Vice President Weeramantry voiced similar concerns. According to Judge Weeramantry, the Court, by allowing the counterclaims to be introduced into the proceedings, in fact makes one case out of two separate cases, each of which involves voluminous evidence in regard to a multitude of facts, thereby imposing an enormous procedural burden upon itself. Both judges pointed out that problems related to the introduction of counterclaims, especially in cases involving alleged criminal conduct attributable to a state, are of a different kind than those normally confronting the Court as a tribunal of essentially civil, as opposed to criminal, jurisdiction. It begs the question: How well is the Court equipped to deal with such problems and make complex determinations of fact in what are essentially criminal cases? Will it transform the traditional process in the Great Hall of Justice where testimony by witnesses and experts, cross-examination and an active bench are the exception rather than the rule?

THOMAS FRANCK

That covers a lot of territory and some of it is "no-go" territory, since the matter is still before the Court. But some of it is not. First of all, Bosnia's objection to the insertion of the counterclaim by Yugoslavia was not primarily because it burdened the counsel or burdened the Court, although quite obviously, if you have a case that is heavily fact-based there is going to be a tremendous burden on the counsel and the Court. There are going to be real problems about how the Court manages that burden and, even though it is not entirely a new subject, it has a new dimension in that case because you would be talking about many hundreds of witnesses that the parties want to bring forward and the Court would have to somehow manage that, to get it down to a level that is reasonable. The Court would have to deal with the probative weight of decisions by the International Criminal Tribunal for the former Yugoslavia which has dealt with many of the same factual issues that will be raised if merits are faced, and so on. So the insertion of a counterclaim into the same action vastly increases those problems that are already inherent in the case *ab initio*. Then there is a rather different question which is one of the timing of the bringing of the counterclaim. As you pointed out, the litigation has been going on for seven years and it was only after 5-1/2 of those years that the counterclaim was raised. It was our feeling that Yugoslavia might have come forward with its counterclaim a little earlier. Everyone had accepted at that point the fact that the Court had jurisdiction, and the jurisdictional argument took several years. We would have been quite willing to entertain the counterclaim much earlier in the proceedings. Why were they coming along now as free riders, as we were sort of coming down to the wire? That is an interesting question and the Court gave it an answer in this case. It could give quite another answer in another case. But the real heart of the matter in this particular insertion of a counterclaim was whether it was, in fact, best managed as a counterclaim. Again, both of the parties were before the Court, both were before the Court after a finding of jurisdiction had been made on the basis of a treaty which gave the Court jurisdiction, or so the Court had found. There was absolutely nothing to stop Yugoslavia from bringing an action against Bosnia. And the question in this genocide case to me is almost a visceral one, that is, if I bring an action against you, the Government of X, for the massive deliberate killings of persons in order to destroy in whole or in part an ethnic group, and in the middle of that you say to me, "But you did it, too!", since that is not the defense it should not be managed as a counterclaim. In other words, even if that were true, which of course we are not willing to concede for a moment, what has that got to do with the case that is before the Court? Unless there were some theory of set-off, exculpation or some theory that links the two, other than the fact that both parties happen to be arguing about massive killing of persons with the intent to destroy in whole or in part. But they are not the same people who are being killed. It is not as if both parties were killing the same person or as if there were a real question of a particular person, if they have been killed at all, which party killed that person. That is nowhere the issue. The Yugoslav argument was that the Bosnians also killed people, but not the same people. So, we felt that, as a matter of case management, it should have been handled as a separate case. The facts were different, there did not seem to us to be any real nexis, and as a matter of manageability for the Court it practically doubled the case – but we were not going to call 800 witnesses, the other side was. And so it vastly complicated the fact-finding problems of the Court.

PIETER BEKKER
Keith, how will it affect your case between Cameroon and Nigeria where also a counterclaim was held to be admissible and joined to the principal proceedings?

KEITH HIGHET
Well, it will obviously make the case bigger. A case is a case. We must in this whole discussion separate the procedures, the way in which the Court manages a counterclaim, considers it as a valid counterclaim, and the substance.

I noticed that they slop over into each other here. The fact that the *Genocide* Case features counterclaims of enormous dimensions which require large amounts of fact-finding does not necessarily mean that a counterclaim will always have that problem. It is really the question of a human rights case, or a question where intent is provable or criminal intent attributable to a state organ. I remember in the *South West Africa* Cases in 1965 being confronted with 64 potential witnesses by the South African Government. With 64 witnesses, it would take 2-3 days of Court time to deal with each one, including cross-examination, re-direct and re-cross. We were looking at about an additional 14 months of Court time. It was totally unmanageable and yet South Africa was only not filing a counterclaim but was merely saying "you have drawn into question the state of mind of the Republic of South Africa as the Mandatory, whether we intended to deliberately oppress the people of South West Africa by applying apartheid and if indeed, we are therefore bound to advance witnesses that prove that we have a purer state of mind." A very interesting question, not that far from the problem faced in the Bosnia case. A counterclaim is a counterclaim. Nigeria presumably would have had jurisdiction to file a separate case against Cameroon and chose instead to file it in the context of one case. How the Court manages it, how the judges and the Registry manage to solve it, and counsel too, is going to vary from case to case.

PIETER BEKKER

Let me turn to the final question and leave room for questions from the audience and perhaps we can tie that in with the final question. We have talked about the role and the record of the Court, and some of the problems it faces with the current record. What about the future? What might be done to improve the Court? French President Jacques Chirac in his address to the Court on February 29, 2000, expressed his wish to see the Court invested with a "regulatory role, advising international organizations with advisory opinions requested to reconcile in cases where the international law of the environment, trade and labor standards conflict." He also suggested that when treaties containing dispute mechanisms set up a new jurisdiction, that jurisdiction should be endowed with the power to refer questions to the Court for preliminary ruling, much like the Court of Justice of the European Communities. In his final General Assembly speech as ICJ President, Judge Schwebel suggested that there might be a virtue in enabling other international tribunals to request, through the Security Council or the General Assembly, advisory opinions of the Court on issues of international law arising before such tribunals that are important to the unity of international law. So the question is: How likely is it that the Court will be endowed with a preliminary ruling mechanism? Also, how likely is it that there may be other amendments to the ICJ Statute, because obviously this would require an amendment of the Statute and as you know the Statute being an integral part of the United Nations Charter, it is subject to the same rigorous procedures for amendment. What other amendments, besides preliminary rulings, would you like to see?

JUDGE SCHWEBEL

I am cautious about any amendments. Frankly, I think that if the amendment process is opened up, the Statute could emerge in worse shape than it is. For example, there might well be a move to expand the size of the Court, particularly if agreement is ever reached on expanding the size of the Security Council. I will not comment on whether it is a good idea to expand the size of the Security Council. But I will say that, in my view, it would be a very poor idea to expand the size of the International Court of Justice which already is burdened with reaching a majority among as many as 15 judges. It is not necessary to amend the Statute to permit other tribunals to seek the opinion of the Court on issues of international law arising before those tribunals. Whether in fact that is a practicable idea, is difficult to say. I do not think it is a very likely consummation, but it may be a desirable one. It will only work if other tribunals wish to make it work, and whether they will or not is altogether uncertain.

EDUARDO VALENCIA-OSPINA

I think the question is a fundamental one. It has to do with what is the role of the Court not only in the future, but today. And I think the premise, it has been alluded to by Steve, has to be that we should look at it in terms of how the Court has been organized and functions under its present Statute and leave all speculation about reform of the Statute aside, because of the political almost impossibility of reforming the Charter of the UN of which the Statute is an integral part. I do not think the position of the Court and its role is necessarily a question of, or depends upon, amendments to the Statute, especially on expansion of the jurisdiction, in terms of standing questions. The position of the Court is already a preeminent one. It is the highest judicial organ of the United Nations. And even *vis-à-vis* tribunals that are not part of the United Nations system, it holds that position. It is a position based on its authority as the Court endowed with general competence in international law, unlike most other tribunals whose competence is restricted either *ratione personae* or *materiae*. So it is up to the Court, in the final analysis, to maintain this position. Again, one observes a trend in the Court toward limiting itself to settling the dispute at hand, more often than not, lately, on the narrowest of grounds, leaving aside its other very fundamental role, that is, the development of international law. Of course, there are questions about the binding nature of a decision being limited to the parties to the case, and only in connection with the particular case. But that aside, the value of the opinions of the Court is measured in terms of how tightly reasoned it should be. There, again, one is to be careful about another tendency, namely, to try to reduce the reasoned judgments of the Court to its minimum expression. The Court has a role to play in persuading the parties that it has arrived at a conclusion by the best possible legal reasoning and at the same time make sure that, in the confines of the jurisdictional parameters of the case, it does not retreat from facing challenges in terms of the development of international law. When one looks at the work of codification of international law by the International Law Commission and how much it was enriched by pronouncements of the Court in the past, one would like that trend to continue.

PIETER BEKKER
I think I should hand it over to the audience, now that I have questioned this very distinguished panel for some time.

[*Question from the audience:*] My question has to do with provisional measures. I wonder what has been the reaction of the Court in cases where provisional measures have not been complied with? I think it poses a big challenge for an international court. With many people saying that orders indicating provisional measures are not legally binding, how do you assess the role of provisional measures, in particular in reference to the cases of *LaGrand* and *Breard*, both against the United States, arising under the Vienna Convention on Consular Relations?

KEITH HIGHET
That is an excellent question. I am glad you asked it. I cannot obviously answer that from the point of view of the Court, but from the point of view of an interested bystander. It seems to me, and has seemed to me for many years, that the Court really should bite the bullet and say in a judgment of some kind that provisional measures are more than merely hortatory. It is really embarrassing to me to read briefs filed by certain governments where they say that provisional measures are merely hortatory. After all, what on earth do you think happens when the Court assembles to decide provisional measures? Why these judges have to come from all over the world. They have to convene themselves

quickly. They have to set aside all the other cases on the calendar. The Court is faced with a priority question. And in *Breard* and *LaGrand*, you are dealing with death penalty cases. In both cases the people involved were put to death in spite of the provisional measure requesting the United States not to do so. I find it extraordinary. I think it is a very small point, and a very good point, but a very, very big point at the same time, because it relates to whether or not states are prepared to take the Court seriously. I think it goes to Article 94 of the Charter. Article 94, paragraph 1 of the Charter says that "each Member of the United Nations undertakes to comply with the decision of the International Court of Justice in any case to which it is a party." Article 94, paragraph 2 provides for recourse to the Security Council. The question, of course, is: Is a determination on provisional measures, since it is an ancillary proceeding or something which is not itself a "decision" of the Court, one that has a binding quality? There are many arguments that can be made on both sides, but I have a strong emotional, perhaps not entirely rational, commitment to feeling that the Court should express itself now once and for all and we should get rid of this problem.

PIETER BEKKER
I would add that the Court might actually be chasing away potential litigants by not addressing the issue. For instance, in nearby Hamburg, there is an International Tribunal for the Law of the Sea that offers binding provisional measures. In cases of maritime jurisdiction, especially the release of vessels, the matter might also be brought before the Court if there is jurisdiction.

JUDGE SCHWEBEL
I understand Keith's instincts and they are laudable, but there are problems, first, in the wording of the Statute in respect of provisional measures, which is worded in more hortatory than binding terms. Second, it should be recalled that in the, I believe, first case of provisional measures in the current Court, at least an early case, and certainly the first one brought to the Security Council under Article 94, the *Anglo-Iranian Oil Company* Case, the Security Council ducked. It was not willing to treat the Court's Order of provisional measures as one to be enforced by the Council, but said "let's wait for the Court's judgment on jurisdiction." One must bear in mind that if the Court were to reach a decision on this, of the sort that Keith would like it to reach, it is inconceivable in my view that it would be a unanimous decision. On the contrary, it would sharply divide the Court and a positive decision would be open to substantial attack. I will not say where the better view lies. I think that

views on this subject have been traditionally divided. But the Statute does read as it reads. Perhaps it should not, but it does.

THOMAS FRANCK

I also want to say to my friend Keith that, while I understand the instinct, I think that if the Court had somehow worked it into its *Breard* decision, that that decision was binding on the Supreme Court, the result would have been identical. I think that the argument that this was not a binding decision was a make-weight argument and that the outcome would have been exactly the same. And so there is an organic problem here – an organic problem that is different in respect of each case but in connection with *Breard* the organic problem is how to reorient our judiciary to take decisions of international tribunals, particularly of the International Court, seriously.

EDUARDO VALENCIA-OSPINA

Two cases were mentioned and of course we have to realize that, even though the import of the provisional measures was to delay or suspend the execution, the ICJ was not sitting as a court of appeal in terms of the eventual execution of these individuals. What was at stake was the Vienna Convention on Consular Relations and I would like to say that, from the point of view of the states parties, the fact that the provisional measure was not complied with in the *Breard* Case was no impediment for Germany to bring the *LaGrand* Case. Even though there the provisional measures were again not complied with, the case has remained and is going into the merits.

[*Question from the audience:*] Professor Franck mentioned the legitimacy surplus and deficit questions which are so important. I am interested in the eyes of the players inside and around the Court. What has been the legitimacy surplus or deficit *vis-à-vis* the *Nuclear Weapons* Case, which was a very profoundly important case in the history of the Court and the history of international law? It has been four or five years now since that decision. How does that play into issues of surplus and deficit?

JUDGE SCHWEBEL

Well, since the opinions – and I think every judge of the Court filed an opinion in that case – go in every possible direction, I do not think the impact on policy has been very marked, even if the Court's advisory opinion had been coherent. It might not have been very marked, but in these circumstances the more so.

THOMAS FRANCK

I think it may not have affected the behavior of states, but it has affected certain other constituencies. That is, there are now books on the subject, it is taught in law schools, it has become part of the fermentation process of the law.

PIETER BEKKER

Having reached the end of our program, I would like to thank the audience for their patience and, of course, today's very distinguished panelists for their very useful insights. I can only say that I look forward to continue being educated by them. Thank you very much.

5

THE YEAR 2001

THE 2001 JUDICIAL ACTIVITY OF
THE INTERNATIONAL COURT OF JUSTICE

This introductory section summarizes the judicial work of the International Court of Justice during 2001, using the updated General List, pleadings filed, Orders and Judgments issued, and hearings held at the Peace Palace in The Hague to describe the Court's record in 2001.[1]

THE WORK OF THE COURT

General List

During the calendar year 2001, the Court was seised of 2 new contentious cases: *Application for Revision of the Judgment of 11 July 1996 in the Case concerning* Application of the Convention on the Prevention and Punishment of the Crime of Genocide (Bosnia-Herzegovina v. Yugoslavia), Preliminary Objections *(Yugoslavia v. Bosnia-Herzegovina)*[2], *Certain Property (Liechtenstein v. Germany)*[3] and a case concerning title to territory and maritime delimitation in the western Caribbean between Nicaragua and Colombia.[4] In 2001 a total of 26 cases appeared on the General List at any particular time. Besides the new cases referred to, the contentious proceedings before the full

---

1   Most of the information contained in this Note is available from the ICJ's Web site, <www.icj-cij.org>.
2   Application filed by Yugoslavia in the ICJ Registry on April 24. *See* ICJ Communiqué 2001/12 (April 24, 2001).
3   Application filed by Liechtenstein in the ICJ Registry on June 1. *See* ICJ Communiqué 2001/14 (June 1, 2001).
4   Application filed by Nicaragua in the ICJ Registry on December 6, *See* ICJ Communiqué 2001/34 (December 6, 2001).

P.H.F. Bekker, World Court Decisions at the Turn of the Millennium (1997-2001), p. 279-284.
© 2002 *Kluwer Law International. Printed in the Netherlands.*

Court were *Maritime Delimitation and Territorial Questions between Qatar and Bahrain (Qatar v. Bahrain)*; *Questions of Interpretation and Application of the 1971 Montreal Convention arising from the Aerial Incident at Lockerbie (Libya v. United Kingdom) (Libya v. United States)* (hereinafter *Lockerbie Cases*); *Oil Platforms (Iran v. United States)* (hereinafter *Oil Platforms* case); *Application of the Convention on the Prevention and Punishment of the Crime of Genocide (Bosnia-Herzegovina v. Yugoslavia)* (hereinafter *Genocide (Bosnia)* case); *Land and Maritime Boundary between Cameroon and Nigeria (Cameroon v. Nigeria)*; *Gabčíkovo-Nagymaros Project (Hungary/Slovakia)*; *Sovereignty over Pulau Ligitan and Pulau Sipadan (Indonesia/Malaysia)*; *Ahmadou Sadio Diallo (Republic of Guinea v. Democratic Republic of the Congo)*; *LaGrand Case (Germany v. United States)*; *Legality of Use of Force (Yugoslavia v. Belgium) (Yugoslavia v. Canada) (Yugoslavia v. France) (Yugoslavia v. Germany) (Yugoslavia v. Italy) (Yugoslavia v. the Netherlands) (Yugoslavia v. Portugal) (Yugoslavia v. United Kingdom)*; *Armed Activities on the Territory of the Congo (Democratic Republic of the Congo v. Burundi) (Democratic Republic of the Congo v. Rwanda) (Democratic Republic of the Congo v. Uganda)*; *Application of the Convention on the Prevention and Punishment of the Crime of Genocide (Croatia v. Yugoslavia)* (hereinafter *Genocide (Croatia)* case); *Maritime Delimitation between Nicaragua and Honduras in the Caribbean Sea (Nicaragua v. Honduras)* (hereinafter *Caribbean Sea* case); and *Arrest Warrant of 11 April 2000 (Democratic Republic of the Congo v. Belgium)* (hereinafter *Arrest Warrant*). No advisory or chamber proceedings were brought or pending in 2001.

Pleadings

In 2001 pleadings were filed in the following instances. On January 4, Nigeria filed a Rejoinder in *Land and Maritime Boundary between Cameroon and Nigeria*, while Cameroon filed an additional pleading on Nigeria's counterclaims on July 4. In the same case, Equatorial-Guinea filed a written statement on its Application to intervene in the case on April 4, followed, on July 4, by the written observations of Cameroon and Nigeria. On March 2, Indonesia and Malaysia each filed a Reply in *Sovereignty over Pulau Ligitan and Pulau Sipadan*, followed, on May 2, by their written observations on the March 13 Application to intervene of the Philippines. Croatia filed a Memorial in its *Genocide* case against Yugoslavia on March 14. Nicaragua filed its Memorial in *Maritime Delimitation between Nicaragua and Honduras in the Caribbean*

Sea on March 21. On March 23, the United States filed a Rejoinder in *Oil Platforms*. On April 21, Uganda filed its Counter-Memorial, which included counterclaims, in *Armed Activities on the Territory of the Congo (Dem. Rep. of the Congo v. Uganda)*. Also on March 23, Guinea filed a Memorial in *Ahmadou Sadio Diallo*. On May 18, the Democratic Republic of the Congo filed a Memorial in *Arrest Warrant of 11 April 2000*, followed by a Counter-Memorial of Belgium on September 17. The United Kingdom and the United States each filed a Rejoinder in each of the *Lockerbie* cases on August 3. On September 24, Iran submitted an additional pleading relating solely to the counterclaim submitted by the U.S. in *Oil Platforms*.

Orders

A total of 19 Orders were made by the Court, the President and the Vice President in 2001, most of which concerned time limits.[5] The Court's Order fof November 29 addressed the admissibility of Uganda's counterclaims in Armed Activities on the Territory of the Congo. On January 30, the President issued two separate Orders placing on record the discontinuance by the DRC of the *Armed Activities* cases against Burundi and Rwanda as Respondents and ordering the removal of the cases from the General List. The President's Order of September 10 officially recorded the withdrawal by Yugoslavia of its counterclaims in the *Genocide (Bosnia)* case.

Hearings

In 2001 the Court held public sittings (hearings) on the Philippines' request for permission to intervene in *Sovereignty over Pulau Ligitan and Pulau Sipadan* (June 25-26, 28-29) and in *Arrest Warrant of 11 April 2000* (Oct. 15-19).

---

5   The Court issued Orders fixing time limits in the *Land and Maritime Boundary between Cameroon and Nigeria* (Feb. 20), *Sovereignty over Pulau Ligitan and Pulau Sipadan* (Mar. 14), and *Certain Property* (June 28) cases. It issued eight separate Orders extending time limits in the *Legality of Use of Force* cases (Feb. 21) and two in the *Arrest Warrant of 11 April 2000* case (March 14 and June 27). The President issued an Order extending time limits in the *Arrest Warrant* case on April 12. The Vice President issued an Order fixing time limits in the *Oil Platforms* case on August 28.

Decisions

In 2001 the Court handed down three decisions. The Court's Judgment of March 16 determined the merits in *Maritime Delimitation and Territorial Questions between Qatar and Bahrain* (Qatar v. Bahrain),[6] as did its Judgment of June 27 in the *LaGrand Case* (Germany v. U.S.). The Court's Judgment of October 23 rejected the Philippines' Application for permission to intervene in *Sovereignty over Pulau Ligitan and Pulau Sipadan* (Indonesia/Malaysia).

ELECTIONS

On February 20, it was announced that Jean-Jacques Arnaldez (France) was re-elected to another seven-year term as Deputy-Registrar at the Court's private meeting held on February 19.[7] On October 12, after a single round of balloting, the UN General Assembly and Security Council elected Nabil Elaraby (Egypt) to hold office for the remainder of Judge Mohammed Bedjaoui's term expiring on February 5, 2006, following Judge Bedjaoui's resignation with effect from September 30.[8] The composition of the Court as at December 31, 2001 is as follows (in order of seniority): Gilbert Guillaume (France), President; Shi Jiuyong (China), Vice President; Shigeru Oda (Japan); Raymond Ranjeva (Madagascar); Géza Herczegh (Hungary); Carl-August Fleischhauer (Germany); Abdul Koroma (Sierra Leone); Vladlen Vereshchetin (Russian Federation); Rosalyn Higgins (United Kingdom); Gonzalo Parra-Aranguren (Venezuela); Pieter Kooijmans (the Netherlands); Francisco Rezek (Brazil); Awn Shawkat Al-Khasawneh (Jordan); Thomas Buergenthal (United States); Nabil Elaraby (Egypt).

PRESIDENT'S ADDRESS

On October 30, Judge Guillaume addressed the General Assembly of the United Nations again as ICJ president on the occasion of the Assembly's examination

---

6   *See* ICJ Communiqués 2001/19-19*bis* (March 16, 2001).
7   *See* ICJ Communiqué 2001/03 (Feb. 20, 2001).
8   *See* ICJ Communiqué 2001/20 (July 6, 2001).

of the Court's annual report.[9] His presentation built on topics addressed in previous speeches by ICJ presidents.

Referring to the need to find solutions designed to avoid excessive delays in the Court's examination of cases and to accelerate its work, the president summarized recent initiatives taken by the Court and announced that the Court is seeking the cooperation from states parties to ICJ cases by issuing "Practice Directions" to them (see below). He said that the Court was particularly desirous to see a decrease in the number of pleadings exchanged, the volume of annexes to pleadings, and the length of oral argument. He acknowledged that the various administrative and procedural innovations introduced by the Court are not sufficient in themselves to address the situation with which the Court is confronted and renewed his plea for a substantial increase in the Court's budget and staff. In this respect, he called on the Assembly to reaffirm its support of the Court.

Pointing out that access to international justice should not be impeded by financial inequality, the president argued for easier access of countries with limited financial resources to the Court and, specifically, brought the ICJ Trust Fund, established by the UN Secretary-General in 1989 to assist states unable to meet the expenses involved in submitting a dispute to the Court, to the renewed attention of the UN membership.[10]

He again referred to the phenomenon of the recent proliferation of international courts and tribunals, which, besides reflecting greater confidence in justice, may also jeopardize both the unity of international law and its role in inter-state relations. In this context, he re-introduced the idea of empowering and encouraging both existing and future courts to request advisory opinions from the ICJ, the only judicial body vested with universal and general jurisdiction, through the intermediary of the UN Security Council and General Assembly.

---

9   The full text of the Address by the President of the International Court of Justice, Judge Gilbert Guillaume, to the United Nations General Assembly, Oct. 30, 2001, is available on the ICJ's Web site, *supra* note 1. For a summary by the ICJ Registry, see ICJ Communiqué 2001/31 (Oct. 30, 2001).
10 For a description of the ICJ Trust Fund, see Peter H.F. Bekker, *International Legal Aid in Practice: The ICJ Trust Fund*, 87 AJIL 659 (1993) (with additional literature references).

NEW "PRACTICE DIREC rIONS"

Within one day from the announcement by the ICJ president that the Court would issue "Practice Directions" for use by states parties to ICJ cases, the Registry announced the adoption and dispatch of such directions "with immediate effect."[11] These "Practice Directions," which the Court will review at regular intervals, are additional to the Rules of Court and are meant to guide the parties in their conduct during both the written and oral phase of a case. The rationale for issuing the "Practice Directions" was "the congested state of [the Court's] List and the budgetary constraints it continues to face."

In the "Practice Directions," which the Court "wishes the parties to follow," the parties are strongly urged to annex to their written pleadings only strictly selected documents. Parties are also requested to provide the Registry with any available translation of the pleadings into the other official language of the Court. Each party is to include a short summary of its reasoning at the conclusion of the written pleadings.

The "Practice Directions" also discourage the practice of simultaneous deposit of pleadings in cases brought jointly through the notification of a special agreement. Special agreements should specify the number and order of pleadings.

In the context of preliminary objections asserting lack of jurisdiction or inadmissibility of the application, the "Practice Directions" state that the time limit for the presentation by one party of its written observations and submissions on the preliminary objections of the other party "shall generally not exceed four months."

Finally, with regard to the oral phase of a case, the "Practice Directions" emphasize that oral arguments must retain their succinct character, as stipulated in Article 60(1) of the Rules of Court, and oral proceedings on objections of lack of jurisdiction or inadmissibility must be limited to statements on those objections.

---

11 *See* ICJ Communiqué 2001/32 (Oct. 31, 2001). The "Practice Directions" are included in the "Note containing important information for parties to new cases," which replaces the "Note containing recommendations to the parties to new cases." For the text, see the ICJ Web site, *supra* note 1.

*Territorial and maritime boundary delimitation – interpretation of British
Government decisions concerning protectorates-drawing of single maritime
boundary-delimitation of various maritime jurisdictions based on
customary international law-equidistance/special circumstances rule in
territorial sea delimitation-equitable principles/relevant circumstances rule
in delimitation of continental shelf and exclusive economic zone-difference
between islands and low-tide elevations-right of innocent passage*

MARITIME DELIMITATION AND TERRITORIAL QUESTIONS BETWEEN QATAR
AND BAHRAIN (Qatar v. Bahrain)

Merits, Judgment
Obtainable from <www.icj-cij.org>
International Court of Justice, March 16, 2001

When Qatar and Bahrain failed to negotiate their maritime boundary, sovereignty over certain islands and sovereign rights over several shoals in the
Arabian/Persian Gulf (Gulf), Qatar filed an Application with the International
Court of Justice instituting proceedings to delimit the maritime and territorial
boundary between the two states on July 8, 1991. By two Judgments rendered
in 1994 and 1995, the Court, having found that the parties had undertaken to
submit to it the whole of their dispute, ruled that it had jurisdiction to adjudicate
upon the dispute, that it was seised of the whole of the dispute, and that Qatar's
Application was admissible.[1] Finally, after two full rounds of written pleadings,
the Court heard the arguments of both parties on the merits in May-June 2000,
some nine years after the institution of proceedings. Qatar and Bahrain put
forward competing claims on sovereignty over Zubarah, the Hawar Islands,
Janan Island, and other territorial and maritime features. They also proposed
different lines as the single maritime boundary between them. On March 16,
2001, the Court found (1) unanimously, that Qatar has sovereignty over Zubarah, (2) (*a*) by 12 votes to five, that

---

[1]   *See* 1994 ICJ REP. 112 (July 1) and 1995 ICJ REP. 6 (Feb. 15). For a detailed
analysis of both decisions, see COMMENTARIES ON WORLD COURT DECISIONS (1987-
1996) 191 (P.H.F. Bekker ed., 1996) (co-authored by Keith Highet and Pieter
Bekker).

P.H.F. Bekker, World Court Decisions at the Turn of the Millennium (1997-2001), p. 285-312.
© 2002 *Kluwer Law International. Printed in the Netherlands.*

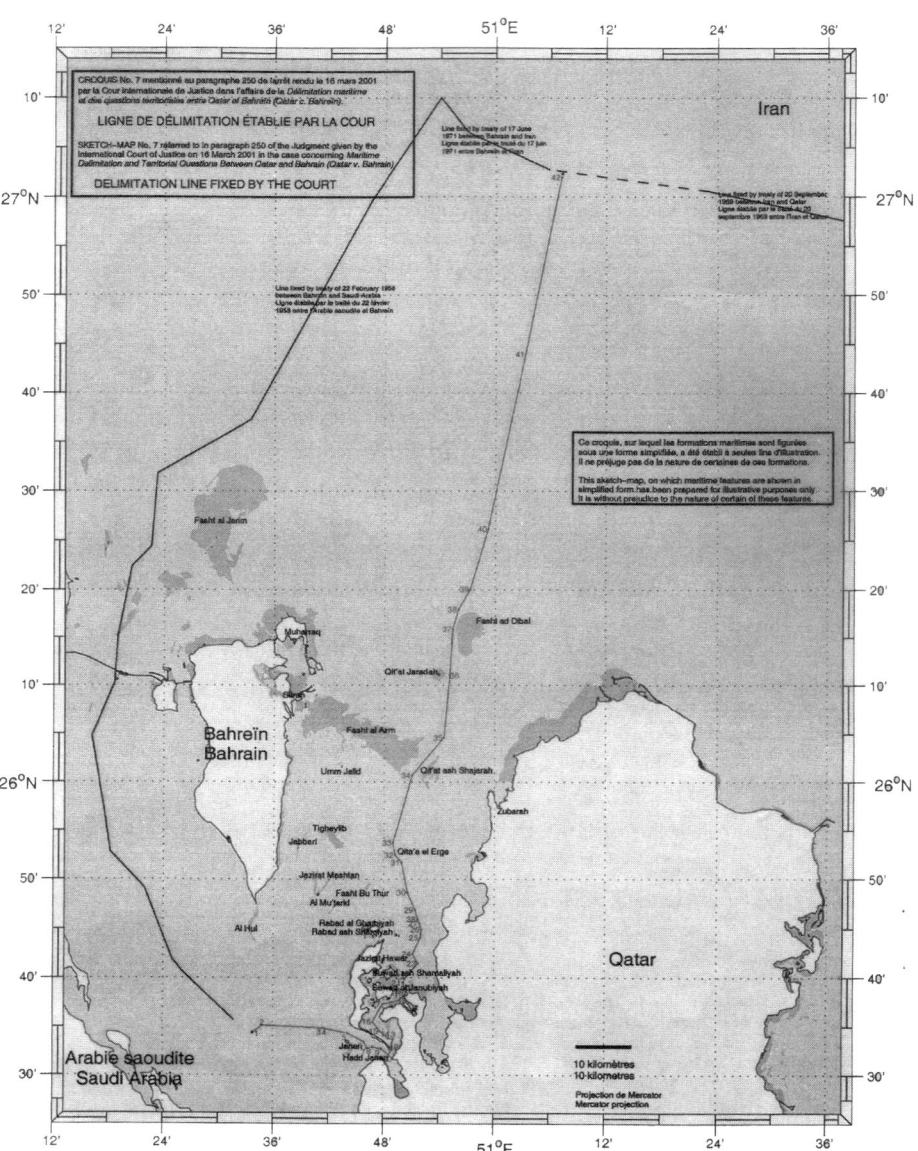

Bahrain has sovereignty over the Hawar Islands,[2] (2) (*b*) unanimously, that vessels of Qatar enjoy in the territorial sea of Bahrain separating the Hawar Islands from the other Bahraini islands the right of innocent passage, (3) by 13 votes to four, that Qatar has sovereignty over Janan Island, including Hadd Janan,[3] (4) by 12 votes to five, that Bahrain has sovereignty over the island of Qit'at Jaradah,[4] and (5) unanimously, that the low-tide elevation of Fasht ad Dibal falls under the sovereignty of Qatar. The Court also fixed, by 13 votes to four,[5] the single maritime boundary that divides the various maritime zones (territorial sea, continental shelf and exclusive economic zone) of Qatar and Bahrain.[6]

Qatar and Bahrain both are located in the southern part of the Gulf. The Qatar peninsula, which projects northward into the Gulf, borders on the Kingdom of Saudi Arabia to the south. Bahrain consists of a number of islands, islets and shoals.

The Court's Judgment is divided into two main parts, one dealing with a determination of the parties' territorial sovereignty over Zubarah, the Hawar Islands and Janan Island, and the other concerning the Court's determination of the single maritime boundary dividing the maritime zones of the two parties.

Before determining the issue of sovereignty over Zubarah, the Hawar Islands and Janan Island, the Court summarized the complex history that formed the background to the dispute between the parties.[7] Following Portugal's century-long monopoly of trade in the Gulf area, which lay along one of the trading routes with India, Great Britain began to consolidate its presence in the region at the beginning of the seventeenth century in an effort to protect the growing commercial interests of the East India Company. The British signed separate agreements with the various sheikhs and chiefs in the region whereby the latter undertook to abstain from plunder and piracy against British and local ships. This practice was followed by the conclusion of exclusive agreements between

---

2   Judges Bedjaoui, Ranjeva, Koroma and Vereshchetin and Judge *ad hoc* Torres Bernárdez (appointed by Qatar) voted against this part of the holding.

3   Judges Oda, Higgins and Kooijmans and Judge *ad hoc* Fortier (appointed by Bahrain) voted against this part of the holding.

4   Judges Bedjaoui, Ranjeva, Koroma and Vereshchetin and Judge *ad hoc* Torres Bernárdez voted against this part of the holding.

5   Judges Bedjaoui, Ranjeva and Koroma and Judge *ad hoc* Torres Bernárdez voted against the single maritime boundary fixed by the Court's Judgment.

6   Judgment of March 16, 2001, slip opinion available from the ICJ Registry and the ICJ Web site, <www.icj-cij.org> [hereinafter Judgment].

7   *See* Judgment, *supra* note 6, at paras. 36-69.

the British, represented by a "British Political Resident" in the Gulf, and most sheikhdoms as part of a general policy of protection in the Gulf. "British Political Agents" subsequently were stationed in each of these sheikhdoms.[8] In September 1868, the Chiefs of Bahrain and Qatar each signed an agreement with Great Britain following hostilities on the Qatar peninsula. The Chief of Bahrain recognized that certain acts of piracy had been committed by his predecessor and promised to appoint an agent with the British Political Resident. In a separate agreement, the tribal chiefs "residing in the province of Qatar" agreed to pay certain annual sums to the Chief of Bahrain through the British Political Resident.[9] While Bahrain believed that the foregoing demonstrates that Qatar was not independent from Bahrain, Qatar viewed the agreements of 1868 as the first formal recognition of Qatar's separate identity.[10]

Toward the end of the seventeenth century, the Ottomans made Qatar an administrative division of their empire, remaining for over 40 years on the Qatar peninsula, while the British increased their influence over Bahrain. On March 13, 1892, Great Britain and Bahrain concluded an "Exclusive Protection Agreement."[11] Desirous to determine their respective interests in the Gulf and surrounding territories, Great Britain and the Ottoman Empire signed a treaty on July 29, 1913. Although Section II of the 1913 convention dealt with Qatar and defined a line separating the Ottoman territory from the "peninsula of al-Qatar," it was never ratified.[12]

Following the departure of the Ottomans in 1915, Great Britain signed an exclusive protection treaty with Sheikh Al-Thani of Qatar on November 3, 1916. Although the British undertook to protect the Sheikh and his subjects against attacks by land within the territories of Qatar, the treaty did not define the extent of those territories.[13] Starting in 1925, the Ruler of Bahrain granted oil concessions to private companies, which practice was followed in the mid 1930s by the Ruler of Qatar. In connection with Bahraini concession negotiations, the British were asked whether the Hawar Islands belonged to Bahrain or Qatar. In communications between British officials and Petroleum Concessions Ltd. (a prospective oil concessionaire), which were not conveyed to the Sheikh of Qatar, the British took the position in 1936 that Hawar belonged

---

8   *See id.*, at para. 38.
9   *See id.*, at para. 40.
10   *See id.*, at paras. 41-42.
11   *See id.*, at para. 44.
12   *See id.*, at para. 45.
13   *See id.*, at para. 48.

to Bahrain.[14] This position was later confirmed, at the request of the Rulers of Qatar and Bahrain, in a British decision of July 11, 1939.[15] In connection with the division of the sea-bed between Qatar and Bahrain by the British Government in 1946, the parties were informed that Janan Island was not regarded as being included in the islands of the Hawar group.[16]

Qatar and Bahrain ceased to be British protected states in 1971 and joined the United Nations in September of that year.[17] When the mediation or "good offices" by the King of Saudi Arabia, which had started in 1976, did not lead to the desired outcome, Qatar instituted proceedings before the ICJ against Bahrain.[18]

The Court turned first to the issue of territorial sovereignty over Zubarah, which is located on the north-west coast of the Qatar peninsula, opposite the main island of Bahrain. Whereas Qatar asked the Court to hold that Bahrain had no sovereignty over Zubarah, Bahrain requested the Court to adjudge and declare that Bahrain is sovereign over Zubarah.[19] Bahrain argued that from 1783 until 1937, it had full title to the region *inter alia* by effective occupation and that its rights to sovereignty over Zubarah had been recognized by Great Britain. In its view, the forceful eviction of the Naim tribesmen loyal to Bahrain by the Al-Thani of Qatar in 1937 constituted an unlawful use of force from which no legal rights could arise. Therefore, Qatar's continued physical control of Zubarah since 1937 did not give rise to a valid title of sovereignty over Zubarah.[20] Qatar disputed Bahrain's historical account of the occupation of Zubarah and invoked various international agreements in support of its claim to sovereignty over Zubarah. Even though Qatar acknowledged that it imposed

---

14   *See id.*, at paras. 49-54.
15   *See id.*, at para. 57.
16   *See id.*, at para. 61.
17   *See id.*, at para. 65.
18   *See id.*, at paras. 66-69.
19   *See id.*, at paras. 71-72. As Judge Oda points out in his separate opinion, the issue of Zubarah was not included in Qatar's Application of July 8, 1991, but was added in Qatar's "Act to comply with paragraphs (3) and (4) of the operative paragraph 41 of the Judgment of the Court dated 1 July 1994" filed on November 30, 1994. This addition made it possible for Bahrain to accept referral of this case to the Court. *See* separate opinion of Judge Oda, at para. 2. Zubarah was the power base of the present ruling family of Bahrain before they moved to the main Bahrain Island. *See* separate opinion of Judge Kooijmans, at para. 35.
20   *See id.*, at paras. 73-76.

its authority over Zubarah by force in 1937, it justified this as being an internal matter concerning a territory that was under its sovereignty at the time.[21]

Noting that the parties agreed that the Al-Khalifa occupied Zubarah in the 1760s before settling in Bahrain, the Court observed that there was disagreement as to the legal situation after this period and especially around 1937. In the Court's view, the terms of the Agreement of September 6, 1868 between the Chief of Bahrain and Great Britain showed that any attempt by Bahrain to pursue its claims to Zubarah through military action at sea would not be tolerated by the British. There was no evidence of Bahrain asserting direct sovereign authority over Zubarah after 1868.[22] Article 11 of the Anglo-Ottoman Convention of July 29, 1913 stated that "it is agreed between the two Governments that the [peninsula of al-Qatar] will, as in the past, be governed by the Sheikh Jasim-bin-Sani and his successors."[23] Qatar and Bahrain differed on the treaty's value as evidence of Qatar's sovereignty, the treaty never having been ratified. Observing that signed but unratified treaties may constitute an accurate expression of the parties' understanding at the time of signature, the Court concluded that the Anglo-Ottoman Convention represented evidence of the views of Great Britain and the Ottoman Empire as to the factual extent of the authority of the Al-Thani Ruler in Qatar up to 1913.[24] Thus, Article 11 made it clear that Great Britain and the Ottoman Empire did not recognize Bahrain's authority over the Qatar peninsula, including Zubarah.[25] Even though the 1913 convention was never ratified, Article 11 was referred to in Article III of the Anglo-Ottoman treaty of March 9, 1914, which was ratified that same year and did not contemplate any authority over the Qatar peninsula other than that of Qatar.[26] As to the events that took place in Zubarah in 1937, after the Sheikh of Qatar had tried to impose taxation on the Naim tribe, British internal communications concluded that Bahrain's claim to Zubarah failed.[27] Referring to the 1868 agreement, the 1913 and 1914 conventions and the British internal communications, the Court rejected Bahrain's contention that Great Britain had always regarded Zubarah as belonging to Bahrain. In the Court's view, the authority of the Sheikh of Qatar over Zubarah definitively was established

---

21 *See id.*, at paras. 77-81.
22 *See id.*, at para. 84.
23 *See id.*, at para. 87.
24 *See id.*, at para. 89.
25 *See id.*, at para. 90.
26 *See id.*, at para. 91.
27 *See id.*, at para. 92.

in 1937 and his actions were not an unlawful use of force against Bahrain. For these reasons, the Court concluded that Qatar has sovereignty over Zubarah.[28]

The Court next determined which of the two parties has sovereignty over the Hawar Islands, which are located in the immediate vicinity of the central part of the west coast of the Qatar peninsula, to the south-east of the main island of Bahrain and at a distance of approximately 10 nautical miles from the latter. The Court's answer to this question would have important ramifications for the single maritime boundary to be fixed by the Court, as Qatar had based its proposed boundary on its alleged sovereignty over the Hawar Islands.[29]

Qatar's claim of sovereignty over the Hawar Islands was based on the alleged priority to be accorded to its original title and the principle of proximity and territorial unity. Qatar pointed out that each of the islands in the Hawar group was nearer to its mainland territory than to the main island of Bahrain, which it saw confirmed by both geology and geomorphology. In Qatar's view, history showed that Great Britain in effect recognized the existence of the separate entity of Qatar, including its mainland and immediate offshore islands such as the Hawar Islands. Qatar relied on a number of maps that it believed confirmed that its territory encompassed the entire Qatar peninsula, including the Hawar Islands.[30] Referring to international precedents, Bahrain argued that the geographical proximity of inhabited islands was irrelevant.[31] For its part, Bahrain claimed to have had title to the Hawar Islands since the eighteenth century and to have maintained such title continuously and uninterruptedly by possession and control, citing a number of examples of the alleged exercise of its authority from both before and after 1938-1939. Bahrain also submitted the testimony of former Hawar Islands residents in support of its claim and pointed to the consistent inclusion of the islands in oil concession discussions

---

28 *See id.*, at paras. 95-97.
29 Judge Oda points out in his separate opinion that the issue of the Hawar Islands arose out of the discovery of potential oil and natural gas reserves in this area of the Gulf region, making it the most important issue in these proceedings. *See* separate opinion of Judge Oda, at para. 3.
30 *See id.*, at para. 99.
31 *See id.*, at para. 100 (citing Island of Palmas (U.S./Neth.), 2 RIAA 829, 869 (1928) (Perm. Ct. Arb.) ("[t]he title of contiguity, understood as a basis of territorial sovereignty, has no foundation in international law"), and Minquiers and Ecrehos (Fr. v. UK), Judgment, 1953 ICJ REP. 47 (Nov. 17)).

between Bahrain, Great Britain and prospective oil concessionaires during the 1930s.[32]

In particular, Bahrain relied on a July 11, 1939 decision of Great Britain that the Hawar Islands belonged to Bahrain and not to Qatar. In Bahrain's view, this decision must be regarded as an arbitral award, which is *res judicata* and therefore not subject to review by the Court,[33] or at least as a binding political decision and part of the colonial heritage based on the *uti possidetis juris* principle applicable to states born of decolonization.[34] According to Qatar, the *uti possidetis* principle is inapplicable to this case given that Qatar and Bahrain at all times were independent states both before and after the 1971 agreements that ended their status as British protectorates. Qatar claimed that the British decision of 1939 was null and void based on the absence of its consent to the process, bias on the part of the British officials involved, and the decision's lack of reasoning. Moreover, it claimed that the Ruler of Qatar had repeatedly protested against the decision, so that the decision was not opposable to Qatar.[35]

The Court first examined the nature and validity of the 1939 decision. Observing that no agreement existed between the parties to submit their case to an arbitral tribunal made up of judges chosen by them, the Court concluded that the decision did not constitute an international arbitral award and that, consequently, it did not need to consider Bahrain's argument concerning the

---

32   *See id.*, at paras. 101-02.

33   *See id.*, at paras. 103 and 111 (citing Société Commerciale de Belgique, 1939 PCIJ (ser. A/B) No. 78 at 160 (June 15); Arbitral Award Made by the King of Spain on 23 December 1906 (Hond. v. Nica.), 1960 ICJ REP. 192 (Nov. 18); Arbitral Award of 31 July 1989 (Guinea-Bissau v. Sen.), 1991 ICJ REP. 53 (Nov. 12)). Qatar argued that the 1939 British decision was not an arbitral award but at best an administrative decision of a binding character, except that it did not have that character in this case (citing Dubai/Sharjah Border Arbitration, arb. award of Oct. 19, 1981, *reprinted in* 91 ILR 543, 579 (1993)). *Id.*, at para. 112.

34   The *uti possidetis juris* principle was described by the Court's Chamber formed to deal with the case concerning the Frontier Dispute (Burkina Faso/Mali) in 1986 as follows: "The essence of the principle lies in its primary aim of securing respect for the territorial boundaries at the moment when independence is achieved ... [By this principle] administrative boundaries [were] transformed into international frontiers in the full sense of the term." 1986 ICJ REP. 554, at 566, para. 23 (Dec. 22).

35   *See* Judgment, *supra* note 6, at paras. 105-06.

Court's jurisdiction to examine the validity of arbitral awards.[36] The Court noted that the comprehensive "Bahraini formula" accepted by both parties embraced all questions relating to the Hawar Islands, including the parties' dispute concerning the British decision of 1939.[37] The Court next pointed out that the fact that a decision is not an arbitral award does not mean that it is devoid of legal effect, which may be determined from the events preceding and immediately following its adoption.[38] After a detailed description and examination of the circumstances leading to the British decision holding that the Hawar Islands belonged to Bahrain and its aftermath,[39] the Court considered Qatar's argument challenging the validity of the decision. In connection with Qatar's argument that it never gave its consent to have the question of the Hawar Islands decided by the British Government, the Court observed that, following an official exchange of letters, the Ruler of Qatar had consented on May 27, 1938 to entrust decision of the Hawar Islands question to the British Government, as had the Ruler of Bahrain. Thus, the jurisdiction of the British Government to decide the question derived from these two consents.[40] As to Qatar's complaint that the procedure followed violated the rule prohibiting bias in a decision-maker on the international plane (the British officials responsible for the Hawar Islands question allegedly were biased and had prejudged the matter) and that the parties had not been given an equal and fair opportunity to present their argument, the Court noted that the validity of the

---

36 *See id.*, at paras. 113-15. As Judge Kooijmans explains in his separate opinion, "[a]rbitration as a procedure for dispute settlement with a final and binding character has for centuries been seen as requiring an agreement concluded by two parties to a dispute on the basis of formal equality to entrust the resolution of that dispute to a mutually agreed third party and to comply with the decision given by that party," pointing out that "[i]t is the combination of consent to the procedure and of commitment to compliance which produces the *res judicata* character of the decision, although the procedure itself is subject to certain requirements of fairness and equality of arms." *See* separate opinion of Judge Kooijmans, at para. 45.

37 *See id.*, at para. 116. According to the "Bahraini formula," proposed by Bahrain on October 26, 1988 and accepted by Qatar at the annual meeting of the Co-operation Council of Arab States of the Gulf at Doha in December 1990, "[t]he Parties request the Court to decide any matter of territorial right or other title or interest which may be a matter of difference between them; and to draw a single maritime boundary between their respective maritime areas of seabed, subsoil and superjacent waters."

38 *See id*, at para. 117 (citing Dubai/Sharjah Border Arbitration, arb. award of Oct. 19, 1981, *reprinted in* 91 ILR 543, 577 (1993)).

39 *See id.*, at paras. 118-35.

40 *See id.*, at para. 137.

decision, not being an arbitral award, was not subject to the procedural principles governing the validity of arbitral awards.[41] The Court was satisfied that Qatar had been informed and had consented in advance that the British Government would proceed on the premise that Bahrain possessed *prima facie* title to the Hawar Islands and that the burden of proving the opposite lay on the Ruler of Qatar. Qatar and Bahrain both had the opportunity to present, and had indeed presented and commented on, their arguments in relation to the Hawar Islands and the evidence supporting them.[42] Finally, as regards Qatar's complaint that the decision was not reasoned, the Court noted that this circumstance has no influence on the validity of the decision taken, given that no obligation to state reasons had been imposed on the British Government when it was entrusted with the settlement of the matter. The Ruler of Qatar did not claim that the decision was invalid for lack of reasons after he was informed of its contents, and his protests could not render the decision not opposable to him.[43] The Court thus concluded that the 1939 decision was binding on the parties and that Bahrain has sovereignty over the Hawar Islands.[44]

The Court next considered the parties' claims to Janan Island, located off the south-western tip of Hawar Island.[45] Qatar based its claim of sovereignty

---

41   *See id.*, at paras. 138-40.

42   *See id.*, at paras. 141-42.

43   *See id.*, at paras. 143-45.

44   *See id.*, at paras. 146-47. Even though the Court noted that the parties' lengthy arguments on the issue of sovereignty over the Hawar Islands had raised other legal issues, including the existence of an original title and *effectivités* and the applicability of the *uti possidetis juris* principle to the case, it concluded that its findings on the British decision of 1939 made it unnecessary for it to rule on any of those arguments. *See id.*, at para. 148 and paras. 107-09. The Court's Chamber formed to deal with the case concerning the Frontier Dispute (Burkina Faso/Mali) defined the term *effectivités* as being "the conduct of the administrative authorities as proof of the effective exercise of territorial jurisdiction in the region during the colonial period." The Court's Chamber formed to deal with the case concerning the Land, Island and Maritime Frontier Dispute distinguished between *effectivités coloniales* and a state's post-independence *effectivités*. *See* Land, Island and Maritime Frontier Dispute (El Sal./Hond.; Nicar. interv.), Merits, Judgment, 1992 ICJ REP. 351, 398, para. 61 (Sept. 11).

45   As Judge Oda points out in his separate opinion, Qatar's Application of July 8, 1991 did not refer to Janan. Janan instead was mentioned in Qatar's "Act to comply with paragraphs (3) and (4) of the operative paragraph 41 of the Judgment of the Court dated 1 July 1994" filed on November 30, 1994. *See* separate opinion of Judge Oda, at para. 4. *See also* separate opinion of Judge Kooijmans, at paras. 80-81. Whereas Qatar referred to "Janan Island" as one island situated 1.6 nautical miles

over Janan Island on the principles governing proximity and sovereignty over islands in territorial waters, and alleged that any island falling partially within a three-mile limit drawn from the low-water line along the mainland enjoys the benefit of the regime applicable to islands located wholly within that three-mile limit.[46] Pointing out that only half of Jannan lies within the three-mile limit, Bahrain argued that proximity is not a basis for title in international law and that, in any event, Janan is closer to the Hawar Islands, over which Bahrain has sovereignty.[47] Qatar also argued that letters dated December 23, 1947 by the British Political Agent in Bahrain, in which the British Government informed the Rulers of Qatar and Bahrain of the delimitation of the seabed between Qatar and Bahrain effected by the British Government, noted that "Janan Island is not regarded as being included in the islands of the Hawar group."[48] According to Bahrain, however, the 1939 decision recognized Bahrain's sovereignty over Janan as part of the Hawar Islands and Bahrain had in fact established its sovereignty over Janan Island, including by permitting fishing activities and by beaconing it in 1939. Qatar countered that the latter activities cannot serve as an indication or manifestation of sovereignty.[49]

The Court first considered the effects of the 1939 British decision on the question of sovereignty over Janan Island. The 1939 decision made no mention of Janan Island, nor did it specify what was to be understood by the expression "Hawar Islands." The Court next examined the documents cited by each party, including the 1947 British letters invoked by Qatar and a series of lists regarding the composition of the Hawar Islands on which Bahrain relied.[50] Noting that no definite conclusion could be drawn from the various lists introduced by Bahrain, the Court turned to the 1947 letters. In the Court's view, the statement that "Janan Island is not regarded as being included in the islands of the Hawar group" contained in the letters meant that the British Government did not recognize the Sheikh of Bahrain as having sovereign rights over Janan

---

off the southwestern tip of the main Hawar Island, for Bahrain the term covered two islands, Janan and Hadd Janan. Since, in Qatar's view, Hadd Janan is a small area of sandy bottom below water at low tide, and Bahrain viewed it as forming one island with Janan at low tide, the Court considered itself entitled to treat Janan and Hadd Janan as one island. *See id.*, at paras. 149-50.

46   *See id.*, at para. 151.
47   *See id.*, at para. 152.
48   *See id.*, at para. 153.
49   *See id.*, at paras. 154-56.
50   *See id.*, at paras. 158-62.

Island and, based on points fixed and maps enclosed in the letters, that Great Britain regarded Janan as belonging to Qatar. By its letters, the British Government had provided an authoritative interpretation of its 1939 decision and of the situation resulting from it. Based on the decision taken by the British Government in 1939, as interpreted in 1947, the Court found that Qatar has sovereignty over Janan Island including Hadd Janan.[51]

In the second part of its Judgment, the Court addressed the question of the maritime delimitation of the disputed area. It noted that the "Bahraini formula" adopted by the parties in December 1990 requested the Court "to draw a single maritime boundary between their respective maritime areas of seabed, subsoil and superjacent waters," which was confirmed by the parties in their written pleadings. Given that none of the law of the sea conventions are applicable to both parties, customary international law was the applicable law to be applied by the Court in this case.[52]

Noting that in the present case the single maritime boundary would be the result of the delimitation of various jurisdictions, the Court observed that the delimitation to be effected by it was partly a delimitation of the territorial sea and partly a combined delimitation of the continental shelf and the exclusive economic zone.[53] The Court followed the parties' differentiation between a

---

51 *See id.*, at paras. 163-65.

52 *See id.*, at para. 167. Bahrain and Qatar have neither signed nor ratified the 1958 Geneva Conventions on the Law of the Sea (i.e., the Convention on the Territorial Sea and the Contiguous Zone, the Convention on the High Seas, the Convention on Fishing and Conservation of the Living Resources of the High Seas, and the Convention on the Continental Shelf). Whereas Bahrain has signed and ratified the United Nations Convention on the Law of the Sea of December 10, 1982 (1982 Convention), Qatar has only signed it. The Court noted that both parties agreed "that most of the provisions of the 1982 Convention which are relevant for the present case reflect customary law."

53 Art. 2(1) of the 1982 Convention describes the territorial sea as a belt of sea adjacent to a state's land territory and internal waters. The exclusive economic zone, "an area beyond and adjacent to the territorial sea" up to 200 nautical miles from the baselines from which the breadth of the territorial sea is measured (Arts. 55 and 57), is governed by Part V of the 1982 Convention. Art. 76, which opens Part VI of the 1982 Convention, defines the continental shelf of a coastal state as "the sea-bed and subsoil of the submarine areas that extend beyond its territorial sea throughout the natural prolongation of its land territory to the outer edge of the continental margin, or to a distance of 200 nautical miles from the baselines from which the breadth of the territorial sea is measured where the outer edge of the continental margin does not extend up to that distance." *See*, generally, GERARD TANJA, THE LEGAL DETERMINATION OF MARITIME BOUNDARIES (1989).

southern sector and a northern sector. In the *southern* part of the delimitation area, situated where the coasts of the parties are *opposite* each other, the distance between the coasts is nowhere more than 24 nautical miles, so that the boundary drawn by the Court would delimit exclusively their territorial seas over which they enjoy territorial sovereignty. Due to the parties extending the breadth of their territorial sea to 12 nautical miles in 1992-93, the waters in the southern sector at the time of the Court's delimitation consisted exclusively of partially overlapping territorial seas.[54] In the *northern* sector, the coasts of the two states instead are comparable to *adjacent* coasts, making the delimitation one between the continental shelf and exclusive economic zone belonging to each of the parties.[55] The latter are areas in which states have only sovereign rights, as opposed to territorial sovereignty, and functional jurisdiction. As a consequence of this fundamental difference, delimitation of territorial seas, where territorial sovereignty entails sovereignty over the sea-bed and the superjacent waters and air column and the rules of customary law govern, does not present the problems inherent in the determination of a single boundary of coincident jurisdictional zones.[56] In the latter case, the determination of a single boundary for the different objects of delimitation "can only be carried out by the application of a criterion, or combination of criteria, which does not give preferential treatment to one of these ... objects to the detriment of the other, and at the same time is such as to be equally suitable to the division of either of them."[57]

As to the delimitation of the territorial seas, which the Court undertook first, it noted that the parties had confirmed the customary character of Article

---

54 The Court's approach drew sharp criticism from its senior Member, Judge Oda. In Judge Oda's view, it was clear that Qatar and Bahrain never thought that they would be engaged in a dispute concerning the delimitation of their respective territorial seas (as opposed to the sea areas for oil exploitation), so that the Court was incorrect in applying the rules and principles governing the boundary of the territorial sea in the southern sector. *See* separate opinion of Judge Oda, at paras. 13-15.

55 *See* Judgment, *supra* note 6, at paras. 169-72.

56 *See id.*, at para. 174.

57 *See id.*, at para. 173 (citing Delimitation of the Maritime Boundary in the Gulf of Maine Area (Canada/U.S.), Judgment, 1984 ICJ REP. 246, 327, para. 194 (Oct. 12) (involving drawing of single line delimiting continental shelf and superjacent water column)).

15 of the 1982 Convention.[58] According to the "equidistance/special circumstances" rule embodied in Article 15, the most logical and widely practiced approach is first to draw provisionally an equidistance line[59] and to consider next whether that line must be adjusted in the light of the existence of special circumstances. However, the equidistance line can be drawn only when the baselines from which the breadth of the territorial seas of each of the two states is measured are known. In this case, the parties had neither specified the baselines nor produced official maps or charts reflecting such baselines. They only provided the Court with approximate basepoints during the proceedings.[60]

In order to determine the location of the baselines and the pertinent basepoints enabling it to measure the equidistance line, the Court first determined the relevant coasts of the parties. Qatar advocated the use of the mainland-to-mainland method in constructing the equidistance line. This method would take no account of the islands (except for the main Hawar Island, Bahrain Island, al-Muharaq and Sitrah), islets, rocks, reefs or low-tide elevations in the relevant area, and would lead to construction of the equidistance line by reference to

---

58   *See id.*, at paras. 175-76. Art. 15 states: "Where the coasts of two States are opposite or adjacent to each other, neither of the two States is entitled, failing agreement between them to the contrary, to extend its territorial sea beyond the median line every point of which is equidistant from the nearest point on the baselines from which the breadth of the territorial seas of each of the two States is measured. The above provision does not apply, however, where it is necessary by reason of historic title or other special circumstances to delimit the territorial seas of the two States in a way which is at variance therewith."

59   The equidistance line has been defined as "[a] line composed of relatively short segments connecting points that are equidistant from the normal baselines, or from claimed (or assumed) baselines from which the breadth of the territorial sea is measured. This is sometimes called a median line." INTERNATIONAL MARITIME BOUNDARIES xix (Jonathan I. Charney & Lewis M. Alexander eds., 1993). In his separate opinion, Judge Oda charges the Court with a mistaken and confusing interpretation of the applicable rules and principles, pointing out that the equidistance/special circumstances rule has not been referred to in connection with the delimitation of the territorial sea. In his view, the "true median line" is the general rule, which does not apply when historic title or other special circumstances so necessitate. *See* separate opinion of Judge Oda, at paras. 16-21.

60   *See* Judgment, *supra* note 6, at para. 177. As Judge Oda points out in his separate opinion, however, the Court also does not specify any precise baselines showing how it decided on the final line of demarcation: of the 42 coordinates listed by the Court, no explanation is given as to how they were selected. *See* separate opinion of Judge Oda, at paras. 24 and 28.

the high-water line (the line on the shore reached by the sea at high tide), which Qatar believed was justified on both technical and legal grounds.[61] Bahrain, on the other hand, pointed out that it is a *de facto* archipelago or multiple-island state, characterized by a variety of maritime features of diverse character and size, and since it is the land that determines maritime rights, the relevant basepoints were situated on all those maritime features over which Bahrain has sovereignty. Bahrain thus advocated the use of the low-water line.

Based on its *de facto* status, Bahrain considered that it was entitled to declare itself an archipelagic state under Part IV of the 1982 Convention and to draw the baselines that Article 47 permits, i.e., "straight archipelagic baselines joining the outermost points of the outermost islands and drying reefs of the archipelago."[62] Qatar contested this alleged entitlement, arguing that Part IV is not part of customary law and consequently is not opposable to Qatar as a non-party to the 1982 Convention. Qatar also claimed that Bahrain did not meet the requirements of Article 47, in particular the required ratio "between 1 to 1 and 9 to 1" of the area of water to the area of land. Qatar thus asked the Court to declare that any claim by Bahrain concerning archipelagic baselines was irrelevant for the purpose of maritime delimitation in this case.[63] The Court simply observed that Bahrain had not made this claim one of its formal submissions and that it therefore was not requested to take a position on this issue. The Court pointed out that it was merely to apply customary international law in carrying out the delimitation and that its decision would have binding force between the parties pursuant to Article 59 of the Statute. This meant that the Court's decision could not be put in issue by the unilateral action of either of the parties.[64]

The Court confirmed that international law dictates that the normal baseline for measuring the breadth of the territorial seas between two states is the low-water line along the coast.[65] It is the terrestrial territorial situation that must be taken as the starting point for the determination of the maritime rights of a coastal state.[66] Islands, no matter their size, thus enjoy the same status, and generate the same maritime rights, as other land territory. A determination of

---

61 *See id.*, at para. 179.
62 *See id.*, at paras. 180-81.
63 *See id.*, at para. 182.
64 *See id.*, at para. 183.
65 *See id.*, at para. 184 (citing Art. 5 of the 1982 Convention).
66 *See id.*, at para. 185 (citing North Sea Continental Shelf (FRG/Den.; FRG/Neth.), Judgment, 1969 ICJ REP. 3, 51, para. 96 (Feb. 20); Aegean Sea Continental Shelf (Gr. v. Turk.), Judgment, 1978 ICJ REP. 3, 36, para. 86 (Dec. 19)).

Bahrain's relevant coasts and baselines required a finding as to which islands come under Bahraini sovereignty. The Court already had concluded that Bahrain has sovereignty over the Hawar Islands and that Janan belongs to Qatar. In the southern sector of the delimitation area, Bahrain claimed uncontested sovereignty over the islands of Jazirat Mashtan and Umm Jalid. The parties having presented differing viewpoints, the Court had to decide, however, whether Fasht al Azm must be deemed to be part of the island of Sitrah, as claimed by Bahrain, or whether it is a low-tide elevation that is not naturally connected to Sitrah Island. In Qatar's view, Fasht al Azm is a low-tide elevation that has always been separated from Sitrah Island by a natural channel. Bahrain disagreed with Qatar's contention that this channel is navigable even at low tide. Having analyzed the various reports, documents and charts submitted by the parties, the Court concluded that it was unable to establish whether a permanent passage separating Sitrah Island from Fasht al Azm existed before Bahrain undertook reclamation works for the construction of a petrochemical plant in 1982. However, the Court considered that it was nonetheless able to undertake the requested delimitation in the southern sector without determining the question whether Fasht al Azm is to be regarded as part of Sitrah Island or as a low-tide elevation.[67]

The parties also offered opposing views on whether Qit'at Jaradah, another maritime feature located off the north-western coast of the Qatar peninsula and to the north-east of Fasht al Azm and the main island of Bahrain, is an island or a low-tide elevation. In its 1947 letters announcing the delimitation of the sea-bed of the two states, the British Government stated that the Dibal and Jaradah "shoals should not be considered to be islands having territorial waters."[68] Bahrain nonetheless argued that Qit'at Jaradah had recovered its island status by natural accretion, submitting an expert report in support. Submitting its own expert evaluations, Qatar refuted the Bahraini report and pointed out that Qit'at Jaradah always had been reflected on nautical charts as a low-tide elevation. Based on the legal definition of an island as "a naturally formed area of land, surrounded by water, which is above water at high tide" in Article 121 of the 1982 Convention, and having weighed the evidence presented by the parties, the Court concluded that the maritime feature of Qit'at Jaradah satisfied the criteria of the definition and was, therefore, an island that as such should be taken into consideration in the drawing of the equidistance

---

67   *See id.*, at paras. 188-90.
68   *See id.*, at para. 191.

line.[69] Noting that Qit'at Jaradah is a very small island situated within the 12-mile limit of both states and recalling an earlier precedent of its predecessor, the Court considered that the totality of the activities carried out by Bahrain on the island (including the erection of a beacon, the ordering of the drilling of an artesian well, the granting of an oil concession, and the licensing of fish traps) were sufficient to support Bahrain's claim of sovereignty over it.[70]

Bahrain invoked similar acts of authority (not necessarily performed à titre de souverain) in support of its claim of sovereignty over Fasht ad Dibal, which both parties agreed is a low-tide elevation. Whereas Qatar maintained that low-tide elevations cannot be appropriated, Bahrain contended that such maritime features by their very nature are territory and therefore can be appropriated in accordance with the criteria pertaining to territorial acquisition.[71]

The Court observed that a low-tide elevation is defined by international law to mean a naturally formed area of land surrounded by and above water at low tide but submerged at high tide.[72] The low-water line of a low-tide elevation may be used as the baseline for measuring the breadth of the territorial sea if it is situated wholly or partly at a distance not exceeding the breadth of the territorial sea from the mainland or an island.[73] The 1958 and 1982 Conventions provide that straight baselines shall not be drawn to and from low-tide elevations, unless lighthouses or similar installations that are permanently

---

69 *See id.*, at para. 195.
70 *See id.*, at paras. 197-98 (citing Legal Status of Eastern Greenland, 1933 PCIJ (ser. A/B) No. 53, at 46 ("in many cases the tribunal has been satisfied with very little in the way of the actual exercise of sovereign rights, provided that the other State could not make out a superior claim.")). In his separate opinion, Judge Parra-Aranguren points out that the drilling of an artesian well and the construction of navigation aids do not constitute acts of sovereignty *per sé* (citing Minquiers and Ecrehos (Fr. v. UK), Judgment, 1953 ICJ REP. 47, 71 (Nov. 17)). Separate opinion of Judge Parra-Aranguren, at paras. 5-6.
71 *See id.*, at paras. 199-200. Judge Oda points out in his separate opinion that there was no dispute between Qatar and Bahrain regarding title to Qit'at Jaradah and Fasht ad Dibal and that no diplomatic effort had been undertaken to negotiate the matter of territorial sovereignty over these features, which were mentioned only in connection with Bahrain's claimed maritime boundary. *See* separate opinion of Judge Oda, at para. 5.
72 *See id.*, at para. 201 (citing Art. 11(1) of the 1958 Convention on the Territorial Sea and the Contiguous Zone and Art. 13(1) of the 1982 Convention).
73 *See id.* If it is wholly situated at a distance exceeding the breadth of the territorial sea, it has no territorial sea of its own.

above sea level have been built on them.[74] The Court pointed out that when a low-tide elevation is situated in the overlapping area of the territorial sea of two states, whether with opposite or adjacent coasts, both states in principle are entitled to use its low-water line for measuring the breadth of their territorial sea, so that the same low-tide elevation forms part of the coastal configuration of the two states. In Bahrain's view, however, the *effectivités* presented by the two coastal states dictate which of them has a superior title to the low-tide elevation concerned and is entitled to exercise the right attributed by the relevant provisions of the law of the sea. It claimed that it had proven sufficient display of sovereign authority over all the low-tide elevations situated in the sea between Bahrain's main islands and the coast of the Qatar peninsula.

The Court noted that the validity of Bahrain's claim depended on whether low-tide elevations are territory and can be appropriated in conformity with the rules and principles of the acquisition of territory. In the Court's view, the decisive question in this case was whether a state can acquire sovereignty by appropriation over a low-tide elevation situated within the breadth of its territorial sea when that same low-tide elevation lies also within the breadth of the territorial sea of another state. International treaty law and state practice do not justify a general assumption that low-tide elevations are territory in the same sense as islands. Thus, it could not be established that low-tide elevations can, from the viewpoint of the acquisition of sovereignty, be fully assimilated with islands or other land territory.[75] Since a low-tide elevation that is situated beyond the limits of the territorial sea does not have a territorial sea of its own, such an elevation as such does not generate the same rights as islands or other territory, irrespective of whether the coastal state has treated it as its property and carried out some governmental acts on it. By contrast to a low-tide elevation that is situated within the limits of the territorial sea, an elevation that is situated less than 12 nautical miles from that low-tide elevation but is beyond the limits of the territorial sea may not be used for the determination of the breadth of the territorial sea. The provisions in the 1958 and 1982 Conventions that straight baselines are not to be drawn from low-tide elevations, unless lighthouses or similar installations that are permanently above sea level have been built on them, in the Court's view are another indication that low-tide elevations cannot be equated with islands. Islands, by contrast to low-tide elevations, under all circumstances qualify as basepoints for straight baselines.

---

74   *See id.* (citing Art. 4(3) of the 1958 Convention on the Territorial Sea and the Contiguous Zone and Art. 7(4) of the 1982 Convention).
75   *See id.*, at paras. 203-06.

For these reasons, the Court concluded that there was no ground in this case for recognizing the right of either Bahrain or Qatar to use as a baseline the low-water line of those low-tide elevations that are situated in the zone of overlapping claims, so that it would disregard such low-tide elevations in drawing the equidistance line.[76]

Bahrain further maintained that, as a multiple-island state or archipelago, it was entitled to draw a line connecting the outermost islands and low-tide elevations applying the method of straight baselines. The Court observed that this method, which is an exception to the normal rules for the determination of baselines, may be applied only if a number of conditions are met, and may not be deviated from merely because a state considers itself a multiple-island state or a *de facto* archipelagic state. One of these conditions is that the coastline is deeply indented and cut into, which is not the case here.[77] Another condition, on which Bahrain relied, is that maritime features off the coast may be assimilated to a fringe of islands situated along the coast in its immediate vicinity and constituting a whole with the mainland. In the Court's view, it would be going too far to qualify the maritime features east of Bahrain's main islands as a fringe of islands along its coast. Given that Bahrain has not declared itself to be an archipelagic state under Part IV of the 1982 Convention, the method of straight baselines may not be applied by it. Consequently, each maritime feature had its own effect for the determination of the baselines in this case and the low-tide elevations situated in the overlapping zone of territorial seas were disregarded. The Court made special mention of Fasht al Azm, a maritime feature for which it had not determined whether it forms part of Sitrah Island. If this feature were part of Sitrah Island, the basepoints would be situated on Fasht al Azm's eastern low-water line. If, on the other hand, it were not part of Sitrah Island, Fasht al Azm could not provide such basepoints. The Court therefore drew two equidistance lines, one for each hypothesis.[78]

Having established the basepoints for determining the equidistance line, the Court next examined whether there were special circumstances necessitating an adjustment of the equidistance line as provisionally drawn with a view to obtaining an equitable result in relation to this part of the single maritime

---

76   *See id.*, at paras. 207-09.
77   *See, e.g.*, Fisheries (UK v. Nor.), Judgment, 1951 ICJ Rep. 116, 128-29 (Dec. 18).
78   *See* Judgment, at paras. 210-16.

boundary to be fixed.[79] The Court considered that, under either hypothesis concerning Fasht al Azm, there were special circumstances that justified selecting a delimitation line passing between Fasht al Azm and Qit'at ash Shajarah.[80] With regard to Qit'at Jaradah, a tiny island under Bahraini sovereignty that is situated about midway between the main island of Bahrain and the Qatar peninsula and is uninhabited and lacks vegetation, the Court observed that a disproportionate effect would be given to this insignificant maritime feature if its low-water line were to be used for determining a basepoint in the construction of the equidistance line. The Court thus found that there was a special circumstance in this case warranting the choice of a delimitation line passing immediately to the east of Qit'at Jaradah.[81] Returning to Fasht al Azm, for which the Court had provisionally drawn two equidistance lines, the Court considered it appropriate to draw the boundary line between Qit'at Jaradah and Fasht ad Dibal, the latter falling under Qatar's sovereignty as it is situated in the territorial sea of Qatar.[82]

Before it determined the course of that part of the single maritime boundary delimiting the territorial seas of the parties, the Court noted that it could not fix the boundary's southern-most point, given that its location is dependent upon the limits of the respective maritime zones of Saudi Arabia, which was not a party to the proceedings, and of the parties. Following common practice, the Court also simplified what would otherwise be a very complex delimitation line in the region of the Hawar Islands.[83] Based on all the foregoing, the Court decided that:

> from the point of intersection of the respective maritime limits of Saudi Arabia
> on the one hand and of Bahrain and Qatar on the other, which cannot be fixed,
> the boundary will follow a north-easterly direction, then immediately turn in
> an easterly direction, after which it will pass between Jazirat Hawar and Janan;
> it will subsequently turn to the north and pass between the Hawar Islands and
> the Qatar peninsula and continue in a northerly direction, leaving the low-tide
> elevation of Fasht Bu Thur, and Fasht al Azm, on the Bahraini side, and the

---

79 *See id.*, at para. 217 (citing Maritime Delimitation in the Area between Greenland and Jan Mayen (Den. v. Nor.), Judgment, 1993 ICJ REP. 38, 60, para. 50, 62, para. 54 (June 14)).

80 *See id.*, at para. 218.

81 *See id.*, at para. 219 (citing North Sea Continental Shelf (FRG/Den.; FRG/Neth.), Judgment, 1969 ICJ REP. 3, 36, para. 57 (Feb. 20); Continental Shelf (Lib./Malta), Judgment, 1985 ICJ REP. 13, 48, para. 64 (June 3)).

82 *See id.*, at para. 220.

83 *See id.*, at para. 221.

low-tide elevations of Qita'a el Erge and Qit'at ash Shajarah on the Qatari side;
finally it will pass between Qit'at Jaradah and Fasht ad Dibal, leaving Qit'at
Jaradah on the Bahraini side and Fasht ad Dibal on the Qatari side.

Noting that this line caused Qatar's maritime zones situated to the south of
the Hawar Islands and those situated to the north of those islands to be connected only by the poorly navigable, narrow and shallow channel separating
the Hawar Islands from the Qatar peninsula, forcing local sea traffic between
the northern and southern parts of the western coast of Qatar to follow routes
to the west of the Hawars, the Court emphasized that the waters lying between
the Hawar Islands and the other Bahraini islands are not internal waters of
Bahrain, but are Bahrain's territorial sea. Qatari vessels, like those of all other
states, enjoy in these waters the right of innocent passage accorded by customary international law, just as Bahraini vessels enjoy this right in Qatar's territorial sea.[84]

The Court proceeded to consider and draw the single maritime boundary
in that part of the delimitation area covering both the continental shelf and the
exclusive economic zone, i.e., the maritime zones beyond the 12-mile zone.
Referring to earlier precedents confirming the close relationship between the
continental shelf and exclusive economic zone for delimitation purposes,[85]
the Court concluded that it was proper for it to begin the process of delimitation
in this case by a median line provisionally drawn and then to examine those
factors that might suggest an adjustment or shifting of that line in order to
achieve an "equitable result."[86] Those factors constitute "relevant circumstances" or "special circumstances," i.e., circumstances that might modify the
result produced by an unqualified application of the equidistance principle. The
Court noted that the equidistance/special circumstances rule, applicable to the
delimitation of the territorial sea, and the equitable principles/relevant circumstances rule, as it has been developed since 1958 in case-law and state practice

---

84 *See id.*, at para. 223.
85 *See id.*, at paras. 225-26 (citing Delimitation of the Maritime Boundary in the Gulf
    of Maine Area (Canada/U.S.), Judgment, 1984 ICJ REP. 246, 327, para. 194 (Oct.
    12); Continental Shelf (Lib./Malta), Judgment, 1985 ICJ REP. 13, 33, para. 33 (June
    3)).
86 *See id.*, at paras. 227-30 (citing Maritime Delimitation in the Area between Green-
    land and Jan Mayen (Den. v. Nor.), Judgment, 1993 ICJ REP. 38, 61, para. 51, 62,
    paras. 53, 55 (June 14)).

with regard to the delimitation of the continental shelf and the exclusive economic zone, are closely interrelated.[87]

Recalling that "the equidistance method is not the only method applicable
to the present dispute, and it does not even have the benefit of a presumption
in its favour" and that "under existing law, it must be demonstrated that the
equidistance method leads to an equitable result in the case in question,"[88]
the Court first considered Bahrain's argument that pearling banks constituted
a special circumstance that had to be taken into consideration in carrying out
the delimitation. Qatar denied that Bahrain ever enjoyed exclusive rights over
the exploitation of the pearling banks and pointed out that the pearling industry
effectively ceased to exist a long time ago. Taking note of the latter fact, the
Court observed that pearl diving in the Gulf area traditionally was considered
as a right that was common to the coastal population and that this activity never
led to the recognition of an exclusive quasi-territorial right to the fishing
grounds themselves or to the superjacent waters. Consequently, the pearling
banks did not form a circumstance justifying an eastward shifting of the
equidistance line.[89]

As to the relevance to the current delimitation of the line dividing the sea-
bed of Qatar and Bahrain described in the British letters of December 23, 1947
advocated by Qatar and contested by Bahrain, the Court simply noted that
neither of the parties had accepted the "decision" contained in the British letters
as a binding decision, having invoked only parts of it to support their arguments.[90] Given that the 1947 line concerned only the division of the sea-bed,
it could not be considered to have direct relevance to the Court's multi-purpose
delimitation task.

The Court next rejected Qatar's argument relying on the alleged disparity
between the coastal lengths of the parties as a special or relevant circumstance,
based on the fact that it had decided that Bahrain has sovereignty over the
Hawar Islands, which made the lenghts of the relevant coasts almost equal.[91]

Turning to other reasons that might require an equitable adjustment of the
equidistance line, the Court noted that it could not ignore the location of Fasht

---

87 *See id.*, at para. 231. For an examination of the development over recent decades
    of the laws governing the delimitation of the continental shelf, see the separate
    opinion of Judge Oda, at paras. 31-39.
88 *See id.*, at para. 233 (citing Continental Shelf (Lib./Malta), Judgment, 1985 ICJ
    REP. 13, 47, para. 63 (June 3)).
89 *See id.*, at paras. 235-36.
90 *See id.*, at paras. 237-39.
91 *See id.*, at paras. 241-43.

al Jarim, a sizable maritime feature partly situated in the territorial sea of
Bahrain. Whatever the legal nature of this feature, its location dictated that its
low-water line could be used as the baseline from which the breadth not only
of the territorial sea, but also of the continental shelf and the exclusive economic zone, is measured. Recalling an earlier precedent, the Court noted that
in the northern sector the coasts of the parties are comparable to adjacent coasts
abutting on the same maritime areas extending seawards into the Gulf and that
the northern coasts of the parties' territories are not markedly different in
character or extent.[92] However, Fasht al Jarim, being a remote projection of
Bahrain's coastline, would "distort the boundary and have disproportionate
effects" if given full effect.[93] Given that such a distortion due to a maritime
feature located well out to sea and of which at most a tiny part is above water
at high tide would not lead to an equitable result, considerations of equity
required that Fasht al Jarim should have no effect in determining the boundary
line in the northern sector.[94] Accordingly, the Court decided that:

> the single maritime boundary in this sector shall be formed in the first place
> by a line which, from a point situated to the north-west of Fasht ad Dibal, shall
> meet the equidistance line as adjusted to take account of the absence of effect
> given to Fasht al Jarim. The boundary shall then follow this adjusted equi-
> distance line until it meets the delimitation line between the respective maritime
> zones of Iran on the one hand and of Bahrain and Qatar on the other.[95]

---

92 *See id.*, at para. 246 (citing Continental Shelf (Lib./Malta), Judgment, 1985 ICJ
    REP. 13, 48, para. 64 (June 3)).
93 *See id.*, at para. 247 (citing Continental Shelf (Fr./UK), 18 RIAA 114, para. 244).
94 The Court's reference to considerations of equity should not be mistaken to mean
    that it decides the case, not based on the law, but *ex aequo et bono*. Art. 38(2) of
    the ICJ Statute reserves the Court's power to decided a case *ex aequo et bono* to
    situations where the parties explicitly agree to the use of this power. *See* Frontier
    Dispute (Burkina Faso/Mali), 1986 ICJ REP. 554, 567, para. 28 (Dec. 22). For an
    elaborate exposition of the role of equity in law generally and in maritime boundary
    delimitation law specifically, see the separate opinion of Judge Weeramantry
    appended to the Court's Judgment in Maritime Delimitation in the Area between
    Greenland and Jan Mayen (Den. v. Nor.), 1993 ICJ REP. 38 (June 14); *see also*
    R.Y. Jennings, *Equity and Equitable Principles*, 42 ANNUAIRE DE DROIT INTER-
    NATIONAL 27 (1986); NAGENDRA SINGH, THE ROLE AND RECORD OF THE INTER-
    NATIONAL COURT OF JUSTICE 124-28 (1989).
95 *See* Judgment, *supra* note 6, at para. 249.

The penultimate paragraph of the Judgment specifies the exact course of the single maritime boundary fixed by the Court.[96]

* * * *

As the Court's president remarked in a statement he made to the press on the day of the reading of the Judgment, this decision, which is more than 70 pages long, "does not make for easy reading,"[97] prompting him to summarize it for the press and the general public. For this reason, a lengthy review and commentary seemed appropriate here.

It is safe to say that this case will be remembered, not so much for the contents of the Court's Judgment on the merits, but for its ancillary aspects. First, it was the longest ever proceeding in the Court's history: Qatar filed its Application on July 8, 1991 and the Court issued its final decision almost ten years later, on March 16, 2001. The Court issued no less than three Judgments (two on jurisdiction and one on the merits) and seven Orders in the case. Over 6,000 pages of written pleadings were filed by the parties. The oral proceedings on the merits involved some five weeks of hearings. Following its second Judgment on jurisdiction of February 15, 1995, the Court essentially followed the procedure applicable to cases submitted jointly by the parties (consisting of the simultaneous, as opposed to consecutive, filing of written pleadings), even though Qatar had filed the case unilaterally. The case represents the first time that the Court directed the parties to file a second round of written pleadings in an Initial Phase case.[98] Bahrain used three consecutive judges *ad hoc* (Messrs. Valticos, Shahabuddeen and Fortier), the first two having resigned while the proceedings were pending, while Qatar had to replace its original judge *ad hoc*, former ICJ President Ruda, following his death in 1994. Between September 1997 and February 1999, the parties fought an unprecedented battle over the authenticity of some 82 documents produced by Qatar as annexes to its written pleadings, resulting in the withdrawal of these documents.[99]

All but five Judges (President Guillaume, Vice President Shi, and Judges Fleischhauer, Rezek and Buergenthal) appended a declaration or opinion to the Court's Judgment. Judges Herczegh, Vereshchetin and Higgins each

---

96 *See id.*, at para. 250.
97 Statement by the President of the International Court of Justice, Judge Gilbert Guillaume, March 16, 2001, text available from the ICJ Web site, <www.icj-cij.org/icjwww/ipresscom/SPEECHES>.
98 *See* 1992 ICJ REP. 237 (Order of June 26).
99 *See* Judgment, *supra* note 6, at paras. 15-23.

appended declarations to the Judgment in which they explained their vote.[100] The three African Members of the Court, Judges Bedjaoui, Ranjeva and Koroma, complain in their lengthy joint dissenting opinion that the Court's Judgment rules *infra petita* on both the territorial and maritime aspects of the questions before it by ignoring the parties' arguments and wishes, especially on the rules of territorial acquisition.[101] While Judges Oda and Parra-Aranguren focus on the maritime aspects of the Judgment in their separate opinions, Judges Kooijmans and Al-Khasawneh take issue with a number of the territorial issues dealt with by the Court in their separate opinions.[102] The judges *ad hoc* appointed by Qatar and Bahrain, neither of which represented the nationality of the appointing party, appended a dissenting and separate opinion, respectively. Perhaps most significantly, the only Member of the Court of Arab origin, Judge Al-Khasawneh (Jordan), concurred with the view of the majority in this case.

---

100 In his declaration, Judge Herczegh explains that the Court's statements on the right of innocent passage enabled him to vote in favor of the part of the majority's decision to draw a single maritime boundary. Judge Vereshchetin's declaration criticizes the Court's findings on the legal position of the Hawar Islands based on its exclusive reliance on the British decision of 1939, which in his view is not a fully-fledged third-party legal settlement of the parties' dispute and should have been analyzed more carefully on both procedural and substantive legal grounds (including the principle of proximity, *effectivés* and original title). In his opinion, Qit'at Jaradah is not an island but a low-tide elevation, the attribution of which should have been effected after the delimitation of the territorial seas of the parties and not the other way around. In her declaration, Judge Higgins explains her vote based on her belief that sovereignty over Janan lay with Bahrain and points out that the Court also could have grounded Bahraini title in the Hawar Islands on the law of territorial acquisition, especially on the basis of Bahraini *effectivités*.

101 The three African Judges criticize the majority especially for not having analyzed more thoroughly the formal procedural aspects of the British decision of 1939 and for not having assessed whether that decision was well founded in law, including the principle of proximity, *effectivés* and original title.

102 In the view of Judges Kooijmans and Al-Khasawneh, the Court took an unduly formalistic approach by basing itself exclusively on the position taken by Great Britain as the former Protecting Power and not on substantive rules and principles of international law, especially those on territorial acquisition. In Judge Kooijmans' view, the Court did not give the full historical context its due in this case. *See* separate opinion of Judge Kooijmans, at para. 4.

This latest law of the sea decision[103] handed down by the International Court continues a line of previous cases on maritime delimitation and, especially, the practice of the drawing of a single maritime boundary involving a plurality of separate delimitations.[104] The Court's president has remarked that the Court's decisions fixing the boundaries of the different maritime zones appertaining to Bahrain and Qatar "restated the law applicable in this field."[105] By contrast to these prior cases, however, the present decision for the first time relied entirely on customary international law, given that the parties were not both parties to any of the law of the sea conventions.[106] In particular, this case confirms that the maritime practice before the Court has developed from one by which the Court merely undertakes a task preliminary to the determination of a line (indicating legal principles to guide the parties' drawing of the line) to one in which the Court actually draws the line itself.[107] From a law

---

103 With the exception of the Zubarah region, the territorial issues in this case were not distinctly separate from the maritime delimitation. *See* separate opinion of Judge Oda, at para. 1.

104 This is evidenced by the Court's frequent citations from the *Gulf of Maine* (1984) and *Jan Mayen* (1993) cases, which fixed single maritime boundaries dividing the continental shelf and exclusive fisheries/economic zone (in the former case, upon the request of the parties and, in the latter case, at the request of the applicant). In his separate opinion, Judge Oda points out that the phrase "single maritime boundary," which was not mentioned in Bahrain's submissions, "has come to mean an *identical* boundary, being a single line for the two different régimes of the continental shelf and the exclusive economic zone." *See* separate opinion of Judge Oda, at para. 12. *See also* Barbara Kwiatkowska, *Equitable maritime boundary delimitation*, in: FIFTY YEARS OF THE INTERNATIONAL COURT OF JUSTICE 264 (Vaughan Lowe & Malgosia Fitzmaurice eds., 1996).

105 Address by the President of the International Court of Justice, Judge Gilbert Guillaume, to the United Nations General Assembly, Oct. 30, 2001, text available from the ICJ Web site, <www.icj-cij.org/icjwww/ipresscom/SPEECHES>.

106 It must be said, though, that the Court arrived at its conclusions based largely on the customary character of some of the key provisions of the 1958 and 1982 Conventions, so that its conclusions can be said to be anchored indirectly and ultimately in treaty law.

107 Believing that there is no such thing as a single equitable line of delimitation, the Court's senior Member, Judge Oda, favors the former approach, by which the Court merely describes the method by which the maritime boundary line should be measured. *See* separate opinion of Judge Oda, at paras. 26-27 ("the Court should not, in its Judgment, go beyond stating what elements should be taken into account in order to achieve an equitable solution and how these elements should be assessed" and "should always exercise moderation and self-restraint in its decisions on maritime boundaries."). In Judge Oda's view, the Court "should have ordered that a

of the sea point of view, the Court's elaborate treatment of low-tide elevations and their difference with islands is among the most interesting aspects of this Judgment.[108] Time will tell whether the Court will have attracted or instead alienated potential maritime customers by its flexible approach of the maritime aspects of this case.[109] The International Tribunal for the Law of the Sea in Hamburg is yet to emerge as a serious contender in the field of maritime delimitation, having hitherto dealt primarily, and one might add effectively, with vessel arrest cases. So far, states have preferred to submit their maritime delimitation disputes to *ad hoc* arbitration by way of an alternative to the ICJ.

It remains to be seen whether the Court's heavy reliance on administrative decisions by Great Britain, of which the parties in this case were former protectorates, is a victory for third-party dispute resolution or instead must be characterized as a denial of well-developed legal concepts such as *effectivités* and territorial acquisition. In the circumstances, such reliance probably best suited the overall goal of the predictability of the law by which the Court is supposed to be guided in its decision-making.[110]

Judging from the letters that both parties sent to the Court in the days following the delivery of the Judgment,[111] they considered that the Court's decision finally had resolved their long-standing dispute. Both expressed their gratitude to the Court in their letters, Bahrain even twice. However, judging from the dissenting opinion of the judge *ad hoc* appointed by Qatar, and from the fact that Qatar's letter appears to have been prompted by Bahrain's letter, it is Bahrain who can claim a relative victory in this case. This may be

---

panel of experts in the fields of geography and hydrography be appointed, either by the Court or jointly by the Parties, to determine the mathematical or geometric means by which the precise boundary line should be drawn, instead of itself proceeding to the demarcation of a boundary line." *Id.*, at para. 28.

108 In Judge Oda's view, the Court should have dealt more cautiously with the issue concerning islets and low-tide elevations, given that, by contrast to the Court's approach, these issues do not necessarily reflect customary international law as it stands today. *See* separate opinion of Judge Oda, at paras. 6-8.

109 According to Judge Oda, the decision "misconstrues the issues of the maritime boundary and is also mistaken in the manner in which it has applied what it considers to be the appropriate rules." Separate opinion of Judge Oda, at para. 10.

110 *See, e.g.*, Continental Shelf (Lib./Malta), Judgment, 1985 ICJ REP. 13, 64, para. 58 (June 3) (referring to the need for "consistency and a degree of predictability").

111 Letter of March 19, 2001 from Mr. Jawad Salim Al Arayed, Agent of the State of Bahrain, to the ICJ Registrar, and letter of March 27, 2001 from Dr. Abdullah bin Abdulatif Al-Muslemani, Agent of the State of Qatar, to the ICJ Registrar, text available from the Court's Web site, <www.icj-cij.org>.

explained by the fact that the biggest territorial "prize" in this case, the Hawar Islands, was awarded to Bahrain, with important ramifications for the single maritime boundary drawn by the Court and, ultimately, oil exploration and exploitation off the waters of the Hawar group of islands.

U.S. failure to provide consular notification under Vienna Convention on Consular Relations to detained German nationals – treaty creating state and individual rights – diplomatic protection – issues of jurisdiction and admissibility arising from Germany's submissions in merits phase – effect of partial admission of responsibility and formal apology by U.S. – effect of breach of Order indicating provisional measures

LaGrand Case (Germany v. United States)

Judgment
Obtainable from <www.icj-cij.org>
International Court of Justice, June 27, 2001

On March 2, 1999, Germany filed an Application in the Registry of the International Court of Justice instituting proceedings against the United States of America over a dispute concerning alleged U.S. violations of the Vienna Convention on Consular Relations of April 24, 1963 (Convention) with respect to the case of Karl and Walter LaGrand, two German nationals convicted of murder in Arizona. At the time of the filing, Karl LaGrand had already been executed, constituting the first execution of a German national in the U.S. since the founding of the Federal Republic of Germany in 1949, and the execution of his brother Walter was scheduled for the next day. Germany based the Court's jurisdiction on Article I of the Optional Protocol concerning the Compulsory Settlement of Disputes accompanying the Convention.[1] In its Order of March 3, 1999 indicating provisional measures, discussed in Chapter 3 above, the Court found that it had *prima facie* jurisdiction based on this provision. Notwithstanding the Court's Order, Walter LaGrand was executed as scheduled.

Germany requested a declaration from the Court that the United States, by not informing the two Germans without delay following their arrest of their rights under Article 36(1)(b) of the Convention, and by preventing Germany

---

[1] According to Art. I, "[d]isputes arising out of the interpretation or application of the Convention shall lie within the compulsory jurisdiction of the International Court of Justice and may accordingly be brought before the Court by an application made by any party to the dispute being a Party to the present Protocol." Optional Protocol, Convention on Consular Relations, done at Vienna, Apr. 24, 1963, 21 UST 77, 596 UNTS 261.

313

P.H.F. Bekker, World Court Decisions at the Turn of the Millennium (1997-2001), p. 313-333.
© 2002 *Kluwer Law International. Printed in the Netherlands.*

from rendering consular assistance, with the ultimate result of their execution, violated the U.S.' international legal obligations to Germany, in its own right and in its right of diplomatic protection of its nationals, under Articles 5 and 36, paragraph 1, of the Convention (First Submission).[2] Second, Germany asked the Court to declare that the U.S., by applying domestic law rules barring the German nationals from raising their claims under the Convention and by executing them, violated Article 36, paragraph 2, of the Convention requiring each state party to give full effect to the purposes for which the rights accorded under Article 36 are intended (Second Submission). Third, Germany requested the Court to declare that the U.S., by failing to take all measures at its disposal to ensure that Walter LaGrand not be executed pending the Court's final decision in this case, had violated its international legal obligations to comply with the Court's Order of March 3, 1999 indicating provisional measures (Third Submission). Finally, Germany demanded an assurance from the U.S. that it would not repeat its alleged unlawful acts and would ensure the effective exercise of the rights under Article 36 of the Convention and provide effective review of and remedies for criminal convictions impaired by a violation of the rights under Article 36 (Fourth Submission). Although it welcomed a declaration of the Court that it had breached its obligations to Germany under Article 36(1)(b) of the Convention by not promptly notifying the German

---

2   Art. 36, para. 1 provides:
"With a view to facilitating the exercise of consular functions relating to nationals of the sending State:
(*a*) consular officers shall be free to communicate with nationals of the sending State and to have access to them. Nationals of the sending State shall have the same freedom with respect to communication with and access to consular officers of the sending State;
(*b*) if he so requests, the competent authorities of the receiving State shall, without delay, inform the consular post of the sending State if, within its consular district, a national of that State is arrested or committed to prison or to custody pending trial or is detained in any other manner. Any communication addressed to the consular post by the person arrested, in prison, custody or detention shall be forwarded by the said authorities without delay. The said authorities shall inform the person concerned without delay of his rights under this subparagraph;
(*c*) consular officers shall have the right to visit a national of the sending State who is in prison, custody or detention, to converse and correspond with him and to arrange for his legal representation. They shall also have the right to visit any national of the sending State who is in prison, custody or detention in their district in pursuance of a judgement. Nevertheless, consular officers shall refrain from taking action on behalf of a national who is in prison, custody or detention if he expressly opposes such action."

nationals of their rights under the Convention, the U.S. submitted that it had apologized to Germany for this breach and was taking substantial measures aimed at preventing any recurrence. In the U.S.' view, this required that Germany's claims, other than the one relating to Article 36(1)(b), be dismissed.

On June 27, 2001,[3] the Court found (1) by 14 votes to one, that it had jurisdiction to entertain Germany's Application; (2) by overwhelming majorities, that all of Germany's submissions were admissible;[4] (3) by 14 votes to one, that the U.S. breached Article 36, paragraph 1, of the Convention; (4) by 14 votes to one, that the U.S. breached Article 36, paragraph 2, of the Convention; (5) by 13 votes to two, that the U.S. breached the obligation incumbent upon it under the Court's Order of March 3, 1999; (6) unanimously, took note of the commitment undertaken by the U.S. to ensure implementation of the specific measures adopted in performance of its obligations under Article 36(1)(b) of the Convention, which must be considered as meeting Germany's request for a general assurance of non-repetition; and (7) by 14 votes to one, that should German nationals nonetheless be sentenced to severe penalties through a U.S. breach of their rights under Article 36(1)(b) of the Convention, the U.S., by means of its own choosing, must allow the review and reconsideration of the conviction and sentence by taking account of the violation of the rights set forth in the Convention.

Noting that the U.S. had presented a number of objections to the Court's jurisdiction and the admissibility of Germany's Application, even though it had not raised preliminary objections under Article 79 of the Rules of Court during the written phase, the Court first dealt with these issues as a preliminary matter.[5] Germany contended that all four submissions were covered by Article I of the Optional Protocol and that its submissions were admissible.

With regard to Germany's First Submission, Germany alleged that the U.S. failure to inform the LaGrand brothers of their right to contact the German authorities, which was undisputed,[6] prevented it from exercising its rights under clauses (a) and (c) of paragraph 1 of Article 36 of the Convention and violated

---

3   *See* slip opinion, available from the Court's Web site, <www.icj-cij.org> [hereinafter Judgment]. Hearings were held on November 13-17, 2000.

4   The vote on the admissibility of Germany's four submissions was as follows: (a) First Submission: 13-2 (Judges Oda and Parra-Aranguren dissenting); (b) Second Submission: 14-1 (Judge Oda dissenting); (c) Third Submission: 12-3 (Judges Oda, Parra-Aranguren and Buergenthal dissenting); (d) Fourth Submission: 14-1 (Judge Oda dissenting). *See* Judgment, *supra* note 3, at para. 128 (*dispositif*).

5   *See id.*, at para. 35.

6   *See id.*, at para. 15.

Germany's rights under Article 36(1)(b). In addition, by failing to inform the German authorities, the U.S. also violated the individual rights that Article 36(1)(a) (second sentence) and Article 36(1)(b) conferred on the German detainees and for which Germany was claiming by way of diplomatic protection.[7] Although the U.S. acknowledged that its breach of Article 36(1)(b) gave rise to a dispute between Germany and the U.S., it argued that the dispute before the Court and, therefore, the Court's jurisdiction was limited to Germany's own rights. The U.S. characterized Germany's claims of violation of paragraphs 1(a) and (c) of Article 36 as "particularly misplaced" in that the underlying conduct of which Germany complained was the same as its claim under Article 36(1)(b). In the U.S.' view, Germany's claim based on diplomatic protection was outside the Court's jurisdiction under the Optional Protocol because the claim did not concern the interpretation or application of the Convention and the Convention does not deal with diplomatic protection.[8]

The Court rejected the U.S. objections concerning the First Submission, finding that the parties' dispute as to whether Article 36(1)(a) and (c) were violated in consequence of the breach of Article 36(1)(b) and as to whether the latter provision creates individual rights for which Germany has standing both are disputes within the meaning of Article I of the Optional Protocol. The fact that Germany based its claim partly on diplomatic protection, a concept of customary international law, does not prevent a state party to a treaty creating individual rights from taking up the case of one of its nationals and taking legal action on behalf of that national based on a general jurisdictional clause in the treaty concerned.[9]

In connection with the Second and Third Submissions, which were not met with jurisdictional challenges from the U.S., the Court observed that, given that they concerned issues arising directly out of the dispute over which the Court confirmed jurisdiction, they were covered by Article I of the Optional Protocol.[10] The Court confirmed that, where it has jurisdiction to decide a case, it also has jurisdiction to deal with submissions requesting it to determine that a provisional measures order has not been complied with.

---

7   *See id.*, at para. 38.

8   *See id.*, at paras. 39-40.

9   *See id.*, at para. 42.

10 *See id.*, at para. 45 (citing Fisheries Jurisdiction (Fed. Rep. Ger. v. Icel.), Judgment, 1974 ICJ REP. 175, 203, para. 72 (25 July) (Court also may deal with a submission that "is one based on facts subsequent to the filing of the Application, but arising directly out of the question which is the subject-matter of that Application. As such it falls within the scope of the Court's jurisdiction.")).

With regard to the Fourth Submission, the U.S. argued that the Court had no jurisdiction over Germany's request for assurances and guarantees of non-repetition, which in its view went beyond any remedy that the Court can or should grant.[11] Germany sought support in a previous decision for its contention that a dispute as to whether or not the violation of a provision of the Convention gives rise to a certain remedy is a dispute concerning the application or interpretation of the Convention within the scope of Article I of the Optional Protocol.[12] The Court upheld its jurisdiction over the Fourth Submission, considering that a dispute regarding the appropriate remedies for the violation of Convention provisions alleged by Germany is a dispute that arises out of the interpretation or application of the Convention. The Court pointed out that, where it has jurisdiction over a dispute on a particular matter, it needs no separate jurisdictional basis to consider the remedies that a party has requested for the breach of the obligation.[13]

Having affirmed its jurisdiction with respect to the whole of Germany's submissions, the Court next examined the U.S. objections to the admissibility of those submissions.

First, the U.S. contended that the Second, Third and Fourth Submissions were inadmissible because Germany sought to have the Court play the role of ultimate court of appeal in domestic criminal proceedings and correct asserted violations of U.S. law and judgment errors by U.S. judges in such proceedings.[14] The Court observed, however, that the Second Submission merely requested its interpretation of the scope of Article 36, paragraph 2, of the Convention, that the Third Submission sought a finding by it that the U.S. violated a Court Order, and that the Fourth Submission asked it to determine the applicable remedies for the Convention breaches alleged by Germany. In the Court's view, all three submissions required it to do no more than to apply the relevant rules of international law to the issues in dispute between Germany and the U.S. The exercise of this function is expressly mandated by Article 38 of the ICJ Statute and does not convert the Court into a court of appeal of national criminal proceedings.[15]

---

11 *See id.*, at para. 46.
12 *See id.*, at para. 47 (citing Vienna Convention on Consular Relations (Para. v. U.S.), 1998 ICJ REP. 248, 256, para. 31 (Order of Apr. 9)).
13 *See id.*, at para. 48 (citing Chorzów Factory (Ger. v. Pol.), Judgment (Jurisdiction), 1927 PCIJ (ser. A) No. 9, at 22 (July 26)).
14 *See id.*, at para. 50.
15 *See id.*, at para. 52.

Second, the U.S. argued that the manner in which Germany had brought this case before the Court, some 27 hours before Walter LaGrand's execution after having been aware of the LaGrands' case since 1992, rendered the Third Submission inadmissible. In reply, Germany maintained that international law does not lay down any specific time limit for filing a case and contended that it did not become aware of all the relevant facts underlying its claim (especially the fact that the Arizona authorities knew of the German nationality of the brothers since 1982) until one week before the filing of its Application.[16] The Court considered that, notwithstanding the manner of the filing of the case and Germany's timing for which this applicant may be criticized, it had considered it appropriate to issue its Order on March 3, 1999, so that Germany subsequently was entitled to challenge the alleged U.S. failure to comply with it.[17]

Third, the U.S. maintained that the First Submission, to the extent that it concerned Germany's right to exercise diplomatic protection with respect to German nationals, was inadmissible because the LaGrands had not complained at the trial stage that the U.S. had breached its duty to inform them of their right to consular access and thus had not exhausted local remedies.[18] The Court agreed with Germany, however, that the brothers had sought in vain to plead the Convention in U.S. courts after they learned of their rights under the Convention in 1992, but that U.S. procedural law barred them from obtaining any remedy for the breach of their rights.[19] Given that it was the U.S. itself which had failed to carry out its obligation under the Convention to inform the brothers, the U.S. subsequently could not rely on the failure of the brothers to plead the breach in order to preclude the admissibility of the First Submission.[20]

Finally, the U.S. contended that Germany's effort to have a standard applied to the U.S. that was different from its own practice relating to the consequences of the breach of a duty of consular notification was contrary to the basic principles of administration of justice and equality of the parties and rendered Germany's submissions inadmissible. Finding that the evidence adduced by the U.S. did not justify its allegation, the Court considered that it did not need

---

16 *See id.*, at paras. 53-55.

17 *See id.*, at para. 57.

18 *See id.*, at para. 58.

19 According to the "procedural default" rule of U.S. federal criminal procedure, before a state criminal defendant can obtain relief in federal court, the claim must be presented to a state court. *See id.*, at para. 23.

20 *See id.*, at para. 60.

to decide whether the U.S. argument, if true, would result in inadmissibility and pointed out that the remedies for a violation of Article 36 of the Convention are not necessarily identical in all situations (*i.e.*, an apology may be an appropriate remedy in some cases, but it may be insufficient in others).

Having upheld its jurisdiction and the admissibility of Germany's submissions, the Court turned to the merits of each of the four submissions.

With regard to the First Submission, the Court observed that the U.S. acknowledged and did not contest Germany's basic claim that the U.S. had violated its obligation under Article 36(1)(b) of the Convention promptly to inform the LaGrand brothers that they could ask that a German consular post be notified of their arrest and detention. In addition, Germany claimed that the U.S. breach of subsection (b) of paragraph 1 resulted in consequential breaches of subsections (a) and (c) and rendered meaningless all the rights that paragraph 1 confers, and this breach and the execution had caused irreparable harm in violation of international law. The U.S. argued that Germany's claims regarding subsections (a) and (c) were misplaced, because the LaGrand brothers were able to, and did in fact, communicate freely with German consular officers after 1992. In other words, while there was a breach of the U.S. duty of consular notification, there was no deprivation of Germany's right to provide consular assistance. In reply, Germany pointed out that one and the same conduct may result in several violations of distinct obligations and that there was a causal relationship between the U.S. violation of Article 36 and the ultimate execution of the brothers. Germany claimed that, if the U.S. had properly afforded Germany its rights under the Convention, it would have been able to intervene in time and prevented the executions. Germany argued that the U.S. doctrine of procedural default (requiring that claims seeking remedies be asserted at the state trial phase) and the strict post-conviction conditions for proving ineffective counsel under U.S. law prevented Germany, when it intervened after the trial phase, from remedying the prejudice created by counsel appointed by the court to represent the indigent brothers at their trial. The U.S. dismissed the German arguments as speculative.[21]

The Court noted that Article 36, paragraph 1, establishes an interrelated regime designed to facilitate the implementation of the system of consular protection. This provision has a tripartite structure: (1) clause (a) sets forth the right of communication and access, which is the basic principle governing consular protection; (2) clause (b) spells out the modalities of consular notification; and (3) clause (c) lists the measures consular officers may take in render-

---

21   *See id.*, at paras. 65-72.

ing consular assistance to their nationals in the custody of the receiving state. In the Court's view, when the receiving state fails to provide the requisite consular notification without delay so that the sending state is unaware of the detention of its nationals, as happened in this case between January 1982 and June 1992, the sending state in effect is prevented from exercising its rights under Article 36, paragraph 1. Even though a breach of Article 36(1)(b) will not necessarily always lead to a breach of the other provisions of Article 36, the circumstances in this case compelled the opposite conclusion.[22]

The U.S. also questioned the basis for Germany's claim, espoused by way of diplomatic protection, that the individual rights of the LaGrand brothers had been violated. In the view of the U.S., rights of consular notification and access under the Convention are rights of states, not of individuals, and the state's right to communicate with its nationals through its consular officers does not constitute a fundamental right or a human right.[23] Based on the text of Article 36, paragraph 1, of the Convention, the Court concluded that this provision, viewed in its context, creates individual rights which may be invoked by the national state of the detained person by virtue of Article I of the Optional Protocol to the Convention. The Court was satisfied that these rights were violated in this case.[24]

With regard to the Second Submission, Germany argued that Article 36, paragraph 2,[25] of the Convention obligated the U.S. to ensure that its domestic laws and regulations gave full effect to the purposes for which the rights conferred by this provision are intended. Germany contended that the U.S. had breached this obligation by upholding domestic law rules that made it impossible successfully to raise a violation of a right to consular notification after a jury has convicted a defendant. Germany emphasized that it did not question the validity of the U.S. "procedural default" rule as such, but the manner of

---

22 *See id.*, at paras. 73-74. In light of this conclusion, the Court found that it was not necessary for it to deal with Germany's further claim under Article 5 of the Convention.

23 *See id.*, at para. 76.

24 *See id.*, at para. 77. In the light of this conclusion, the Court found that it was not necessary for it to consider Germany's contention that the individual right embodied in Art. 36(1) today has assumed the character of a human right.

25 Art. 36(2) reads:
    "The rights referred to in paragraph 1 of this article shall be exercised in conformity with the laws and regulations of the receiving State, subject to the proviso, however, that the said laws and regulations must enable full effect to be given to the purposes for which the rights accorded under this article are intended."

its application, preventing the LaGrands from effectively raising the violations of their right to consular notification in U.S. criminal proceedings. According to the U.S., the Convention does not obligate states parties to create a national law remedy permitting individuals to assert claims involving the Convention in criminal proceedings; if there is no such obligation, the procedural default rule cannot violate the Convention.[26] The Court rejected the U.S. argument, which was based on the assumption that Article 36, paragraph 2, applies only to the rights of the sending state and not also to those of the detained national. Given that Article 36, paragraph 1, of the Convention creates individual rights in addition to state rights, the reference to "rights" in Article 36, paragraph 2, must be read as applying to both sets of rights. Even though the procedural default rule as such does not violate Article 36, when it does not allow the detained individual to challenge a conviction and sentence by claiming that the receiving state's breach of Article 36, paragraph 1, prevented him from seeking and obtaining consular assistance, the rule has the effect of preventing "full effect [from being] given to the purposes for which the rights accorded under this article are intended" and violates Article 36, paragraph 2, of the Convention.[27]

The Third Submission asked the Court to find that the U.S., through the actions of the U.S. solicitor general,[28] the U.S Supreme Court[29] and the governor of Arizona,[30] had violated its international legal obligation to comply with the Order of March 3, 1999 indicating provisional measures (Order). The parties offered opposing views on the legal obligations flowing from an order indicating provisional measures. Germany contended that the provisional measures indicated by the Order were binding by virtue of the UN Charter (Article 94(1)) and the Court's Statute (Article 41). It also referred to the principle of institutional effectiveness or "*effet utile*" and the procedural pre-

---

26   *See* Judgment, *supra* note 3, at paras. 80-87.
27   *See id*, at paras. 89-91.
28   The Office of the Solicitor General, a section of the U.S. Department of Justice representing the U.S. Government before the U.S. Supreme Court, advised the high court that an order of the ICJ indicating provisional measures is not binding and does not furnish a basis for judicial relief. *See id.*, at paras. 94 and 111-12.
29   The U.S. Supreme Court, which is part of the judicial branch of the U.S., refused to order a preliminary stay of the execution of Walter LaGrand upon Germany's petition to grant such a stay. *See id.*, at paras. 94 and 114.
30   The governor of Arizona, who is part of the executive branch of the U.S., refused to order a stay of the execution of Walter LaGrand, even though the Arizona Executive Board of Clemency had recommended a temporary stay for the first time in its history. *See id.*, at paras. 94 and 113.

requisites for the adoption of provisional measures.[31] The U.S. argued that it had done what was called for by the Order in the light of the extraordinary and unprecedented circumstances in which it was forced to act: there were only a few hours between the issuance of the Order and the time set for the execution of Walter LaGrand and the Government's powers were limited given the character of the U.S. as a federal republic of divided powers. The U.S. maintained that, based on the language and history of Article 41, paragraph 1,[32] of the Statute and Article 94[33] of the UN Charter, the text of the Order, ICJ and state practice, and the literature, orders indicating provisional measures are not capable of creating international legal obligations. The U.S. also complained that basic principles fundamental to the judicial process were not observed in connection with the Order, because of the press of time stemming from Germany's last-minute filing of the case.[34]

After observing that neither it nor its predecessor previously had been called upon to rule expressly on the question of the legal effect of orders indicating provisional measures, which has been the subject of extensive controversy in the literature, the Court proceeded to interpret Article 41 of its Statute in accordance with Article 31 of the 1969 Vienna Convention on the Law of Treaties (the "treaty on treaties"), which reflects customary international law.[35] According to Article 31, paragraph 1, a treaty must be interpreted in good faith in accordance with the ordinary meaning to be given to its terms in their context and in the light of the treaty's object and purpose.[36] Noting that the English and French texts of Article 41 are not in total harmony, the Court pointed out that, based on Article 111 in conjunction with Article 92 of the UN Charter, these texts are equally authentic. Absent guidance from the Charter and the

---

31   *See id.*, at paras. 93-94.
32   Art. 41(1) reads: "The Court shall have the power to indicate, if it considers that circumstances so require, any provisional measures which ought to be taken to preserve the respective rights of either party."
33   Art. 94 reads:
     "1. Each Member of the United Nations undertakes to comply with the decision of the International Court of Justice in any case to which it is a party.
     2. If any party to a case fails to perform the obligations incumbent upon it under a judgment rendered by the Court, the other party may have recourse to the Security Council, which may, if it deems necessary, make recommendations or decide upon measures to be taken to give effect to the judgment."
34   *See* Judgment, *supra* note 3, at paras. 95-97.
35   For the text of the Vienna Convention on the Law of Treaties, *opened for signature* May 23, 1969, *entry into force* January 27, 1980, see 1155 UNTS 331.
36   *See* Judgment, *supra* note 3, at para. 99.

Statute and absent agreement between the parties, the Court turned to Article 33, paragraph 4, of the Vienna Convention, which also reflects customary law. According to this provision, "when a comparison of the authentic texts discloses a difference of meaning which the application of Articles 31 and 32 does not remove, the meaning which best reconciles the texts, having regard to the object and purpose of the treaty, shall be adopted."[37] The Court concluded that the object and purpose of the Statute, which is to enable the Court to fulfill the functions provided for in that document, and especially the basic function of judicial settlement of international disputes by binding decisions in accordance with Article 59 of the Statute, together with the terms of Article 41 read in their context, dictate that provisional measures are binding, inasmuch as the Court's power to indicate such measures is based on the necessity, when the circumstances call for it, to safeguard, and to avoid prejudice to, the rights of the parties as determined by the Court's final judgment.[38] The binding character of such Orders is supported by "the principle universally accepted by international tribunals and likewise laid down in many conventions ... to the effect that the parties to a case must abstain from any measure capable of exercising a prejudicial effect in regard to the execution of the decision to be given, and, in general, not allow any step of any kind to be taken which might aggravate or extend the dispute."[39] The Court pointed out that the preparatory work of the Statute, which it found no need to resort to, and Article 94 of the Charter do not preclude the conclusion that Orders under Article 41 have binding force.[40] The fact that the Court lacks the means to ensure the execution of such Orders is not an argument against the binding nature of such Orders.[41] Based on its review of the steps taken by the U.S. authorities (the Department

---

37   *Id.*, at para. 101. Art. 33 also was featured in Kasikili/Sedudu Island (Botswana/ Namibia) discussed in Chapter 4.

38   *See id.*, at para. 102.

39   *See id.*, at para. 103 (citing Electricity Company of Sofia and Bulgaria (Belg. v. Bulg.), 1939 PCIJ (ser. A/B) No. 79, at 194, 199 (Order of 5 Dec. 1939).).

40   *See id.*, at paras. 104-09. According to the Court, the word "decision" in Art. 94(1) of the Charter could be understood as referring to *any* decision rendered by it, *i.e.*, to both Judgments and Orders indicating provisional measures, thereby confirming the binding nature of such Orders, and also could be interpreted to mean only Judgments rendered by it as provided in Art. 94(2), which still in no way precludes Art. 41 Orders from being accorded binding force under Art. 41 of the Statute. *Id.*, at para. 108.

41   *See id.*, at para. 107.

of State, the solicitor general,[42] the governor of Arizona and the U.S. Supreme Court) following the issuance of the Order,[43] the Court concluded that, given that the various competent authorities had failed to take all steps that they could have taken to give effect to the Order, the U.S. did not comply with the Order.[44] Observing that the Third Submission merely requested a finding that the U.S. violated its international legal obligation to comply with the Order and contained no other request regarding the U.S. breach, the Court stated that, in case Germany had asked for indemnification, it would have taken into account that the U.S. was under great time pressure and that the question of the binding nature of provisional measures orders was unsettled in its jurisprudence and in the literature.[45]

Finally, the Court considered the Fourth Submission, by which Germany sought several assurances: (1) a general demand for an assurance that the U.S. will not repeat its unlawful acts (without specifying the means by which non-repetition is to be assured); (2) an assurance that the U.S. will ensure in law and practice the effective exercise of the rights under Article 36 of the Convention in any future cases of detention of, or criminal proceedings against, German nationals (requiring specific measures as a means of preventing recurrence); and (3) an assurance that the U.S. will provide effective review of, and remedies for, criminal convictions impaired by a violation of the rights under Article 36 in cases involving the death penalty. Germany claimed that these assurances

---

42   By contrast to the solicitor general's advice to the U.S. Supreme Court, the Court reiterated that the March 3 "Order was not a mere exhortation." *Id.*, at para. 110.

43   According to one of the provisional measures indicated in the Order, "[t]he United States of America should take all measures at its disposal to ensure that Walter LaGrand is not executed pending the final decision in these proceedings, and should inform the Court of all the measures which it has taken in implementation of this Order." 1999 ICJ REP. 9, 16, para. 29 (I(*a*)). A letter of March 8, 1999 from the Legal Counsellor of the U.S. Embassy in The Hague informed the Court that the U.S. Department of State had transmitted a copy of the Order to the governor of Arizona without comment on March 3, 1999, but that no further steps had been taken.

44   *See* Judgment, *supra* note 3, at paras. 111-15. The Court indicated that the U.S. could have attached a comment to its transmission of the Order to the governor of Arizona, could have made a plea for a temporary stay of the execution, or could have explained to the competent authorities that there was no general agreement on the U.S. position that ICJ orders on provisional measures are merely hortative and not binding (similar to the position taken by the solicitor general in the case of *Breard v. Greene* before the U.S. Supreme Court in April 1998). *Id.*, at para. 112.

45   *See id.*, at para. 116.

were appropriate in the light of the existence of a real risk of repetition of the acts complained of and the seriousness of Germany's injury, and emphasized that the choice of means to implement the remedy sought was left to the U.S.[46] The U.S. maintained that, by contrast to the character of the relief sought in the first three submissions, which all legitimately sought a Court declaration of the occurrence of a violation of a stated international legal obligation, the assurances of non-repetition sought by Germany in the Fourth Submission had no precedent in the Court's jurisprudence and exceeded the Court's jurisdiction and authority in this case.[47] According to the U.S., it would be inappropriate for the Court to require an absolute assurance as to the application of U.S. domestic law in all future cases, as opposed to the particular case of the La-Grand brothers. The U.S. also pointed out that it had taken substantial measures at the federal, state and local levels aimed at reducing the chances of cases such as the LaGrands' recurring, of which it had informed the Court.[48] Charac-

---

46 *See id.*, at para. 118. Thus, Germany pointed out that appellate proceedings allow for a reversal of the judgment that was impaired by the breach of the right to consular notification and for either a retrial or a re-sentencing.

47 For a comprehensive overview of the concept of guarantees of non-repetition of wrongful acts, a particular form of satisfaction within the law of state responsibility, see the second report on state responsibility by Special Rapporteur Gaetano Arangio-Ruiz, [1989] 2 Y.B. INT'L L. COMM'N 42-47, paras. 148-63, U.N. Doc. A/CN.4/SER.A/1989. *See also* [1990] 1 Y.B. INT'L L. COMM'N 142, paras. 30-33, U.N. Doc. A/CN.4/SER.A/1990.

48 *See* Judgment, *supra* note 3, at para. 119. Such measures include the January 1998 publication and distribution of a booklet entitled "Consular Notification and Access: Instructions for Federal, State and Local Law Enforcement and Other Officials Regarding Foreign Nationals in the United States and the Rights of Consular Officers to Assist Them" and a pocket card designed to be carried by individual enforcement and judicial officers, as well as training programs and the creation of a special office within the U.S. Department of State. *See id.*, at para. 121. For the text, see Marian Nash (Leich), *Contemporary Practice of the United States Relating to International Law*, 92 AJIL 243 (1998). The duty of consular notification under the Convention that is referenced in these materials may be considered the "international supplement" to the so-called "Miranda Warnings" in U.S. criminal procedure. *See* Hofheinz, *Death-Row Cases Of Foreigners Aided by Ruling*, Wall St. J., Aug. 30, 2001, at B1, B4 ("the World Court may have created an extension of the U.S.'s famous Miranda rights of the accused to obtain counsel. This time the right is reserved for foreigners"). The Miranda Warnings, which seek to protect the U.S. Constitution's fifth amendment privilege against compelled self-incrimination, must be given by U.S. enforcement officers, lest any statement made by a during custodial interrogation be inadmissible in court. According to the Miranda Warnings, a person in custody must, prior to interrogation, be clearly informed that:

terizing such measures as inadequate, Germany claimed that an effective remedy required certain changes in U.S. law and practice.[49]

Noting that the U.S. had acknowledged that it had not complied with its obligations to provide consular notification in the case of the LaGrand brothers and that it had presented an apology to Germany for its breach, the Court considered nevertheless that an apology was insufficient in this particular case. In the Court's view, given that no assurance could be given that there never again will be a failure by the U.S. to observe the notification obligation under Article 36 of the Convention and that Germany did not seek such a guarantee or any material reparation, the U.S.' repeated reference to the remedial measures taken by it expressed a commitment to follow through with the implementation of the specific measures devised by it in performance of its obligations under Article 36(1)(b). Thus, the commitment expressed by the U.S., of which the Court took official note, must be regarded as meeting Germany's request for a general assurance of non-repetition.[50]

As for the other assurances sought by Germany, the Court pointed out that it had not found that a U.S. law, whether of a substantive or procedural nature, was inherently inconsistent with the obligations undertaken by the U.S. in the Convention. The U.S. breach of Article 36, paragraph 2, of the Convention "was caused by the circumstances in which the procedural default rule was applied, and not by the rule as such."[51] However, if the U.S. should fail in its obligation of consular notification to the detriment of German nationals notwithstanding the U.S. commitment referred to above, an apology would be insufficient in cases where the individuals concerned have been subjected to prolonged detention or convicted and sentenced to severe penalties. In such cases, the U.S. must allow the review and reconsideration of the conviction and sentence by taking account of the violation of the rights set forth in the

---

(1) such person has the right to remain silent; (2) anything such person says can be used against she or him in a court of law; (3) such person has the right to the presence of an attorney; and (4) if such person cannot afford an attorney, one will be appointed for such person if she or he so desires. The Miranda Warnings were the outcome of the landmark ruling that the U.S. Supreme Court issued in 1966 in *Miranda v. Arizona. See* 86 S.Ct. 1602, 384 U.S. 436. Just like its "international supplement," the Miranda Warnings rose to prominence from a case involving the state of Arizona.

49   *See* Judgment, *supra* note 3, at para. 122.
50   *See id.*, at paras. 123-24, 127.
51   *Id.*, at para. 125.

Convention. The Court pointed out that this obligation can be carried out in various ways and it left the choice of means to the U.S.

* * * *

This is a landmark decision of the Court, especially in the light of its express ruling on the binding nature of orders indicating provisional measures, the first in its history.[52] After a similar case between Paraguay and the United States was discontinued in November 1998 before it reached the merits phase,[53] Germany is to be commended for pursuing its case (despite the execution of the LaGrand brothers by the U.S.) and for including the question of the legal consequences of a breach of an order indicating provisional measures in its final submissions. Such a ruling was long overdue. It will enhance the respect of litigants *vis-à-vis* the Court and may even make potential litigants consider using the Court in cases where they have a viable alternative. For example, the International Tribunal for the Law of the Sea in Hamburg offers litigants the possibility of obtaining provisional measures which Article 290, paragraph 6, of the Convention on the Law of the Sea provides must be complied with promptly. Prior to the present decision, litigants in certain law of the sea cases falling within the jurisdiction of both the Tribunal and the ICJ might have preferred the clarity of Article 290, paragraph 6, over the uncertainty that used to surround Article 41 of the ICJ Statute. As the ICJ president remarked in the aftermath of the Court's decision, "[t]he Court anticipates that in future [provisional] measures will as a result [of the Court's explicit holding] be better executed than when the matter was subject to doubt," expressing the hope "that the Court's contribution to the maintenance of international peace and security will thereby be enhanced."[54]

The Court made its landmark ruling over the objection of its senior Member and the respondent, whose delegation before the Court included the Court's leading commentator, who is on record for supporting the binding nature of

---

52 As Judge Oda points out in his dissenting opinion (para. 29), the Judgment dedicates as many as 25 paragraphs to the question of the binding nature of provisional measures orders.

53 *See* Vienna Convention on Consular Relations (Par. v. U.S.), Order (discontinuance), 1998 ICJ REP. 426 (Nov. 10).

54 Address by the President of the International Court of Justice, Judge Gilbert Guillaume, to the United Nations General Assembly, Oct. 30, 2001, text available from the ICJ Web site, <www.icj-cij.org/icjwww/ipresscom/SPEECHES>.

provisional measures orders.[55] But perhaps even more remarkable is the extra-ordinary statement of the Court's senior Judge that he regrets having voted in favor of the unanimous Order of March 3, 1999, which he admits was done against his judicial conscience.[56]

The American Member of the Court, Judge Buergenthal, voted in favor of all of the Court's rulings in this case, with the exception of the one that upheld the admissibility of Germany's Third Submission relating to the March 3, 1999 Order. He did so, not out of a conviction that orders indicating pro-visional measures are non-binding, but because in his view Germany was to be faulted for its litigation strategy, including by having waited until the last minute to seek the Order, which was issued by the Court *ex parte* without the prior hearing provided for in Article 74, paragraph 3, of the Rules of Court and without an exchange of pleadings.[57] It is not clear what prompted Judge Buergenthal to vote in favor of operative paragraph (5) of the *dispositif* (holding that the U.S. breached the March 3 Order), having voted against operative paragraph (2)(c) (upholding the admissibility of the Third Admission, the merits of which operative paragraph (5) addresses). Normally, if a submission is held to be inadmissible, it does not meet with a positive ruling on the merits of that submission. Although his dissenting opinion does not discuss the question of the binding nature of orders indicating provisional measures, it may be inferred from his positive vote on operative paragraph (5) that he agrees with the

---

55 *See* SHABTAI ROSENNE, 1 THE LAW AND PRACTICE OF THE INTERNATIONAL COURT, 1920-1996, at 215-16 (3rd ed., 1997). Interestingly, the section on provisional measures in Rosenne's book does not take a position on this question. *See id.*, at 1419 *et seq.*

56 *See* dissenting opinion of Judge Oda, at para. 15.

57 *See* dissenting opinion of Judge Buergenthal, at paras. 5 and 7. Judge Buergenthal's reference to "an exchange of pleadings" is puzzling, as the Court's governing documents and practice do not provide for the exchange of pleadings in connection with a request for the indication of provisional measures. According to the American Judge, Germany's lack of diligence in ascertaining the facts which it advanced to justify the late filing of its request deprived the U.S. of an opportunity to be heard on the request and left the Court with little choice but to accept on face value Germany's claim of its lack of knowledge, until late February 1999, about the fact that the Arizona authorities knew as far back as 1984 that the LaGrand brothers were German nationals. Although he did not disagree with the Court's Order of March 3, 2001, he faulted Germany for having seriously jeopardized the principle of procedural fairness and the sound administration of justice, which, in the light of subsequent revelations and Germany's litigation strategy, in his view amounted to misconduct prejudicial to the interests of the U.S. and compelled a finding that the Third Submission was inadmissible. *Id.*, at paras. 12-24.

majority that such orders create binding legal obligations that can be breached and result in state responsibility.

It is interesting to review the comments made by Keith Highet and Stephen Schwebel as part of an ICJ panel discussion, which are reproduced at the end of Chapter 4 of this book, in the light of the Court's ruling. In his remarks, Keith Highet made a strong plea for the binding effect of provisional measures orders, stating that "the Court really should bite the bullet and say in a judgment of some kind that provisional measures are more than hortatory." In his view, this question "relates to whether or not States are prepared to take the Court seriously." Judge Schwebel, who had just retired from the Court, was much more cautious and believed that it was inconceivable that the Court could reach a unanimous decision on this question. In the end, the 13-2 decision that the U.S. breached the obligation incumbent upon it under the March 3, 1999 Order was close enough to prove the retired president wrong.[58]

The Court's decision was handed down at a time when the issue of capital punishment and U.S. adherence to international bodies and agreements is highly contentious between the U.S. and Europe, Germany being one of the strongest opponents of the death penalty.[59] All member states of the European Union

---

58 As a matter of fact, neither of the two Judges who voted against this portion of the *dispositif* expressly stated his opposition to the binding nature of Orders indicating provisional measures. Judge Oda merely refused to accept the specific arguments in favor of the binding nature of such Orders used by the majority and gave expression to his view that "the question as to whether or not the Order of 3 March 1999 indicating provisional measures was complied with should never have been raised," such question bearing no relation to a case concerning alleged U.S. violations of the Vienna Convention on Consular Relations. Nonetheless, he believed that the U.S. complied with the Order. *See* dissenting opinion of Judge Oda, at para. 35. Judge Parra-Aranguren explained that he voted against this particular operative paragraph because of his belief that the Court lacked jurisdiction to decide Germany's Third Submission. *See* separate opinion of Judge Parra-Aranguren, at para. 15.

59 *See also* Int'l Herald Tribune, June 28, 2001, at 1 ("Wading into two of the most emotional trans-Atlantic issues – the death penalty in America and the extent of the United States' willingness to bow to international bodies – the 15-member World Court, the popular name for the court, effectively sought to stake a claim to some influence over the American legal system."). In his opening statement at the hearing of November 13, 2000, the Agent of Germany remarked that Germany's "Application [was not] directed against the practice of capital punishment as such, even though its consequences clearly have a significant impact on the legal matters we are dealing with today." ICJ Doc. CR 2000/26, at 7, para. 2. He further emphasized: "[T]he present case is not about the death penalty in general or its application in

have abolished the death penalty. Closer to home, the U.S. has been faced with opposition on this issue from Canada and Mexico. Just two days before the ICJ issued its Judgment, the governor of Oklahoma issued a 30-day stay of execution for a Mexican national, Geraldo Valdez, who was set to die by lethal injection the following day, reportedly after being advised by the U.S. Department of State that U.S. authorities had failed to inform Valdez of his rights to consular assistance under the Convention.[60] At the hearings, Germany alleged that 14 foreign nationals have been executed in the U.S. since 1993 and that in 11 of these cases violations of Article 36 were asserted.[61] It remains to be seen how U.S. courts, being part of a dualist system,[62] will treat this decision when faced with a U.S. violation of the Convention: as one U.S. commentator has pointed out, the Court's finding that Article 36(1)(b) of the Convention confers individual rights does not automatically mean that individuals in future cases can assert such rights in a U.S. court, even though a U.S. court might consider the ICJ ruling a persuasive interpretation of Article 36(1)(b) that "could tip the scales in favor of enforceable individual rights in a future domestic case."[63]

In his declaration appended to the Judgment, President Guillaume stressed that the Court's finding that the U.S., by means of its choosing, must allow the review and reconsideration of the conviction and sentence to severe penalties of German nationals whose rights under Article 36(1)(b) of the Convention have been violated, must not be made subject to an *a contrario* interpretation:

---

any particular country. However, Germany's stance on capital punishment is clear: together with its EU partners, Germany has for many years been working towards its abolition worldwide." He acknowledged, however, that there is no obligation to abolish the death penalty under international law. *Id.*, at paras. 6-7. Notwithstanding Germany's statements, as Judge Oda points out in his dissenting opinion, "[i]t is unlikely that any human rights group in Germany ever thought that this case involved the Vienna Convention on Consular Relations." Dissenting opinion of Judge Oda, at para. 9.

60   *See* a report dated June 18, 2001 from KOTV Channel 6, *available in* <http://kotv.com/pages/viewpage.asp?id=20370>. *See also* Hofheinz, *Death-Row Cases Of Foreigners Aided by Ruling*, Wall St. J., Aug. 30, 2001, at B1, B4.

61   *See* ICJ Doc. CR 2000/26, at 9, para. 15 (Agent of Germany).

62   *See* OPPENHEIM'S INTERNATIONAL LAW, Vol. I, at 53 *et seq.* (R. Jennings & A. Watts eds., 9th ed. 1996).

63   Frederic L. Kirgis, *World Court Rules Against the United States in LaGrand Case Arising from a Violation of the Vienna Convention on Consular Relations*, text available from the Web site of The American Society of International Law, <www.asil.org/insights>.

it applies only to the obligations of the U.S. in cases of severe penalties imposed upon German nationals. In other words, the Court's ruling does not apply to cases where the penalties imposed are less than "severe" and it has no bearing on cases of severe penalties imposed on non-German nationals.[64] However, Germany did not demand automatic reversal of all U.S. convictions impaired by a violation of Article 36, and it could not have done so: pursuant to Article 59 of the ICJ Statute, which was not mentioned in the president's declaration, the Court's decision in any event "has no binding force except between the parties and in respect of that particular case." It is safe to say, however, that this Judgment, which attracted considerable attention from the world media, will enhance the application of the Convention, at least in the U.S., and contribute to the protection of the rights of detained individuals the world over.

In the same context, Germany's statement that it was bringing these proceedings "not only for the sake of the citizens of [Germany and the U.S.], but for the benefit of human beings worldwide"[65] was misleading: besides the undeniable effect of Article 59 of the Statute referred to above, there is no *actio populais* before the ICJ and the Court did not find it necessary in the present case to address the question of whether the right to consular notification is a human right, as advocated by Germany.[66] In this respect, the U.S. may be

---

64 Although he voted in favor of the Court's holding, Judge Koroma expressed his belief that "everyone, irrespective of nationality, is entitled to the benefit of fundamental judicial guarantees, including the right of appeal or review against conviction and sentence, irrespective of nationality." Separate opinion of Judge Koroma, at para. 8.

65 *See* ICJ Doc. CR 2000/26, at 8, para. 9 (Agent of Germany).

66 In the *South West Africa* cases, the Court stated that contemporary international law does not recognize "the equivalent of an '*actio populais*,' or right resident in any member of a community to take legal action in vindication of a public interest." South West Africa (Eth. v. S. Afr.; Lib. v. S. Afr.), Second Phase, Judgment, 1966 ICJ REP. 6, 47, para. 88 (July 18). In another decision handed down four years later, the Court pointed out that a fundamental distinction should be made between, on the one hand, the obligations of a state arising *vis-à-vis* another state and, on the other hand, the obligations of a state towards the international community as a whole, which by their very nature and importance are the concern of all states, who can be held to have a legal interest in their protection. The latter obligations are truly obligations *erga omnes*. The Court mentioned aggression, genocide, slavery and racial discrimination as examples. *See* Barcelona Traction, Light and Power Company Limited (Bel. v. Sp.), Second Phase, Judgment, 1970 ICJ REP. 3, 32, paras. 33-34 (Feb. 5). Although the Court referred to "the basic rights of the human person" in its 1970 decision, the concept of a human right to

said to have scored a minor victory, in that the Court refused to address Germany's contention that the individual rights provided for by Article 36 of the Convention rise to the level of human rights. In its opposition to the issue of individual rights in relation to the Convention, the U.S. found itself in the odd company of the Chinese Judge.[67]

This decision no doubt also will be cited in the future for its discussion of the legal consequences of an apology within the context of the law of state responsibility, of which not many examples may be found in international case law.[68]

Finally, a word about the length of these proceedings. On the opening day of the hearings, Germany gave expression to "its satisfaction with the decision of the United States not to raise any preliminary objections. This fact demonstrates that both Parties do concur in the objective of having the present dispute settled as expeditiously as possible."[69] Germany did not know at that time that the U.S. would introduce a plethora of objections to the Court's jurisdiction and the admissibility of Germany's Application during the hearings, while the U.S. complained at the same time that "basic principles fundamental to the judicial process were not observed in connection with the Court's 3 March Order."[70] The Court did not sanction the U.S. for its questionable strategy and, as a consequence, 28 paragraphs of the 128-paragraph decision are devoted

---

consular notification was not addressed in the present decision.

67   *See* separate opinion of Vice President Shi, at para. 8 ("it is clear, as the United States has contended, that the *travaux préparatoires* of the 1963 Vienna Convention on Consular Relations [to which the Court did not refer in its interpretation] do not confirm that Article 36, paragraph 1(*b*), is intended to create individual rights."). The views expressed by the Vice President, who served as Legal Adviser to the Chinese Ministry of Foreign Affairs prior to his election to the Court, are in conformity with the traditional Chinese view on individual rights under international law.

68   *See* [1990] 1 Y.B. INT'L L. COMM'N 179, para. 26, 183, para. 56, U.N. Doc. A/CN.4/SER.A/1990. *See also* the second report on state responsibility by Special Rapporteur Gaetano Arangio-Ruiz, [1989] 2 Y.B. INT'L L. COMM'N 31-42, paras. 106-47, U.N. Doc. A/CN.4/SER.A/1989 (offering a comprehensive overview of international jurisprudence and diplomatic practice relating to satisfaction, a form of reparation for an internationally wrongful act that is different from *restitutio in integrum* or pecuniary compensation).

69   *See* ICJ Doc. CR 2000/26, at 17, para. 2 (Mr. Kahn).

70   Judgment, *supra* note 3, at para. 97.

to the U.S. objections, with only 64 paragraphs addressing the merits.[71] More-over, the Court itself cannot be said to have settled this dispute "as expeditious-ly as possible," after taking more than seven months from the close of the hearings to announce its decision. Still, the case was decided on the merits within 28 months from its filing, making it one of the shortest ever, following immediately after the Court's ruling on the longest-ever proceedings.

---

71   In his dissenting opinion, Judge Oda charges the U.S. with having made an error by not raising preliminary objections, notwithstanding the statement in its Counter-Memorial that all of Germany's claims other than the alleged breach of Art. 36(1)(b) of the Convention should be dismissed. *See* dissenting opinion of Judge Oda, at paras. 11-12.

Application by the Philippines to intervene as nonparty in case notified by Special Agreement – examination of parties' objections relying on conditions deriving from Article 62 of Statute, Article 81 of Rules of Court and ICJ jurisprudence – timeliness of filing an intervention request – meaning of "interest of a legal nature which may be affected by the decision" – legal interest not necessarily limited to dispositif *– burden of proof when request does not concern actual subject-matter of dispute – precise object of intervention – jurisdictional link not required for nonparty intervention*

SOVEREIGNTY OVER PULAU LIGITAN AND PULAU SIPADAN
(Indonesia/Malaysia)

Application for permission to intervene, Judgment
Obtainable from <www.icj-cij.org>
International Court of Justice, October 23, 2001

On March 13, 2001, the Government of the Republic of the Philippines (the Philippines) filed an application for permission to intervene as a nonparty in the case brought by Indonesia and Malaysia through the notification of a Special Agreement on November 2, 1998, concerning their territorial dispute over two islands located in the Celebes Sea off the east coast of North Borneo, or the state of Sabah, as it is known today. The application relied on Article 62 of the Court's Statute, which permits a third state to submit a request to the Court to be permitted to intervene in a case if that state considers "that it has an interest of a legal nature which may be affected by the decision in the case."[1]

The Philippines' Application stated that its object was, first, "to preserve and safeguard the historical and legal rights of the Government of the Republic of the Philippines arising from its claim to dominion and sovereignty over the

---

[1]   Article 81 of the Rules of Court requires that an application for permission to intervene (*a*) set out the interest of a legal nature which the state applying to intervene considers may be affected by the decision in the case; (*b*) describe the precise object of the intervention; and (*c*) set out any basis of jurisdiction which is claimed to exist as between the state applying to intervene and the parties to the case. It must also state the name of the agent and contain a list of the documents in support of the application.

P.H.F. Bekker, World Court Decisions at the Turn of the Millennium (1997-2001), p. 335-349.
© 2002 *Kluwer Law International. Printed in the Netherlands.*

territory of North Borneo, to the extent that these rights are affected, or may be affected, by a determination of the Court of the question of sovereignty over Pulau Ligitan and Pulau Sipadan," and, second, "to inform the Honourable Court of the nature and extent of the historical and legal rights of the Republic of the Philippines which may be affected by the Court's decision." The Philippines made clear that it was not asking the Court to determine the issue of North Borneo and that it had no territorial claim with respect to the two islands that form the subject-matter of the dispute between Indonesia and Malaysia, in the outcome of which the Philippines was not interested.

Indonesia and Malaysia both opposed the Philippines' Application on the grounds that it did not meet the various requirements. They argued that the intervention request was made untimely and lacked any documentary or other supporting evidence and that the Philippines had failed to establish that it has an interest of a legal nature that may be affected by the Court's decision on the merits of this case. Hearings on the request were held at the Peace Palace on June 25-26 and 28-29, 2001.

On October 23, 2001, the Court delivered its Judgment finding, by 14 votes to one, that the Philippines' Application for permission to intervene in the case brought by Indonesia and Malaysia could not be granted.[2]

First, Indonesia argued, and Malaysia agreed, that the Philippines' request should be dismissed as being untimely. Article 81, paragraph 1, of the Rules requires that a request for intervention be filed "as soon as possible and not later than the closure of the written proceedings."[3] Indonesia complained that, even though the Special Agreement by which the parties had submitted the case on November 2, 1998 was a public document of which the Philippines must have been aware, the Philippines had never intimated that it had any

---

2   Judgment of October 23, 2001, text available from the Court's Web site at <www.icj-cij.org> [hereinafter Judgment]. The Court's senior Member, Judge Oda voted against the majority's holding and appended a dissenting opinion to the Judgment.

3   Indonesia pointed out that the 1978 version of the Rules of Court incorporates an important amendment from the previous 1972 version in that the former replaced the words "before the commencement of the oral proceedings" with "as soon as possible, and not later than the closure of the written proceedings" in Article 81. In Indonesia's view, this indicates that the current version of the Rules was designed to place a more restrictive time limit on a party wishing to intervene than previously was the case. *See* ICJ Doc. CR 2001/2, at 23 (Mr. Bundy). However, counsel for Indonesia failed to mention that Article 81 also explicitly provides for the Court's admission of a request submitted "at a later stage" in the event of "exceptional circumstances."

interest of a legal nature that could be affected by a decision in the case until it filed its application on March 13, 2001, 11 days after Indonesia and Malaysia had completed their third round of written pleadings through the filing of replies. In Indonesia's view, the application did not comport with the letter or spirit of the Rules of Court and the Court's recent trend to encourage the expedition of proceedings. The Philippines argued that there is no point to asking for documents before they are submitted, so that the proper time was when the bulk of the written submissions were made by the parties.[4] In any event, the so-called Manila Accord, signed on July 31, 1963 by Indonesia, Malaysia and the Philippines, had taken official note "of the Philippine claim [to the territory known as British North Borneo] and the right of the Philippines to continue to pursue it in accordance with international law and the principle of the pacific settlement of disputes,' with the parties agreeing "to bring the claim to a just and expeditious solution by peaceful means, such as negotiation, conciliation, arbitration or judicial settlement as well as other peaceful means of the parties' own choice."[5] The parties, in particular Malaysia and the Philippines, subsequently failed to reach agreement on the submission of the issue of sovereignty over North Borneo to the Court. The Philippines argued that its internationally recognized claim, acknowledged by the parties to the Manila Accord, should suffice for purposes of Article 62.[6]

Addressing this objection *ratione temporis* first, the Court noted that, in the circumstances, "the time chosen for the filing of the Application by the

---

4   Counsel for the Philippines stated during the initial hearing that "[w]hen it was clear that [the Philippines' request to be provided with the pleadings and documents submitted by the parties under Art. 53 of the Rules of Court] was rejected, the Philippines only at that point asked for right of intervention." ICJ Doc. CR 2001/1, at 18, para. 42 (Mr. Reisman). The inaccuracy of this statement is borne out by the facts: by the Philippines' own admission, the intervention request was filed on March 13, 2001, whereas the Court did not deny the Art. 53 request, which was filed on February 22, 2001 and reiterated on March 9, 2001, until March 15, 2001. *See id.*, at 10, para. 7 (Mr. Bello).
5   ICJ Doc. CR 2001/1, at 9, para. 4.
6   The Philippines was conquered by Spain in 1571. It was ceded to the United States by Spain under the Treaty of Paris as part of the settlement of the Spanish-American war of 1898. Indonesia, which is situated between Malaysia and the Philippines and ranks as the fourth most populous country in the world, became known as the Netherlands East Indies after having been conquered by the United Dutch East India Company in 1605. The Dutch colonial regime, except for a short interruption during the 19th century and Japanese occupation during World War II, lasted over 400 years until Indonesia gained independence on August 17, 1945. Malaysia is the successor-in-interest to Great Britain.

Philippines can hardly be seen as meeting the requirements that it be filed 'as soon as possible' as contemplated in Article 81, paragraph 1, of the Rules of Court."[7] This requirement is "essential for an orderly and expeditious progress of the procedure before the Court" and the sound administration of justice demands that an intervention request be submitted in good time.[8] Moreover, there is nothing in the Rules of Court or the Court's practice to support the Philippines' view that there exists an inextricable link between a request for access to the pleadings of the parties under Article 53 of the Statute and one for permission to intervene under Article 62, or that the requirement of the timeliness of the intervention request may be made conditional on whether or not the state seeking to intervene is granted access to the pleadings and documents annexed filed by the parties.[9] Notwithstanding these irregularities, the Philippines could not be held to be in violation of the specific deadline prescribed by Article 81 of the Rules of Court, which calls for the filing of a request for permission to intervene "not later than the closure of the written proceedings." The Court pointed out that neither it nor third states could know on the date of the filing of the Philippine Application whether the written proceedings had come to a definitive end.[10] Thus, the Application was not filed out of time.

In reply to Indonesia's objection that the Philippine Application failed to "contain a list of documents in support, which documents shall be attached" as prescribed by Article 81, paragraph 3, of the Rules of Court, the Philippines explained that it was unable to attach a list of documents in support of its Application, given that the Court on March 15, 2001 had denied its February 22, 2001 request to be given access to the pleadings and documents filed by

---

7   Judgment, at para. 21.
8   *Id.* (citing LaGrand Case (Ger. v. U.S.), Provisional Measures, Order, 1999 ICJ Rep. 9, at 14, para. 19 (Mar. 3)).
9   *Id.*, at para. 22.
10 *Id*, at paras. 23-25 (citing Land, Island and Maritime Frontier Dispute (El Salvador/ Honduras), Application by Nicaragua for permission to intervene, Judgment, 1990 ICJ REP. 92, at 98, para. 12 (Sept. 13) and Continental Shelf (Tunisia/Libyan Arab Jamahiriya), Application by Malta for permission to intervene, Judgment, 1981 ICJ REP. 3, at 6, para. 5 (Apr. 14)). Even though the Special Agreement between Indonesia and Malaysia provided for the possibility of a fourth round of written pleadings in the form of rejoinders, the parties notified the Court on March 28, 2001 that they had agreed that the written pleadings had come to an end with the filing of replies on March 2, 2001. Although this still left open the possibility of the Court prescribing the presentation of rejoinders *ex officio*, as it did in the case between Qatar and Bahrain, the Court refrained from doing so in this case.

Indonesia and Malaysia under Article 53 of the Rules of Court. In any event, Indonesia's objection did not concern the question of the admissibility of the application, but rather that of evidence.

Dismissing the Indonesian objection, the Court observed that Article 81 of the Rules does not require the state seeking to intervene to attach any supporting documents to its application and that it is only where such documents have in fact been attached that a list thereof must be included.[11]

Malaysia also objected to the Philippine Application based on the absence of a jurisdictional link. Although the Philippines acknowledged that there was no basis of jurisdiction in relation to Indonesia and Malaysia, it pointed out that it did not seek to become a party to the case before the Court and that it was not requesting the Court's determination of the sovereignty issue over North Borneo. The Court agreed with the Philippines and referred to earlier precedents holding that the existence of a valid link of jurisdiction between the potential intervening state and the parties is not a requirement for the success of an application to intervene if the would-be intervener is not desirous of itself becoming a party to the case; the procedure of intervention is to ensure that a state with possibly affected interests may be permitted to intervene even though there is no jurisdictional link and for that reason cannot become a party.[12]

The Court next addressed the argument of Indonesia and Malaysia that the Philippines had failed to establish the existence of an "interest of a legal nature" justifying the intervention sought.

The Philippines pointed out that this was an unusual intervention case in that the legal interest involved was not graphic or manifest on the face of the record, but was contingent on further information and specifications and,

---

11 *Id.*, at paras. 27-29. The problem with the Court's approach is that Art. 81, para 3, does not state that the application "shall contain a list of *any* documents in support" or "shall contain a list of the documents, *if any*, in support," but stipulates unambiguously that it "shall contain a list of *the* documents in support," indicating that such documents must, in each case and in fact, be attached. (Emphasis added). The Court found support for its approach in Art. 50, para. 3, of the Rules, governing evidence annexed to a written pleading, and in the consideration that the choice of means whereby the state wishing to intervene seeks to prove its assertions lies in that state's sole discretion. *Id.*, at para. 29.

12 *Id.*, at para. 35 (citing Land, Island and Maritime Frontier Dispute (El Salvador/ Honduras), Application by Nicaragua for permission to intervene, Judgment, 1990 ICJ REP. 92, at 135, paras. 99-100 (Sept. 13) and Land and Maritime Boundary between Cameroon and Nigeria (Cam. v. Nig.), Application by Equatorial Guinea to intervene, Order, 1999 ICJ REP. 1034, para. 15 (Oct. 21)).

therefore, speculative. It complained that, without access to the parties' written pleadings and documents annexed, it could not determine with probability that its interest may be affected by the Court's decision in the case. In this sense, the case was different from a maritime boundary delimitation case (which had triggered previous Article 62 requests), where a third state can more readily determine where prospective delimitations may affect such state's legal interests. It pointed out that its Application might well have been obviated if access to pleadings and documents had not been opposed by the parties under Article 53.[13]

The Philippines explained that the precise object of its Application was to prevent the Court, which had not been informed by the parties to the Special Agreement of the Philippines' claim of sovereignty to territories in North Borneo, from interpreting any treaties, agreements and other documentary evidence relevant to the Philippines' interest in North Borneo on which Indonesia and/or Malaysia might rely in order to sustain a claim to Ligitan and Sipadan in ways that could be prejudicial to the interest of the Philippines.[14] The Philippines' long-standing claim to territory in North Borneo might be implicated by the Court's interpretation of treaties invoked by Indonesia and/or Malaysia. Certain treaties and other agreements may have a direct bearing, not only on the issue of sovereignty over Pulau Ligitan and Pulau Sipadan, but also on the legal status of North Borneo and islands off the coast of North Borneo.[15] For example, if Malaysia's argument for the

---

13   *See* ICJ Doc. CR 2001/3, at 10, para. 16 (Mr. Reisman). The Court simply observed that "the Philippines must have full knowledge of the documentary sources relevant to its claim of sovereignty in North Borneo" and that its lack of access to the parties' pleadings "did not prevent the Philippines from explaining its own claim, and from explaining in what respect any interpretation of particular instruments might affect that claim." Judgment, at para. 63. In other words, in the Court's view there is no correlation between the confidentiality of written pleadings under Art. 53 of the Rules of Court and intervention requests under Article 62 of the Statute.

14   The Special Agreement requested the Court to "determine on the basis of the treaties, agreements and any other evidence furnished by the Parties, whether sovereignty over Pulau Ligitan and Pulau Sipadan belongs to the Republic of Indonesia or to Malaysia." Judgment, at para. 1.

15   The Philippines referred, *inter alia*, to a 1930 Convention regarding the boundary between the Philippine Archipelago and North Borneo concluded by the United States and Great Britain, an 1891 Convention between Great Britain and The Netherlands defining the boundaries in North Borneo, an 1885 Protocol among Great Britain, Germany and Spain, two agreements between two Western businessmen and the Sultans of Brunei and Sulu, respectively, establishing leases to several

islands imports a chain of title that is inconsistent with the claim of title on which the Philippines bases its claim to territories in North Borneo, that interpretation will affect interests of a legal nature. In the event that the Court subsequently is seised of the Philippine claim to North Borneo, the Court cannot deal with that claim if it has already decided it in the present case in the absence of the Philippines.

In the Philippines' view, the contingency for the application of Article 62 is the *subjective* appreciation of the intervening state that it has an interest[16] and the Court's task is to determine whether the intervention would assist it in understanding the implications for a third state of certain possible decisions the Court might take in the case at bar. All that the intervening state must demonstrate, at the threshold, is that the interest is one "of a legal nature," in addition to showing in what way it may be affected.

Malaysia claimed that the Philippines was abusing Article 62 in order to introduce a completely different dispute before the Court, which raises against Malaysia the issue of sovereignty over the whole of the territory of Sabah, one of Malaysia's 13 states situated in North Borneo.[17] In its view, this issue is wholly separate from Indonesia's claim to Ligitan and Sipadan and the territorial titles are different in the two cases. Malaysia also claimed that "the interest of a legal nature must, if affected, be so affected by the *decision* of the Court and not just by its *reasoning*."[18] In what appears to be an ominous warning,

---

territories in North Borneo in 1877-1878, a 1903 agreement between the Sultan of Sulu and the British North Borneo Company formed by one of the businessmen, and a 1907 exchange of notes between Great Britain and the United States. Even though Malaysia acknowledged, during the hearing on June 26, 2001, that Indonesia's claim to Ligitan and Sipadan is based on the 1891 Convention between Great Britain and The Netherlands, it argued that this treaty is irrelevant to the Philippines' claim. *See* ICJ Doc. CR 2001/2, at 26, paras. 7 and 10 (Mr. Mohamad). *See also* Judgment, at paras. 71-73.

16 According to the Philippines, "[t]he criteria are not to *prove* a legal or lawful interest, but to 'identify the interest of a legal nature' and 'to show in what way [it] may be affected." Judgment, at para. 40. Art. 62, para. 2, of the ICJ Statute makes quite clear that "[i]t shall be for the Court to decide upon this request."

17 As the Chamber formed to deal with *Land, Island and Maritime Frontier Dispute* pointed out, intervention under Article 62 of the Statute "is not intended to enable a third State to tack on a new case ... An incidental proceeding cannot be one which transforms [a] case into a different case with different parties." Land, Island and Maritime Frontier Dispute (El Salvador/Honduras), Application by Nicaragua for permission to intervene, Judgment, 1990 ICJ REP. 92, at 133-34, paras. 97-98 (Sept. 13) (cited in Judgment, at para. 35).

18 *See* Judgment, at para. 43.

Malaysia's Agent reminded the Court that this case involves the first joint submission of a dispute by two South-East Asian countries and that:

> [i]ndeed, it is fair to say that there has been as yet hardly any tradition in Asia of solving territorial disputes by judicial means, such as resort to your honourable Court. The present case, which Malaysia and Indonesia have mutually agreed to bring to this Court, is almost the first example -certainly the first example in more than 40 years. Mr. President, permit me to express the hope that Malaysia and Indonesia will be allowed to deal with their bilateral dispute without the distraction of a third party making a claim to a much larger territory, a claim which expressly excludes the two islands which are in dispute between the Parties.[19]

Indonesia, for which these proceedings marked the first appearance before the Court,[20] also pointed out that it received a Note Verbale from the Philippine Embassy in Jakarta on April 5, 2001, whereby the Philippines expressly stated that it does not have any territorial interest with respect to either Ligitan or Sipadan Island. In its view, a determination by the Court of the issue of sovereignty over Ligitan and Sipadan as between Indonesia and Malaysia neither depended on, nor would have implications for, the Philippines' territorial claim to North Borneo.

The Court considered that it was faced with the following question: May a third state intervene under Article 62 of the Statute in a dispute brought to the Court under a special agreement, when the state seeking to intervene has no interest in the subject-matter of that dispute as such, but rather asserts an interest of a legal nature in such findings and reasonings that the Court might make on certain specific treaties that the state seeking to intervene claims to be in issue in a different dispute between itself and one of the two parties to the pending case before the Court?[21] The Court found that the words "affected by the decision in the case" in Article 62 must be read in a broad sense, so that the interest of a legal nature to be shown by a state seeking to intervene is not limited to the *dispositif* alone of a judgment, as Malaysia argued, but may also relate to the reasons that constitute the necessary steps to the *dispositif*

---

19 ICJ Doc. CR 2001/2, at 28, para. 19 (Mr. Mohamad).

20 Indonesia played a prominent role in the case concerning East Timor (Port. v. Austl.), which the Court dismissed in its Judgment of June 30, 1995 citing the absence of Indonesia as a necessary third party to the proceedings. *See* 1995 ICJ REP. 90 (June 30); Peter H.F. Bekker, Case Report: East Timor (Port. v. Austl.), 90 AJIL 94 (1996).

21 *See* Judgment, at para. 46.

or holding in the case.[22] As for the burden of proof, the Court confirmed that "it is for a State seeking to intervene to demonstrate convincingly what it asserts."[23] Not only must the applicant identify the interest of a legal nature which it considers may be affected by the decision in the case, it must also show in what way that interest may be affected. Where a state relies on an interest of a legal nature other than in the subject-matter of the case itself, it must show with a particular clarity the existence of the interest of a legal nature which it claims to have.[24] In the case of the Philippines, it had to show with sufficient clarity and adequate specificity how particular reasoning or interpretation of identified treaties by the Court might affect its own claim of sovereignty in North Borneo, on the basis of the documentary evidence upon which it relies to explain its own claim.[25]

Based on its consideration of various instruments invoked by the Philippines,[26] the Court found that, as regards none of them, had the Philippines discharged its burden of proving that it has an interest of a legal nature specific to it that may be affected by reasoning or interpretations of the Court in the principal case.[27] In the Court's view, either such interests formed no part of the arguments of Indonesia and Malaysia or those parties' reliance on those arguments did not bear on the issue of retention of sovereignty by the Sultanate of Sulu in respect of its claim to North Borneo.[28]

Based on the above, and notwithstanding that the main objects indicated by the Philippines for its intervention were appropriate,[29] the Court decided, by 14 votes to one, that the Philippines was not permitted to intervene as a nonparty in the case brought by Indonesia and Malaysia.[30]

---

22 *See id.*, at para. 47.
23 *See id.*, at para. 58 (citing the two-prong test developed by the Chamber in Land, Island and Maritime Frontier Dispute (El Salvador/Honduras), Application by Nicaragua for permission to intervene, Judgment, 1990 ICJ REP. 92, at 117-18, para. 61 (Sept. 13)).
24 *See id.*, at para. 59.
25 *See id.*, at paras. 60, 81.
26 *See supra* note 15.
27 *See* Judgment, at para. 82.
28 *See id.*, at paras. 64-80. In particular, neither Indonesia nor Malaysia are relying on an 1878 grant by the Sultan of Sulu to two individuals, presented by the Philippines as its primal source of title in North Borneo, as a source of title to Ligitan and Sipadan Islands. *See id.*, at paras. 64-66.
29 *See id.*, at paras. 84-92.
30 *See id.*, at para. 95 (operative paragraph).

* * * *

This is the second time within two years that the full Court ruled on an application for permission to intervene as a nonparty in a case, the former relating to an unopposed request and the latter to a contested one. Prior to this decision, the five-judge Chamber formed to deal with the case concerning the *Land, Island and Maritime Frontier Dispute (El Salvador/Honduras)* unanimously allowed a limited intervention by Nicaragua in 1990[31] and the full Court unanimously permitted Equatorial Guinea to intervene as a nonparty in *Land and Maritime Boundary between Cameroon and Nigeria* in 1999[32] after consistently denying previous requests for intervention pursuant to Article 62 of the Statute.[33] Indeed, reference has been made to "a new appreciation of the utility of Article 62 and an acceptance, in a world of interdependence, more and more of whose disputes are appearing in the docket, that intervention is the other side of interdependence."[34] In his separate opinion, Judge *ad hoc* Weeramantry, who was appointed by Malaysia, predicts that "[t]he closely interknit global society of tomorrow will see a more immediate impact upon all States of relations or transactions between any of them, thus enhancing the practical importance of this branch of procedural law [*i.e.*, intervention]."[35] Judge Kooijmans refers in his separate opinion to some of the fears that have been expressed in respect of such a development, namely, "that a liberal policy of granting permission to intervene might encourage States to attempt to intervene more often, which might lead to a situation at odds with the system of consensual jurisdiction" and that "the risk of potential interventions might

---

31 *See* Land, Island and Maritime Frontier Dispute (El Salvador/Honduras), Application by Nicaragua for permission to intervene, Judgment, 1990 ICJ REP. 92 (Sept. 13).

32 *See* Land and Maritime Boundary between Cameroon and Nigeria (Cam. v. Nig.), Application by Equatorial Guinea for permission to intervene, Order of October 21, 1999.

33 *See* Continental Shelf (Tunisia/Libyan Arab Jamahiriya), Application by Malta for permission to intervene, Judgment, 1981 ICJ REP. 3 (Apr. 14); Continental Shelf (Libyan Arab Jamahiriya/Malta), Application by Italy for permission to intervene, Judgment, 1984 ICJ REP. 3 (Mar. 21). In 1995, the Court dismissed, without consideration or hearings, the Article 62 applications of Australia, Samoa, the Solomon Islands, the Marshall Islands and the Federated States of Micronesia. *See* Request for an Examination of the Situation in Accordance with Paragraph 63 of the Court's Judgment of 20 December 1974 in the *Nuclear Tests (New Zealand v. France)* Case, 1995 ICJ REP. 288, at 306, para. 67 (Order of Sept. 22).

34 ICJ Doc. CR 2001/3, at 11, para. 22 (Mr. Reisman).

35 Separate opinion of Judge *ad hoc* Weeramantry, at para. 1.

make States parties to a dispute less inclined to conclude a special agreement to submit that dispute to the Court."[36]

The competing interests that are at play in the context of a contested application for permission to intervene were aptly described by counsel for the Philippines:

> [F]rom the standpoint of the parties to the litigation and, to an extent, from the standpoint of the Court, an application to intervene under Article 62 is always awkward and likely to be greeted with less than enthusiasm. The intervener is seen as an intruder, an interloper, an uninvited guest, an ill-mannered "party-crasher", a troublemaker. In this sense, intervention is never "timely". The paradigm of the Statute is binary, bilateral: a dispute between two parties and, even if there are more than two, then only two groups of interests. But the drafters of the Statute appreciated that that paradigm is not always true to reality. Even a bilateral dispute may involve the interests of third parties, in the sense that some possible decisions of the Court could affect those interests. When those interests are of a legal nature, the drafters of the Statute decided, in their wisdom, that it is better that the Court, as the principal judicial institution of the world, be informed than remain ignorant of and oblivious to those interests.[37]

This decision is a significant one in that, by contrast to the 1999 precedent, it contains the Court's authoritative views on important procedural and substantive issues arising under Article 62 of the Statute, including especially the question of burden of proof in cases where the claimed interest is not in the actual subject-matter of the dispute before the Court.[38] This is especially important as "the decided cases are all too few to offer any coherent body of

---

36 Separate opinion of Judge Kooijmans, at para. 12.

37 ICJ Doc. CR 2001/3, at 11, para. 21 (Mr. Reisman).

38 In fact, this was the first intervention case in the Court's history in which the claimed interest did not concern the precise subject-matter of the dispute between the parties. In his dissenting opinion, Judge Oda states that "[t]he whole procedure in this case strikes me as being rather unfair to the intervening State." In the view of the Court's senior judge, it is not for the state seeking to intervene to prove in advance of the merits phase that its interest will be affected by the Court's decision in respect of the merits in the principal case, given that that state has no way of knowing the issues involved, especially when it has no access to the written pleadings of the parties. Instead, the burden should be on the parties to assure the third state that its interests will *not* be affected by the decision in their case. *See* dissenting opinion of Judge Oda, at paras. 11, 14, 16.

judicial authority in this important are of procedural law."[39] Counsel and commentators can now turn to both the 1990 and 2001 decisions for helpful guidance on issues of intervention, especially in contested cases. The major novelty represented by this Judgment is the Court's statement that the interest of a legal nature to be shown by a state seeking to intervene is not limited to the *dispositif* alone of a judgment, but may also relate to the findings or reasoning supporting the judgment.[40] Despite this broad interpretation offered by the Court, the applicant in this case was unable to take advantage of it and failed to discharge its burden of proof.[41]

The majority could have been even greater if Judges Bedjaoui and Herczegh had participated in the proceedings. In the case of the former, his resignation effective September 30, 2001 did not prevent him from participating in the deliberations of the case after having attended the hearings, so that his subsequent non-participation may be interpreted as a regrettable lack of interest on his part, or even a failure to exercise his judicial duties.[42] In the case of the latter, no information was made available as to why he did not participate in either the hearings or the deliberations in the case.

This decision confirms that the format of a Judgment is used by the Court if the application for permission to intervene is opposed by one party or both parties to the case. If such an application is unopposed, the Court will issue an Order.[43]

---

39 Separate opinion of Judge *ad hoc* Weeramantry, at para. 2 (also describing precedents in the Permanent Court of International Justice).

40 This statement caused Judge Parra-Aranguren to append a declaration and Judge Koroma to append a separate opinion to the Judgment.

41 In his separate opinion, Judge Kooijmans gives expression to his regret that the Court did not explicitly state that the Philippines had failed to make its claim sufficiently plausible "by not providing answers to the highly pertinent questions which were put during the oral proceedings." Separate opinion of Judge Kooijmans, at para. 16.

42 According to Art. 13, para. 3, of the ICJ Statute, "[t]hough replaced, [Members of the Court] shall finish any cases which they may have begun." The use of the word "shall," as opposed to "may," is significant. In his letter of June 12, 2001 to the ICJ president, Judge Bedjaoui explicitly stated that his resignation was "without prejudice however to the possible application of Article 13 of the Statute." The text of the letter is available at the Court's Web site, <www.icj-cij.org>.

43 *See* Land and Maritime Boundary between Cameroon and Nigeria (Cam. v. Nig.), Order of Oct. 21, 1999. *See also* the Court's decisions on Fiji's application for intervention in the *Nuclear Tests* cases. 1973 ICJ REP. 320; 1973 ICJ REP. 324 (Orders of July 12). *See also* SHABTAI ROSENNE, 2 THE LAW AND PRACTICE OF THE INTERNATIONAL COURT (1920-1996), at 1498 (III.359) (1997).

The incidental proceedings in this case again raise the delicate issue of ethics in the context of the international legal profession.[44] At the time of his installation, the Judge *ad hoc* appointed by Indonesia also appeared as attorney-of-record for Bosnia-Herzegovina in its *Genocide* case against Yugoslavia, while one of Malaysia's advocates simultaneously was serving as a Judge *ad hoc* in the same *Genocide* case. Although the ICJ Statute and Rules of Court do not explicitly prohibit a person who acts as counsel in one active case from accepting an invitation to sit as a Judge *ad hoc* in another unrelated case, the principle of the equality of the Judges (regular Members of the Court and Judges *ad hoc* alike) expressed in Article 31, paragraph 6, of the Statute might guide candidates for a position as Judge *ad hoc* in considering whether or not it would be appropriate for them to appear before the Court in one case and sit with the rest of the bench in another.[45] Given the expression of complete equality in Article 31, perhaps the Court's interpretation of Article 16, paragraph 1,[46] as prohibiting "judges of the Court" from "engaging in the practice of law,"[47] should be applicable with equal force to Judges *ad hoc*.[48] In contrast to Article 16 cases involving regular Members

---

44   *See* Editorial Comment by Detlev F. Vagts in 90 AJIL 250 (1996); Peter H.F. Bekker, Letter to the Co-Editors in Chief, 90 AJIL 645 (1996).

45   Art. 31, para. 6, of the ICJ Statute provides that "[Judges *ad hoc*] shall take part in the decision on terms of complete equality with their colleagues."

46   According to Art. 16, para. 1, of the Statute, "[n]o member of the Court may exercise any political or administrative function, or engage in any other occupation of a professional nature."

47   *Conditions of service and compensation for officials other than Secretariat officials: members of the International Court of Justice*, Report of the Secretary-General, UN Doc. A/C.5/53/11, at 11-12, para. 46 (1998) ("The Court has interpreted the provisions of Article 16 as prohibiting judges of the Court from maintaining or exercising any political or administrative function, whether international, national, or local, whether commercial or otherwise; engaging in any other occupation of a professional nature, *inter alia*, holding a position in a commercial concern, engaging in the practice of law, maintaining membership in a law firm or rendering legal or expert opinions; or holding a permanent teaching or administrative position in a university or faculty of law."). Surely, one who represents a state in proceedings before the Court engages in "the practice of law."

48   The report's use of the words "judges of the Court" as opposed to "member of the Court," as employed in Art. 16, para. 1, lends support to this conclusion. It is not suggested here that law professors or attorneys could never serve as Judges *ad hoc* in ICJ cases; "ethics" issues arise only when counsel in one ICJ case simultaneously serves as a Judge *ad hoc* in another case. It is recognized that states will want to seek out the ablest candidates to serve as a Judge *ad hoc*.

of the Court, the Court is not likely to take any decision or position in a case where a state appoints as a Judge *ad hoc* an individual who simultaneously serves as counsel on behalf of that or another state in an unrelated case: that appointment is considered to be the appointing state's prerogative. Therefore, it is for appointing states and their candidates carefully to consider the appropriateness of such an appointment.

Even though the result of the Court's decision is that the Philippines will not have access to the pleadings and documents filed by the parties in this case, at least not until the Court delivers its Judgment on the merits in the principal case, and will have no direct role in the oral proceedings,[49] it could be that it filed its intervention petition so that either the stated interest of the Philippines would be taken into account, or, as it turned out, the Court would make it clear at this early stage that nothing it does in the case can possibly have any legal effect on the interest that the Philippines sought to protect.[50] If this was the strategy of the Philippines, then it may be said to have been successful. These incidental proceedings at least provided the Philippines with a unique opportunity to present its claim of sovereignty to territories in North Borneo in a world forum, absent willingness on the part of Malaysia to agree to submit the Philippine-Malaysian dispute over North Borneo to the Court. From this perspective, it had nothing to loose and everything to gain.[51]

---

49 These consequences were presented by the Philippines as "the remedies provided for in Article 85 of the Rules of the Court." Judgment, at para. 13. The Court noted, however, that "Article 85 does not provide for 'remedies' as such, but rather deals with the procedural consequences of a decision to accede to an application for permission to intervene under Article 62." *See id.*, at para. 92.

50 Indeed, the Court observed in the final paragraph of the Judgment that "notwithstanding its finding that the Philippines has not demonstrated an entitlement to intervene in the pending case between Indonesia and Malaysia, it remains cognizant of the positions stated before it by Indonesia, Malaysia and the Philippines in the present proceedings." Judgment, at para. 94. This language closely resembles the text included in the Manila Accord of July 1963 signed by Indonesia, Malaysia and the Philippines. *See id.*, at para. 38.

51 According to Judge *ad hoc* Franck, appointed by Indonesia, the Court could also have considered that, in any event, international law bars the very interest that the Philippines sought to have protected, on the ground that, except in the most extraordinary circumstances, modern international law does not recognize the survival of a right of sovereignty based solely on historic title and in derogation of the rights of non-self-governing peoples to claim independence and establish their sovereignty through the exercise of their right to self-determination in accordance with the requisites of international law (here, by the people of North Borneo through a 1963 election). *See* separate opinion of Judge *ad hoc* Franck,

at paras. 2, 15. The appointment of Judge *ad hoc* Franck marks the first time in the Court's history that a U.S. national has served as a Judge *ad hoc*.

Counterclaims – applicant's objections based on formal and admissibility requirements of 1978 version of Article 80 of Rules of Court – condition of direct connection between respondent's counterclaims and subject-matter of applicant's claim

ARMED ACTIVITIES ON THE TERRITORY OF THE CONGO
(Dem. Rep. of the Congo v. Uganda)

Counterclaims, Order
Obtainable from <www.icj-cij.org>
International Court of Justice, November 29, 2001

On April 20, 2001, the Government of the Republic of Uganda (Uganda) duly filed its Counter-Memorial in the case brought against it by the Democratic Republic of the Congo (DRC) through an Application filed in the ICJ Registry on June 23, 1999. The case concerns a dispute over state responsibility for acts of armed aggression and other unlawful acts allegedly perpetrated by Uganda on Congolese territory. Chapter XVIII of Uganda's Counter-Memorial contains three counterclaims based on alleged violations of customary international law and the UN Charter. First, Uganda accused the DRC of being responsible for acts of armed aggression against Uganda since 1994. Second, it referred to alleged attacks by the DRC on Ugandan diplomatic premises and personnel in Kinshasa and on Ugandan nationals. Third, Uganda asked the Court to hold the DRC responsible for alleged violations of the Lusaka Agreement signed by both parties on July 10, 1999.[1] While the DRC did not deny that Uganda's counterclaims fulfill the jurisdictional condition laid down in Article 80, paragraph 1, of the Rules of Court, it asked the Court to rule that those counterclaims are inadmissible for failure to satisfy the other conditions set out in Article 80, especially that of a "direct connection" between the counterclaim and the subject-matter of the applicant's claim. After a meeting with the ICJ president on June 11, 2001, the DRC filed its written observations on the ques-

---

1   The DRC's claims contained in its Application are summarized on pp. 231-232 in Chapter 4 above.

P.H.F. Bekker, World Court Decisions at the Turn of the Millennium (1997-2001), p. 351-357.
© 2002 *Kluwer Law International. Printed in the Netherlands.*

tion of the admissibility of Uganda's counterclaims on June 28, 2001, followed by Uganda's observations on August 15, 2001.[2]

The Court's Order of November 29, 2001, found (1) unanimously, that the first counterclaim is admissible as such and forms part of the proceedings between the two parties; (2) by 15 votes to one, that the second counterclaim also is admissible as such and is joined to the main proceedings; and (3) unanimously, that the third counterclaim is inadmissible, because it is not directly connected with the subject-matter of the DRC's claims.[3] The Order also fixed time limits for the filing of further written pleadings addressing the claims of both parties.

At the outset, the Court determined that Uganda's claims constitute "counterclaims" within the meaning of Article 80 of the Rules of Court on the basis that they "seek, over and above the dismissal of the claims made by the Congo, a ruling establishing the Congo's responsibility and awarding reparations on that account."[4]

The DRC did not challenge Uganda's right to submit counterclaims or the Court's jurisdiction over such claims, but objected to the admissibility of the counterclaims. The DRC's principal argument was that Uganda's contentions were defective on formal grounds, because they were not identifiable as claims and were not presented correctly in Uganda's submissions.[5] While the Court agreed that "Uganda's counterclaim could have been presented in a clearer manner,"[6] it was satisfied that their presentation, in various sections of Uganda's Counter-Memorial and in its final submissions, does not deviate from the requirements of Article 80, paragraph 2, of the Rules of Court, which provides that "[a] counter-claim shall be made in the Counter-Memorial of the party

---

2   The Order mentions that the DRC submitted comments on Uganda's written observations by letter of September 5, 2001, and that Uganda objected to such comments by letter of October 8, 2001. *See* Order of November 29, 2001, *infra* note 3, at para. 25. In its Order, the Court does not address Uganda's objection to the filing of the DRC's comments. Considering that it was sufficiently well informed of the parties' positions concerning the admissibility of Uganda's counterclaims, the Court proceeded without hearing the parties orally. *See id.* at para. 26.

3   Armed Activities on the Territory of the Congo (Dem. Rep. of the Congo v. Uganda), Counterclaims, Order of November 29, 2001, at para. 51 (*dispositif*), *available from* the Court's Web site at www.icj-cij.org. [hereinafter Order].

4   Order, *supra* note 3, at para. 29 (citing Application of the Convention on the Prevention and Punishment of the Crime of Genocide (Bos.-Herz. v. Yugo.), Counterclaims, Order, 1997 ICJ REP. 243, 256, para. 27 (Dec. 17).

5   *See* Order, *supra* note 3, at para. 7.

6   *Id.* at para. 33.

presenting it, and shall appear as part of the submissions of that party." In the Court's view, Uganda was permitted to refer to a request for reparation in its submissions without the modalities thereof being indicated at this stage of the proceedings.

The Court next examined the DRC's alternative argument that Uganda's counterclaims are not "directly connected" with the subject-matter of the DRC's original claims, as required by Article 80, paragraph 1, of the Rules of Court.

The DRC conceded that the first counterclaim meets the requirement of a "direct connection" under Article 80, paragraph 1, of the Rules of Court, but only inasmuch as it relates to its alleged aggression during the period from May to August 1998. It maintained that events featured in Uganda's claim relating to alleged aggression by the DRC otherwise (i.e., as concerns the period from early 1994 to May 1997 and from August 1998 onwards) did not take place during the same period as the events of which the DRC complained in its Application.[7] Uganda pointed out, however, that its first counterclaim describes the continued and uninterrupted use of force against Uganda for which the DRC bears responsibility from 1994 to the present, so that there is no basis for limiting the scope of the counterclaim to the period running from May to August 1998. Even though the heads of the Congolese state have changed and the state itself has been renamed, the illegal activities and the main actors identified in the counterclaim have continued without interruption since 1994. Hence, all these activities conducted or supported by the Congolese state are part of the same complex of facts as those upon which the DRC's illegal use of force claim is based. Uganda also pointed out that its counterclaim and the DRC's claim are based on the same legal prohibition against the use of force in international relations and against providing military support to irregular armed forces embodied in Article 2, paragraph 4, of the UN Charter.[8]

The Court observed that the Rules of Court do not define what is meant by "directly connected." In these circumstances, it is for the Court to assess whether the counter claim is sufficiently connected to the principal claim both in fact and in law.[9] Contrary to the DRC's contention, the establishment of this connection is not subject to the additional condition "that the counterclaimant's arguments must both support the counterclaim and be pertinent for the purposes of rebutting the principal claim."[10] The Court was satisfied that the DRC's

---

7   *See id.* at paras. 11-12.
8   *See id.* at paras. 20-21.
9   *See id.* at para. 36.
10 *See id.* at paras. 10 (DRC), 19 (Uganda) and 38 (ICJ).

claims and Uganda's first counterclaim relate to facts of the same nature (i.e., the use of force and support allegedly provided to armed groups) and, even though Uganda's claim ranges over a longer period than that covered by the DRC's claim, both claims concern a conflict that has been ongoing between the two states, in various forms and of variable intensity, since 1994. Both claims form part of the same factual complex and pursue the same legal aims (i.e., the establishment of each party's responsibility based on the violation of the principles of the non-use of force laid down in Article 2, paragraph 4, of the UN Charter and forming part of customary international law, and the non-intervention in matters within the domestic jurisdiction of states).[11] On this basis, the Court found, unanimously, that Uganda's first counterclaim is admissible as such and forms part of the main proceedings.[12]

The DRC argued that Uganda's second counterclaim –referring to alleged attacks on Ugandan diplomatic premises, property and personnel in Kinshasa for which the DRC is responsible– is devoid of any connection whatsoever, whether legal or factual, with the subject-matter of the DRC's claims. While these attacks occurred during the same period as the events complained of by the DRC, they do not constitute facts of the same nature and cannot be considered as pursuing the same legal aim.[13] The Lusaka Agreement was signed after the filing of the DRC's Application, so that Uganda's counterclaim refers to a period of time different from that referred to in the Application.[14] Uganda maintained that the facts referred to in its counterclaim are of the same nature as many of the facts on which the DRC's claims rely and are all part of the same factual complex (i.e., the events complained of by both parties took place at the same time and on the same territory). Uganda claimed that the direct connection in this case is demonstrated by the fact that the attacks on its embassy commenced just days after the invasion of Congolese territory of which the DRC's Application complains, being a direct outgrowth of the hostilities

---

11 *See id.* at para. 38.

12 *See id.* at paras. 39 and 51(A)(1) (*dispositif*).

13 In the DRC's view, the events referred to in the Ugandan counterclaim relate to legal rules that are radically different from those underlying its Application (namely, the prohibition on the use of force, the principles of non-intervention in internal affairs and respect for the permanent sovereignty of states and their peoples of their natural resources, and the general obligation to respect and enforce fundamental human rights). *See id.* at paras. 13-14.

14 *See id.* at para. 14.

on Congolese territory. Moreover, it is pursuing many of the same legal aims as the DRC.[15]

The Court observed that is was evident from the case file that the facts on which Uganda is relying occurred in August 1998, immediately after its alleged invasion of Congolese territory. In the Court's view, the parties' claims of responsibility for various acts of oppression allegedly accompanying an illegal use of force concern facts of the same nature and form part of the same factual complex. Given that they assert responsibility for alleged illegal use of force based on rules of conventional or customary international law, the parties are pursuing the same legal aims. On this basis, the Court found, by 15 votes to one, that Uganda's second counterclaim is admissible as such and forms part of the main proceedings.[16]

With respect to Uganda's third counterclaim, alleging DRC violations of the 1999 Lusaka Agreement, the DRC argued that this counterclaim involves neither facts of the same nature nor the same legal rules as those complained of in the DRC's Application. The DRC claimed that Uganda should refer any alleged dispute concerning violation of the Lusaka Agreement to the Court in the normal way, i.e., through the filing of an application pursuant to Article 40 of the ICJ Statute.[17] Uganda maintained that the Lusaka Agreement relates to the very same armed conflict that is the subject-matter of the DRC's Application and Memorial.[18]

In the Court's view, Uganda's third claim concerns quite specific questions that relate to the methods for solving the conflict in the Great Lakes region agreed at a multilateral level in a ceasefire accord. Such questions concern facts of a different nature from those relied on in the DRC's claims, which relate to acts for which Uganda allegedly was responsible during that conflict. Consequently, the parties' respective claims do not form part of the same factual complex and do not pursue the same legal aims, given that Uganda sought to base the DRC's responsibility on the violation of specific provisions of the

---

15 *See id.* at para. 22.
16 *See id.* at paras. 40-41 and 51(A)(2) (*dispositif*). Judge *ad hoc* Verhoeven, appointed by the DRC, voted against this part of the *dispositif*. In his declaration appended to the Order, he explains that the attack against Uganda's embassy in Kinshasa in his view does not throw any useful light for the Court on the armed aggression and unlawful occupation of which the DRC has complained. The mere fact that this attack is part of a multifaceted history of conflict in his view is insufficient for the admissibility of Uganda's counterclaim.
17 *See id.* at para. 14.
18 *See id.* at para. 23.

Lusaka Agreement. Consequently, the Court, by unanimous vote, dismissed Uganda's third counterclaim as inadmissible.[19]

The Court next rejected the DRC's argument that the requirements of the sound administration of justice (especially, expediency) dictate that Uganda's counterclaims not be joined to the main proceedings. In the Court's view, the sound administration of justice and the interests of procedural economy call for the simultaneous consideration of the respondent's counterclaims and the applicant's principal claims in cases where their direct connection has been established.[20]

As has become the Court's usual practice relating to counterclaims, it reserved the applicant's right to present its views on the respondent's counterclaims a second time in an additional written pleading and instructed the ICJ Registrar to transmit a copy of the Order to third states entitled to appear before the Court with a view to protecting any interests they might have.[21]

Finally, the Court unanimously fixed May 29, 2002, as the time limit for the filing by the DRC of a Reply and November 29, 2002, as the time limit for the filing by Uganda of a Rejoinder addressing the claims of both parties.[22]

* * * *

This straight-forward Order is further evidence of the steady increase of the instrument of counterclaims in "involuntary" cases before the ICJ, except that, by contrast to the previous instance involving counterclaims introduced by Nigeria against Cameroon as applicant, the Court had not rejected preliminary objections in this case. This marks the sixth time that the Court has ruled on counterclaims, and the fourth time since 1997.[23] This Order for the first time focuses entirely on the test of direct connection laid down in Article 80 of the Rules of Court.[24] Even though this was the first counterclaims ruling since

---

19 *See id.* at paras. 42-43 and 51(A)(3) *(dispositif)*.

20 *See id.* at paras. 15-16 and 44.

21 *See id.* at paras. 47-50.

22 *See id.* at para. 51(B) *(dispositif)*.

23 For the four earlier precedents, see footnote 1 on page 185 of Chapter 3 above.

24 The Court's Order of June 30, 1999, dealing with Nigeria's counterclaims against Cameroon, contained an examination *proprio motu* of the requirements of Article 80 in the absence of any objections by Cameroon. Whereas the Court's Order of March 10, 1998, addressing U.S. counterclaims against Iran, dealt with Iran's objections based on lack of direct connection *and* lack of jurisdiction, its Order of December 17, 1997, relating to Yugoslavia's counterclaims against Bosnia-

the most recent amendment of Article 80 of the Rules of Court, the Order still was governed by the 1978 version of the Rules, given that the amended version is not applicable to cases pending on February 1, 2001, the date on which the amendment took effect.[25] While Uganda filed its counterclaims after the effective date of the amendment, the case itself already was pending at the time of the amendment.

The resemblance with the previous Orders on counterclaims reviewed in this book confirms the development of a procedural jurisprudence on counterclaims that is consistently applied by the Court. This Order, in which the Court's senior Member, Judge Oda, did not participate,[26] firmly establishes the Court's practice of settling the issue of the admissibility of counterclaims at a preliminary stage of the proceedings on the basis of the parties' written observations and without oral proceedings. The speed with which the Court did so in this case is remarkable: whereas it took the Court between five and nine months to announce its rulings in the two previous cases introducing counterclaims, the current Order was issued after only 2.5 months from the filing of the counterclaimant's written observations on the applicant's objections to admissibility.

Herzegovina, focused on direct connection and the qualification of the respondent's claim as a "counterclaim."

25 The amendment merely assigns priority to the jurisdictional requirement over the "direct connection" requirement.

26 The Order does not indicate why Judge Oda was absent from the proceedings. It would be helpful if the Court (in its decision) or the Registry (in a press communiqué) would indicate why a Member of the Court did not participate in the vote, thereby putting an end to any speculation regarding the reasons for such absence.

ANNEXES

A

COMPOSITION OF THE ICJ (1997-2001)

PRESIDENCY

Eighteenth Period (1997-2000):

President Stephen M. Schwebel (United States)

Vice President Christopher Weeramantry (Sri Lanka)

Nineteenth Period (2000-2003):

President Gilbert Guillaume (France)

Vice President Shi Jiuyong (China)

JUDGES (1997-2001)

Shigeru Oda
(Japan; 1976; term expires on 2/5/2003)

Stephen Schwebel
(United States; 1981-2000)

Mohammed Bedjaoui
(Algeria; 1982-2001)

Gilbert Guillaume
(France; 1987; term expires on 2/5/2009)

Christopher Weeramantry
(Sri Lanka; 1991-2000)

Raymond Ranjeva
(Madagascar; 1991; term expires on 2/5/2009)

Géza Herczegh
(Hungary; 1993; term expires on 2/5/2003)

Shi Jiuyong
(China; 1994; term expires on 2/5/2003)

Carl-August Fleischhauer
(Germany; 1994; term expires on 2/5/2003)

Abdul Koroma
(Sierra Leone; 1994; term expireson 2/5/2003)

Vladlen Vereschchetin
(Russian Federation; 1994; term expires on 2/5/2006)

Rosalyn Higgins
(United Kingdom; 1995; term expires on 2/5/2009)

Gonzalo Parra-Aranguren
(Venezuela; 1996; term expires on 2/5/2009)

Pieter Kooijmans
(The Netherlands; 1997; term expires on 2/5/2006)

Francisco Rezek
(Brazil; 1997; term expires on 2/5/2006)

Awn Shawkat Al-Khasawneh
(Jordan; 1999; term expires on 2/5/2009)

Thomas Buergenthal
(United States; 2000; term expires on 2/5/2006)

Nabil Elaraby
(Egypt; 2001; term expires on 2/5/2006)

JUDGES *AD HOC* (1997-2001)
(with case title and appointing state)

Prince Bola Ajibola
Land and Maritime Boundary (Nigeria);
Request for Interpretation (Nigeria)

Ahmed Sadek El-Kosheri
Libya v. U.S. (Libya)
Libya v. UK (Libya)

Yves Fortier
*Maritime Delimitation and Territorial
Questions between Qatar and Bahrain*
(Bahrain)

Sir Robert Jennings
Libya v. UK (UK)

Milenko Kreća
Genocide (Bosnia) (Yugoslavia)
Genocide (Croatia) (Croatia)
Legality of Use of Force (Yugoslavia)

Marc Lalonde
Fisheries Jurisdiction (Canada)
Legality of Use of Force (Canada)

Sir Elihu Lauterpacht
Genocide (Bosnia) (Bosnia-Herzegovina)

Kéba Mbaye
Land and Maritime Boundary
(Cameroon);
Request for Interpretation (Cameroon)

B.P. Jeevan Reddy
Aerial Incident of 10 August 1999
(India)

François Rigaux
Oil Platforms (Iran)

Krzysztof Skubiszewski
Gabčíkovo-Nagymaros Project
(Slovakia)

Santiago Torres Bernárdez
*Maritime Delimitation and Territorial
Questions between Qatar and Bahrain*
(Qatar)
Fisheries Jurisdiction (Spain)
Legality of Use of Force (Spain)

Syed Sharif Uddin Pirzada
Aerial Incident of 10 August 1999
(Pakistan)

Christine Van den Wyngaert
Arrest Warrant of 11 April 2000
(Belgium)

Sayeman Bula-Bula
Arrest Warrant of 11 April 2000 (DRC)

Mohamed Shahabuddeen
*Sovereignty over Pulau Ligitan and
Pulau Sipadan* (Indonesia; resigned
3/20/2001)

Thomas Franck
*Sovereignty over Pulau Ligitan and
Pulau Sipadan* (Indonesia (2001))

Christopher Weeramantry
*Sovereignty over Pulau Ligitan and
Pulau Sipadan* (Malaysia)

Patrick Duynslaeger
Legality of Use of Force (Belgium)

Giorgio Gaja
Legality of Use of Force (Italy)

Jean Salmon
*Armed Activities on the Territory of the
Congo* (Burundi)

John Dugard
*Armed Activities on the Territory of the
Congo* (Rwanda)

Joe Verhoeven
*Armed Activities on the Territory of the
Congo* (DRC)

James Kateka
*Armed Activities on the Territory of the
Congo* (Uganda)

Budislav Vukas
Genocide (Croatia) (Croatia)

Ian Brownlie
Certain Property (Liechtenstein)

B

GENERAL LIST OF ICJ CASES (1997-2001)

A. CONTENTIOUS CASES

Source in *I.C.J. Reports*

I CASES TERMINATED BY A JUDGMENT ON THE MERITS

Gabčíkovo-Nagymaros Project (Hungary/Slovakia)
(September 25, 1997) (but still pending on
implementation issues)   1997, 7

Kasikili/Sedudu Island (Botswana/Namibia)
(December 13, 1999)   1999, 1045

*Maritime Delimitation and Territorial Questions between Qatar
and Bahrain (Qatar v. Bahrain)* (March 16, 2001)   2001

LaGrand Case (Germany v. U.S.) (June 27, 2001)   2001

II CASES TERMINATED BY A JUDGMENT ON A JURISDICTIONAL
POINT/JUDGMENTS ON QUESTIONS OF JURISDICTION AND
ADMISSIBILITY ("INITIAL PHASE")

Fisheries Jurisdiction (Spain v. Canada) (December 4, 1998)   1998, 432

Aerial Incident of 10 August 1999 (Pakistan v. India)
(June 21, 2000)   2000

VII ORDERS RELATED TO COUNTERCLAIMS

Land and Maritime Boundary between Cameroon and Nigeria (Cameroon v. Nigeria; Equatorial Guinea intervening)

Sovereignty over Pulau Ligitan and Pulau Sipadan (Indonesia/Malaysia)

Ahmadou Sadio Diallo (Guinea v. Dem. Rep. of the Congo)

Legality of Use of Force (Yugoslavia v. Belgium)

Legality of Use of Force (Yugoslavia v. Canada)

Legality of Use of Force (Yugoslavia v. France)

Legality of Use of Force (Yugoslavia v. Germany)

Legality of Use of Force (Yugoslavia v. Italy)

Legality of Use of Force (Yugoslavia v. the Netherlands)

Legality of Use of Force (Yugoslavia v. Portugal)

Legality of Use of Force (Yugoslavia v. United Kingdom)

Armed Activities on the Territory of the Congo (Dem. Rep. of the Congo v. Uganda)

Application of the Convention on the Prevention and Punishment of the Crime of Genocide (Croatia v. Yugoslavia)

Maritime Delimitation between Nicaragua and Honduras in the Caribbean Sea (Nicaragua v. Honduras)

Arrest Warrant of 11 April 2000 (Dem. Rep. of the Congo v. Belgium)

Application for Revision of the Judgment of 11 July 1996 in the Case concerning Application of the Convention on the Prevention and Punishment of the Crime of Genocide (Bosnia-Herzegovina v. Yugoslavia), Preliminary Objections, *(Yugoslavia v. Bosnia-Herzegovina)*

Certain Property (Liechtenstein v. Germany)

[Title to Territory and Maritime Delimitation in the western Caribbean]
(Nigeria v. Colombia)

B. ADVISORY PROCEEDINGS

Source in *I.C.J. Reports*

1 *Difference Relating to Immunity from Legal Process of a*
   Special Rapporteur of the Commission on Human Rights
   (April 29, 1999)   1999, 62

C

STATES PARTIES TO CASES (1997-2001), BY REGION

AFRICA (10)

Botswana[1]
Burundi[2]
Cameroon[3]
Congo (Dem. Rep. of)[4]
Guinea[5]
Libya[6]
Namibia[7]
Nigeria[8]

---

1 Party in *Kasikili/Sedudu Island (Botswana/Namibia)*.
2 Respondent in *Armed Activities on the Territory of the Congo (Dem. Rep. of the Congo v. Burundi)*.
3 Applicant in *Land and Maritime Boundary between Cameroon and Nigeria*; Respondent in *Request for Interpretation*.
4 Applicant in *Armed Activities on the Territory of the Congo (Dem. Rep. of the Congo v. Burundi), Armed Activities on the Territory of the Congo (Dem. Rep. of the Congo v. Rwanda), Armed Activities on the Territory of the Congo (Dem. Rep. of the Congo v. Uganda)* and *Arrest Warrant of 11 April 2000 (Dem. Rep. of the Congo v. Belgium)*; Respondent in *Ahmadou Sadio Diallo (Guinea v. Dem. Rep. of the Congo)*.
5 Applicant in *Ahmadou Sadio Diallo (Guinea v. Dem. Rep. of the Congo)*.
6 Applicant in *Questions of Interpretation and Application of the 1971 Montreal Convention arising from the Aerial Incident at Lockerbie (Libya v. United Kingdom)* and in *Questions of Interpretation and Application of the 1971 Montreal Convention arising from the Aerial Incident at Lockerbie (Libya v. United States)*.
7 Party in *Kasikili/Sedudu Island (Botswana/Namibia)*.
8 Respondent in *Land and Maritime Boundary between Cameroon and Nigeria* and Applicant in *Request for Interpretation*.

Rwanda[9]
Uganda[10]

ASIA (7)

Bahrain[11]
India[12]
Indonesia[13]
Iran[14]
Malaysia[15]
Pakistan[16]
Qatar[17]

---

9   Respondent in *Armed Activities on Territory of the Congo (Dem. Rep. of the Congo v. Rwanda)*.

10 Respondent in *Armed Activities on Territory of the Congo (Dem. Rep. of the Congo v. Uganda)*.

11 Respondent in *Maritime Delimitation and Territorial Questions between Qatar and Bahrain (Qatar v. Bahrain)*.

12 Respondent in *Aerial Incident of 10 August 1999 (Pakistan v. India)*.

13 Party in *Sovereignty over Pulau Ligitan and Pulau Sipidan (Indonesia/Malaysia)*.

14 Applicant in *Oil Platforms (Iran v. United States)*.

15 Party in *Sovereignty over Pulau Ligitan and Pulau Sipidan (Indonesia/Malaysia)*.

16 Applicant in *Aerial Incident of 10 August 1999 (Pakistan v. India)*.

17 Applicant in *Maritime Delimitation and Territorial Questions between Qatar and Bahrain (Qatar v. Bahrain)*.

EASTERN EUROPE (5)

Bosnia-Herzegovina[18]
Croatia[19]
Hungary[20]
Slovakia[21]
Yugoslavia[22]

LATIN AMERICA (4)

Colombia[23]
Honduras[24]
Nicaragua[25]
Paraguay[26]

---

18 Applicant in *Application of the Convention on the Prevention and Punishment of the Crime of Genocide (Bosnia-Herzegovina v. Yugoslavia)*; Respondent in *Application for Revision of the Judgment of 11 July 1997 in the Case concerning* Application of the Convention on the Prevention and Punishment of the Crime of Genocide (Bosnia-Herzegovina v. Yugoslavia), Preliminary Objections *(Yugoslavia v. Bosnia-Herzegovina)*.

19 Applicant in *Application of the Convention on the Prevention and Punishment of the Crime of Genocide (Croatia v. Yugoslavia)*.

20 Party in *Gabčíkovo-Nagymaros Project (Hungary/Slovakia)*.

21 Party in *Gabčíkovo-Nagymaros Project (Hungary/Slovakia)*.

22 Applicant in *Legality of Use of Force (Yugoslavia v. Belgium) (Yugoslavia v. Canada) (Yugoslavia v. France) (Yugoslavia v. Germany) (Yugoslavia v. Italy) (Yugoslavia v. Netherlands) (Yugoslavia v. Portugal) (Yugoslavia v. Spain) (Yugoslavia v. United Kingdom) (Yugoslavia v. United States)*; and in *Application for Revision of the Judgment of 11 July 1997 in the Case concerning* Application of the Convention on the Prevention and Punishment of the Crime of Genocide (Bosnia-Herzegovina v. Yugoslavia), Preliminary Objections *(Yugoslavia v. Bosnia-Herzegovina)*; Respondent in *Application of the Convention on the Prevention and Punishment of the Crime of Genocide (Bosnia-Herzegovina v. Yugoslavia)*; and *Application of the Convention on the Prevention and Punishment of the Crime of Genocide (Croatia v. Yugoslavia)*.

23 Respondent in the case filed by Nicaragua on December 6, 2001.

24 Respondent in *Maritime Delimitation between Nicaragua and Honduras in the Caribbean Sea (Nicaragua v. Honduras)*.

25 Applicant in *Maritime Delimitation between Nicaragua and Honduras in the Caribbean Sea (Nicaragua v. Honduras)* and the case against Colombia filed on December 6, 2001.

26 Applicant in *Vienna Convention on Consular Relations (Paraguay v. United States)*.

WESTERN EUROPE AND OTHER STATES (11)

Belgium[27]
Canada[28]
France[29]
Germany[30]
Italy[31]
Liechtenstein[32]
The Netherlands[33]
Portugal[34]
Spain[35]
United Kingdom[36]
United States[37]

---

27 Respondent in *Legality of Use of Force (Yugoslavia v. Belgium)* and *Arrest Warrant of 11 April 2000 (Dem. Rep. of the Congo v. Belgium)*.
28 Respondent in *Fisheries Jurisdiction (Spain v. Canada)* and *Legality of Use of Force (Yugoslavia v. Canada)*.
29 Respondent in *Legality of Use of Force (Yugoslavia v. France)*.
30 Applicant in *LaGrand Case (Germany v. U.S.)* and Respondent in *Legality of Use of Force (Yugoslavia v. Germany)* and *Certain Property (Liechtenstein v. Germany)*.
31 Respondent in *Legality of Use of Force (Yugoslavia v. Italy)*.
32 Applicant in *Certain Property (Liechtenstein v. Germany)*.
33 Respondent in *Legality of Use of Force (Yugoslavia v. The Netherlands)*.
34 Respondent in *Legality of Use of Force (Yugoslavia v. Portugal)*.
35 Respondent in *Legality of Use of Force (Yugoslavia v. Spain)* (discontinued).
36 Respondent in *Questions of Interpretation and Application of the 1971 Montreal Convention arising from the Aerial Incident at Lockerbie (Libya v. United Kingdom)* and *Legality of Use of Force (Yugoslavia v. United Kingdom)*.
37 Respondent in *Questions of Interpretation and Application of the 1971 Montreal Convention arising from the Aerial Incident at Lockerbie (Libya v. United States), Oil Platforms (Iran v. United States), Legality of Use of Force (Yugoslavia v. United States), Vienna Convention on Consular Relations (Paraguay v. United States)* and *LaGrand Case (Germany v. United States)*.

D

BACKGROUND READING

Listed below is a selection of some of the most informative writings on the World Court.

J. Douma, *Bibliography on the International Court including the Permanent Court, 1918-1964* (1966).

Arthur Eyffinger, *The International Court of Justice 1946-1996* (The Hague, 1996).

Sir Gerald Fitzmaurice, *The Law and Procedure of the International Court of Justice* (repr., Cambridge, 1995).

Geneviève Guyomar, *Commentaire du Règlement de la Cour internationale de Justice adopté le 14 avril 1978 – Interprétation et pratique* (Paris, 1983).

Manley O. Hudson, *The Permanent Court of International Justice 1920-1942* (repr., New York-London, 1972)

I. Hussain, *Dissenting and Separate Opinions at the World Court* (The Hague, 1984).

Eduardo Jiménez de Aréchaga, *The Amendments to the Rules of Procedure of the International Court of Justice*, 61 AJIL 1 (1973).

Vaughan Lowe and Malgosia Fitzmaurice (eds.), *Fifty Years of the International Court of Justice* (Cambridge, 1996).

Connie Peck and Roy S. Lee (eds.), *Increasing the Effectiveness of the International Court of Justice* (Proceedings of the ICJ/UNITAR Colloquium to Celebrate the 50th Anniversary of the Court) (The Hague, 1997).

Shabtai Rosenne, *Procedure in the International Court – A Commentary on the 1978 Rules of the International Court of Justice* (The Hague, 1983).

Shabtai Rosenne, *The World Court – What it is and how it works* (5th rev. ed., The Hague, 1995).

Shabtai Rosenne, *The Law and Practice of the International Court 1920-1996*, volumes I-IV (3rd ed., The Hague, 1997) (updates available from Kluwer's Web site, <www.wkap.nl/kapis/appendices/lawpracticeupdate>).

Nagendra Singh, *The Role and Record of the International Court of Justice* (Dordrecht, 1989).

Brigitte Stern, *20 ans de jurisprudence de la Cour internationale de Justice 1975-1995* (The Hague/London/Boston, 1998).

J. Sztucki, *Interim Measures in the Hague Court* (Deventer, 1983).

Giuliana Ziccardi Capaldo, *Repertory of Decisions of the International Court of Justice (1947-1992)* (Dordrecht, 1995).

E

JUDICIAL STATISTICS (1987-2001)

YEAR	GENERAL LIST		NEW CASES		ORDERS			JUDGE-MENTS	ADVISORY OPINIONS	CHAMBER CASES	OPTIONAL CLAUSE ACCEPTANCE
	contentious	advisory	contentious	advisory	Full Court	President	Chamber				
1987	6	1	1	0	5	2	2	0	1	3	46
1988	5	1	1	1	3	1	0	1	1	2	49
1989	8	1	3	1	5	3	2	1	1	2	50
1990	8	0	1	0	3	2	1	1	0	1	51
1991	12	0	4	0	3	6	0	1	0	1	53
1992	13	0	3	0	8	4	0	2	0	1	56
1993	12	1	2	1	6	4	0	1	0	0	56
1994	11	2	1	1	1	3	0	2	0	0	58
1995	12	2	2	0	6	4	0	2	0	0	59
1996	10	2	1	0	4	5	0	2	2	0	62

YEAR	GENERAL LIST		NEW CASES			ORDERS			JUDGE-MENTS	ADVISORY OPINIONS	CHAMBER CASES	OPTIONAL CLAUSE ACCEPTANCE
	contentious	advisory	contentious	advisory	Full Court	President	Chamber					
1997	9	0	0	0	2	0	0	1	0	0	62
1998	13	1	5	1	11	8	0	4	0	0	62
1999	29	1	17	0	35	0	0	2	1	0	63
2000	25	0	1	0	4	16	0	1	0	0	63
2001	27	0	3	0	14	5	0	3	0	0	63

TABLE OF CASES

International Court of Justice

PERMANENT COURT OF INTERNATIONAL JUSTICE

INDEX OF SUBJECTS

List of Errata

The Publisher regrets that the following errors appear in this book, all of which are outside the Author's responsibility.

Page 7 (Introduction): in footnote 5, the word "that" accidentally was left out between "fact" and "cases"

Page 8: in footnote 9, "Nvember" should read "November"

Page 19: at the end of footnote 59, the word "in" accidentally was left out between "*Honduras*" and "*the Caribbean Sea*"

Page 176: in footnote 176, the words "1999 ICJ REP. 124" accidentally were left out after "Order of June 2, 1999,"

Page 177: in footnote 2, a comma accidentally was left out after "139"

Page 181: in footnote 15, a comma accidentally was left out after "137"

Page 247: in footnote 30, a comma accidentally was left out after "124" and "139"

Page 279: in the first line under "*General List*," the words "2 new contentious cases" should read "three new contentious cases"

Page 279: in the eighth line under "*General List*," the words "26 cases" should read "27 cases"

Page 279: in footnote 4, "Nicragua" should read "Nicaragua"

Page 281: in the seventh line from the top, "September 17" should read "September 28"

Page 281: in the third line under "*Orders*," "fof" should read "of"

Page 325: in the 17th line in footnote 48, the word "suspect" was accidentally left out before "during custodial interrogation"

Page 367: under "VII," after "*Oil Platforms*," "198, 190" should read "1998, 190"

Page 368: under "VIII," after *Legality of Use of Force (Yugoslavia v. Spain)*," "1999" should read "1999, 761"

Page 368: under VIII, after *Legality of Use of Force (Yugoslavia v. U.S.)*," "1999" should read "1999, 916"

Page 370: in the third line, "(Nigeria v. Colombia)" should read "(*Nicaragua v. Colombia)*"

Page 372: after "ASIA," "(1)" should read "(7)"
